# REASSESSING THE LIBERAL STATE
## READING MARITAIN'S *MAN AND THE STATE*

# American Maritain Association Publications

## General Editor: Anthony O. Simon

*Jacques Maritain: The Man and His Metaphysics*
Edited by John F. X. Knasas, 1988
Distributed by the University of Notre Dame Press   ISBN 0-268-01205-9 (out of print)

*Freedom in the Modern World: Jacques Maritain, Yves R. Simon, Mortimer J. Adler*
Edited by Michael D. Torre, 1989, Second Printing 1990
Distributed by the University of Notre Dame Press   ISBN 0-268-00978-3

*From Twilight to Dawn: The Cultural Vision of Jacques Maritain*
Edited by Peter A. Redpath, 1990
Distributed by the University of Notre Dame Press   ISBN 0-268-00979-1

*The Future of Thomism*
Edited by Deal W. Hudson and Dennis Wm. Moran, 1992
Distributed by the University of Notre Dame Press   ISBN 0-268-00986-4

*Jacques Maritain and the Jews*
Edited by Robert Royal, 1994
Distributed by the University of Notre Dame Press   ISBN 0-268-01193-1

*Freedom, Virtue, and the Common Good*
Edited by Curtis L. Hancock and Anthony O. Simon, 1995
Distributed by the University of Notre Dame Press   ISBN 0-268-00991-0

*Postmodernism and Christian Philosophy*
Edited by Roman T. Ciapolo, 1997
Distributed by The Catholic University of America Press   ISBN 0-8132-0881-5

*The Common Things: Essays on Thomism and Education*
Edited by Daniel McInerny, 1999
Distributed by The Catholic University of America Press   ISBN 0-9669226-0-3

*The Failure of Modernism: The Cartesian Legacy and Contemporary Pluralism*
Edited by Brendan Sweetman, 1999
Distributed by The Catholic University of America Press   ISBN 0-9669226-11

*Beauty, Art, and the Polis*
Edited by Alice Ramos, 2000
Distributed by The Catholic University of America Press   ISBN 0-9669226-2-X

*Reassessing the Liberal State: Reading Maritain's* Man and the State
Edited by Timothy Fuller and John P. Hittinger, 2001
Distributed by The Catholic University of America Press   ISBN 0-9669226-3-8

# REASSESSING THE LIBERAL STATE
## READING MARITAIN'S *MAN AND THE STATE*

Edited by
Timothy Fuller and John P. Hittinger

AMERICAN MARITAIN ASSOCIATION
Distributed by The Catholic University of America Press
Washington, D.C. 20064

Copyright © 2001

American Maritain Association

All Rights Reserved

Library of Congress Cataloging-in-Publication Data

Reassessing the liberal state: reading Maritain's Man and the state/ edited by Timothy Fuller and John P. Hittinger.
    p. cm. — (American Maritain Association publications)
Includes bibliographical references and index.
ISBN 0-9669226-3-8 (alk. paper)
    1. Maritain, Jacques, 1882-1973 Man and the state. 2. State, The. 3. Democracy. 4. Human rights. 5. Liberalism. 6. Church and social problems—Catholic Church. I. Fuller, Timothy, 1940-. II. Hittinger, John. III. Series.

JC261.M323 R43 2002
320.1'5—dc21

2001028145

Manufactured in the
United States of America

Distributed by The Catholic University of America Press

*In Memoriam*

Horace Shepard Fuller
1908-2001

Francis Russell Hittinger, Jr.
1926-1968

# Contents

**Introduction**
John Hittinger and Timothy Fuller
**Maritain and the Reassment of the Liberal State**   1

## I. Politics and Community in the Modern World

1. Russell Hittinger
   Reasons for a Civil Society   11

2. Timothy Fuller
   Jacques Maritain and Michael Oakeshott on the Modern State   24

3. William Haggerty
   The Question of Modernity in the Political Thought
   of Heinrich Rommen   34

4. Catherine Green
   Work, Rest, and Generosity   49

5. Desmond FitzGerald
   Maritain and Gilson on the Challenge of Political Democracy   61

## II. Liberalism Reconsidered

6. Henk E.S. Woldring
   Constitutional Democracy in Search of Justification   73

7. Jeanne M. Heffernan
   Acknowledging Ambiguity and Difference in Politics:
   A Christian Realist Challenge to Thomists   87

8. John R. Goodreau
   Kant's Contribution to the Idea of Democratic Pluralism   99

9. James Hanink
   Liberalism and Legitimacy: An Indictment   113

III. **Natural Law Foundations for Liberalism**

10. Gregory Doolan
    Maritain, St. Thomas Aquinas, and the First Principles
    of Natural Law — 127

11. V. Bradley Lewis
    Liberal Democracy, Natural Law and Jurisprudence:
    Thomistic Notes on an Irish Debate — 140

12. J. Budziszewski
    Denying What We Can't Not know — 159

13. John Trapani, Jr.
    Different Music–The Same Keyboard:
    Obscene Art/Pornography and the First Amendment Debate — 166

IV. **The Church in the Modern World**

14. John Hittinger
    The Cooperation of Church and State:
    Maritain's Argument from the Unity of the Person — 179

15. Joseph M. de Torre
    Maritain's "Integral Humanism" and Catholic Social Teaching — 202

16. Deborah Wallace Ruddy
    Christian Humility and Democratic Citizenry:
    St. Augustine and Jacques Maritain — 209

17. Nicholas C. Lund-Molfese
    Maritain's Contribution to the Development
    of the Magisterium of Means — 228

V. **Appendix: Pope Paul VI, Discourse and Messages at the Close of Vatican II**

18. Pope Paul VI
    Message to Men of Thought and Science — 245
    Message to Heads of State — 246
    Discourse at the Last General Session of Vatican II — 247
    Contributors — 255
    Index — 259

# Acknowledgements

The cover painting, "The American Thanksgiving Day Service, Westminster Abbey – 1944" by Frank E. Beresford, is provided through the Courtesy of the United States Air Force Art Collection. Frank Ernest Beresford was born in Derby, England in 1881 and died in 1967. His most famous work was "The Princes' Vigil," showing the four sons of King George V guarding their father's coffin at the King's lying in state in Westminster Abbey in 1936. It was named "Painting of the Year" by the Royal Academy. He painted for four years during World War II with the United States Army Air Force and was awarded the Exceptional Service Award of the United States Air Force for the painting used on the cover. We find in this painting some suggestive parallels with the work of Jacques Maritain. The sense of urgency to defend liberal democracy in speech and deed during the crisis of World War II sets the tone for much of Maritain's work in political philosophy. The framing of the American Flag by the sacred symbols of Christendom also is found in Maritain's admiration for the United States and his attempt to reconnect the case for liberty with the ancient and medieval philosophical tradition. Finally, the painting conveys something of Maritain's attempt at "reassessing the liberal state" by depicting the important affairs of state in the more expansive context of the transcendent.

We wish to thank the following people for their assistance in producing this book: Suzanne Tregarthen for her patient and careful work with the manuscript; Keith Emmons, Rick Specht, and Todd Wilson of Colorado College for their work in the compositing of the text and cover; J. Dennis Mulqueen for his initial cover design; Peter Greenman for his proof-reading and indexing; and Anthony O. Simon for his proof-reading and his general editorship of the American Maritain Association book series. We acknowledge the generous funding support of The Colorado College Studies at Colorado College for the initial conference and for the preparation of the book for publication.

Chapter 12, "Denying What We Can't Not Know," by J. Budziszewski, was originally published in *First Things* 84 (June/July 1998), pp. 21-27. The photo of Jacques Maritain and Pope Paul VI found on page 244 was taken by Pontificia Fotografia / Felici.

# Introduction

## Maritain and the Reassessment of the Liberal State

### John Hittinger and Timothy Fuller

The book we commemorate and critically engage in these essays, Jacques Maritain's *Man and the State*, is one volume in the remarkable series of lectures sponsored by the Charles Walgreen Foundation at The University of Chicago in the mid twentieth century. The Walgreen Lectures prompted a set of books that set the agenda for political philosophy for fifty years, having guided now three generations of students of political philosophy. *Man and the State* finds its place alongside Leo Strauss's *Natural Right and History*, Eric Voegelin's *New Science of Politics*, and Yves R. Simon's *Philosophy of Democratic Government*, among others.[1] Ex-patriots from war torn-Europe, these seminal thinkers combined European scholarship with deep admiration for the American constitution, aiming to show, through the recovery of classical and medieval thought, the true foundation of modern liberal democracy.[2] In order to do this, they had to outline a classically grounded political science adequate to understand the prospects and perils of the modern achievement of liberal democracy in a century that had crushed the easier optimism of the enlightenment tradition. Especially they sought to refute the prevalent modes of political science, especially those fostered by positivism and Marxism. What seems more obvious to us today about the shortcomings of such reductionist modes of thought is so because of what these thinkers accomplished fifty years ago when it was by no means obvious.

Nevertheless, all were influenced by, and took seriously, contemporary philosophy (for Maritain it was Bergson) and sought to make the case for the ancient wisdom in the deepest issues of philosophy and politics in awareness of what had been said against the ancient wisdom. They had to make sense of the incessant experience of war, the onset of the Cold War, and to chart a future for

---

[1] Eric Voegelin, *The New Science of Politics* (Chicago: The University of Chicago Press, 1952), Leo Strauss, *Natural Right and History* (Chicago: The University of Chicago Press, 1953), Yves R. Simon, *Philosophy of Democratic Government* (Chicago: The University of Chicago Press, 1951).
[2] Timothy Fuller, "Reflections on Leo Strauss and American Education," in *Hannah Arendt and Leo Strauss: German Emigres and American Political Thought after World War II*, eds. Peter Graf Kielmansegg, Horst Mewes and Elisabeth Glaser-Schmidt (New York: Cambridge University Press, 1995), pp. 61-80.

the defenders of liberty against the totalitarianisms of left and right. Neither the positivism nor the historicism of the day could provide the tools for the job. These thinkers, in attempting to recover the ancient wisdom, did not necessarily agree with each other at the level of speculation. But they came to a profound convergence on what ought to be opposed in thought and action.

For Maritain, the principal inspiration was Thomas Aquinas.[3] Thus Maritain's work bears a double mission of enlightening American citizens as to a deeper, sounder philosophy of government, but also of representing modern liberal democracy to the Church, whose conflicts with, and suspicions of the modern liberal, democratic state (the suspicions were, of course, reciprocal) date back centuries at least to the English and French revolutions as well as to numerous other skirmishes in both political and philosophic matters.[4]

*Man and the State* is a double achievement, for both the city of man and the city of God, for both its political philosophy and its theology. Sadly this double achievement has waned in its proper recognition. His achievement does not set the debate in the sphere of political thinking, in part, because the exponents of natural law philosophy, with claims about a stable nature and natural ends, continue to focus on the reductionism of social science and the deconstruction of post-modern philosophy. Maritain has, of course, in other works, launched a defense of natural foundations and an elaborate critique of the positivist mentality and the shortcomings of existentialist and historicist approaches. These achievements may wax again since they are, in principle, compatible with the revival of interest in natural law.

What may be surprising is the neglect with which Maritain is treated in his own historic tradition. Applauded before Vatican II as a source of renewal, yet disdained by some as too liberal, Maritain saw his reputation and influence slip after the Council, even though he was chosen by Paul VI to receive the Conciliar "Message to Men of Thought and Science."[5] A post-conciliar work entitled *The Peasant of the Garonne*, subtitled, "an old laymen questions himself about the present time," was received with much disappointment and rejection.[6] The great enthusiasm and readiness for experimentation was not yet ready for the words of caution and criticism. Many seemed to embrace change for the sake of change. But perhaps a passage from Burke's *Reflections* would help to indicate Maritain's attitude about the "revolution" – the experience of change and liberation is likened to a "wild gas" and Burke cautions that we "suspend our judgment until the first

---

[3] See Jacques Maritain, "The Apostle of Modern Times," in *St. Thomas Aquinas*, trans. Peter O'Reilly (New York: Meridian Books, 1958), pp. 88-118
[4] See John P. Hittinger, "Jacques Maritain and Yves R. Simon's Use of Thomas Aquinas in Their Defense of Liberal Democracy," in *Thomas Aquinas and His Legacy*, ed. David M. Gallagher (Washington, D.C.: The Catholic University of America Press, 1994), pp. 149-72. On Maritain's critique of the origins of modernity see his *Three Reformers: Luther, Descartes, Rousseau* (New York: Charles Scribner's Sons, 1929) and *Antimoderne* (Paris: Editions de la Revue des Jeunes, 1922).
[5] See new translation in the Appendix, "To Seekers of Truth: Message to Men of Thought and Science," p. 245.
[6] Jacques Maritain, *The Peasant of the Garonne: An Old Layman Questions Himself About the Present Time*, trans. Michael Cuddihy and Elizabeth Hughes (New York: Holt, Rinehart and Winston, 1968).

effervescence is a little subsided, and until we see something deeper than the agitation of a troubled and frothy surface."[7] But Maritain's caution was not heeded. Many reviewers focused on the tone, which they found bitter, or on its occasional *ad hominem* arguments.[8] Some declared that he had lost his wit as an old man who fearfully returned to a conservative position. Few seemed to appreciate the significance of the work as a completion of a lifetime project of engaging modernity as a 20th century disciple of Thomas Aquinas.

Maritain's project attempted to unite Thomistic and Aristotelian traditions with the human rights thrust of modern political philosophy. Maritain wished to reassess the liberal state in light of ancient and medieval political traditions, seeking to find what is true, enduring, and practical in the modern liberal state, while criticizing its excesses and reconceptualizing its philosophical foundations. This great project, whose trajectory begins with the criticism of the French right wing, runs through *Integral Humanism* and *Man and the State*. *The Peasant of the Garonne* displays the spiritual and intellectual center of Maritain's work and reveals many of the ideas that shaped Vatican II. There is a great myth concerning the intellectual life of the Church prior to Vatican II–specifically that it was impoverished by a lack of imagination, narrowly focused on scholastic hair-splitting, rigidly enclosed by dogma and irrelevant to the contemporary world. Many clerics and religious, educated by scholastic text books, were very susceptible to this view, and they found it liberating to read more progressive writers such as Karl Rahner, Teilhard de Chardin and Hans Kung. And while Rahner and Chardin may have kept faith, many of their enthusiasts followed the new methods and sources into dissent and often out of the Church and beyond Christianity itself. The attempt to reconcile the Tradition with the intellectual trends of the day is risky business. More often than not, the new element (be it Heidegger, Wittgenstein, or now Kolhberg and Derrida) comes to predominate and the Tradition is transformed beyond recognition or rejected outright. This is not always the case. John Paul II is a case in point; thoroughly steeped in phenomenology, John Paul is faithful and has successfully combined the old and the new. He was deeply influenced by prior generations of faithful scholars such as Garrigou-Lagrange and Jacques Maritain. Thus, while it is the case that textbook Thomism often ruled the day with a formulaic approach to the big questions, the deep intellectual germination of Leo XIII's encyclical *Aeterni Patris* (1890) came to bear extraordinary fruit during the 1930s and 1940s in the works of a number of French Thomists, including Father Garrigou LaGrange, Jacques Maritain, and Yves R. Simon.[9] The fruits of their scholarship, along with

---

[7] Edmund Burke, *Reflections on the Revolution in France*, ed. Conor Cruise O'Brien (New York: Penguin, 1969), p. 90.
[8] See Brooke W. Smith, *Maritain: Antimodern or Ultramodern?* (New York: Elsevier Scientific Publishing, 1976) and Bernard Doering, *Jacques Maritain and the French Catholic Intellectuals* (Notre Dame, Indiana: University of Notre Dame Press, 1983).
[9] See Leo XIII, "On Christian Philosophy," in *The Church Speaks to the Modern World: The Social Teachings of Leo XIII*, ed. Étienne Gilson (Garden City, New York: Image, 1954), pp. 29-54, and Victor B. Brezik, ed. *One Hundred Years of Thomism: Aeterni Patris and Afterwards - a Symposium* (Houston, Texas: Center for Thomistic Studies, 1981).

many other initiatives in liturgy, education, and politics gave rise to the great renewal of Vatican Council II. Maritain's books remain to give a sound interpretation in a time of a wildly swinging pendulum from one extreme to another, from an outright rejection of Vatican II by the traditionalists to the strained interpretation of the progressive wings of liberation theology and biblical deconstruction. In *The Peasant of the Garonne* Maritain humorously refers to these extremes as "the ruminators of the holy alliance" and the "sheep of the panurge."[10] But this is yet the "frothy surface" after a great council.

Maritain refers to the need for "a great and patient work of revitalizing in the order of intelligence and the order of spirituality."[11] Such a revitalization or renewal has tremendous political significance. It may be perhaps claiming too much to be reminded of Augustine's reference to his own work, *The City of God*, as a "great and arduous task."[12] But Maritain's scope and ambition, his inspiration and method, are no less. In *the Peasant of the Garonne* Maritain describes the post-Vatican II political and theological scene as follows: "In truth, every vestige of the Holy Empire is today liquidated; we have definitely emerged from the sacral age and the baroque age. After sixteen centuries which it would be shameful to slander or repudiate, but which have completed their death agony and whose grave defects were incontestable, a new age begins."[13] The collapse of the Roman empire and the emergence of the post-Constantinian era are of decisive historical weight. Perhaps the mid-twentieth century, after a second world war, a surprising ecumenical council, and the collapse of the Marxist empire prove the need of a new Augustinian effort. Maritain certainly thought so, as does John Paul II. We should not allow the contemporary lull and drift of world events at the beginning of a new century, or the sordidness of recent American public life, to discourage us from seeing the new possibilities for thought and action on behalf of liberty and human fulfillment and the new risks and challenges that loom on the horizon.

It is at just such a time that Maritain's freshness and purity of vision provides such charm and attraction. In the Preface to the new edition of *Man and the State*,[14] Ralph McInerny challenges us to ask why we have lost the optimism of Maritain. It strikes us, upon re-reading *Man and the State*, how much the climate has changed in this country since these lectures were initially given. Then there was a bold openness about the theological questions. In the 1940s and 1950s, it was part of common public philosophy to acknowledge the importance of religion for the democratic polity. All the Walgreen Lecturers were fully conversant with the Theological/Political question as it had emerged over the centuries of modern

---

[10] *Peasant*, p. 25.
[11] Ibid., p. 53.
[12] "Magnum opus et arduum, sed Deus adiutur noster est." Augustine, *The City of God against the Pagens*, trans. George E. McCracken, 7 vols. (Cambridge: Harvard University Press, 1957), vol. 1, p. 10. See Peter Brown, *Augustine of Hippo* (Berkeley: University of California Press, 1969), pp. 299-312.
[13] *Peasant*, p. 4
[14] Jacques Maritain, *Man and the State* (Washington, D.C., The Catholic University of America Press: 1998).

European history. It is a historic fact that religion has played no less a role than science or modern philosophy in the conception and founding of liberal democracy. The Theological/Political question is part of a broader, fuller political analysis, as Tocqueville, with characteristic perception, noted long ago. We should find it is an ever-present predicament, under the rubric of separation of church and state, that must realistically be resolved in a pluralistic society. It is a complex issue requiring legal and constitutional, as well as sociological, philosophical and theological approaches for a comprehensive solution. It is unremarkable, then, that Maritain chose as a central theme of *Man and the State* the importance of the religious and the theological to the health and vitality of liberal democracy.

But no longer is the Theological/Political question even seriously considered. Religion and irreligion have been reduced to the narrow confines of partisanship. Mainstream accounts of public philosophy now seek to exclude religion from the public square, formulating criteria by which religion can have no place in public reason. Our jurisprudence looks with suspicion upon religious expression, often declaring it hostile to the rights of citizens. Our education seeks to neutralize religious expression or even attacks it as politically incorrect. The very situation against which Maritain warned us fifty years ago has come to pass: the isolating antagonism of church and state. But his is a voice which should continue to be heard; he demonstrates the possibility of a public philosophy that is religious in its deepest inspiration and yet rational in its presentation, maintaining the possibility of dialogue in truly pluralistic conditions. He is an example of a noble and magnanimous soul who loves what is best in liberal democracy and who provides for its defense in speech and deed. He provides a historical and metaphysical perspective on the nature and prospects for liberal democracy, and at the same time points the way to a higher source of heroism and good citizenship so necessary for the vitality of liberal democracy. And this all centers on a constructive engagement between church and state, liberal democracy and the kingdom of God.

### Reading *Man and the State*

There are many paths into Maritain's account of, and defense of, liberal democracy, many of which are traversed by the authors of the papers in this collection. But let us consider the structure of *Man and the State*. Chapter One reflects on the notion of the people and the body politic. The very notion of the common good, Aristotelian in form, evidences the source of politics in the experience of polity. So, too, the notion of a pluralist conception of society with various forms of community, pre-political as well as intermediate groupings, grounds the limit on state power in a naturally multifaceted human situation and allows us to see afresh alternatives to monistic accounts of the state and its power. Maritain sharply distinguishes the "state" as the "topmost" administrative function from the "body politic" which is steeped in heritage and characterized by "structural pluralism." Maritain achieves in this chapter a fresh application of Aristotle's account of the political regime to the complexities of modern political life.

In Chapter Two, Maritain criticizes the notion of sovereignty insofar as it excludes accountability to the people, and reminds us of the limits to power exercised under God. In Chapter Three, Maritain offers a profound critique of Machiavelli as the ingenious advocate of technical artistry, to which he counters with a notion of the moral rationality of politics, by which he means that a regime must draw upon the vital energies and generosity of its citizens. Freedom and conscience will prove to be more politically enduring than the Machiavellian mode of manipulation and hypocrisy. Writing in 1950 Maritain serenely anticipates the demise of such "gigantic Machiavellian robots" as the Soviet Union, which must become "more perfect and ruthless in techniques of oppression, universal mutual spying, forced labor, mass deportation and mass destruction."[15] He says that "they do not possess lasting inner force; their huge machinery of violence is a token of their inner human weakness." He asks "how long can the power of the state endure which becomes more and more of a giant as regards the external or technical forces, and more and more of a dwarf as regards the internal human actually vital forces?" He confidently concludes, circa 1950, "I doubt that it can take root in the historic duration of nations." By way of contrast, Maritain proposes the "moral rationalization" of political life — a recognition of the human ends of political life and at the same time the use of human means — the use of "human energies as energies of free men." Maritain cites his mentor, Henri Bergson, who suggested that the gospel is the deepest root for democratic feeling and philosophy. "Democracy can only live on Gospel inspiration."[16] Without that inspiration, we would deprive democracy of its lifeblood, of faith in supra-material, supra-mathematical, and supra-sensory realities.

In the central and key chapter, Chapter Four, we encounter the orienting idea in Maritain's account of liberal democracy: the natural law foundation for human rights. It is well known that Maritain helped to draft the United Nations Charter on Human Rights. He explores this theme in various works.[17] Here we find a listing of basic rights and an explanation of human rights in light of natural law. He explains how human rights presuppose some notion of a stable human nature and an order of human goods. Again he proposes the thesis that the gospel leads to the greatest clarity concerning natural law, human rights and the dignity of the person.[18]

Now Maritain does not claim that this account is the only account; indeed he says that a secularist or a rationalist may give another account. But this leads to the next

---

[15] Ibid., p. 58. For recent comments on Maritain's refutation of Machiavelli, see James V. Schall, *Jacques Maritain: The Philosopher in Society* (Lanham, Maryland: Rowman & Littlefield, 1998) and his article "Was Maritain a Crypto-Machiavellian?" in *The Failure of Modernism: The Cartesian Legacy and Contemporary Pluralism*, ed. Brendan Sweetman (Washington, D.C.: American Maritain Association/The Catholic University of America Press, 1999), pp. 87-100; also see Markus Fischer, *Well-Ordered License: On the Unity of Machiavelli's Thought* (Lanham, Maryland: Lexington Books, 2000), pp. 199-205.
[16] Ibid., p. 61. For an elaboration see Jacques Maritain, *Christianity and Democracy*, trans. Doris C. Anson (New York: Charles Scribner's Sons, 1950) and *On the Use of Philosophy* (Princeton: Princeton University Press, 1961), chapter three.
[17] See in particular, *The Rights of Man and Natural Law*, trans. Doris C. Anson (New York: Charles Scribner's Sons, 1943).
[18] *Man and the State*, p. 90. See John P. Hittinger, "Three Philosophies of Human Rights," in *In Search of a National Morality*, ed. William Bentley Ball (Grand Rapids, Michigan: Baker Book House, 1992), pp. 246-58.

chapter on the democratic charter, expounding a key element of Maritain's philosophy of the pluralist state. No longer will there be a religious belief that gives unity to the political society. In fact, the society will be pluralist and have many diverse spiritual families, institutions and bodies. But they must share a common "secular faith" concerning the essentials of liberal democracy. Basic tenets at the core of our life together include the dignity of the human person, involving the enjoyment of basic rights but also the acceptance of civic responsibility individually, in the family and in our voluntary associations. We must adhere to the rule of law, to human equality, ideals of justice and fraternity, religious freedom and mutual tolerance.

These are practical tenets, points of practical convergence. In our common subscription to these we will, nevertheless, both have and confront varying theoretical justifications, given the diverse groups that must appear in political society. We can agree on the temporal or secular order of things to a substantial degree, and yet be divided on the theological issues or philosophic justifications for them. By the same token, Maritain doubts that a purely rational or scientific creed will be able to justify the practical convergence sufficiently. He urges that "religion and metaphysics are an essential part of human culture, primary and indispensable incentives in the very life of society;" the individualist and neutral approach to rights he thinks (incorrectly) is a thing of the past, although he correctly notes the weakness of such an approach. The polity can defend itself and its creed through democratic means — censorship, he says, is the worst way to seek unity. Inner energies, reason and conscience, are best. Education is key because it is the primary means to foster a "common secular faith." But the State's competency is severely limited. The "creed" must be "intrinsically established in truth."[19] Hence the State cannot help but resort to "philosophical and religious traditions and schools of thought that are spontaneously at work in the consciousness of the nation." It is an illusion to think our convictions can be taught effectively if abstracted from their metaphysical root. Do we not wish to allow for full understanding and personal inspiration in teaching? Jacques Maritain is perhaps the finest example of such a teacher: a defender of democracy using the full range of philosophical and theological arguments, a dialectical partner whose aim is not victory but discovery of the common truths of our lives together.

In the chapter on the Church and State Maritain outlines the significance of the "post Constantinian" approach that came to characterize offical Church teaching at Vatican II. Maritain explains the enduring principles of the roles of Church and state and yet provides a very effective argument concerning the different historical context in which they are to be applied. No longer is religion the basis for civil unity. But religion has a tremendous role to play in the field of education, morality and culture. One must read this chapter and then look at Paul VI's "Message to Guardians of Temporal Power,"[20] to fully appreciate the influence of Maritain.

---

[19] See Ralph McInerny, *Art and Prudence: Studies in the Thought of Jacques Maritain* (Notre Dame, Indiana: University of Notre Dame Press, 1988), chapter nine.
[20] For the content of the message see Appendix, p. 246.

The closing chapter is perhaps the most controversial. As we noted above, Maritain was instrumental in drafting the United Nations Declaration on Human Rights. In Chapter Seven Maritain makes a case for world government. As an associate of the Adler and Hutchins group, Maritain was deeply attracted to the idea of world government. I believe the reader will find a careful analysis of the problems and promises; he does not expect an overnight solution. He rejects a "super state" notion and he would undoubtedly deplore the centralized bureaucratic approach to world problems which has emerged of late from the United Nations. But he meditates deeply upon the problem of war and the exaggerated claims for state sovereignty. He argues for a "political" approach to world unity. Such an approach will undoubtedly take much time and generations of effort. But Maritain referred to himself as "a kind of spring finder pressing his ear to the ground in order to hear the sound of hidden springs, and of invisible germinations."[21] *Man and the State*, for all of its flaws and shortcomings, has indeed discovered some hidden springs for democratic politics and contains yet more invisible germinations for the city of God and the city of man.

## The Present Collection of Essays

These essays were inspired by the 1998 conference of the American Maritain Association whose theme was *Man and the State*. We have arranged the essays into four areas. The first group concerns politics and community in the modern world. Maritain's retrieval of Aquinas is articulated and applied to contemporary issues and compared with other thinkers such as Michael Oakeshott, Heinrich Rommen and Étienne Gilson. In Part II, entitled "Liberalism Reconsidered," Maritain's approach to liberalism is further applied and compared to problems concerning the meaning of democracy today. Part III takes up the theme of a natural law foundation for liberalism. The essays range from a critique of Maritain's use of Aquinas and a defense of a natural law approach to politics to specific applications of the natural law approach to contemporary issues in politics. Part IV ends with a consideration of Maritain and the Church in the Modern World. The essays explore Maritain's influence on Catholic social doctrine and some new paths in Christian approaches to the political regime. In the appendix we provide some new translations of remarks by Paul VI on the religious and political significance of Vatican II and the new approach to the city of man heralded by Vatican II. One of the statements, the "Message to Seekers of Truth," was received by Jacques Maritain from the hand of Paul VI.

It is our hope that this collection of essays, commemorating Maritain's *Man and the State*, will lead the reader to turn to Maritain's book and to join the project of intellectual and spiritual renewal which he helped to germinate. This will lead to a constructive reassessment of the liberal state.

---

[21] Jacques Maritain, *Notebooks*, trans. Joseph W. Evans (Albany, New York: Magi Books, 1984), p. 3.

# I

# Politics and Community in the Modern World

# 1

## Reasons for a Civil Society

### *Russell Hittinger*

In *Man and the State* (1951), Jacques Maritain argued that the political "madness" of twentieth-century Europe can be traced to the fact that modern democracies had never truly renounced the ideology of "substantialism"[1] — the myth "that the state is the people personified."[2] The so-called "absolutist" regimes of the sixteenth and seventeenth centuries claimed absolute sovereignty on the basis of a theological myth, the divine right of kings; the new regimes claimed the same powers, but now as a donation of the people themselves. For Maritain these different myths generated the same result: the state is *not* the relatively higher power within a network of authorities constituting the body politic; rather it is a separate and transcendent power entitled to act upon the body politic. At the end of World War II, Maritain felt that it was time to admit that one despotism had been exchanged for the other. Insofar as ideologies compete to produce a separate and transcendent state, history teaches that non-democratic ideologies can produce such a state more effectively. In a famous sentence at the conclusion of chapter three of *Man and the State*, Maritain asserted: "The two concepts of Sovereignty and Absolutism have been forged together on the same anvil. They must be scrapped together."[3]

Maritain's alternative is an instrumentalist conception of the state. By this, he certainly did not mean that the political common good is a merely instrumental good; rather, he meant that the apparatus of public law is an instrument serving the rights and liberties of various societies, which, together, form a whole that

---

[1] Jacques Maritain, *Man and the State* (Chicago: The University of Chicago Press, 1951), p. 14; p. 16, n. 11.
[2] Ibid., p. 52. Maritain deploys the older papal criticism that the modern state rests upon a "fiction." "Since there is no such thing as the general popular will," Von Ketteler argued, "one has to rely on a fiction." "The Labor Problem and Christianity" (1864), in *The Social Teachings of Wilhelm Emmanuel Von Kettler*, trans. Rupert J. Ederer (Lanham, Maryland: University Press of America, 1981), p. 363. Von Ketteler's critique of the modern state as a "fiction" was adopted by Leo XIII twenty years later. "It is plain, moreover, that the pact which they allege is openly a falsehood and a fiction." *Diuturnum*, §§ 11-12; Leo XIII, "On Civil Government," in *The Church Speaks to the Modern World: The Social Teachings of Leo XIII*, ed. Étienne Gilson (Garden City, New York: Image, 1954), pp. 40-56. Pope Pius XII, too, continues the Leonine critique of the modern state as "fiction." In his 1942 Christmas address, he refers to "superimposed and fictitious" order.
[3] *Man and the State*, p. 53.

cannot be equated with the state. In Maritain's view, the post-war repair of the nations — achieving a "pluralistically organized body politic"[4] — requires us to say both yes and no to the modern political experiment. No, to the concept of absolute sovereignty; yes, to the eighteenth-century Enlightenment's notion of inalienable rights — viz. rights which cannot be transferred to the state.[5]

I will emphasize in this paper that Maritain's critique of substantialism represents an important moment in the history of Catholic political theory. He was by no means the only Catholic thinker to move in this direction.[6] In the late 1940s, the idea of the "juridical state," distinct from the body politic, was advanced by John Courtney Murray. Pope Pius XII, too, moved the Church in this same direction. In his Christmas addresses of 1944, he asserted that democracy "appears to be a postulate of nature imposed by reason itself,"[7] chiefly because it can serve as a check upon despotism. The Pope did not use the word "instrumental," but in context it is clear that he and Maritain were advocating the same position. Democracy can be recommended insofar as it checks the despotism of the state, *and* (here is the crucial qualification) insofar as social unity does not model itself on this instrument. Social unity, Pius warned, always must be regarded as an intrinsic perfection of human beings. The state is an instrument of different modes of solidarity; it is neither the substance nor the exemplar of society. Hence, by convergent lines of argument, Catholic thinkers decisively shifted away from solidarist (or exemplarist) conceptions of the state in favor of solidarist conceptions of the body politic. This change of perspective would prevail at Vatican II. In *Gaudium et Spes*, for example, we read: "As for public authority, it is not its function to determine the character of the civilization, but rather to establish the conditions and to use the means which are capable of fostering the life of culture[8] …. The political community exists, consequently, for the sake of the common good, in which it finds its full justification and significance, and the source of its inherent legitimacy. Indeed, the common good embraces the sum of those conditions of the social life whereby men, families and associations more adequately and readily may attain their own perfection."[9]

To really appreciate the importance and novelty of this move away from solidarist conceptions of the state to solidarist conceptions of civil society it would be necessary to understand how long it took for the modern (post-1789) Church to come to this insight. From 1789 to 1939, Roman authorities understood perfectly well the despotic

---

[4] Ibid., p. 23.
[5] Ibid., p. 95.
[6] This is what John Courtney Murray quite accurately called the "juridical state." For this discussion, see Murray's essays: "The Problem of Religious Freedom," *Theological Studies* 25 (December 1964), pp. 503-75; "The Issue of Church and State at Vatican Council II," *Theological Studies* 27 (December 1966), pp. 580-606.
[7] "1944 Christmas Message of His Holiness Pope Pius XII: Addressed to the People of the Entire World on the Subject of Democracy and a Lasting Peace." §19. He says that the world would not have been "dragged into the vortex of a disastrous war" had there been "efficient guarantees in the people themselves." §12.
[8] *Pastoral Constitution on the Church in the Modern World (Gaudium et Spes)* (Boston: Daughters of St Paul, 1965), §59.
[9] Ibid., §74.

and even totalitarian impulses of the new regimes. They also understood that the doctrine of royal absolutism had produced its mirror image in the revolutionary regimes. Papal encyclicals usually defended the rights of society against the states born in the revolutions. Even so, theologians like Bishop Von Ketteler, and popes from Pius IX to Pius XI, were unwilling to completely abandon what then was called a corporativist conception of the state. For one thing, their imaginations were still informed by the sacral model of kingship, and it would take the Great War to make that model practically obsolete.[10] The more important reason, however, was the one mentioned by Pius XII in his 1944 Christmas address: they feared that once the state is depicted in instrumentalist terms, the other organs of society would inevitably follow suit. In other words, they feared that the liberal state, even in its most favorable depiction as an instrument rather than the substance of the common good, would produce atomism and instrumentalism in every other sector of society. The disaster of World War II made it necessary to reconsider. Maritain's work deeply influenced this reconsideration of the nature of the state. Today, one can discern the stamp of his mind on the encyclicals of John Paul II, who, if anything, expounds the instrumentalist conception of the state more aggressively than did Maritain himself.

If the theory of the instrumental state represents a decisive adaptation of Catholic thought to the best of liberal tradition, what sense are we to make of the rest of the liberal tradition which does tend to view civil society in terms similar to the state? As Von Ketteler asserted in the mid-nineteenth century: "The associations that modern liberalism sponsors ... are mechanical assemblages of people who are thrown together merely for some superficial, utilitarian end."[11]

A perusal of current literature on civil society would indicate well enough that this problem has not been entirely put to rest. Take, for example, Ernest Gellner's *Conditions of Liberty: Civil Society and its Rivals*. Ernest Gellner sets out to explain (for a central and eastern European audience) what makes polities of the west so much more successful than their rivals in the east. He insists that the correct answer is not democracy or capitalism — nor even a constitutional scheme of legally protected individual liberties — but rather the "miracle of Civil Society."[12] "Civil society," as Gellner defines it, "is that set of diverse non-governmental institutions which is strong enough to counterbalance the state and, while not preventing the state from fulfilling its role of keeper of the peace and arbitrator between major interests, can nevertheless prevent it from dominating and atomizing the rest of society."[13]

We notice that Gellner's definition focuses our attention on the instrumental function and value of civil society. It checks the powers of the state and of the extended family. This view is traceable to Montesquieu who held that liberty is found only in

---

[10] Pius XI inaugurated the Feast of Christ the King in the encyclical *Quas Primas*, issued on Dec. 11, 1925; Pius recognized the futility of speaking of the sacral kingship of temporal authority; indeed, the gist of this encyclical is that church rather than the state exemplifies that Kingship; Pius XI, "On the Kingship of Christ," in *The Church and the Reconstruction of the Modern World: The Social Encyclicals of Pius XI*, ed. Terence P. McLaughlin (Garden City, New York: Image, 1957), pp. 53-72.
[11] "The Labor Problem and Christianity," in *The Social Teachings of Wilhelm Emmanuel Von Kettler*, pp. 408-9. The next sentence reads: "Whatever future it may have, therefore, the cooperative idea belongs to Christendom."
[12] Ernest Gellner, *Conditions of Liberty: Civil Society and its Rivals* (New York: The Penguin Press, 1994), p. 32.
[13] Ibid., p. 5.

moderate governments, "where power must check power by the arrangement of things."[14] Intermediate powers (*pourvoirs intermeditaires*), especially in aristocratic societies, contribute to the scheme of power checking power. Tocqueville, who more than anyone else set the terms of discussion about civil society, perhaps was more appreciative than Montesquieu of the intrinsic value of free, non-governmental institutions.[15] Yet his famous discussion of intermediate associations in *Democracy in America* is framed almost entirely in the terms of how they remedy the destructive consequences of modern democracy, especially its bent toward centralization and uniformity. Tocqueville never fully transcends the instrumentalist conception of civil society.

The problem with the instrumentalist depiction of civil society is that it leaves few options for defending civil society other than showing that useful goods, including liberty, are more efficiently produced and distributed by non-governmental agents. As Gellner says, civil society is the "social residue left when the state is subtracted."[16] So, if there are socially useful goods better achieved in the private sector, it becomes necessary either to give power-checking-power reasons, or to give cost-benefit reasons why we ought to subtract from the state's power. We are all familiar with such policy arguments: e.g., that education is better attained if parents have more options for where to send their children to school, or that security for the elderly is best effected through private investment than by state mandated social security. The author of a recent book entitled *More Guns, Less Crime* goes so far as to argue that citizens ought to be able to carry concealed weapons because private citizens, acting in self-defense, kill three times as many criminals each year as are killed by the police.[17] In an ingenious new book, *Membership and Morals*, Nancy Rosenblum advances the escape valve model of civil society, once again in reference to the state.[18] A pluralism of private associations, including those that are incongruent with ideals of liberal democracy, are useful, she explains, because they let off the steam of illiberal impulses.

The main problem with the policy-oriented view of civil society is what it leaves out of the picture. The power-checking-power and economistic reasons typically leave out of the picture the intrinsic perfections which make solidarity worth undertaking for its own sake.

Let us briefly consider a thirteenth-century treatise which may be the first, or at least one of the first, systematic defenses of civil society. Medieval thinkers, of course, had no single linguistic equivalent for our terms "civil society." Theologians like Thomas used variations on the word *societas: societas oeconomica, societas politica, societas privata,*

---

[14] Montesquieu, *The Spirit of the Laws*, trans. Anne M. Cohler, Basia Carolyn Miller, and Harold Samuel Stone (Cambridge: Cambridge University Press, 1989), 11.4.
[15] "The morals and intelligence of a democratic people would be in as much danger as its commerce and industry if ever a government wholly usurped the place of private associations. Feelings and ideas are renewed, the heart enlarged, and the understanding developed only by the reciprocal action of men one upon another." Alexis de Tocqueville, *Democracy in America*, trans. George Lawrence (Garden City, New York: Doubleday & Co., 1969), II.2.5
[16] *Conditions of Liberty*, p. 212.
[17] John R. Lott, *More Guns, Less Crime* (Chicago: The University of Chicago Press, 1998).
[18] Nancy L. Rosenblum, *Membership and Morals: The Personal Uses of Pluralism in America* (Princeton: Princeton University Press, 1998).

*societas publica, societas saecularis*, and so forth. But they did understand the value of free associations not reducible to the family or the state. The case in point is *Contra impugnantes*, Thomas's apologetic for the Dominican vocation.[19] First, allow me to say a few words about *Contra impugnantes*, and then I will show why it is relevant to modern Catholic social and political theory.

In the year 1256, Thomas and Bonaventure were summoned to the court of Pope Alexander IV to defend the newly formed mendicant orders. William of Saint-Amour, a doctor of the Sorbonne, charged that the "double spirit" of action and contemplation embodied by mendicants is a novel way of life that perverts the principles of both civil and ecclesiastical society. In *De periculis novissimorum temporum* ("The Perils of these most novel [or, Last] times," 1256), William of Saint-Amour launched a number of criticisms of the mendicants. The mendicants, he asserted:

- Violate the principle of a society of contemplatives by seeking to act on others rather than being purely receptive of divine grace;
- Violate civil and ecclesiastical jurisdictional authority by moving from place to place, unlike secular and monastic clergy;
- Violate the virtue of humility by acquiring and communicating learning in universities;
- Violate monastic order by refusing to engage in manual labor;
- Violate principles of justice by dispensing wisdom for alms;
- Violate principles of familial order by recruiting young men and women.

Thomas's response comes down to us in the *Opusculum* entitled *Contra impugnantes*, written in 1256, and probably summarized orally for the Pope in that same year. Here, I will outline the main thrust of his response. Thomas contends the "active life" consists of more than political rule and mercantile pursuits.[20] Granted that religious are neither magistrates or businessmen, they are "active" in other ways, including the communication of knowledge and wisdom by teaching and preaching. The active life, generically understood, is the communication of gifts. In this, all agents imitate God. Strictly speaking, there is no such thing as a society that is in every respect receptive. Although *societas* is an analogous term, every society, he argues, is constituted by "communications"[21] whereby goods are given and received. In Thomas's works, every analogous use of the word *societas* is mirrored by uses of the word *communicatio: communicatio oeconomica, communicatio spiritualis, communicatio civilis*, and so forth. The word communicatio simply means making something common, one rational agent participating in the life of another. Society, for Thomas, is not a thing, but an activity.

---

[19] Thomas Aquinas, *Contra impugnantes Dei cultum et religionem* (Rome: Marietti, 1954) *Opuscula Theol.*, vol. 2, pp. 5-110; *An Apology for the Religious Orders*, trans. J. Proctor (Westminster, Maryland: Newman, 1950). See discussion by James A. Weisheipl, *Friar Thomas D'Aquino: His Life, Thought, and Works* (Garden City, New York: Doubleday, 1974), pp. 88-91, 383-84.
[20] *Contra impugnantes*, II.7
[21] Ibid., I.3

The multiplicity of vocations and skills whereby men engage in different common projects for the benefit of all society, Thomas argues, is grounded "primarily in Divine Providence, and, secondarily, in natural causes whereby certain men are disposed to the performance of certain functions in preference to others."[22] Thus, he argues for a "right" of men to associate for good works across classes and states of life: "any person who is competent to perform some special function, has a right to be admitted to the society of those who are selected for the exercise of that function." That Dominicans would sit and teach in schools alongside the laity and the youth was a point of scandal in the controversy. It seemed that the fixed order of social classes was being jumbled. But Thomas contended: "an association of study is a society, established with the object of teaching and of learning; and as not only laymen, but also religious, have a right to teach and to learn, there can be no doubt that, both these classes may lawfully unite in one society."[23]

Therefore, to prevent free men and women from associating for the purpose of communicating gifts is contrary to the natural law. It is tantamount to denying to rational agents the perfection proper to their nature, and denying to the commonweal goods it would not enjoy were it not for free associations. To the argument that the active-contemplative would no longer possess the fruit of his contemplation, Thomas points out that the giving of knowledge does not deplete the gift possessed by the giver. The contemplative is not less graced when he preaches what he receives from God; nor is the teacher less learned when he communicates knowledge to the student; nor is anyone less "free" by virtue of imparting a gift to another. Thomas here quotes Augustine's *De doctrina christiana*: "Everything that is not lessened by being imparted, is not, if it be possessed without being communicated, possessed as it ought to be possessed."[24]

But, what about authority? Isn't it depleted if multiplied? This, in fact, was one of the major fears of local church authorities about Dominicans taking the fruit of contemplation into universities and pulpits. Thomas answers that this charge makes sense if authority is thought to consist only in the power to make laws. The free society of mendicants does nothing of the sort, for Dominicans do not usurp the authority of magistrates or bishops, but rather enjoy authority that naturally supervenes upon doing a job well. Interestingly, Thomas mounts an argument against the creation of monopolies in academic professoriate.[25] Indeed, he even makes cost-benefit argument in behalf of mendicant teachers and preachers. Mendicants work for the social good, taking only freely given alms: they make no effort to legally compel compensation for their efforts; rather, they only argue at law for the right to receive those donations freely given to them.[26]

---

[22] Ibid., I.5
[23] Ibid., I.3
[24] Ibid., I.4
[25] Ibid.
[26] Ibid., I.7

Though this is a rather compact summary of Thomas's argument, nonetheless we can draw into view a picture of the kind of he society has in mind. It is a society constituted by a voluntary reciprocal action for the common good; a society that multiplies associational authorities without usurping the authority properly belonging to law-making authorities (ecclesiastical and civil). But it is also a society distinguished from the more sedentary pattern of rights, obligations, and classes which characterize the family and extended kinship. Thomas's argument for voluntary societies must be sharply distinguished from the pre-modern understanding of the "ancient constitution." Based upon charters, customs, and local privileges, the ancient constitution preserved plural authorities, and it had considerable resources for resisting centralization — but it was essentially conservative. As in the *Magna Carta*, the prince was forbidden to make incursions into those spheres of aristocratic liberty and authority where he had never been before. In effect, the prince was forbidden to introduce novel forms and applications of authority. Thomas's argument for liberty is of an entirely different sort, for he argues for the invention of new forms of associational liberty despite the claims of vested privilege and class. And as I have already mentioned, he claims "rights" not only for the corporate mission of the mendicants, but also for individuals.

With remarkable clarity and prescience, Thomas saw what was at stake in the charges that mendicants travel too much, refuse manual labor, and recruit the young. Let us examine briefly comment on each of these three charges before I move back to the main point of this paper.

Mendicants are unlike secular clergy, who are bound to their diocese, and unlike monks who are bound by a vow of stability to their monastery. Thomas understood that *societas* cannot be absolutely constrained to such places and boundaries. The body politic of Christendom was international, and the good of that body politic transcended the relatively static conditions of feudal order. The diocesan clergy and monks reduplicated feudal order in their respective organizations. The mendicants broke free of that feudal order not only by their mobility — their portable authority, as it were — but also by refusing to be bound to the monastic practice of manual labor. The effort of critics to keep religious in a single place, under the drudgery of manual labor, was nothing less than an effort to block the introduction of new social forms in society. Here, of course, the new "form" was evangelical. It concerned purely voluntary societies brought into being neither by commerce, by positive law, nor by matrimonial procreation, but by free response to grace. Such societies of gift-givers do not cancel out, but by the same token, are not reducible to either legal or paternal authority. As Thomas understood in his own case, the bid to prevent Dominicans from recruiting the young was motivated by the desire to shield authority from novelty, from freedom, ultimately from grace.

It might seem to be a long stretch from medieval societies of mendicants, living in voluntary poverty, to modern issues of civil society. But this is not true. In *Rerum Novarum* (1891), Pope Leo XIII's argument for the rights of association by laborers relies directly on *Contra impugnantes*.[27] Some scholars have suggested that Pope Leo borrowed the language of "rights" from John Locke.[28] Perhaps there is some truth to this interpretation with respect to Leo's understanding of property rights. The main argument in *Rerum novarum*, however, is not from the right of property but the right of association. As for the rights of private association, Leo's use of rights language is drawn directly from Thomas's *Contra impugnantes*.

In *Centesimus Annus*, written both to celebrate the centennial of *Rerum novarum* the recent collapse of Communism in Eastern Europe, Pope John Paul II continues this line of argument. Pope John Paul II refers to "intermediate communities [which] exercise primary functions and give life to specific networks of solidarity."[29]

> When man does not recognize in himself and in others the value and grandeur of the human person, he effectively deprives himself of the possibility of benefiting from his humanity and of entering into that relationship of solidarity and communion with others for which God created him. Indeed, it is through the free gift of self that one truly finds oneself. This gift is made possible by the human person's essential "capacity for transcendence".... As a person, one can give oneself to another person or to other persons, and ultimately to God, who is the author of our being and who alone can fully accept our gift. A person is alienated if he refuses to transcend himself and to live the experience of self-giving and of the formation of an authentic human community oriented towards his final destiny, which is God. A society is alienated if its forms of social organization, production and consumption make it more difficult to offer this gift of self and to establish this solidarity between people.[30]

Perhaps it would not be entirely misleading to say that there has been a laicization of the idea of society as *communicatio* — a laicization already begun in *Rerum novarum* when Leo XIII took the defense of mendicant liberty as a model for a defense of the rights of workers to organize. This laicization is especially necessary in societies where so many things are mediated by free choice, and where the primary model of free choice is drawn from economic markets. In this kind of society, it is necessary to provide something more than merely instrumental reasons for free, social order. Indeed, it becomes necessary to give reasons for what is *perfected*, rather than merely *maximized*, by free choice. The modern mind has little trouble understanding what is maximized by a zone of free society, that is, by a zone of freedom that is not reducible to the law of the state. Gellner, for example, will

---

[27] See Leo XIII, "On the Rights and Duties of Capital and Labor," in *The Church Speaks to the Modern World: The Social Teachings of Leo XIII*, ed. Étienne Gilson (Garden City, New York: Image, 1954), pp. 200-44.
[28] Ernest L. Fortin, "'Sacred and Inviolable': *Rerum Novarum* and Natural Rights." *Theological Studies* 53 (1992), pp. 202-33.
[29] John Paul II, *On the Hundredth Anniversary of Rerum Novarum (Centesimus Annus)* (Washington, D.C.: United States Catholic Conference, 1991), § 49.
[30] Ibid., §41.

propose that this zone of liberty constitutes a check upon the power of the state, which, in turn, gives rise to economic associations, which, in turn, maximize productivity, which, to close the circle, immunize society against the overweening administrative ambitions of state power. But what is perfected in this process? Or to put the question slightly differently, what would be missing from the world if the state were to be the primary agent in charge of bringing about social goods? Except to say that life would be suffocating, and our private choices reduced in scope, Gellner does not tell us.

Taking Isaiah Berlin's celebrated distinction between positive and negative liberty in "Two Concepts of Liberty", we can frame the question in this way.[31] Liberalism has triumphed in Catholic political theory insofar as the state is no longer considered the end, substance, or exemplar of positive liberty (freedom *for*). There is an entirely appropriate way to express liberty in negative terms (freedom *from*) vis-à-vis the state. But how do we understand the liberty of society itself?

I read the work of the present papal magisterium as an effort to answer that question. The question is not whether it is useful to enjoy "private" liberties insofar as they are distinguished from the power of the state. Since the collapse of the Communist experiment, the argument from utility has been won. The question today is what to do with liberty and how to understand it on something more than the grounds offered by economists.

Solidarity is an inherently complex notion.[32] To provide only a short list, in contemporary papal encyclicals solidarity can mean: (i) common material *things*, which are subject to distributive justice; (ii) sociological or economic *states of affairs*, such as technological and economic interdependence; (ii) *personal attitudes*, dispositions, or virtues with regard to what is, or should be, common; (iv) *activities*, in the sense of teamwork and collaboration toward common ends; (v) loving *communion* between persons, where the communion is the very goal of action.

If we examine recent encyclicals, we discover three main foci for the terms "solidarity" or "common good." Undoubtedly, there are others. But these three can be gathered easily from the texts.

First, the common good can consist of goods realized in individuals, which are called "common" by virtue of a common species. For example, human beings share a common humanity, even though there is no "humanity" existing independently of individuals, nor a "humanity" distributed to persons. This ontological perfection is only "in" individuals; so, from individuals we gather the predicate that is common.

---

[31] Isaiah Berlin, "John Stuart Mill and the Ends of Life," in *Four Essays on Liberty* (Oxford: Oxford University Press, 1969), pp. 173-206.
[32] "In this way what we nowadays call the principle of solidarity, the validity of which both in the internal order of each nation and in the international order I have discussed in the encyclical *Sollicitudo Rei Socialis*, is clearly seen to be one of the fundamental principles of the Christian view of social and political organization. This principle is frequently stated by Pope Leo XIII, who uses the term 'friendship,' a concept already found in Greek philosophy. Pope Pius XI refers to it with the equally meaningful term 'social charity.' Pope Paul VI, expanding the concept to cover the many modern aspects of the social question, speaks of a 'civilization of love'." *Centesimus Annus*, §10

By virtue of our common humanity, three notions arise: (i) common status, in the sense that no person is more or less human than another; (ii) common ontological perfections, such as health, knowledge, and religious devotion; (iii) common utilities, such as money, food, and technology. Each of these can be the ground of moral and legal rights; each can express a reason for solidarity. In *Sollicitudo Rei Socialis*, the "virtue" of solidarity is described (initially) as the willingness to make a moral response to common goods as we have just described them: "It is above all a question of interdependence, sensed as a system determining relationships in the contemporary world in its economic, cultural, political and religious elements, and accepted as a moral category. When interdependence becomes recognized in this way, the correlative response as a moral and social attitude, as a 'virtue,' is solidarity."[33]

Thus, when John Paul II speaks of "solidarity towards society's weakest members,"[34] he emphasizes our common humanity, which prohibits us from cutting corners in the distribution of legal rights and economic resources. When, in *Pacem in Terris* John XXIII speaks of "the requirements of universal common goods,"[35] and when *Gaudium et Spes* refers to one person depending on another "in needful solidarity,"[36] the common utilities are being emphasized.

I place these three diverse notions of "common" into one set, because they are either properties realized in individuals (e.g., human, life, knowledge, health), or useful goods (food, computers, health care plans) which are made common by virtue of a just order of distribution.[37] If we restrict ourselves to this first set of meanings, we shall understand that we are all human, and that there are cords of interdependence in realizing our perfections. We conduct most of our debates about civil society at this level, for here we engage the persistent issues in public policy, including the characteristically instrumental problems about how best to distribute and nurture fundamental human goods and utilities. Here, too, in the Anglo-American world, we typically consider the question of where the agency of the state ought to begin and end.

The second set of meanings for solidarity and common good can be described generally as *common activities*. The notions of "collaboration," "cooperation," the

---

[33] John Paul II, *On Social Concerns (Sollicitudo Rei Socialis)* (Washington, D. C.: United States Catholic Conference, 1987), §38.
[34] John Paul II, *The Gospel of Life (Evangelium Vitae)* (New York: Times Book/Random House, 1995), §8.
[35] John XXIII, *Peace on Earth (Pacem in Terris)* (Boston: Daughters of St. Paul, 1963), §7.
[36] *Gaudium et Spes*, §4.
[37] Thomas Aquinas argued that the ontological perfection of being human is common according to what reason understands (*secundum rationem*), or common by predication (*commune in praedicando*). The same can be said for health, temperance, and knowledge, which are in individuals, but "take on a universal character in the intellect." Useful goods are not necessarily public; indeed such things as food and money are usually the things privately exchanged in commutative justice. They can be made common, however, to ensure their distribution to the welfare of the community. If "common" is exhausted by the aforesaid notions, we face the problem of a conflict between the good of the individual and the public good. This is why St. Thomas argues that the common good immediately relevant to social order is not the good common by community of genus or species, but rather the good "common by the community of final cause" (*non quidem communitate generis vel speciei, sed communitate causae finalis*), ST, I-II, 90.2.

"spirit of creative initiative," and the "expanding chain of solidarity" express, in different ways, and at different levels, common goods as common activities. Depending on the particular encyclical, the idea of solidarity as common activities is applied to domestic political order, international relations, the initiatives of intermediate societies, and economic life. In *Centesimus Annus*, John Paul II emphasizes that the market represents not only the good of things to be distributed, but also the good of reciprocal actions:

> By means of his work a person commits himself, not only for his own sake but also for others and with others. Each person collaborates in the work of others and for their good. One works in order to provide for the needs of one's family, one's community, one's nation, and ultimately all humanity. Moreover, a person collaborates in the work of his fellow employees, as well as in the work of suppliers and in the customers' use of goods, in a progressively expanding chain of solidarity.[38]

Here, our main focus is not given to the external good to be commonly distributed, but rather goods inherent to activity. It raises the issue of subsidiarity. If the common good is constituted by the common activity, then whenever "higher" powers intervene in such a way that the common activity is supplanted, or whenever the result of common activity is achieved behind the back, as it were, of the collaborative activity itself, the distinctive good of society is lost. Take, for example, the common activities which go into the work of an orchestra. Every part needs to be harmonized with the others in order to produce the desired result. If the good being aimed at were simply the external result, however, then there is no reason, other than aesthetic preference, why a computer-generated concerto wouldn't suffice. But we all know that common activity constitutes part of the good being aimed at.

The point is that where collaboration is not an inherent, but a merely useful good, the grounds for subsidiarity are greatly weakened. Except on contingent grounds of efficiency, there is no good reason why the state should do everything, or by the same token, do nothing. Therefore, it seems that a truly useful concept of subsidiarity depends upon a concept of solidarity that preserves the intrinsic value of collaborative activity. Without that value, discussion about subsidiarity easily becomes, as in our American policy debates over "federalism," an issue of magnitudes concerning money and power.

Suppose, for example, that a policy expert could show that "welfare" is most efficiently accomplished delivered by sub-contracting the work to a private firm. In this case, care of the indigent is neither by the state nor by civil society. Would we be missing anything by commissioning others to do this work? The same question can be asked with respect to a wide array of collaborative activities. For example, why shouldn't parent's sub-contract acts of parenting to someone else? If solidarity were restricted to the first set of notions (common nature, perfections,

---

[38] *Centesimus Annus*, §43.

and utilities) we could satisfy (hypothetically) the requirements of the common good by adopting whatever policies most efficiently distribute the useful goods. The fact that we do not engage common activities is neither here nor there, except perhaps as a matter of individual preference. It is only when we identify goods of common activities that we can discover a principled limit to the power of the state as well as to the subcontracting (or "out-sourcing") mentality characteristic of markets.

At this juncture it is appropriate to introduce John Paul II's understanding of the "subjectivity" of society. In *Centesimus*, he refers to the subjectivity of society in terms of "structures of participation and shared responsibility"[39] He writes, "the social nature of man is not completely fulfilled in the State, but is realized in various intermediary groups, beginning with the family and including economic, social, political and cultural groups which stem from human nature itself and have their own autonomy, always with a view to the common good. This is what I have called the 'subjectivity' of society which, together with the subjectivity of the individual, was canceled out by 'Real Socialism'."[40] Notice that the argument against socialism is not chiefly an argument about its inefficiency: viz., that the common good, as a just distribution of resources, was not met. Rather, what was "canceled out" was the common good(s) constituted by free, collaborative agents.

The expressions "subjectivity of society" and "expanding chain of solidarity" often sit adjacent to yet another idea of common good. Earlier, I quoted John Paul II's rather flat definition of the virtue of solidarity as a certain moral attitude taken toward interdependence. Now, consider the following definition, which crops up two sections later in *Sollicitudo*:

> Solidarity is undoubtedly a Christian virtue. In what has been said so far it has been possible to identify many points of contact between solidarity and charity, which is the distinguishing mark of Christ's disciples ... Beyond human and natural bonds, already so close and strong, there is discerned in the light of faith a new model of the unity of the human race, which must ultimately inspire our solidarity. This supreme model of unity, which is a reflection of the intimate life of God, one God in three Persons, is what we Christians mean by the word "communion."[41]

We immediately see that a distinct notion has been added to the idea of a common good. Although this third range of meanings is almost always discussed in theological terms, the idea of a *common good as communion*, where the communion is the very good being aimed at. To be sure, marriage is at least a matter of collaborative activities. But a marriage can be understood as something more than a common good constituted by collaborative activity. It is also a communion, a flesh of one flesh unity. Married people can use their relationship as

---

[39] Ibid., §46.
[40] Ibid., §13. See also *Sollicitudo Rei Socialis*, §15.
[41] *Sollicitudo Rei Socialis*, §40.

a useful means for the distribution of goods (for themselves, for children, and for wider society); married people also constitute an essential cell, indeed a model, for the goods of mutual deliberation; but if they do not achieve the unity of one flesh they simply do not do what married people do *qua* married. For the Catholic Church, marriage is a sign and instrument of the union of God and man.[42]

The encyclicals and conciliar documents speak of "spiritual unity," or "interior unity," or "communion" typically in reference to marriage, eucharistic fellowship, and baptism through which the individual is grafted into the body of Christ. The "civilization of love" includes all of these diverse notions of common good, and not just the theological one. But the theological concept of communion is the main model for what the papacy means by the proposition that man is inherently social.

Maritain's generation had to win the argument about the nature of the state. It represented a long over-due reckoning with the Anglo-American experiment. Now that Catholic thought has been liberated from any temptation to sacralize or substantialize the state, attention can be given to the pressing issue of society itself.

---

[42] Ibid., §31.

# 2

# Jacques Maritain and Michael Oakeshott on the Modern State

## *Timothy Fuller*

For present purposes I shall stipulate that the object of investigation of classical political philosophy is the ancient city and that the object of investigation of modern political philosophy is the modern European state. Jacques Maritain in *Man and the State* investigates the character of the modern state but also proposes a third possible object of investigation, the world political society.[1] Michael Oakeshott, on the other hand, explores, especially in *On Human Conduct*, the character of the modern European state as it has come to be, without speculating on what it may become in the future.[2] Maritain is proposing something that might be called post-modern, in a peculiar sense of the term, though he expresses this in terms of a philosophy of history that has ancient roots and an evolutionary character. Michael Oakeshott is a modern in seeking to understand the premises upon which the modern state has been conceived and modern politics have operated, and in distinguishing those premises from ancient alternatives. Both Maritain and Oakeshott recognize the emergence of the individual as a defining feature of the modern situation, although Oakeshott does not make the idea of natural rights central to this and Maritain does.

To speak somewhat loosely, one might say that Maritain engages in philosophizing that is idealistic in suggesting to us what we ought to be doing and what we ought to be aspiring to based on his analysis of what he finds to be the providential lessons of history, while Oakeshott philosophizes in the indicative mood: he seeks to explain what we have been doing and what we understand ourselves to be about, refusing to prescribe, because he does not think that one can, as a philosopher, prescribe a direction to take.

Maritain, although speaking within the Catholic tradition, is in many respects rooted in a nineteenth-century liberal progressivism reminiscent at times of both Immanuel Kant and John Stuart Mill, leavened by a Wilsonian internationalism

---

[1] Jacques Maritain, *Man and the State* (Chicago: The University of Chicago Press, 1951).
[2] Michael Oakeshott, *On Human Conduct* (Oxford: Clarendon Press, 1975).

preoccupied with the advent of the cold war and the bipolarity of the nuclear age; Oakeshott is conservative and a political realist, less willing to take his philosophical understanding of politics from the events that were immediately contemporary to both Maritain and himself. He did not, for example, think that the atomic bomb was a revelatory experience. I am not seeking to make a judgment of better or worse at this point, but rather to highlight what seems to me to be obvious differences in their understanding of the philosophical task and its relation to contemporary events, and to set them in dialectical relation. Maritain is a neo-Thomist progressive while Oakeshott is an Augustinian skeptic. What I propose to do is to set out the thesis of each on the modern state to see what we may learn from the comparison.

## I

From the outset in *Man and the State*, Maritain wishes to characterize the idea of the modern state correctly, thereby establishing the scope, and thus the limits, of the modern state. He does this by putting the state in a grand historical context that is for him nothing less than the materialization of the Gospel in world history, with the emergence of natural rights in modern times as the articulation of what was implicit in the medieval natural law tradition, indeed in the very being of humanity. In this way, modernity at its best would be the implementation of the Christian recognition of the dignity of all persons.

For Maritain, the modern state is the topmost element of the body politic.[3] It represents the whole but, as an instrument in service to the whole and as a symbol of unity in the complex arrangements over which it presides, cannot be a substitute for or superior to the whole. The state is not the whole, but a representation of the whole.[4] At the same time, the state is to enact defense against foreign threats and is to be the means by which social justice is to be achieved, yet without being paternalistic. The state's activity is to be limited with respect to business, arts, culture, science and philosophy, but it is to be a welfare state. The aim of the body politic is "to better the conditions of life itself ..." to seek a proper, civilized life for every member through the establishment of civilization and culture and the cultivation of faith, righteousness, wisdom and beauty."[5] The state must serve this aim in giving formal articulation to the body politic.

To make this clear, Maritain sets out to criticize and reject the concept of sovereignty, because sovereignty involves attributing to the state the character of a separate and transcendent whole which it cannot have. Only God is sovereign. No earthly power can claim the divine attribute. The state, he says, has supreme independence and power only with regard to the other parts of the body politic, subject to its laws and administration. To understand the modern state, then, requires one not only to identify its character but also to define the scope of its

---

[3] *Man and the State*, pp. 13, 15-19.
[4] Ibid., pp. 12-13.
[5] Ibid., pp. 54-55.

power. It is the organizer of the constituent elements of the body politic, but it cannot supersede them or substitute for them. The state is not absolute—no political institution can be absolute—but is comprehensive procedurally, supreme within its scope, but having no natural right or transcendent power, and it is always accountable to the people since its legitimacy depends on their acknowledgment of its authority.

For Maritain, the closest approximation to the right understanding of the state appears in the western democracies where there is participation in governance of both rulers and ruled, and where in principle there is possible a collaborative relationship between liberal democracy and Christianity, the former being the practical matrix within which the aspirations of the latter are to be realized, to the degree possible, on earth. For Maritain there is an evolution in thought and aspiration to be traced from Aristotle through Aquinas to liberal democracy. As he says, "democracy is the only way of bringing about a *moral rationalization* of politics ... democracy is a rational organization of freedoms founded upon law."[6] This is an unmistakable reference to the Kantian aspiration to replace political morality with moralized politics, or to solve once and for all the Machiavellian problem.

Moreover, the road to moral rationalization is "the highest terrestrial achievement of which the rational animal is capable here below ... the only way through which the progressive energies in human history do pass."[7] For Maritain, democracy is the use of means worthy of the end sought, in which rulers and ruled participate jointly in self-governance. The evolution is towards practical truths coming to universal recognition in acknowledging the "rights possessed by man in his personal and social existence."[8]

Yet, at the same time, the process of materializing the Gospel message is ambiguous because modernity is not simply Christian; is indeed in many respects anti-Christian and secularizing. At best, then, we enjoy an emergent agreement on some practical truths in the midst of powerful metaphysical and theological oppositions.[9] There is, Maritain says, "notable progress in the process of world unification" at the level of practical formulations, but no theoretical position can "claim to establish in actual fact universal ascendancy over men's minds."[10] The most important "factor in the moral progress of humanity is the experiential development of awareness which takes place outside of systems ..."[11]

Yet, there are problems. The increasing recognition of natural rights, which is a necessary feature in Maritain's scheme, has been deformed by the failure to remember that natural law is the foundation of the rights of man. By losing that insight we moved towards abstract ideas of autonomy and then to disillusion over the conflicting abstract claims. We must, Maritain says, will to act in conformity

---

[6] Ibid., p. 59.
[7] Ibid., pp. 59-60.
[8] Ibid., p. 76.
[9] Ibid., p. 76.
[10] Ibid., p. 79.
[11] Ibid., p. 80.

with what is appropriate for our fulfillment. Moral law involves recognizing what is best for us as what is established independently by nature. This means that visions of an "ideal order" are generated out of our responses to the natural human character under varying historical conditions. To articulate an ideal order is to respond to the disposition in all human beings to live as they should. If this is universal, one might still expect that it would yield considerable, if not infinite, variety of response. But according to Maritain, "there is, by the very virtue of human nature, an order or a disposition which human reason can discover and according to which the human will must act in order to attune itself to the essential and necessary ends of the human being. The unwritten law, or natural law, is nothing more than that."[12]

There is a developing, not a finished, moral conscience because knowledge of the law is imperfect, and that development is necessarily towards "essential and necessary ends."[13] Natural law has to acquire the force of law, inclination has to be clarified and made specific. This has been happening through time and thus explains why there is both commonality and variability in the moral understanding. Maritain asserts that the "progress of moral conscience is indeed the most unquestionable instance of progress in humanity."[14] Unfortunately, however, rights now overshadow obligations in the common understanding. Thus the moral progress is vitiated by the way in which it has been understood and pursued in practice. The rights of human beings emerged by inclination, but the discussion and specification have been defective. Despite this, Maritain insists "there is a dynamism which impels the unwritten law to flower forth in human law, and to render the latter ever more perfect and just in the very field of its contingent determinations."[15]

It is difficult to know how to respond to Maritain's tension-ridden argument. It is by no means self-evident, even if we accept the idea that there is an evolving materialization of the Gospel message, that the materialization or practical realization of that message can or will have a necessary and unambiguous temporal outcome that approaches the ever more perfect and just. Dialectically speaking, Maritain seems to share with Hegel – I do not mean of course that Maritain is an Hegelian – a particular sort of incarnational theology in which the Idea, as Hegel would say, is not so impotent as to remain only an Idea, but he does not accept that what actually happens in the process is all that can happen, that it is open-ended and contingent, and that we may either fail to realize our aspirations or realize them in ways that are not at all what we expected or had hoped for, that, so to speak, our successes may turn into our failures. To posit "essential and necessary ends" is to say that there is an ideal or correct unfolding of moral conscience through time that is not alterable by its actualization in time. This evolution is thus a revealing of what is not subject to time and is supra historical. History is supposed to confirm the faith expressed.

---

[12] Ibid., p. 86.
[13] Ibid., p. 91.
[14] Ibid., p. 94.
[15] Ibid., p. 100.

On a different Christian outlook from Maritain's, the historically experienced combination of success and failure, of gain and loss, might be exactly what we should expect because it is what it means to be temporal beings. This does not mean that there are no better and worse results, better and worse regimes; but it may well mean that judgment in these matters will always be arguable and argument interminable; stipulating what is progressive is by no means self-evident.

Earlier, I mentioned the link of Maritain's outlook to the liberal tradition of Kant, Mill and Woodrow Wilson. We must return to this in light of the fact that Maritain criticizes the liberal tradition in this context. He laments that faith no longer unites us, and that we now see that reason alone cannot successfully replace faith. Religion, to be sure, has not disappeared, but it has become plural, and there is no religious expression which can claim successfully to be authoritative for us all. As we have been moving from a "sacral" age to a "secular" age the integrating force of Christianity has been constrained or excluded even while its residual, leavening effects remain. We are in a post-Constantinian age.[16] It is obvious why Maritain would not accept this outcome as a realization in practice of the Gospel message, unlike some Protestant theorists or those theorists of secularization who believe that secular democracy is, in fact, a realization of the truth contained in the Christian tradition. But here again Maritain is unclear about whether, or in what sense, there can be in practice any such thing as the ideal order on earth. Of course, he accepts that the heavenly kingdom is not of this world, but does he fully explore the implications of this for earthly political life?

Maritain does recognize this insofar as he speaks of the need for Christian fortitude in a democratic society, and insofar as he commits himself to what he calls long-term success, rejecting what he calls the Machiavellian "illusion of immediate success."[17] What he is proposing is to be taken as an ideal of permanent, inspirational value. We might choose to acknowledge this without expecting ever to enjoy anything but an ambiguous and arguable practical result. But the question remains as to how much this view is contingent upon our response to the actual historical conditions we experience. The ideal may be maintained apart from our view of our rising and falling fortunes in history, but the very assessment itself will be subject inevitably to endless debate and argument. Given the joint participation in governance of rulers and ruled, the limitations on any claims to political authority and the plural character of religious expression, it is hard to see how practical consensus on defining the true fulfillment of our destiny, so far as it is earthly, is to be achieved. One may admire the nobility of Maritain's aspiration but wonder whether he has fully absorbed, or was willing to admit, the true implications of the emergence of individuality in the realm which Hegel described as that in which all are free. The realm of universal freedom invests human beings with the responsibility to determine for themselves what is essential and necessary to them.

---

[16] Ibid., p. 162.
[17] Ibid., p. 71.

Social structures, Maritain says, must constantly be altered to allow the full emergence of the articulation and exercise of rights that are always present awaiting a forum for realization. The end is predetermined, and it is only our awakening to that end and full understanding of it that is still to be achieved. Yet there are also constraints on how this may happen – recognizing the need to use means worthy of the end sought – in preserving the rights of property, of education, constitutional dispersion of power to prevent claims of sovereignty, and so on. The manner in which we conduct our affairs is crucial. That has to be part of the end, constraining any determination of what the end is for us, since it has to be for us. But it would seem that the end has to be grasped as we can grasp it, that we must participate in defining the end in order to guide our action. Under these circumstances, Maritain might be seen as a sober progressive, like John Stuart Mill, continually seeking to reconcile order with innovation, and, as also with Mill, believing that ultimately there would be a convergence on truth.

The largest political innovation would be the establishment of Maritain's world political society under the moral leadership of a supreme advisory council to "organize international opinion," to articulate a common good that will supersede the common good of each body politic, and to subordinate the state as the principal unit of politics and world history.[18] This would presumably constitute a concrete manifestation of the growing moral unity of mankind. One might describe this as the restatement of the Kantian ideal of the cosmopolitan point of view and perpetual peace as the solution to the Hobbesian problem, namely, how to gain a covenant without the sword. Yet it remains unclear, as in previous explorations of this ideal, how to achieve the covenant without the sword by means of agents of world history which inevitably employ the sword. At this point, one might think of the Augustinian critique of efforts at to transform politics by means of politics within world history. And here I shall turn to Michael Oakeshott.

II

Oakeshott famously has said that "in political activity, then, men sail a boundless and bottomless sea; there is neither harbour for shelter nor floor for anchorage, neither starting-place nor appointed destination. The enterprise is to keep afloat on an even keel; the sea is both friend and enemy; and the seamanship consists in using the resources of a traditional manner of behaviour in order to make a friend of every hostile occasion."[19] Oakeshott described himself as a skeptic who would do better if only he knew how. Politics, an object of lifelong philosophic investigation for him, especially aroused his skepticism. In this he followed that strain of the Augustinian tradition which sees politics as a necessary evil for fallen humanity, something we cannot do without but also something not to be overrated, and

---

[18] Ibid., p. 215.

[19] Michael Oakeshott, "Political Education" in *Rationalism in Politics,* new and expanded edition (Indianapolis, Indiana: Liberty Fund Press, 1991), p. 60.

certainly not a source of salvation. He was skeptical of all ideologies, including schemes for world government or perpetual peace; more generally, he criticized the modern rationalism we associate with the legacy of Francis Bacon and René Descartes, first because he thought it promoted, especially in those less adept than Bacon and Descartes themselves, a philosophically mistaken understanding of human reason and how it works, and derivatively because he thought it magnified the dangers of political misjudgment in assuming that we can know where we are going and how to get there, what he called the pursuit of perfection as the crow flies. The political manifestation of this rationalism is to be found in the progressive and utopian tendencies of modern thought, not only in the extreme case of totalitarian regimes, but also the less obvious perfectionist idealism within the liberal tradition itself. Oakeshott's use of the term "rationalism" corresponds to Eric Voegelin's use of the term "gnosticism" in describing a misplaced claim of the autonomy of human reason, when armed with "appropriate methods," to remake the world according to our independently premeditated goals.

This rationalism and utopianism Oakeshott called the "politics of faith."[20] His point was that a *politics* of faith is contrary to faith as Christianity understands faith because it is faith in the things of this world. Oakeshott thought that what he called the "politics of skepticism," which tends towards minimalism in government because it thinks the primary issue is to constrain the use of governmental power rather than to expand it, is more appropriate to the human condition. At the same time, he thought that modern politics was a polarized field of tension between the "politics of faith" and the "politics of skepticism," that these dispositions emerged at the same time at the start of the modern period, roughly four hundred to five hundred years ago, and that they counterbalance each other, although the politics of faith has dominated in our era. It is this continuing polarity that constitutes the field of modern political life. Arguments over the scope of the state's activity, what it should or should not try to do, are shaped by this underlying field of tension within which we operate.

For Oakeshott, philosophy is the effort to understand in other terms what we already understand, to explain not to prescribe, to discern and describe the premises that clarify why we think and act as we do. Philosophical examination of politics led Oakeshott to formulate the explanation of modern politics as the tension between the politics of faith and the politics of skepticism. Yet this philosophical explication of modern politics cannot prescribe an ideal or generate a plan for improving the world. Oakeshott did not think that exploring politics philosophically could produce a simple, unified doctrine. He did not think we have access to a plan or a vision for reconciling the tension between the politics of faith and the politics of skepticism. His analysis seeks to clarify the way we live, but it leaves that

---

[20] Michael Oakeshott, *The Politics of Faith and the Politics of Scepticism*, ed. Timothy Fuller (New Haven: Yale University Press, 1996).

as it is. The philosophical study of politics, as he saw it, is not a higher, more abstract way to advocate policies. In wanting to understand politics philosophically Oakeshott sought to examine politics in detachment from the specific issues which, at any given moment, dramatize or reveal the character of political activity. To understand politics in this way is to adopt a stance that is difficult, perhaps impossible, for political actors to take up so long as they remain political actors.

Equally, the philosophic inquirer, if drawn to one side or another in political debate, can only present that inclination by disclosing the reasons he finds persuasive, exposing his position to further philosophic investigation. In this, Oakeshott was unquestionably influenced by Socratic dialectic and accepted the limitations that dialectical inquiry imposes on equipping oneself for political action. To seek more is to abandon philosophic reflection, favoring persuasion and action over prolonged, unfinished conversation. One cannot simply unify philosophic understanding with practical action. The attempt to do so will necessarily sacrifice the philosophic endeavor, and corrupt political action insofar as it takes on a misplaced sense of certainty that it can leap over the contingency and uncertainty inherent to political action. On these grounds, an Oakeshottian would be bound to say that Maritain has mixed politics and philosophy, and has justified the mixture by stipulating a shape and direction of world history through a particular reading of the implications of Christianity.

What Maritain asserts, therefore, would become for Oakeshott an invitation to a conversation of questioning. Among the questions that might arise from an Oakeshottian standpoint are these: Is it definitive for Christianity that there be an evolving materialization of the Gospel message in world history? Is it not likely that to think in such terms is to engage in stipulating the revelatory significance of one's own historical era, even to claiming to have an authoritative insight into what is relevant and irrelevant to the advance of world history?

At the same time, there is no doubt that Oakeshott and Maritain would agree on the validity of the western polities. But Oakeshott would put less emphasis on the democratic element, and, rather than exalting rights, he would find the greater achievement in the rule of law and the constitutional limits on power that derive from a deep rooted skepticism about politics that is itself prompted by Augustinian Christianity. He would see an error in thinking that one could advocate rights and also control the evolving understanding of what they mean to those who exercise them. For Oakeshott, the defect in the realization of rights, lamented by Maritain, is inherent to the idea of rights when rights are abstractly rather than locally and customarily understood. Maritain then could not assert that there is a "correct" realization of rights available to us. In this sense, Oakeshott acknowledges more fully the open-endedness of existence in world history, and did argue that Christian faith is not tied to the episodic character of historical existence. Like Maritain, Oakeshott would say that the state is not an independent entity but rides atop a complex whole that could never be comprehended in formal expression alone. Let us say that in practice they could be in friendly tension.

Maritain recognizes something that we surely cannot ignore: the universalism of thought that dominates our time. One may wonder whether Oakeshott adequately absorbed this phenomenon for he surely did not speculate on what could or might supersede the modern state. To understand philosophy as Oakeshott did, precludes speculation of this sort because it falls into the realm of the "ought to be" rather than the "is." Speculation on the future is an inevitable part of political activity, and there it makes a difference whether such speculation is sober and cautious or expansive and utopian, whether it is confident or alarmist, and so on. Thus to introduce such speculation into philosophical analysis is to confuse what, for Oakeshott, are two categorically different activities, amounting to carrying on politics by other means. Politics can overtake philosophy, but philosophy cannot overtake politics.

How then did Oakeshott characterize the modern state? In simplest terms, he articulated an ideal type of the modern state that he thought to be implicit in the actual practices of modern European states. It is a procedural state, largely intent on the tasks of minimal legislation and adjudication of disputes. In principle, it has at its disposal very little to redistribute. It is not the representative of a world historical purpose, or, perhaps, of any purpose but civil peace. Modern bodies politic, to use Maritain's term, are brought together by chance or choice, and are basically coercive associations bringing together people who need not and often do not agree on what their lives are for, but for whom exit is seldom a likely alternative. They are not voluntary associations which may be animated by a common purpose or a specified goal, and which one may enter and also exit. The civil condition is one in which many are bound together without agreement on common purposes or specified goals.

Moderns understand themselves as individuals entitled to recognition from each other, who are "in themselves what they are for themselves." The last thing people with such self-understanding want is to have a common purpose, justified as essential and necessary, imposed upon them. Nor is it likely that an agreement on the essential and necessary would arise spontaneously from the endless exchanges among them. Nor is there an agreement on anyone's claim to the authority to articulate such an agreement on behalf of the participants in the body politic. In short, the modern state in this view does not, and could not have, a telos. The modern state is organized precisely for people who do not think they can have such a thing. From the Oakeshottian perspective, one would ask Maritain if he is not confusing Christianity with an historicized neo-Aristotelianism.

In a way, the difference between Maritain and Oakeshott, to a degree, illustrates the distinction between the politics of faith and the politics of skepticism, as Oakeshott developed that distinction. It is clear that Maritain is not simply an exponent of what Oakeshott would call the politics of faith since that would mean the collapsing of the sacred into the secular. This clearly is not the case with Maritain as an orthodox Christian. Maritain appears in some measure to be drawn to the politics of faith. On the other side, insofar as Oakeshott would be in practice an exponent of the politics of skepticism, even though philosophically speaking he cannot advocate either position, he could be questioned as to whether he has grasped sufficiently the need to respond to what are thought to be the unprecedented conditions of the twentieth century.

The point is, however, that here we enter into political discourse within the range of what has characterized our politics for several centuries. Philosophical reflection on these matters has both clarified some features of the situation and also led us into the uncertainty that philosophy imposes upon us when we seek its aid in deciding what we mean to ourselves.

# 3

# The Question of Modernity in the Political Thought of Heinrich Rommen

## William Haggerty

### Introduction

For every thoughtful student of Catholic political theory, modernity must remain a problem, a question. Given its close association with the history and traditions of the pre-modern world, the Church has never had an easy or uncomplicated relation with the political ideas and movements of the modern era. And insofar as most of the intellectual architects of the modern horizon established their teaching in response (if not in direct opposition) to the theological and philosophical positions embodied in orthodox Christianity, it seems an essential task for the Catholic theorist to attempt, in some manner or form, to come to terms with their claims.

The German political thinker, Professor Heinrich A. Rommen, is no exception to this rule. In his magisterial study, *The State in Catholic Thought*, he presents an exhaustive account of the Catholic tradition in political and social philosophy. Though he does not ignore the history of modern practice, he is more interested in examining the response of Catholic thought to modern political philosophy and its intellectual challenges. Along with other theorists in the mid-century Neo-scholastic revival, he would maintain that the orthodox Christian teaching provides a helpful corrective to possible excesses in modern theory partly because it places or locates "politics" within a certain designated sphere. But what are the grounds of his criticism of modernity? What does he consider to be the characteristic excesses or abuses in modern political philosophy? And what remedy, in his estimation, can Catholic political thought offer to cure the ills of modernity?

In responding to a criticism in *The State in Catholic Thought*, Rommen refers to an idea that helps answer these questions. Critics have often accused the Catholic political-philosophical tradition of being a *"complexio oppositorum,"* a confused jumble, as Rommen calls it, of "contradictory borrowings from different philosophical and theological schools."[1] To the more acute observer, he suggests, there is rather a "complete unity in these principles"; what appears at first sight to be "diametrically contradictory opinions" are merely "parallel courses of reasoning on account of oscillations" that reside or "rest in the polar unity of the general principles." He immediately frames these comments within an historical context: in the Catholic intellectual tradition, there occur variations on central theoretical points that represent opposing poles. The account of human nature, for example, can be dominated by a philosophical anthropology that stresses intellect or one that stresses will. Historically, the Thomist tradition has emphasized the pole of intellect, promoting "a strong rationality," which, however instrumental in the development of natural law, "can lead to an undervaluation of the dynamism of history." At the other pole, the nominalist school of the *via moderna* promoted the "superiority of the will" to such a degree that, though it restored "the dynamism of historical evolution," it unfortunately "disparaged the importance and range of natural reason."[2] The imbalance toward volition would finally degenerate into a crude Occamism that produced "nihilism in natural ethics, a transformation of the *fides rationalis* into an emotional faith of sentiment, the negation of natural theology and a one-sided supernaturalism."[3] Theoretical and practical difficulties arise only when the tradition, focusing on one aspect or part of the problem, ignores the other side. Rommen cites a second historical example, one with clear political overtones: the dispute between Thomists and Molinists on the question of grace reflects the "tension between the individual and the community." The Molinists represent the "more individualist school that stresses freedom and self-initiative," the Thomists prefer "*ordo* and authority." These intellectual tendencies, polar contrasts, Rommen maintains, define the tradition and "are admissible as long as the accentuation of the one element does not result in the disappearance of the other." They "may be conditioned by historical circumstances," but they are more often "typical of the differences about the philosophic premises that result from theological and philosophical schools within the Church."[4] Whatever their source, such "internal disputes," "do not destroy the unity of polar tension." The Catholic tradition, especially in political theory, lives and breathes between the polar accentuations, trying to unite apparent contradictions. Now though it is never systematically developed in his work, I contend that the idea of a "polar unity of tension" is central to understanding Rommen's treatment of modernity, his judgment of his fellow Catholic theorists, and his appraisal of the uniqueness of the Catholic political-philosophical tradition.

---

[1] Heinrich Rommen, *The State in Catholic Thought* (St. Louis, Missouri: B. Herder, 1945), p. 16.
[2] Ibid., p. 17.
[3] Ibid., p. 18.
[4] Ibid., p. 19.

### Linear and Spheric Thinking

Let us begin with his examination of modernity. In a revealing comment early in *The State in Catholic Thought*, Rommen connects the idea of polar unity with two characteristic ways of political thinking:

> What may be called linear thinking goes straight out from one pole or from one idea of the cosmos of ideas, which every true philosophy is. This idea, cut off from its interrelations and interdependencies with the cosmos, [linear thinking] then fanatically thinks to a finish. Then it becomes radical individualism or socialism or totalitarianism or anarchism. This linear thinking, so characteristic of the modern mind and its countless -isms, is a stranger to Catholic political philosophy. For Catholic political philosophy is spheric thinking.[5]

The distinction between linear and spheric thinking provides Rommen with a useful image. The logic of modernity is the logic of linear thinking; this kind of theorizing is a trait so "characteristic of modernity" that at one point Rommen suggests that "an interesting history of modern political philosophy" could be written as a "philosophy of separations, of antinomies."[6] What is central to linear thinking is its "monistic opposition of necessary human elements." At its core, it is exclusive: it "exaggerates" or exalts one pole by forgetting or neglecting the other side. Perhaps the best illustration is the prototypical modern antithesis "individual versus state" that has its political counterparts in the modern trends of liberal individualism and social collectivism. Inasmuch as liberal individualism emphasizes the autonomy of the individual, it rejects the classical Christian understanding of the common good. Because all political and moral duties serve the self-interest of the individual, because in fact "individuals are the only reality," the state in liberal thought possesses a "service value," and the common good as such cannot be an "objective and qualitatively different reality."[7] Moreover, since it claims the individual is "inherently self-sufficient," liberal individualism restricts the state to "merely a legislative order" without "moral character," and without a specifically "moral end."[8] The maximization of the individual demands the "minimizing of the state."[9] Not surprisingly, most liberal theorists look forward to the eventual disappearance of the state; their fervent hope resides in their belief "in the final overcoming of any form of society that demands any kind of sacrifice of (the) individual's subjective interests and any restrictions on his liberty."[10]

At the other extreme, "social collectivism" forgets or denies the individual to such a degree that, in embracing the idea of the collective, it allows the individual to disappear "completely submerged in society or state." The maximization of the

---

[5] Ibid., pp. 22-23.
[6] Ibid., p. 283.
[7] Ibid., p. 315.
[8] Ibid., pp. 315, 331.
[9] Ibid., p. 331.
[10] Ibid., p. 315.

state demands the minimizing of the individual: "the individual is nothing; the party, the proletariat, the nation is all." Social collectivism, identified at times with the "Hegelian ideal," makes of the state a "moral absolute, the divine representation of absolute morality itself."[11] Curiously, adherents of this pole manifest the "same Messianic complex" as liberal theorists; they too embrace the dreams of a "paradisiac millenium of freedom," where the "state will wither away." And seen at least from this secular eschatological perspective, collectivism appears "only socialistic as a means"; it seems as "utterly individualist" as its polar opposite. When collectivism envisions the "final society" as "an amorphous multitude of socialized individuals, classless and egalitarian," and liberalism speaks of its economic utopia as "an atomistic aggregation of individuals formally equal," the extremes touch one another.[12] In both cases, the final vision is thoroughly "non-political."

Often, the antinomies of modernity vary in Rommen's analysis, but they always involve a narrowing of vision. At one point, he contrasts liberal individualism with political romanticism by focusing on the "one-sided exaggeration" in the antinomy of nature and will. Impressed by the "silently working powers of history," the political romantics of the nineteenth century developed a teaching that ignored the place of "human rational will." For them, enlightened self-interest could never provide the standard for political legitimacy; rather "tradition, history and duration" remain "the sufficient and best tests." But their reliance on tradition, and their unfortunate neglect of rationality in response to the exaggerated rationalism of Enlightenment thinkers, too often led them to "embrace authoritarian ideas." On the other hand, in championing the will, liberal theorists ignored or even suppressed "nature, the urge of nature and nature as the final cause of the social process." The "free and rational production of human will" developed in liberal theory arrogates to itself "all forms of socio-political life." Natural law in such a view is emptied of content, transformed into "a set of subjective individual rights wholly abstracted from the socio-political order." As such, by the eighteenth century it becomes an ideological instrument for "perpetual revolution."[13]

But the characteristic reductionism of linear thinking is not defined merely by the pursuit of one extreme and the neglect of another. Rommen finds the modern position "abstract and unreal" largely because it sees in the "polemic antithesis of individual versus state" the "total political problem."[14] In doing so, it sees only the individual and the state and omits important "intermediary" communities, associations that are undoubtedly part of the political landscape and thus part of the "total political problem." By ignoring the rich matrix of political reality and human action, linear modernity fails to see "the family, the free, religious, neighborhood, professional and vocational groups, the free educational and cultural

---

[11] Ibid., p. 331.
[12] Ibid., pp. 316, 300.
[13] Ibid., p. 246.
[14] Ibid., p. 300.

organizations." If political theorizing is analogous to a kind of vision, one could say that linear thinking suffers from ideological myopia; it lacks peripheral vision. The modern schema thus "contains dangerous dissolving tendencies." For example, liberal individualism measures every political category against its "service value to the profit interest of the individual." But there are no "abstract individuals" in any political community. The liberal individual *qua individual* has no face, bears no flesh; in the end, the human person is "always a father or a mother, a son or a daughter, a brother or a sister, a farmer or a townsman."[15] Marriage becomes in this moral horizon "a sale contract" serving the "subjective pleasure and will" of the partners; the family becomes the equivalent of a joint stock company.[16] But at the other pole, the view is equally myopic: inasmuch as it ensures "the complete surrender of the individual person," collectivism erases the family and intermediary associations just as completely as its opposite. And the "socialized individual of the classless society" is as faceless an abstraction as the "free and absolutely autonomous individual" of liberalism. In eliminating any social form that lies outside of its chosen antithesis, both sides so closely resemble each other that they merge into one. In light of these remarks, one is not surprised to find Rommen associating linear modernity with all types of "perfectionism and progressivism" in political life. By cutting itself off from the "cosmos of ideas," linear thinking divorces itself from the complexity of political reality; it cannot comprehend the "total political problem." And, as a result, all difficulties are easily dissolved: progress towards the perfect society is assured when traveling in a straight line.[17]

Spheric thinking, emblematic of Catholic political thought, is altogether different; it "rests on the existential way of thinking"; it is "discursive and dialectical."[18] By its very nature, it is inclusive; in demanding that two poles be thought together, it rejects wholeheartedly any "monistic opposition of necessary human elements." Unlike the linear extremes of modernity, it does not see political reality as a set of artificially constructed abstract "antitheses": it does not posit "freedom or order, freedom or authority, the rights of the individual or the rights of the state," but joins together "freedom in order, the rights of the individual

---

[15] Ibid., p. 297.
[16] Ibid., p. 300.
[17] Rommen does not restrict this analysis to the political realm. He argues that the linear extremes of modernity apply to the epistemological problem as well. Occam's denial of the "validity of the universal concept" led initially to the "disappearance of the ontological order" and the "denial of natural law" in late scholasticism, and eventually to the complete separation of the ontological and moral orders in modern thought. Underlying this nominalist view, however, is another polar extreme. The nominalists lacked "confidence in the human intellect"; they replaced the natural law with a kind of "moral supernaturalism" grounded solely upon Scripture. (Ibid., p. 176.) Occamism, for Rommen, is the necessary first step in an epistemological slide down hill in modern thought: if the world is "not accessible to the human mind," it remains a "chaos of phenomena, but *sine fundamentam in re*." "Human nature as causa finalis and exemplaris" becomes "man as an empirical entity in its factuality." The intellect, now separated from any grounding in objective reality, considers itself "as a sovereign versus the world," a relation that reaches its speculative apotheosis in the Kantian analysis of "the thinking subject that produces its world in autonomy as the object of possible experience in space and time." And it is the will that inevitably dominates in this horizon, "producing and even finally creating ... moral rules"; the idea of the "free and autonomous" individual, who "creates for himself a subjective order of ends," is a concept that arises from the polar extreme of late nominalism. Ibid., p. 177.

corresponding to the duties of the state and the rights of the state corresponding to the duties of the individual."[19] In his chapter on the origin of the state, Rommen provides a cogent example of spheric thinking. The two modern claims concerning this question exhibit typically polar positions. One theoretical tendency, biologicism or organicism, proceeds from "a purely biological concept of human nature," and dismisses the efficacy of "reason and free will." Though there are a number of variations, all forms of biologicism trace the beginning of the political community to "the blind forces of biological life," to "irresistible natural forces."[20] The alternative theory adopts the other extreme, ignoring human nature as "*bios*," and stressing the complete autonomy of free will. This position, of course, informs the view of various social contract theories. In its especially radical form, which finds its fullest expression in the political thought of Hobbes, social contract theory denies any ground to nature at all—at least with respect to the formation of the political community. It is radically "individualist, utilitarian, and anti-historical."[21] As a creature of abstract modernity, it possesses an "entirely political" and "unphilosophic character."[22]

It is only in the light of these extremes that Rommen can illustrate the traditional Catholic position on the origin of the political community. While maintaining that the state "arises with moral necessity out of (the) dynamic teleological growth of human nature," the tradition also claims that the "concrete coming into existence" of the political order is the result of human initiative and will.[23] The tradition binds together the elements that the linear extremes of social contract and biological theory "exaggerate or forget"; it does not separate "*bios*" from "*logos*" or nature from will, but considers them together "in interaction." "The state is thus the result of a driving power of man's biological life and of the free rational activity of man recognizing his nature's realization as the ideal of his moral existence."[24] To set the natural over the intentional order, or to assert the intentional over the natural order, is to lose, as Rommen suggests in a felicitous phrase, "the fruitful polar tension of natural urge and freedom."[25]

This analysis, however, does not go as far as it should. Rommen has indicated that linear thinking fixes on one "polemic antithesis" mistaking it for the "total political problem." Spheric thinking cannot be reduced or confined to the mere union in tension of antinomies. It takes place within a "cosmos of ideas" where "the interdependencies and interrelations between ideas" are seen as united.[26] But what does this mean? Rommen appears to ground the dialectic of spheric thinking

---

[19] *The State in Catholic Thought*, p. 436.
[20] Ibid., pp. 231-32.
[21] Ibid., p. 333.
[22] Ibid., p. 236.
[23] Ibid., p. 236.
[24] Ibid., p. 237.
[25] Ibid., p. 247.
[26] Ibid., p. 23.

in the traditional natural law understanding of the state as a *unitas ordinis* arranged according to a "hierarchical economy of ends."[27] In doing so, he adopts the Thomistic understanding of causality: form "as active agent is the nature, the *causa finalis*," and "as final end," it becomes the criterion of judgment for any being: "the most perfect realization of its nature, of its idea, becomes the end of the thing."[28] He applies this teleological view to the political and social nature of man and to the understanding of the state: as social life is "an intentional form of life for the individual," so the state in this conception is "the *terminus ad quem* of the teleological perfection of nature." For all its focus on individualism, modernity neglects the possibility that the "individual's very individuality," his neediness, points to natural sociality.[29] And, given this understanding of the state, the Catholic position does not begin with "the concept of the individual" or the idea of the collective, those "modern abstractions" so "unable to explain reality." Rather, at its heart there abides the "idea of a cosmos of the spheres of life," stretching from the individual as person, touching upon the "intermediary" associations, and leading finally to "the comprehensive political sphere."[30] Insofar as the state represents an economy of ends, every social form, however secondary, contributes its own unique good to the political community as a whole. The Catholic principle of subsidiarity, with its traditional emphasis on the independence and autonomy of various social forms, has its roots in this conception. The state may indeed possess a comprehensive end, but it must never interfere with, let alone abolish, the lower forms; "the upper form does not make the lower forms superfluous."[31] There is no idea more central to Rommen's analysis than the principle of subsidiarity. He speaks eloquently of the "three essentially different circles of human existence," finding in them a "symbiotic" relation, where each circle is distinct, yet not "utterly separated" from the others.[32] The first circle, "the intimate sphere" of the "individual person as such," is the locus of the human personality, "immortal and in himself an individual and irreplaceable value."[33] The idea of the person is the "starting point of all social philosophy," whether one begins with "natural rights" or civic duties. The family, despite all its cultural and historical variation, occupies a "second circle." Though its domain may be confined initially to the *vita economica*, its traditional emphasis

---

[27] Ibid., p. 15.
[28] Ibid., p. 135. It would be wrong to claim that Rommen identifies the Catholic political tradition with Thomism. While he sometimes associates it with the Thomist tradition (at one point contrasting the antinomies of modernity with the "great harmony of Thomism"), in other passages, as we have noted, he assigns the Thomist position to a specific pole in the "cosmos of ideas." There is no contradiction here, for he ultimately regards the Thomistic synthesis as an example of "Christian theory": "Every high point in Christian theory is a time of concordance. St. Thomas produced a concordance between Aristotle and Christian tradition; the late Scholastics, of Thomism and Augustinianism; modern times have produced concordances in social philosophy." Ibid., p. 84.
[29] Ibid., p. 136.
[30] Ibid., p. 151.
[31] Ibid., p. 301.
[32] Ibid., p. 376.
[33] Ibid., p. 377.

on the procreation and care of children must necessarily include "spiritual goods" as well as material ends.³⁴ Nevertheless, the "social relations between families and individual adults," and the resulting "conflicts of interests and rights," cannot be resolved through the limited means available to the *paterfamilias*. The comprehensive political circle, over which the state rules, must provide "a protective coordinating and mediating organization with supreme authority."³⁵ Responsible for the "common good" understood as the "order of peace and justice," the state can never be a substitute family.

In their interpenetration, the "circles of human existence" form the *unitas ordinas*, an interdependent community that is also a *unitas diversitas*.³⁶ The very complexity of this understanding of the state assures the failings of linear modernity: if "social life moves in indestructible concentric circles," as Rommen suggests, then political thinking must respect the outlines, the boundaries, that political life presents to it; it must embrace the "total political problem" in all its complexity. This is exactly what the spheric thinking of the tradition sets out to do; and this is also why the utopianism and progressivism, so typical of modernity, is absent from the mainstream Catholic political tradition.

### The *Distinctio Christiana* of Catholic Political Thought

Throughout his study, Rommen repeatedly attempts to defend the tradition against the charge that it is a "*complexio oppositorum*." But if the unity of polar tension is the *distinctio christiana* of Catholic political thought, it cannot help but avoid "one-sided exaggerations"; shifting back and forth between poles, it will exhibit at one and the same time "conservative principles and flexible progressivism."³⁷ It is never a "static and brittle system"; its "polarism" is subject to "an everlasting process."³⁸ In light of modern categories, this tension in political thought reveals itself in the conservative/ liberal dichotomy. The terms "conservative" and "liberal" are open to misunderstanding, but their significance for Rommen has to do with their peculiar judgment on the status of modern liberal democracy. He maintains that the tradition is "philosophically and morally indifferent" to the question of "the forms of government." The status of any regime, whether democracy or traditional monarchy, ultimately "depends on (its) actual service ... to the realization of the common good."³⁹ Liberal democracy may foster "a great perhaps too optimistic faith in freedom," nevertheless its "institutions and political principles" are defensible in terms of Catholic political thought.⁴⁰

---

³⁴ Ibid., p. 378.
³⁵ Ibid., p. 379.
³⁶ Ibid.
³⁷ Ibid., pp. 20, 23.
³⁸ Ibid., p. 22.
³⁹ Ibid., p. 477.
⁴⁰ Ibid., pp. 484-85.

What is striking in Rommen's account of the conservative/liberal split is the balance he brings to his discussion of political imbalance. The prototypical conservative mind-set rejects liberal democracy for "its easy-going optimism," and for its over-emphasis on the individual. The conservative adopts a "delicate cultural pessimism" because he knows that "culture" cannot be discovered "in the mass civilization of a mass production era"; it is rather nurtured through a tradition, through "the wisdom and learning" transmitted through time. It demands a "stable, solid order." The modern idea of infinite progress represents the very negation of the "traditional way of life, of the historical culture of a particular nation."[41] The conservative distrusts democracy because he distrusts "the sovereignty of the masses": a democratic mass possesses "no dignity and therefore no gift of distinction." He longs nostalgically for the ancestral, for "the soils and the forests, the farms and old small towns, the guilds of the Middle Ages."[42] Similar to his secular counterpart, the Catholic conservative engages in an "unjustified glorification" of the medieval period, forgetting that "the social and economic life" of that era left much to be desired.[43] He "dislikes capitalism" not only because it subjects "the laborer to a cruel and inescapable rule of the profit motive, " but also because its promised egalitarianism is illusory; it does not produce a free-market utopia, but "a hideous economic hierarchy ... without regard to moral value." It is only the presence of the Church, "the greatest conservative power," that sustains the Catholic conservative: the Church remains for him "the continuous admonition" to the world "that there are higher values than profit and material pleasures."[44] The historical embodiment of this mind-set Rommen identifies with the Catholic political romantics of the nineteenth century. Reacting to the "overwhelming rationalism and anarchism" of the French Revolution, they pressed the "traditional rights of the crown" against "the concept of popular sovereignty." They did so "with some sacrifice of balance," forgetting in their rejection of the political ideas of the Enlightenment, that the underlying political institutions may not only be morally indifferent, but "may be defended and upheld on the basis of Catholic political thought."[45]

Rommen's analysis of the liberal mind-set of the Catholic tradition is equally instructive, and especially prescient. The Catholic liberal, though aware of the importance of custom, will be "free from an overesteem of tradition." He does not promote "the abstract liberty" of modernity, but political liberty "under the rule of law equal for all." The liberal will choose "progressive justice" even though, in doing so, he knows it may be "risking a threat to the public order." While seeking "to enlarge in social and political life the sphere of consent," he works at the same

---

[41] *The State in Catholic Thought*, p. 493.
[42] Ibid., p. 494.
[43] Ibid., p. 488.
[44] Ibid., p. 495.
[45] Ibid., p. 437.

time "to restrict the sphere of domination and compulsion."[46] He is "less pessimistic" than the conservative regarding human nature, and holds "an unconditional reverence" before "the dignity of the individual person." He does not distrust "democratic opinion" because, believing as he does in the rationality of each man, he knows each has "access to objective truth."[47] Rejecting romantic nostalgia, he has no longing for "a precapitalistic and pre-democratic era."[48] Since he values most "justice *hic et nunc*," he is a "great champion of social reform," and "of the rights of the socially underprivileged."[49] Unfortunately, this liberal tendency also is "subject to extremes." If the conservative attitude risks "mummification" in its praise of traditional forms, the liberal attitude neglects the "value of tradition." If the conservative attitude fosters an indifference to "social justice," the liberal "might underestimate the growth of state activity," placing the Church completely "at the service of a social gospel activism."[50] Throughout his study, Rommen finds ample evidence of this corresponding pole: from the "democratic Americanism" of Father Hecker to the Catholic liberalism of Lord Acton, and the "pro-democratic" natural law writings of Jacques Maritain.

Rommen does not see this polarity as a negative, but as a source of vitality necessary for the life of the Church. The "continuous defense and attack" between conservative and liberal prevents either side "from monopolizing political philosophy." By keeping "the other from falling into extremes," each side can learn from its opposite.[51] The conservative, prone to "inflexibility and complacency," should "seek counsel from the liberals"; the liberal, given to novelty and social change, should consider conservative prejudices. To fail to do so is to risk losing the "*distinctio christiana*": to raise the possibility of the conservative uncritically approving any regime he deems sufficiently anti-democratic, or the liberal "forgetting that social progress and secular happiness are not enough as the goal of life." The ever-present danger is to fall into a type of linear thinking that destroys the fruitful polarity of the Catholic tradition.

### The Unity of Polar Tension and the Idea of Man.

The unity of polar tension is not only the *distinctio christiana* of Catholic political philosophy, it remains for Rommen the distinctive mark of human nature. The tradition maintains that man himself possesses an "antithetic character"; he "lives in a sphere of tension," "a tension arising from a polar opposition of diverse principles." These "antithetical concepts" represent "the poles out of which life comes, between which arises its stresses and strains, between which it goes on." Both as believer and citizen, a human being must seek ever "to unite," to balance

---
[46] Ibid., pp. 496-97.
[47] Ibid., p. 497.
[48] Ibid., p. 498.
[49] Ibid., p. 496.
[50] Ibid., p. 499.
[51] Ibid., p. 500.

in a "*concordantia discordantia*" these "haunting antitheses."[52] Thus, the unity of tension that is man remains an imperfect image of the unity of God: the "ceaseless effort" to unite the poles of reason and will, or nature and will, is nothing less than "a perpetual striving to produce the *concordantia* as it lives in God who is pure intellect, omnipotent will, perfect goodness and unlimited love."[53] The consideration of man leads by ascent to a contemplation of the perfect goodness and unity in God. Catholic political theory is thus grounded in an anthropology that reflects theology; and it is no surprise that Rommen is fond of quoting Proudhon that "all political problems are at last theological problems." He makes this connection explicit in his chapter on "The Idea of Man," a remarkable discussion that serves both as a philosophical anthropology and an example of spheric thinking at its best. He divides the chapter into two parts. In the first half, he examines a series of modern philosophical positions: in his analysis, each modern claim not only represents a polar extreme, a turning away from "unity," but also contains an underlying theological problem. In the second part, he explores the idea of man in Catholic thought. By showing how the tradition balances the polar tendencies in modernity, Rommen skillfully weaves together a history of modern positions, a critique of linear extremes, and a presentation of the *concordantia discordantia* that is Catholic political philosophy.

He begins with a short treatment of Hobbes and Rousseau who occupy opposite poles on the question of the "natural goodness of man." Rousseau's optimistic portrait of the "natural status," among other things, denies the possibility of Christian theology, because theology "knows the force of evil, knows that the nature of man is weak, inclined to evil and in need of supernatural help and redemption."[54] Hobbes' "deep pessimism concerning human nature," however, presents a philosophical anthropology that serves as the basis for "the origin of the state and its lasting justification."[55] The Leviathan's power must be "unlimited" and unrestrained because of the "selfish, reckless and evil" character of man; in order to control that nature, the Sovereign must control the civic theology.[56] Since Hobbes holds a "pre-Christian contempt for the specific Christian virtues of truth, charity, and humility," the "contradictory" poles of Hobbes and Rousseau are equally "unchristian."[57]

Rommen next examines two theological positions that hold extreme views on the relation of nature and grace. For Luther, "original sin had so utterly destroyed the goodness of human nature that even grace did not reform its inner malignity." In his theology, nature "is separated from the realm of supernature," and the lone

---

[52] Ibid., p. 282.
[53] Ibid., p. 85.
[54] Ibid., p. 60.
[55] Ibid., pp. 61-62.
[56] Ibid., p. 61.
[57] Ibid., p. 62.

"guiding principle" for human action becomes the "revealed Word."[58] When the state is considered "a consequence of sin," political theory suffers: once human reason is unable "to recognize natural law," and the human will unable to "strive for it," the state lacks any basis in rationality, and consequently, any political order could be "sanctioned at least as long as the integrity of the gospel is not wholly destroyed."[59] Calvinism agrees at most points with this theology, but it possesses "a less pessimistic attitude" toward political things partly because the Old Testament for Calvin is "exclusively a source of political theory." The state cannot be established on natural law principles, but Scripture provides a divine "pattern of the constitutional life in its most minute particulars."[60] The citizens of the Calvinist theocracy or "bibliocracy" are "the holy people of God, the chosen people." The Calvinist doctrine of predestination lends credence to the "political predestination" of the rule of the "noble, wise and virtuous." The notion of the "holy people" may give Calvinism a "republican character," but it is, in essence, "an aristocracy of the redeemed."[61] Central to both Reformers, however, is "the separation of nature and grace": because of their emphasis on the utter depravity of the human condition, they could not employ the "social nature of man" as a basis "for any morally good act."[62] It is finally their interpretation of the doctrine of original sin that compels them to deny any ground to natural law and political philosophy.

Yet Enlightenment rationalism revived both natural law and political theory, replacing the "theological basis" of the Reformers with "secularized rights" and "a more optimistic idea" of human nature. It introduced an understanding of natural law that provided a novel "philosophical basis" for liberal democracy.[63] Unfortunately, the good rationalist of the eighteenth century became the good pagan agnostic of the nineteenth century, who "abandoned his smiling optimism" for a "disillusioned" relativism.[64] This happened, Rommen suggests, because modern rationalism neglected the "*homo religiosus*": that is, in seeking to avoid the sectarian extremes of the Reformers, it forgot that the foundation of its political theory was built upon a "Christian inheritance," that its principles were "secularized Christian ideals." The "mild skepticism" of the nineteenth century became the "irrationalism" of the early twentieth. The emptying of the "religious sphere" resulted both in the recognition of a "*horror vacui*," the realization that the gods that "animated" modernity had "fallen," and in a corresponding longing for new gods. "Quasi-religious collectivism" attempted to fill this vacuum with "new myths," yet its political "mysticism" was no substitute for the Christian tradition. Its idea of man was thoroughly "depersonalized"; it lacked "an interior life," and "that vivid feeling

---

[58] Ibid., p. 63.
[59] Ibid., pp. 63-64.
[60] Ibid., p. 66.
[61] Ibid., p. 67.
[62] Ibid., p. 69.
[63] Ibid., p. 70.
[64] Ibid., p. 71.

of finiteness and imperfection."[65] This "new politicized faith" was "extroverted and secularized ... anti-intellectual and non-moral." It exploited an "aimless political dynamism" in man, a nihilistic "inner restlessness" that issued only in "external destruction." At this point, Rommen reminds the reader of "the invisible but quite real connection between man as a religious being and man as a rational being." But the decline of modern rationalism into totalitarian "irrationalism," the transformation of "useless autonomy" into "the individual's unconditional surrender to irrational mass feelings," began with the Reformers' separation of nature and grace. This separation triggered the consequent depreciation of the religious sphere in modern political thought. The neglect of the *homo religiosus*, the separation of reason and religion, which for Rommen is the separation of man from his creatureliness, paved the way for "quasi-religious collectivism" and its creation of the God-state. "Any political philosophy neglecting the truth that man is 'religious' cannot avoid the alternative of either anarchy or God-state with all its consequences."[66] The "irrationalism" of totalitarianism is a direct result of the linear extremes of modernity.

Rommen now contrasts his critique of modernity with a presentation of the philosophical anthropology underlying Catholic thought. The tradition grounds its view in the rational, social nature of man. Sociality embraces every aspect of life, even "the innermost thinking" of the individual person.[67] Human nature is so radically social that "there is no experience of the community through which individuality does not shine, and no experience of individuality which is not borne by community and open to it."[68] Moreover, the traditional notion of law "as an order of reason" implies that law is addressed to, and established for, "rational beings" who can judge the reasonableness of its commands. Rommen clearly frames this position in direct opposition to the theological view taken by the early Reformers: the state in Catholic thought does not arise from original sin, but is the natural end of human beings, both "redeemed and unredeemed." Though nature is damaged by the effects of sin, it is not destroyed. The Reformers' separation of nature and grace is contrasted with the "famous Thomist principle" that "grace presupposes nature and perfects it." The Catholic position thus provides a "bridge between religion as grace and the world as the field of reason and natural ethics."[69]

The attributes of rationality and sociality, Rommen now argues, embody "the whole content of the concept of the natural law and the idea of human dignity."[70] For the first time in this chapter, he explicitly refers to the idea of polarity, and it arises in a surprising context. In assessing this understanding of human dignity,

---

[65] Ibid., p. 72.
[66] Ibid., p. 73.
[67] Ibid., p. 76.
[68] Ibid., p. 77.
[69] Ibid., p. 63.
[70] Ibid., p. 77.

critics contend that it is contradicted by the Catholic tradition's casual acceptance of political exigencies like capital punishment. Rommen responds that the paradoxical "coincidence of human dignity and political power" in Catholic thought is nothing less than the "same polarity" found in the idea of human nature. Man may not be thoroughly corrupted, but he is nevertheless "inclined to evil, to a selfishness threatening the just peaceful order." In the end, the polarity in man is a consequence of his fallen condition.[71] More important for our study is the rhetorical movement of Rommen's discussion here: just after he condemns the Reformers for their extreme position, he reminds the reader that a consideration of original sin remains a significant factor in Catholic political theory. The tradition embraces the Thomistic position on nature and grace, but it must still think between two poles; it must measure the rational and social nature of man against the revelational fact of original sin. And it is this understanding that gives Catholic political theory its "characteristic elasticity": it can accept "almost all political forms as they appear in the history of nations. "[72]

But Rommen is not finished with his examination of modern extremes. The "dignity of man as a rational and free being," receives "a more exalted meaning" in the understanding that the "human person is an image of God."[73] This "addition," of "incomparable importance," is "revolutionary," involving as it does "a new concept of freedom" and the "ultimate equality of all" before God. Rommen here addresses the problem in modern rationalism: because the understanding of man as "*imago dei*" must include the idea of man as "homo religiosus," the Catholic position connects rationality and religion; and it thus avoids the exaggerated rationality so disastrous for modern rationalism. For the second time in the chapter, he refers to the idea of polarity. Critics charge that conservative Catholic thinkers (De Maistre and Cortes), far from finding the roots of liberal democracy in the idea of "imago dei," appear more sympathetic to authoritarian or anti-democratic regimes. Rommen points out that those thinkers focused almost exclusively on one polar extreme: they "overstressed the wounding of human nature by sin" and doubted the capacity of human reason to "control dangerous passions." This

---

[71] Rommen here obviously includes certain revelational factors in his philosophical examination of "The Idea of Man." Yet, in his preface, he denies that Catholic political philosophy "is based on theology or revelation." Given all this, one wonders about the specific character of philosophy in his account: in other words, what is the relation between political theory and revealed theology? There is no space here to discuss the question at length, but I might suggest that, while Rommen supports the traditional distinction between philosophy and theology, he allows for the possibility that political theory remain open to, and thus may be influenced by, the truths of revelation. After rejecting the "political theology" of nineteenth- century Catholic conservatives, he notes: "This repudiation of political theology follows the traditional Thomistic doctrine of the distinction between ... natural reason and revelation. This distinction does not mean 'separation' as if 'theology,' the revealed word of God, and the positive divine law as distinguished from natural law, were under no circumstances of any influence on political philosophy and political ethics and on political institutions ... Theology will always be of help and assistance to political philosophy." Ibid., pp. 114-15.
[72] Ibid., p. 79.
[73] Ibid., p. 81.

interpretive digression is much like the earlier one. When critics questioned the Catholic "coincidence of human dignity and political power" with respect to the issue of capital punishment, Rommen stressed the polar tendency of original sin; here, after responding to criticism suggesting the anti-democratic character of Catholic thought, he swings back to the other pole, admitting that the emphasis on original sin has been, and can be, exaggerated in the tradition.

On the question of "the idea of man," then, modernity does involve a "philosophy of antinomies, of separations." And each imbalance, each extreme, harbors a corresponding theological problem. Reformation thinking separates nature and grace, denying the possibility of natural law and political theory. Modern rationalism divides rationality from religion only to remove the underlying basis for that very rationality. And, after the degeneration of rationalism, collectivism ushers in a new "irrationalism" and the "politicized faith" of the God-state. By contrast, the spheric thinking of the tradition joins together, in a harmonious "cosmos of ideas," nature and grace, reason and revelation, religion and rationality. The distance between the Catholic understanding and the ideological tendencies of late modernity is especially striking when one juxtaposes Rommen's comments on the unity of tension with his remarks about collectivism. The collectivist man suffers, he says, from an "aimless political dynamism" and "an inner restlessness" that results in "external destruction." To Catholic political philosophy, man lives in tension, but this "inner restlessness" embodies a "dynamic life" striving for restfulness in God. Thus "life and philosophy remain venturesome" for Rommen, since "only the final redemption, the lasting rest in God, will end the striving."[74] While the antinomies of modernity issue in the loss of man, the loss of the creature, the "unity of polar tension" is finally a metaphor for man's limitations, and "that vivid feeling of finiteness and imperfection."

---

[74] Ibid., p. 473.

# 4

## Work, Rest and Generosity:

### *Catherine Green*

Everywhere we see evidence of the increasingly fast-paced nature of our society. More people are working at second and even third jobs, not just to survive, but in order to accomplish the various financial and personal goals they might have. Many of us find it hard to find time to visit with friends and family. Our holidays, both religious and secular, historically devoted to rest and contemplation, are increasingly given over to recreation. It seems as if we are literally trying to create ourselves anew *in order* to be able to return to work. We say to ourselves "I *have* to take a vacation or I'll never make it through the fall!"

This scenario brings up questions about the nature of work and its meaning in our lives. What does it mean when work takes up all of our time and energies? Is there no need for rest and contemplation in the modern world, or is it more a matter of no space for it? In order to think about these issues, I turned to several of the essays by Yves Simon on the problem of work and the modern man. In *Work, Society and Culture*, Simon notes that the modern "ethic of the worker" leaves little room for contemplation and he suggests that the weakness of this ethic is "to be found in its tendency to identify useful activity with the exploitation of physical nature for human purposes."[1] The only activities we are interested in are those aimed at changing the natural world to make it satisfy our human needs and desires. Simon's suggestion brings to mind Rene Descartes who stands as one of the most compelling authors of the mastery of nature thesis. In the *Discourse on Method*, Descartes argues explicitly that if we use his method consistently we can learn to "use these objects [of the natural world] for all the purposes for which they are appropriate and thus make ourselves, as it were, masters and possessors of nature."[2] Simon argues that both work and contemplation are inherently acts of

---

[1] Yves R. Simon, *Work, Society and Culture*, trans. Vukan Kuic (New York: Fordham University Press, 1971), p. 45.
[2] Rene Descartes, *Discourse on Method and Meditations on First Philosophy*, trans. Donald Cress (Indianapolis, Indiana: Hackett, 1980), AT 62. Future references to the *Discourse* will be to this edition unless otherwise noted. All references to the *Discourse* will cite Adam & Tannery numbers.

generosity. Interestingly, Descartes argues that the "ripest fruit" of his philosophy is *generosity* which is the virtue that "serves as the remedy for all the disorders of the Passions."[3]

In this paper I will use Simon's understanding of the nature and the generosity of work, rest and contemplation along with Descartes' theory of the science of human activity and generosity to examine the issue of work in our modern culture. To do this I will ask several questions. Of Simon I will ask: What are the natures of work, rest, and contemplation? Of Descartes I ask: What is the nature of the activity of the modern scientist and the generous person? And, what is the role of contemplation and rest in this world and how does this differ from the view expressed by Simon? The paper will have three sections. I will begin by examining Simon's understanding of the metaphysics of work and rest as they apply to the actions of laborers, scientists and contemplatives. Next, I will examine Descartes' understanding of the kind of work that is carried out by the modern scientist and then look at the various activities and passions of the human soul in order to understand where work, rest and contemplation might be found. Finally, I will argue that while Descartes' language is familiar to our ears, his meaning seems to have taken what I will call a Copernican turn. The goal of work and its good and the goal of meditations, both scientific and theological, are all directed to the person in a way vastly different from the way they perfect the person in the traditional model explicated by Simon. Because of this turn, we will see that in the modern Cartesian world there really is no possibility for rest or play and certainly no room for contemplation.

To begin, then, in "Work and Workman" Simon poses the problem of how to identify what human endeavors qualify as work; e.g. is a scientist a worker?[4] To answer this question he begins with an examination of the kind of work carried out by a day laborer, the clearest example of a worker. He uses the classic Aristotelian-Thomistic metaphysics of action and rest to argue that work is characterized by two essential features. First, work "is a useful activity, whose end does not lie within itself, but in a result distinct from itself."[5] The good of work accrues to the product of the work. That is, the good of road building is found in the finished road. This means that work is an inherently generous activity. The worker "labors for his work rather than for himself."[6] In the terms of Aristotle's causes, the worker gives his efficiency to the world by effecting a good therein. In the essay "Work and Wealth" Simon notes that the day laborer is primarily working to produce wealth, that is to attain the physical realities necessary and favorable for supporting and expanding his life.[7] This shows the reciprocal nature of the relation between the

---

[3] Rene Descartes, *The Passions of the Soul*, trans. Stephen H. Voss (Indianapolis, Indiana: Hackett, 1989), article 156. Future references to *The Passions of the Soul* will refer to this edition by article number unless otherwise noted.
[4] Yves R. Simon, "Work and Workman," in *The Review of Politics* 2 (January 1940), pp. 63-86.
[5] Ibid., p. 65
[6] Ibid., p. 66.
[7] Yves R. Simon, "Work and Wealth," in *The Review of Politics* 2 (April 1940), p. 198.

worker and his work. The worker gives his efficiency to the world in his work and is rewarded for this activity by achieving some physical good that supports his life. When he plants seeds he makes the world more productive and is rewarded with food for his family. When he picks the fruits of nature's trees, even as he gathers food for his own table he accomplishes the task of dispersing the seeds of that tree such that others may grow. The *good* of work accrues primarily, then, in the product and the world, and only secondarily to the worker. Second, Simon argues that work is by its nature a moving activity, "intrinsically subjected to the laws of Becoming and Time."[8] When we work, we are always adding some new aspect to an unfinished project. When the project is complete, the work ceases. Thus work is incompatible with rest. Work, then, changes the object to which it is applied and ceases when the desired change has been effected.

Simon then develops the characteristics of contemplation in the same tradition and in sharp distinction from work. Here he speaks about contemplation understood in its broadest sense. He is not speaking of theological contemplation as such or speculation but rather of any terminal activity of the soul, that is; any activity of the soul that is completed within itself and that pursues no goal beyond the activity. Both love and intellectual speculation are included in this category. Since contemplation is a terminal activity of the soul, while it achieves the greatest good, it is essentially useless. By useless Simon means, of course, any activity not ordered to an ulterior end.[9] In contemplating his knowledge the knower gives himself up to the form of the thing known. He does not search for the concept or theory that follows from this formal determination, but simply accepts the object as it is; without limitation or change. The lover does not seek some good from the beloved beyond being with her. In true love the lover conforms his good with the good of the beloved to make himself *worthy* of the beloved. Simon argues that the generosity of contemplation "consists in [this] self-renouncement in behalf of the term known or loved."[10] The goods of knowing and loving, then, accrue primarily to the agent who enjoys his unity with his object and secondarily results in the production of concepts or theories or in a multitude of loving and generous activities. Again we see a kind of reciprocity between the agent and the world. By giving himself over to the other, as known or as beloved, the agent achieves his own good, while by that same action a gift is given in the form of ideas and actions.

It becomes clear from this discussion, then, that all activity that seeks an end that is distinct from the activity itself is a form of work. Thus, Simon argues that mental activity which is for the sake of changing the world, is as decidedly work as is road building. The engineer who designs the road as well as the scientist who develops the chemicals that are used to complete it are each engaged in discursive mental activity for the sake of an end beyond their activities and are thus workers.

---

[8] Yves R. Simon, "Work and Workman," p. 66.
[9] Ibid.
[10] Ibid., p. 67.

In this understanding, even the "pure researcher" who is trying to solve a problem simply to know truth nevertheless engages in a kind of work. The achievement of that truth remains an end distinct from the activity that produces it for him. When he achieves that truth, he then rests in his contemplation of the good he has achieved.

It is important to note that new theories or concepts and good actions can result from both discursive or transitive actions of knowing and loving as well as from their immanent and contemplative counterparts. These transitive actions are for the sake of the truth they pursue or for the sake of the beloved with whom they seek to be united. They represent the struggle to know or to be joined with the beloved. Contemplative actions also may, in fact they regularly do, result in new ideas or an increase of love and good action. However, these effects remain beyond the goal of the action which was simply to know or to love. Such effects represent the accidental bounty that overflows the nature of contemplation. By this definition any action that is for its own sake, that achieves its good within the action itself is not work. Thus contemplation, rest, and simple play would all fall into this category.

To review, then, Simon argues that work in a broad sense encompasses all activity that is ordered to an end beyond itself. Such activity is in motion and results in a change in the object: theoretically, at least, this is a perfection of the object. When the object is perfected the work is completed. Rest is thus incompatible with all forms of work. Contemplation is a kind of motionless activity where the good of the action is achieved within the nature of the action itself. It pursues no end beyond itself. The contemplative, in the form of a knower or a lover, effaces himself to the form of the known object or to the goodness of the beloved and changes himself to know that thing as it is or to be good enough to be with the beloved as she is without changing the known or the beloved. The agent changes while the other remains unchanged. The generosity of contemplation is the giving up of oneself in the face of truth and of making oneself good in order to be worthy of love.

We will turn now to a brief examination of Descartes' theory of the pursuit of science and his understanding of the generosity of this endeavor. In Descartes' preface to the French translation of *The Principles of Philosophy*, he tells us that "the whole of philosophy is like a tree. The roots are metaphysics, the trunk is physics, and the branches, emerging from the trunk are all the other sciences…"[11] The most important of these sciences, he tells us, are mechanics, medicine and moral philosophy. The good of the tree is not the roots or the trunk though clearly the tree could not exist without them. The good is in the fruits that can be picked from this tree. He is clear in this discussion that the highest good that comes from this tree and that presupposes all the other sciences is moral philosophy.[12]

---

[11] John Cottingham, Robert Stoothoff, Dugald Murdoch and Anthony Kenny, *The Philosophical Writings of Descartes*, 3 vols. (Cambridge: Cambridge University Press, 1985-1991), vol. 1, p. 186. All references to his *Principles of Philosophy* and his correspondence will cite page numbers and will refer to this edition unless otherwise noted.
[12] Ibid.

"By 'morals' I understand the highest and most perfect moral system, which presupposes a complete knowledge of the other sciences and is the *ultimate level of wisdom*."[13] Metaphysics is for the sake of physics and physics is for the sake of the "useful" sciences. This is consistent with his assertion in the preface to *The Passions of the Soul* where he tells us that his goal is to explain the passions, *not* as a moral philosopher, but rather as a physicist! It is *by means* of physics that we come to understand how to live a good life!

The question, then, is whether all the activities of the scientist and the moral person are what Simon would classify as work? Is all Cartesian activity for the sake of some end exterior to the action itself? Is there any place here for contemplation or for rest? To answer these questions we will briefly look first at Descartes' discussion of the method of his science, primarily in the *Discourse on Method*. Then we will look at his discussion of the actions and passions of the soul. Here we will explore his ideas about the activities of meditation, veneration, and happiness.

In the *Discourse on Method*, Descartes sets himself in sharp contrast to Aristotle and the Scholastics. They were interested in speculative philosophy, knowledge for its own sake, where he is interested in practical philosophy.[14] His philosophy is aimed at arriving at the knowledge of everything that is useful in life. Probably the most memorable passage where he articulates the mastery of nature thesis is in part six of the *Discourse*. The reason we would want to master nature, he tells us, is that we could invent an infinity of devices that would allow us to enjoy the fruits of the earth without pain and we could maintain our health which is necessary for all the other goods including wisdom.[15] The highest wisdom as we saw is moral wisdom. Wisdom, then, is not good for itself or for the scientist as a knower but is good for his ability to make the world better for himself and for others. Wisdom is for the sake of change. All our scientific activity, then, meets Simon's criteria for work; it means to change things in the world.

The next problem is to examine Descartes' discussion of the soul where we can address the question whether there is any place for contemplation in Descartes' theory of the activities of the soul. According to Descartes, all the functions of the soul are thoughts.[16] Of these thoughts there are two broad categories; the passions which include perceptions and knowledge, and actions which include volitions and meditations.[17]

Descartes distinguishes between the passions of the soul and those of the body. In article 132 he discusses the usefulness of the six primary passions of the body. All the other passions are species or combinations of these six.[18] These passions

---

[13] Ibid., emphasis mine.
[14] *Discourse on Method*, AT 62, p. 35.
[15] Ibid.
[16] *The Passions of the Soul*, art. 17.
[17] Ibid., art. 27.
[18] Ibid., art. 69.

inform the soul of things useful or harmful to the body. In the end hatred or repugnance is the most important passion of the body since it is "more important to repel the things that harm and can destroy than to acquire those that add some perfection without which one can survive."[19] Thus the usefulness of the bodily passions is simply the preservation of life.

Descartes then turns to the usefulness of the passions of the soul. Here love is the most important passion, and he argues that the most immoderate love is extremely good if, of course, it inclines us toward things that are truly good. What this love does is to "join us so perfectly to those [true] goods *that the Love we have for ourselves in particular* makes no distinction between us and them…"[20] Because we love ourselves and our own good we join ourselves as intimately as possible to things that are good for us. We strive to possess those things. The usefulness of love is that it helps us achieve the things that are good for us. This is not loving the other above ourselves, but rather *for ourselves*. All the passions, as Descartes so clearly tells us, "*dispose* the soul to will the things nature tells us are useful and to persist in this volition…"[21] All the passions of both the body and the soul are explicitly useful. They are clearly and completely directed to a good beyond themselves.

We turn now to the actions of the soul, its volitions and meditations. Are they also for the sake of an end external to them? The answer again is yes. We will begin with a brief discussion of volitions which, of course, make the clearer case. In article 29 he tells us that our volitions are excitations of the soul which are caused by the soul and which have reference to it.[22] Clearly all volition is for the sake of some effect, and since volitions number among the thoughts of the soul, they are directed by what Descartes understands to be the teachings of nature to will things useful to us.[23] He tells us that the "whole action of the soul consists in this: merely by willing something, it makes the little gland to which it is closely joined move in the way required to produce the effect corresponding to this volition."[24] Volitions produce effects. These effects are those things that are useful to us as a whole.

The more difficult problem, of course, is meditation where we might expect to find a kind of rest or contemplation. In fact in both joy and veneration, Descartes suggests just such a rest. However, further review reveals that these actions are as clearly purposeful as the others. Clearly, if we are to take seriously Descartes' discussion of his metaphor of the tree of philosophy, philosophical meditations that give us the metaphysical ground of science are *for the sake of* the various mechanical, medicinal and moral fruits. However, we would wonder about theological meditation. Surely it must be simply contemplative. Such does not appear, however, to be the case.

---

[19] Ibid., art. 137.
[20] Ibid., art. 139, emphasis mine.
[21] Ibid., art. 52, emphasis mine.
[22] Ibid., art. 29.
[23] Ibid., art. 52.
[24] Ibid., art. 41, emphasis mine.

In a letter to Chanut, Feb. 1, 1647, Descartes takes up the question; "Does the natural light by itself teach us to love God?"[25] He answers in the negative, arguing that the way to reach the love of God is to consider what He must be. We begin by considering that God is a being that thinks and that we resemble him. We then consider that our own knowledge seems to grow by degrees to infinity. Now, since God's knowledge is infinite, we might make the mistake of believing that we could become gods. But we are prevented from that "disastrous mistake" when we reflect on the infinity of his power. By such reflection we recognize His omnipotence and our own limitations. "If a man meditates on these things and understands them properly, he is filled with extreme joy."[26] Meditation leads to the recognition of our place in the world. This recognition fills us with joy. Meditation is a means to joy! This would not be surprising except that he has just argued that, "*with regard to the present life*, this love itself is the most delightful and *the most useful passion* possible..."[27] If even the love of God is useful to us, clearly the meditation that achieves such love is doubly useful! There is no allusion here to any suffering that might follow from our love of God. The only issue at hand is that of usefulness here and now. Love, he argued in the *Passions* erases the distinction between ourselves and the beloved and the joy that necessarily follows from the immoderate love of a truly good being "represents to us what we love as a good that belongs to us."[28] The meditation that allows us to love God would result in our recognition that *He belongs to us*. This is certainly no ordinary view of what it would mean to love God!

Descartes' language takes a similar turn in his discussion of veneration in *The Passions of the Soul*, article 162. Here he tells us that veneration inclines us "not only to esteem the object it reveres but also to submit to it with a certain apprehension, in order to try to render it propitious."[29] Now, we only revere beings whom we recognize to be free causes and whom we judge to be capable of doing us good or evil! And we do so in the hope that our veneration will result in a favorable response. Now surely God can do us good, and given his omnipotence, perhaps evil as well. Thus it would be with the hope that our veneration will effect a change in His action that we might submit to Him. Devotion is of a similar sort. According to Descartes, we are devoted to one "from which we expect only good."[30] Devotion, then, is an attitude of expectation of our own good from another. To a God from whom we expect only good we give devotion. To one who might punish us we give veneration in hopes of mitigating our punishment. Devotion, veneration, meditation: all are actions that might appear to be contemplative but in fact are useful for achieving rather immediate and concrete goods.

---

[25] *Philosophical Writings*, vol. 3, p. 309.
[26] Ibid.
[27] Ibid., emphasis mine.
[28] *The Passions of the Soul*, art. 139.
[29] Ibid., art. 162.
[30] Ibid.

Well then, what about happiness or joy? Is not happiness, the simple awareness of our unity with our beloved, a strictly contemplative action? In his discussion of happiness both in the *Discourse* and in a letter to Princess Elizabeth, he takes what appears to be a rather stoic view: our own happiness is within the power of our thoughts. He argues that happiness consists "in a perfect contentment of mind and inner satisfaction which is not commonly possessed by those who are most favoured by fortune, and which is acquired by the wise without fortune's favor."[31] He argues that, "each person can make himself perfectly content by himself without any external assistance..."[32] In order to do this, the person must satisfy three conditions. First he must use his reason to establish how he should act in each situation. Then he must have a "firm and constant" resolve to act as reason dictates without being diverted by the passions. Finally he must bear in mind that if he does these things the goods he does not possess "are one and all entirely outside his power."[33] This suggests, certainly, a rest and a contentment within the limitations of one's situation.

It is interesting to note however that in the *Discourse on Method*, to which he refers us in this discussion, Descartes states the last condition somewhat differently. "After having done our best regarding things external to us, everything that fails to bring us success, from our point of view, is absolutely impossible."[34] The qualifier, "*from our point of view*" seems to add a different dimension. Beyond the fact that desires for impossible objects are fruitless and frustrating and thus not supportive of our contentment as is clearly suggested in both his letter to Elizabeth and *The Discourse*, there may be another reason to believe that only our thoughts are in our power. That is, if our thoughts are in our power, then we are free to direct them as we see fit. Thus, perhaps from another point of view the goal may not be so impossible after all.[35] As we know, Descartes was aware of the Copernican theory and the wealth of possibilities that arose because of it. If in fact our will is as unlimited as Descartes argues in both the *Meditations*[36] and in the *Passions*[37] then perhaps it is more useful for us not to limit our desires but rather to search for a different path by which to reach the desired goal. In fact, in a letter to Elizabeth written in May or June, 1645, Descartes advises her to do just that. He tells her to concentrate her thoughts on distracting her imagination and senses from the problems that are distressing her. By this maneuver, he suggests, she may be able to restore herself to health as he had done in a similar situation when he was in his twenties. Here he points out that he has "always had an inclination to look at things from the most favourable angle and make [his] principal happiness depend

---

[31] *Philosophical Writings*, vol. 3, p. 257.
[32] Ibid.
[33] Ibid., p. 258.
[34] *Discourse on Method*, AT 25, p. 15.
[35] *Philosophical Writings*, vol. 3, p. 98.
[36] *Discourse on Method and Meditations on First Philosophy*, AT 57, p. 83.
[37] *Passions*, p. 41.

upon [him]self alone..."³⁸ This change of perspective along with the help of medical remedies, he suggests, would allow her to have hope that she would "recover perfect health, which is the foundation of all the other goods of life."³⁹ He is not suggesting she should rest quietly in her condition but rather she should change her perspective in order to effect a cure.

This view of the world is again presented in his discussion of generosity. At the end of the second part of *The Passions*, he argues that we need not be limited by fortune. In effect, we are the masters of our own fortune. We have two remedies for dealing with what he terms our "less useful desires." The first remedy is generosity. The second is to reflect on divine providence. We will begin with the latter. In our reflection on divine providence, he tells us that we "represent to ourselves that it is impossible that anything should happen otherwise than has been determined by this Providence for all eternity; thus it is like a fate or immutable necessity which must be opposed to Fortune, in order to destroy it, as a chimera arising only from error in our understanding."⁴⁰ Divine providence is by immutable necessity opposed to fortune. We can consider to be possible those things that *do not depend* on us, *only* if we think they do depend on fortune and thus fortune could grant them to us. To give up fortune is, of course, to consider these things impossible. In this discussion he tells us that those things are impossible that have failed to happen in the past because a necessary cause for their happening was absent. By this account any future event would remain possible if the necessary cause were present. With fortune ruled out, there remain two possible causal agencies in this account; divine Providence and ourselves. In article 146 he notes that some things are willed by divine Providence to depend on our own free will and that we "ought to think that *from our point of view*, nothing happens which is not necessary and as it were fated, so that we cannot without error desire it to happen otherwise."⁴¹ He goes on to argue that if it were the case that divine Providence has willed that we should be robbed if we choose to take a path that reason tells us is usually the safest path, we should yet follow our own reason. This suggests that since we do not know what divine Providence has decreed, we must always follow our own best judgment. By this account we would discard the idea of fortune because in believing things possible by it we may fail to act resolutely on our own best judgments. Further, we would not worry about divine Providence because we do not know its decree. Rather, we must concentrate on what is within our own power and use our reason to determine how to achieve what we desire. Then, he argues, for those issues that do not rest on our own power alone, we would still act resolutely and hope for the best. In article 144 he argued that the most serious error we commit is to "fail to distinguish sufficiently the things that depend entirely

---

[38] *Philosophical Writings*, vol. 3, p. 251.
[39] Ibid., p. 250.
[40] *Passions*, art. 145.
[41] Ibid., art. 146.

on us from those that do not..." This would suggest two changes in our thinking. First we will not struggle against those things that are done and finished, nor will we concern ourselves with things outside our power, including, of course, divine Providence. Second, we consider possible, perhaps by our own actions, those things that are not finished and done. One of the remedies for our useless desires, then, would be to distinguish clearly those desires that are truly vain and to conceive as possible those that are not.

Generosity, the other remedy for vain desires, is to act resolutely to achieve those things we judge to be good. It allows a man to think as highly of himself as it is legitimate to do.[42] This generosity has two facets. The first is the understanding that nothing truly belongs to a man other than his free control of his volitions and that there is no reason for him to receive praise or blame "except as he uses [his will] well or badly."[43] The generous man recognizes that his true power is in the control of his own will and he deserves praise or blame insofar as he exercises this control. The second facet is in his feeling "a firm and constant resolution to use [his will] well, that is, never to lack the volition to undertake and execute all the things he judges best—which is to *follow virtue perfectly*."[44] That is, he recognizes his true power and he executes it resolutely to achieve all the goods he judges to be best. The good he judges to be best is, of course, his own good. This may sound little different from Aristotle's formulation that "the good of man is an activity of the soul in conformity with excellence or virtue"[45] Yet clearly Descartes places himself in sharp distinction to this ancient model.

How, then, is Descartes' notion of virtue different? Descartes describes his generous man as one who is both naturally "inclined to do great things" and who "undertake[s] nothing [he] does not feel [him]self capable of."[46] If our understanding of Descartes' theory of scientific activity and the soul is correct, the apparent tension between these two attributes is not so great. The generous man who recognizes his own power and executes it resolutely for his own good also recognizes that everything or almost everything that is not a finished issue may yet be open to achievement by the action of his will. He does not *feel* incapable of anything, really. He recognizes that he is truly powerful. In a letter to Queen Christina, dated 20 November, 1647, Descartes argues that "free will is in itself the noblest thing we can have, since it makes us in a way equal to God and seems to exempt us from being his subjects. And so its correct use is the greatest of all goods we possess..."[47]

---

[42] Ibid., art. 153.
[43] Ibid.
[44] Ibid., emphasis mine.
[45] Aristotle, *Nicomachean Ethics*, trans. Martin Ostwald (Indianapolis, Indiana: Bobbs-Merrill, 1985), I.7.
[46] *Passions*, art. 156.
[47] *Philosophical Writings*, vol. 3, p. 326.

Descartes goes on to describe the generous man as "esteeming nothing more highly than doing good to other men."[48] In doing so he would scorn his own interest. How can he scorn his own interest and at the same time be, as I have argued, pursuing with all resolution precisely his own interest? I would argue that if the recognition of and resolute execution of his will for the best end is always his goal, then it is the case that every action he exercises for the good of others in fact achieves his highest good, the exercise of his will. What is primarily at issue here is power and the exercise of power. The highest good is not knowledge or love, but rather it is the exercise of a powerful will!

Generosity, here, can be seen as having itself taken a Copernican turn. In Simon's model of the generosity of work, the efficiency of the agent produces a gift in the world for which the agent is secondarily rewarded by the world. The act is for the sake of the perfection of the object in the world. The perfection of the laborer himself both as an agent and financially are by-products of the efficiency. Work is necessarily change and motion that only accidentally leads to perfection of the agent while it is inherently generous. It is not by accident that the best work reflects the good character of the worker. This good is seen in the world and is measured by external standards. For Descartes, however, the goal of the work, that is, the resolute exercise of the will for truly good action, is for the good of the agent himself primarily and the byproduct of this exercise would be the mass of good actions that occur in the world. This is not an expression of love for another, but is solely an expression of self-love. Cartesian generosity is not measured by any external standard, but is always and only a measure of self-esteem.

Similarly, with contemplation, rather than being an activity that perfects the agent directly by knowing the world as it is and by making himself good in order to be worthy of the beloved, Cartesian meditation and love are for the sake of changing the world to make it better for the knower and again changing the world in order to make it good enough for the lover. This is another Copernican turn. In Simon's view of contemplation, we completely give ourselves over to the form of the thing known and make ourselves over to be good enough to be with the beloved. We change only ourselves leaving the known and the beloved unaltered; not because they are good for us, but because they are good in themselves and as they are. For Descartes the world can only be understood as it relates to the agent. There is no seeing the other as it is or loving the other because it is good in itself. We see the other and how it is good for us. We change it to make it useful to us. The goal is the good of the agent and all the good actions that he carries out are the accidental means to that end.

Perhaps, you might suggest, this is not such an important turn as a Copernican turn. I would argue otherwise. Let us look at the ancient model of work. There we work to accomplish a finite good in the world. We work until that goal is

---

[48] Ibid.

accomplished, then we rest. We necessarily rest because there is nothing more to do to complete the project. By this same action, we are led to reflect on and contemplate the good that we have achieved. We experience the joy that comes with accomplishment. By our actions, we have made ourselves worthy of the good that then comes to us from the world in the form of honor or money or goods. While it may be the case that the final good we desire is infinite, each particular good is clearly finite. We can see and rejoice in the reality of the mediate goods we achieve even as we continue the pursuit of our ultimate good. There are clearly defined and necessarily achieved rest stops along the way! In the Cartesian model, all this is different. If all action of my soul is for the sake of satisfying my desire for my own good and if my will and that desire is in fact infinite as Descartes argues, then it is the case that no particular work can ever satisfy that will. My work is as infinite as my will. Furthermore, because it is the case that, by my actions, I constantly open up new possibilities for the exercise of my will, the possibility for actions I should resolutely enact grows exponentially. The more I achieve, the more I can achieve and the more I can achieve, the more I must resolutely pursue. There is no room here for rest. By its very nature the process becomes increasingly frenetic. It is not without reason, so to speak, that Descartes regarded his work as infinite. By this account, as an unreflective Cartesian, I cannot, of course, rest on labor day or on any other day, for that matter.

# 5

## Maritain and Gilson on the Challenge of Political Democracy

### *Desmond FitzGerald*

This collection of essays is dedicated to reflecting on the achievements of Jacques Maritain in political philosophy, especially considering *Man and the State*, the series of lectures he gave at Chicago. These 1949 lectures went a long way toward integrating the political and social themes he had been developing since the 1920s in works such as *The Things That Are Not Caesar's, Integral Humanism, Scholasticism and Politics, The Rights of Man and Natural Law, The Person and the Common Good, Freedom in the Modern World, Christianity and Democracy* and "The End of Machiavellianism," an article in *The Review of Politics*.[1]

This was a tremendous production, and this along with his writings on epistemology, philosophy of art, ethics and metaphysics inspire awe and admiration.

In proposing to bring to your attention some of the reflections on politics of Maritain's friend and co-worker in the Thomistic revival, Étienne Gilson, I undertook a task which proved more difficult than I had originally imagined; for in contrast to the volume of Maritain's writings, what was available in Gilson's *ouevre* proved rather slight. Gilson not only reflected on the political issues of his time in various talks he was invited to give to different groups, he participated in the politics of post-World War II France and so his reflections, while slight, had some grounding in his practical experience. But these talks were not published as books, and the many articles he wrote for French papers and periodicals, such as *Le Monde* and *Sept* were not available to me.[2] What I did have were photocopies of his own typed speeches sent to me by Fr. Fred Black, CSB, the archivist of the Pontifical Institute of Mediaeval Studies, Toronto.

---

[1] Jacques Maritain, *The Things That Are Not Caesar's*, trans. J. F. Scanlan. (London: Sheed and Ward, 1939); *The Range of Reason* (New York: Charles Scribner's Sons, 1952); *The Rights of Man and Natural Law*, trans. Doris C. Anson (New York: Scribners, 1943); *Freedom in the Modern World*, trans. Richard O'Sullivan (New York: Charles Scribner's Sons, 1936); *Christianity and Democracy*, trans. Doris C. Anson (New York: Charles Scribner's Sons, 1950); *Scholasticism and Politics*, trans. Mortimer J. Adler (Garden City, New York: Image Books, 1960); *The Person and the Common Good*, trans. John J. Fitzgerald (Notre Dame: University of Notre Dame Press, 1966); *Integral Humanism*, trans. Joseph W. Evans (Notre Dame: University of (Notre Dame Press, 1973).

[2] Étienne Gilson, *Pour un Ordre Catholique* (Paris: Desclée de Brouwer, 1934). This work was a strong rhetorical work Gilson addressed to his fellow Catholics in France whom he believed were neglecting their opportunity to participate in the French politics of the 1930's, and consequently were leaving the contemporary civil scene to be

To appreciate the similarities and differences of Maritain and Gilson, who were great friends and who admired each other very much, it is well to consider their different origins and ambitions. Thanks to Fr. Laurence Shook, the author of the Gilson biography,[3] this was beautifully done in an article which appeared in a 1979 *Notes et Documents*.[4]

Maritain, born in 1882, was the son of Paul Maritain, a lawyer, and Genevieve Favre, the daughter of the great statesman of the Third Republic, Jules Favre. It was an intellectual not a religious family, the father being something of a liberal Catholic and the mother a Protestant. In this atmosphere of the salon, and what Shook calls the *haute* or *grande bourgeosie*, Jacques was well to do enough to embrace the social causes of the workers far from his own status enjoying the ideals of a Tolstoy as he began university life occupied with the causes his mentor, Charles Péguy, espoused.

Gilson was born in 1884 into a *petite bourgeosie* family of no distinguished lineage that would be comparable to Maritain; it was, however, a hard-working, practicing Catholic family. Gilson, a bright son, was drawn to studies and early on conceived the ambition to become a teacher in the French educational system—with all the financial security a position as a civil servant, a *fonctionnaire*, could promise.

Where Maritain and his fianceé, Raissa, the daughter of Russian-Jewish immigrants, were disappointed in the Sorbonne, Gilson threw himself into the opportunity he had to succeed within the system. He worked hard to climb the steps which eventually led to his first teaching positions within the French educational organization where, as I understand it, all was ultimately controlled by the Ministry of Education in Paris. Gilson's middle class background was such that he was pleased to be employed in an educational system where one began teaching in some provincial city looking toward Paris as the ultimate rung on the ladder of success should one be so fortunate to return to the Sorbonne or a comparable institute of learning.

This is not the place to review Gilson's climb to the top by listing a series of teaching posts. I shall rather go on to several extra academic events which must have shaped his political reflections. Like most other healthy French youths at the turn of the century, Gilson took his year of military training at the age of eighteen. Then he went on with what we think of as his graduate studies. Like Maritain,

---

dominated by other parties who had only a confused and caricature understanding of what Catholics stood for. It was, as if, in the post-revolution era Catholics had abdicated their responsibility to stand up and be counted for the political positions to which they should give support. Given the intellectual and moral tradition the Church had developed, he particularly argued that Catholics had failed to have the impact they might have in the field of education, and he was attempting to rally them to do something in this cause. Gilson invited those of his readers who were persuaded by him that it was time to take action toward bringing Catholic educational principles to the contemporary social milieu to give their support to the Dominican Fathers' journal *Sept*. By aiding the journal Gilson believed there would be a focal point for Catholic intellectuals to work to change what had become, no longer a Catholic France, but a secular, pagan France dominated by free-thinkers and anti-clerics.

[3] Laurence K. Shook, *Étienne Gilson* (Toronto: Pontifical Institute of Mediaeval Studies, 1984).
[4] *Notes et Documents* (Rome) 17 (October-December, 1979), p. 12ff.

Gilson attended and was fascinated with the lectures of Henri Bergson. Particularly exciting were Bergson's affirmations of the validity of metaphysical thinking.

Embarked on his career and hard at work on his dissertation on Descartes, Gilson was called to military service in 1914 with the outbreak of what became World War I in 1914. In the light of his later work in philosophy I have always found it interesting that his specialty was machine gun instruction. He came also to serve in the trenches, and in the historic battle of Verdun, he was almost killed. He was captured and spent the rest of the war as a prisoner of war, where in addition to polishing his German he made use of the chance to learn Russian from fellow prisoners.

In June 1940, during World War II, Gilson was home in France when it collapsed and surrendered to the German army. He was approached several times during the occupation by the Nazi authorities but he refused to co-operate with them. Instead he devoted his energies to teaching and the revision of his writings. The famous fifth edition of *Le Thomisme* appeared in 1944. With the liberation of Paris in the late summer of 1944, he was able to make contact again with some colleagues in North America.

Here also is when what might be considered his political activity began. The government of Charles de Gaulle made him a member of the French delegation that went to San Francisco in April 1945 to work on the creation of the United Nations. Gilson's remarkable language skills (he was quite fluent in English and could understand and speak Russian) proved of great help to the delegation. With the completion of the conference it was a great joy to him that he was able to stop in Toronto and renew his friendships with colleagues at the Institute on his way home.

Returning to France in late summer 1945 and looking forward to returning full-time to teaching he was again prevailed upon to serve his country as a participant in an October London conference on education and intellectual co-operation. This conference later became the originating organization of UNESCO. Once more he was gaining experience with international politics. Incidentally, about the time Gilson was preparing to go to San Francisco for the United Nations, Charles de Gaulle appointed Jacques Maritain French ambassador to the Vatican in March, 1945.

Maritain's influence on European politics in that post-war period was significant. In the different countries there were active Communist parties which benefited from the fact that some of their members had established heroic records during the occupation as members of the Resistance. But balancing them were the Christian Democratic parties which had been inspired by Maritain's writings, and these parties were, in fact, forming the governments of the Netherlands, Belgium, West Germany and Italy. In France, the party took the name of Mouvement Republicain Populaire (MRP) led by such ex-professors as Georges Bidault and Maurice Schumann.

In fact Gilson was invited to stand for election in 1947; he consented but lost the nomination. However, there was some provision whereby the MRP could appoint a certain number of members to a Senate-like Counsel, and in 1947 Gilson was appointed. He served two years, 1947-1949, during which he found himself in the middle of the legislative process and party politics; years he considered his least productive in a political sense. He felt as if he had accomplished nothing.

In an interview some years later he said:

> What I realized most is that there is no difference between being a senator and being nothing. In a few cases I risked giving advice to some minister, but I was not listened to ... I feel I got nothing at all out of my experience as a senator. It might have been better had I been able to do something ... but I felt no satisfaction. For the most part, in France, deputies and senators don't count for much.[5]

While his actual experience of politics was disappointing, his participation in the political process provided an occasion for Gilson to crystallize his thinking about political democracy.

In Canada during the fall semester, 1947, he accepted the invitation of two groups to speak on the philosophy of liberalism. The first group was a National Summer Conference of the Liberal party at the McMaster University, Hamilton, Ontario and the second was the Political Science Society, at the University of Toronto. While they were two different talks, the structure and the message of the talks was the same: how political democracy must work for economic democracy, not in the Marxist way of State Capitalism, but by using state power to promote the economic welfare of the various societies, such as the families and unions, to better achieve social justice.

Now that sentence summarizes, but does not do justice to, some twenty-five pages of closely reasoned text of which I will give a precis in a moment. But before I do I shall make a couple of comments to set the scene.

First, unlike Maritain in *Man and the State*, Gilson does not give a deep analysis of political terms such as: body politic, sovereignty, state and so on. He uses ordinary political words in an ordinary, conversational way. He does at one point use the distinction between "individual" and "person," and here his clarification is along the same lines as Maritain as they both reflect traditional Thomistic teaching.

Second, remember Gilson is speaking in 1947, just two years after the end of World War II. The Western nations had not had time to enjoy their military success before they were confronted with a militant Marxism that came to fruition in the Soviet Union and the People's Republic of China. Even from within various European countries vigorous Marxist political groups rose as opposition parties to the Christian Democratic governments. Gilson was most concerned with the threat of Marxist successes even at the polls.

Gilson's 1947 lecture begins with the recognition that democracy with its promise of political liberty had been generally successful in the civilized countries. Now people have the vote and can choose their governments. But this political

---

[5] Shook, *Étienne Gilson*, p. 275.

equality has not brought social and economic equality; while many have political liberty they have not economic liberty; some have and enjoy much greater power than others in virtue of their economic status. This, he recognizes, is the strength of the Marxist critique of capitalistic social system. Gilson is not attracted to Marxism: "I quite agree that Marxism is a plague, but so long as we don't know what germ is the cause of a catching disease, we are unable to stop it ... If we want to remove Marxism we should first remove its cause."[6]

In other words Gilson takes the temptation for Marxism on the part of many workers very seriously; he sees further that the solution the Marxists propose to gain economic equality leads to the denial of political liberty, and so that is no solution. We must, he argues, invent an alternative to unfettered capitalism and Marxism, and that alternative is the full realization of political democracy. "...The creating of social and economic democracy will mean nothing else than our firm resolution to carry justice everywhere into all orders of human relations. Such is the full meaning of the word: Democracy."[7]

This assertion provides the occasion for Gilson to clarify for his audience the distinction between "individual" and "person" which, as I have mentioned he does in such a fashion as Maritain would approve. Gilson concludes: "I would say that fully to own oneself is, for every human person, the very essence of its own liberty."[8]

Keep in mind Gilson is speaking as a philosopher, not a member of a political party; he is also a Frenchman addressing a Canadian audience, and he is careful to keep a certain level of abstraction—and not to identify with the political program of any party in any country—yet he does not want to be so abstract that his thinking could be dismissed as pious generality. It is here that he turns to the groups we belong to as social animals, especially our families, and speaks of the obligation of the state to protect and foster such groups, including our professions and churches, so that they can function well and enable us to become worthy of being human persons.

While he repudiates Marxism, which could cancel human or personal liberty, Gilson is concerned with providing some area for state intervention that would enhance the common good. "... The proper function of the modern State is to insure the common good of all, by putting at the disposal of various social groups all the legal and technical means which they need in order to achieve themselves their own ends."[9]

He sees the state's role as being the protector and helper of those social groups outside of which there can be no personal liberty. Again it is the family he has especially in mind as it has the first responsibility to feed, clothe, house and educate its children. And Gilson is not against State intervention to preserve the economic

---

[6] This is from a photocopy of the text Gilson typed himself for delivery to the Political Science Society, Toronto, pp. 7-8. The original is in the Gilson Archives, Pontifical Institute of Mediaeval Studies, Toronto.
[7] Ibid., p. 14.
[8] Ibid., p. 15.
[9] Ibid., p. 19.

functioning of a country in crisis situations. He makes reference to two situations: a coal laborers' strike in Great Britain in 1947 and a railroad workers' strike in France that same year. He approved of using state power to end what could be regarded as economic anarchy. Again it is the State's role to promote conditions of social justice.[10]

Reporting on Gilson's lecture at McMaster University, Shook states: "Gilson's address drew a tremendous response from his audience. He reported to Thérèse [his wife] that 'never have I received such an ovation' " and one journalist who attended reported some young liberals were moved to dedicate themselves to a life of public service."[11]

Let us now compare Maritain and Gilson on world government.

With respect to the problem of world government, or as Maritain prefers to call it, "a genuinely political organization of the world," Maritain is cautiously favorable in *Man and the State*. He quotes approvingly his friend Mortimer Adler's 1944 book *How to Think About War and Peace*[12] and agrees with the basic argument that absent some world organization we are doomed to international anarchy. The price of peace is some sort of world government; however, the investment nations have in their political autonomy remains for the time being a barrier to such an organization. It is recognized that in a different way there is a world economic interdependence, and no nation is self-sufficient. For Maritain the logic of the fact that no nation is a perfect society complete unto itself dictates a conclusion of some sort of World State despite contemporary obstacles towards its achievement.[13]

Some twenty years later, in 1970, Mortimer Adler was editor-in-chief of *The Great Ideas Today*, a yearbook sold to purchasers of the Britannica set, *The Great Books of the Western World*. The purpose of the yearbook was to relate the so-called great ideas to the events of the contemporary world. To that end, a theme, often a question or controversy, would be chosen as an organizing principle and leading thinkers would be invited to contribute their thoughts to some aspect of the question. Thus their essays would constitute a symposium on the topic. In 1970 Otto Bird, Adler's assistant at that time, wrote Gilson to invite him to contribute his thoughts on "the world community, not world government—where it stands today, the chances for its further development and obstacles to it, the necessity for it, its feasibility etc..." Gilson, then in his mid-80's, was living in retirement in his country home, Vermenton, and the honorarium for the essay ($1,000) was inviting. So he set to work and wrote a dozen typewritten pages which were never published, since there was apparently a change of mind on the part of the editors. The manuscript exists amongst Gilson's papers in Toronto, and I shall

---

[10] This is from a photocopy of the text Gilson typed himself for delivery to the Political Science Society, Toronto, p. 22. The original is in the Gilson Archives, Pontifical Institute of Mediaeval Studies, Toronto.
[11] Shook, *Étienne Gilson*, chap. 8, p. 279.
[12] Mortimer Adler, *How to Think About War and Peace* (New York: Simon and Schuster, 1944).
[13] *Man and the State*, chap. 8.

use it as an indication of his mature reflections on this issue. To summarize, Gilson was much more skeptical and pessimistic on the feasibility of a world community than Maritain had been.

Perhaps here is the place to mention that Gilson had given a series of lectures at Louvain University, Belgium, in 1952, which were published as *Les Métamorphoses de la Cité de Dieu*[14] in which he explored the role of Christendom in the universal community of men. He examined the different forms the concept of a universal community had taken in the Western tradition, citing the writings, not only of Augustine, but Roger Bacon in the 13th century, Dante in his *De Monarchia* and so on.[15] The book was never translated into English, and in a note to Bird, Gilson refers to it saying: "The book fell still born from the press; it has taken it nearly twenty years to get out of print." In *Les Métamorphoses* Gilson was somewhat more optimistic of an ecumenical project of the three monotheistic religions, Judaism, Christianity, and Islam working together.

On the "world community" Gilson was quite pessimistic. "The chief obstacle to the founding of a world community lies in the artificiality of the project. Of itself, nature would not produce such a community, only human minds can think of it and, if needs be, proceed to the elimination of those of the actually given societies of which the destruction is required on order to make room for the universal one."[16]

A few lines later Gilson continues:

> To substitute an artificially conceived world community for the teeming multiplicity of the national groups would be to lessen the culture of the earth in both quantity and quality. The history of past civilizations shows this to be true.[17]

Gilson seemed to believe that even a united states of Europe (something that today one can say is being created with the creation of a common currency) would be "positively frightening." He says:

> One can lay down as a sort of rule that the fecundity of world culture is directly proportional to the number of its centers and in inverse ratio to their sizes. To the question, where does the project of a world community stand today? The obvious answer suggested by the preceding remarks is that it exists only under the form of a pious wish unsure of the exact nature of its object ... True societies are born, not made.[18]

There is more, of course, but this indicates the contrast between the optimism of Maritain and the realism of Gilson on this matter.

An account of Gilson's political thinking would be incomplete if no reference were given to what his biographer, Shook, calls *"l'Affaire Gilson."* In 1950, a year after his wife, Therese, had died of leukemia he returned to his teaching in Toronto,

---

[14] Louvain: Publicationes Universitaires de Louvain, 1952.
[15] Shook, *Étienne Gilson*, p. 315.
[16] The original paper is in Gilson's Toronto Archives.
[17] Shook, *Étienne Gilson*, p. 5.
[18] Ibid., p. 6.

and in the course of the year decided to resign his Paris professorship at the Collége de France. He had been working on Duns Scotus for some time, and along with this book, his lectures and seminars dealt with different aspects of Scotus' thought.

What I shall report here is almost entirely taken from Shook's biography of Gilson, and I shall largely be summarizing his account.[17] At the invitation of his old friend, Gerald B. Phelan, Gilson went in late November, 1950, to give a short series of four lectures sponsored by the University of Notre Dame Medieval Institute. Along with the lectures there was a busy series of luncheons and dinners to celebrate Gilson's visit, and winding up the parties was a dinner hosted by a Professor James Corbett and his wife, Suzanne, on a Saturday evening. As the give and take of the conversation flowed Gilson presented his position of "neutralism" as the best course for France in this era of the Cold War between the Soviet Union and the United States.

This was not an off the cuff remark; in a series of articles in *Le Monde* earlier in 1950, Gilson had argued that were there to be an armed conflict between the United States and Russia, France should try to remain neutral. To better put this in context it has to be remembered how challenged the free world had been by the success of communist takeovers in Eastern Europe and China, and the tensions arising in Korea and Greece. Also, Gilson had been a prisoner of war in World War I and had lived through the Nazi occupation of France in World War II. Gilson feared what he considered a real possibility of war between the United States and Russia and the consequences for his country, his family, and himself. In those days NATO was still in formation, and Gilson had little confidence that France could resist invasion if a military conflict occurred, and he was afraid the USA could not protect France.

With hindsight we can recognize that Gilson was mistaken; NATO and the deterrence of the bomb helped to keep what peace we had during this Cold War period, but do not forget the United Nations' armies were fighting in Korea. The United States was fully engaged in the Korean conflict, which had begun the previous June, and, at best, was just holding its own in that conflict.

The day following that dinner party Gilson, Phelan, and Peter O'Reilly drove to Milwaukee where Gilson presented a lecture at Marquette University. The lecture was one of those he had just given at Notre Dame. He then returned to Toronto on December 4th to enjoy the company of Jacques Maritain, who had just arrived to spend a short visit. On December 12th, Gilson wrote the French Ministry of Education to announce his decision to retire from his professorship at the Collége de France, something he was quite entitled to do, however, he did it without first discussing his intent with his Parisian colleagues. From their point of view, he appeared to be deserting France for North America, and it was not a welcomed move.

---

[17] Shook, *Étienne Gilson*, pp. 301-10.

A few days later, December 15, 1950, the Catholic weekly *Commonweal* published an "Open Letter to Étienne Gilson" by Waldemar Gurian, distinguished professor of political philosophy at Notre Dame, the editor of *The Review of Politics*, and a regular contributor to *The Commonweal*. While complimenting Gilson on his Scotus lectures he accused him "of spreading the sad gospel of defeatism." Gurian continued: "You have stunned those whom you have met with your prophecy that France will be occupied by the Red Army without much resistance and that the United States will not do much about it." There is more, of course, but that is enough for our purposes: the article was picked up and reprinted in the French press, as well as other papers and journals and Gilson was treated like a traitor. It stunned the poor man (he was in his late sixties) and he was devastated by the controversy. Of course some rushed to his defense but *The Commonweal* refused to publish a retraction even after it became clear that Gurian had not himself attended the social event on which he based his article but had apparently written it upon hearing the gossip of someone else who had been present at the dinner conversation.

Gilson was deeply hurt and while Phelan and others who were there put out the correct version of what was actually said, Gilson had to suffer the humiliation of seeing his distinguished reputation damaged. More than that, the feelings in France ran so hotly against him that when his colleagues at the College de France gathered to vote on what his pension would be he was denied it. Later the pension was restored and later also Gurian wrote Gilson to apologize for the harm he had done and for the way he did it. As Shook reports it, the *"l'Affaire Gilson"* was a depressing event that damaged his reputation in France.[18]

Gilson, as I have indicated, did not offer a fully developed political philosophy such as Maritain offered, but he took his role as a philosopher and Catholic citizen seriously. And when invited he not only participated in the political life he shared his reflections. Most of these reflections were in French daily papers which are not easily accessed in the English speaking world. However thanks to the Gilson archives in Toronto I have tried to present a sample of Gilson's thinking about political democracy in comparison to that of Jacques Maritain.

---

[18] Ibid., p. 310. Anthony O. Simon at the Maritain conference in Colorado Springs in 1998 spoke informally of the role his father, Yves R. Simon, had played in prompting Gurian to write his apology. It was Yves Simon who composed a letter of apology and forced Gurian to sign and send it to Gilson.

# II

# Liberalism Reconsidered

# 6

# Constitutional Democracy in Search of Justification

## *Henk E.S. Woldring*

Jacques Maritain writes in favour of democracy because the word stands for a political ideal. He argues that a pluralist democracy needs more than a set of formal or practical rules and procedures. First, a pluralist democracy needs a common thought and a public morality. Second, citizens should justify the formal rules from different philosophical or religious comprehensive outlooks that give them more consistency and vigour. The central questions of this article read as follows: What does Maritain understand by comprehensive ideas of democracy and how could they strengthen the practical democratic rules? What relevance does his theory of democracy have for the contemporary democracy debate being held by Jean-Marie Guéhenno, Claude Lefort, John Rawls and Philip Selznick? After answering the first question I shall discuss the relationship between the formal and substantial conception of democracy. Finally, I shall illustrate this relationship by an analysis of democratic defects of the European Union.

### Maritain on Democracy

Maritain argues that the word "democracy" has a wider meaning than that implied or stated in many political-scientific treatises of government. It refers first and foremost to a general philosophy of human and political life and state of mind. Like Abraham Lincoln, Maritain summarizes democracy as a "government of the people, by the people, for the people."[1] However, he knows from history that many theories of democracy that employ this device contain at the same time contrary consequences.

Maritain rejects Rousseau's idea of sovereignty of the people. Like Rousseau, he resists despotism and he defends the rights and liberties of the people, but he rejects Rousseau's theory because it leans toward the totalitarian state. Rousseau refuses to recognize a deeper ground of political life than what is found in the

---

[1] Jacques Maritain, *Man and the State* (Chicago: The University of Chicago Press, 1951), p. 24.

people as an aggregate of individual human beings.[2] Maritain rejects the idea of sovereignty of the state as well. This idea means that everything must bow before the will and the aim of the almighty state. There is no other right but the immanent right that is written down in law. The law is right not because its content is in harmony with principles of right but because it is law. According to Maritain, the sovereignty of the state implies the danger of centralization of power of the government at the cost of the rights and liberties of citizens. In this case the government becomes a totalitarian one that takes over many responsibilities of citizens and undermines the vitality of society.[3]

In his own philosophy of democracy Maritain discusses a pluralist type of democracy. Citizens who belong to a variety of autonomous social groups and associations participate in this type of democracy. However, it does not admit that the state is a superpower to incorporate all authority and to impose its authority from above upon human life. It tends to sustain the idea of civil society that requires that autonomous groups, in possession of authority commensurate with their function, have their proper rights and responsibilities. Moreover, in a pluralist democratic state citizens participate who belong to very different philosophical and religious creeds, and who should cooperate for the common welfare.[4] He argues that a genuine democracy implies a fundamental agreement between minds and wills on the basis of life in common. Democracy needs such a common thought; "[I]t must bear within itself a common human creed, the creed of freedom."[5] This faith is not a religious faith but a *secular* or *civic* one. He criticizes libertarian theories which conceive democratic society as an arena in which all private conceptions of communal life are met without a common thought of society.[6]

This secular faith deals with practical tenets or a *practical charter* that contains a legal structure, articles, formal rules and procedures that together converge citizens toward the political organization of a democratic state. Next, citizens can try to justify this *practical charter* from very different philosophical or religious outlooks. Moreover, Maritain argues that notwithstanding the diversity of worldviews the democratic sense should be kept alive by the adherence of minds, however diverse, to a *moral charter*. This *moral charter* or the code of social and political morality deals for instance with the following items: social and political rights and liberties of human persons and corresponding responsibilities; rights and liberties of persons who are members of a family and associations and the liberties and obligations of the latter to the body politic; government of the people, by the people and for the

---

[2] *Man and the State*, pp. 45-49.
[3] Jacques Maritain, *Christianity and Democracy* (San Francisco: Ignatius Press, 1986), p. 61.
[4] *Man and the State*, p. 11-12. *Christianity and Democracy*, pp. 58-59.
[5] *Man and the State*, p. 109. See Jacques Maritain, *The Range of Reason* (New York: Charles Scribner's Sons, 1952), pp. 165-71.
[6] See also the articles of Mortimer J. Adler and George Anastaplo in Michael D. Torre, ed., *Freedom in the Modern World: Jacques Maritain, Yves R. Simon, Mortimer J. Adler* (Notre Dame, Indiana: University of Notre Dame Press/ American Maritain Association, 1989).

people; human equality, fraternity, mutual tolerance and respect, obligations of each person and the state towards the common good.[7] Moreover, Maritain also discusses a *common ethos*: the inner energy of both the secular democratic faith and the socio-political morality to revitalize the practical charter.[8]

In short, Maritain distinguishes between the secular faith of a common democratic thought, a moral charter, a common ethos, a practical charter and theoretical justifications of the latter. Moreover, when Maritain is discussing only a "democratic charter" in general, these subjects are included.

When discussing theoretical justifications of the practical charter Maritain acknowledges that people hold very different fundamental theoretical conceptions of democracy. He also acknowledges that neither the state nor any party may impose a philosophical or religious creed. Therefore, he argues that these justifications "must cling only to the common practical recognition of the merely practical tenets upon which the people have agreed to live together, despite the diversity or the opposition between their spiritual traditions and schools of thought."[9]

These practical tenets of agreement (the practical charter) are reduced to a mere series of abstract or formal formulas, if they are not beared and sustained by citizens from their philosophical or religious worldviews and moral motives. Therefore, Maritain argues that democracy needs education: citizens should learn to justify theoretically those practical tenets from their philosophical or religious convictions. By this justification citizens contribute to the enforcement of the moral charter at the same time.[10] This enforcement of the practical and the moral charter will promote social and moral cohesion in a pluralist democracy. Otherwise a pluralist democracy runs the risk of disintegration. The state should encourage citizens to develop their own diverse justifications of the practical charter in order to strengthen this charter, and to revitalize both the secular faith and the moral charter of democracy.

### Maritain's Comprehensive Conception of Democracy

Maritain argues that a constitutional democracy advances thanks to the vitalization of moral energy springing from the spirit of human dignity, liberty and brotherly love. This means that progress of a constitutional democracy will take place by the ascent of moral consciousness that is linked to a superior level of organization: the quality of the practical charter. Thus, the quality of this charter cannot be achieved by coercion but only by the progress of moral consciousness and by development of social relationships which are characterized by human dignity, liberty and brotherly love. This consciousness is "the soul of democracy."[11]

---

[7] *Man and the State*, pp. 111-13.
[8] Ibid., p. 145.
[9] Ibid., pp. 120-21.
[10] Ibid., pp. 121-22.
[11] *Christianity and Democracy*, p. 27. See Jacques Maritain, *The Rights of Man and Natural Law* (San Francisco: Ignatius Press, 1986), pp. 114-15.

An important reason for the failure of the modern democracies to realize democracy is "the fact that this realization inevitably demanded accomplishment in the social as well as in the political order, and that this demand was not complied with."[12] This means, according to Maritain, that modern democracies have failed to achieve both a constitutional democracy and a democracy of social organizations. However, the reason for the failure of this nexus of political and social democracy is that in modern society common life is disintegrated by economic selfishness.[13]

Moreover, social and political democracy are not only methods of organizing society but they designate first and foremost a general philosophy of human and political life and a state of mind, in which human dignity, inalienable human rights, justice, equality and brotherhood are essential. According to Maritain, the principal reason for the failure of modern democracies is a spiritual one, and he continues: "This form and this ideal of common life, which we call democracy, springs in its essentials from the inspiration of the Gospel and cannot subsist without it."[14]

Maritains's own comprehensive ideas of democracy consist of his understanding of the meaning of the Gospel for democracy and its revitalization: the unity of the human race, the natural equality of all men, the inalienable dignity of human beings, of labor, and of the poor, compassion with the weak and the suffering, the inviolability of conscience, and viewing every human being as our neighbor. These characteristics are the basis of his ideal of "personalist democracy": the conception of democracy that is concentrated upon the dignity of human beings. Moreover, from his religious and comprehensive worldview Maritain gives a theoretical justification of the practical charter to strengthen it and the common ethos as well.[15]

Maritain argues that by virtue of the "hidden work" of the evangelical inspiration secular political philosophical theories contain the following widespread ideas of inalienable rights of the person; equality; the government as representative of the multitude; political rights of the people whose consent is implied by any political regime; relations of justice and the legal order at the base of society; the ideal of fraternity, and promotion of the "common good" of the multitude.[16] By virtue of his theoretical justification Maritain wishes to strengthen these ideas. He acknowledges that the democratic state of mind stems not solely from the inspiration of the Gospel, but he holds that it cannot exist without this inspiration.[17]

---

[12] *Christianity and Democracy*, p. 19.
[13] See Yves R. Simon, *Philosophy of Democratic Government* (Notre Dame, Indiana: University of Notre Dame Press, 1993), p. 88.
[14] *Christianity and Democracy*, pp. 19-20.
[15] Jacques Maritain, *Integral Humanism: Temporal and Spiritual Problems of a New Christendom* (Notre Dame, Indiana: University of Notre Dame Press, 1973), pp. 201-202.
[16] *Christianity and Democracy*, pp. 34-41, 57-59.
[17] *Christianity and Democracy*, p. 49. See John DiJoseph, *Jacques Maritain and the Moral Foundation of Democracy* (Lanham, Maryland: Rowman and Littlefield, 1996), pp. 1-3, 80-93, 96-98. Also Gerald A. McCool, "Maritain's Defense of Democracy," *Thought* 54, 213 (June 1979), pp. 132-42.

Next, I shall discuss the contemporary debate on the formal conception of democracy (the practical charter) and its justification from various worldviews including comprehensive conceptions of democracy.

## Formal Conceptions of Democracy

The French political philosopher Claude Lefort argues that in a democracy the legitimacy of power is based on the people. However, the image of sovereignty of the people is linked to the image of an empty place, impossible to occupy. Those who exercise public authority can never claim to appropriate it. Democracy is sustained by two contradictory principles: on the one hand, political power emanates from the people; on the other, it is the power of nobody. This paradox of democracy came to the fore when universal suffrage was introduced: at the moment that sovereignty of the people would manifest itself by suffrage, solidarity faded away. Sovereignty of the people was reduced to a sum of mathematical units; "the idea of number as such is opposed to the idea of the substance of society. Number breaks down unity, destroys identity."[18]

The principle that power belongs to nobody is reflected in the institutionalized competition between political parties. However, this paradox of democracy cannot be conquered by any institutional arrangement. Lefort argues that if the place of power appears genuinely empty, then those who exercise power are perceived as mere ordinary individuals, as forming a faction at the service of group interests.[19] How can abuse of political power be avoided?

When answering this question many citizens propose formal-legal democratic rules and procedures as the solution. They acknowledge that in Western societies concepts of democracy are closely connected with plurality of worldviews and comprehensive political outlooks. This plurality does not mean that various worldviews only accomplish or partially overlap each other, although this may be the case in some respects, but in the public debate representatives of different worldviews demonstrate that they hold opposite opinions and different social and political ideals. In the liberal political tradition democracy is a form of government that is neutral to the worldviews citizens hold.

Francis Fukuyama, for example, defends such a "strictly formal definition of democracy" that is worldview neutral. This means that citizens and the government should follow correctly certain rules without questioning moral values that could underlie democracy. He admits that democratic procedures can be manipulated by elites but he fears a much greater danger in abolishing the formal concept of democracy. Refering to Lenin, who held comprehensive ideas of democracy, Fukuyama fears oppression and misuse of power in the name of "democracy."[20]

---

[18] See Claude Lefort, *The Political Forms of Modern Society: Bureaucracy, Democracy, Totalitarianism* (Cambridge: Polity Press, 1986), p. 303.
[19] *The Political Forms*, p. 279.
[20] Francis Fukuyama, *The End of History and the Last Man* (New York: The Free Press/Macmillan, 1992), p. 43.

However, formal-legal democratic rules appear not to be only formal. There are many moral values which underlie this formal conception of democracy: for instance, freedom of speech, press and association, equality of human beings for the law, the right of all citizens to vote and to participate in politics, tolerance, mutual respect, cooperation, respect for privacy, social peace, and individual tastes, talents, interests and life plans.[21] I call these politico-moral values minimal values: they are based upon fundamental human rights and/or interests of individual citizens, they underlie a constitutional democracy, and make it possible. This implies that a purely formal conception of democracy does not exist. Sure, there are formal democratic rules and procedures but they presuppose minimal substantial moral values. In Maritain's phrase, a practical charter presupposes a moral charter.

John Rawls argues, and rightly so, that constitutional democracy does not consist of only formal legal rules. He holds that the political conception of justice is a *moral* conception that ought to underlie the basic structure of a constitutional democracy. By this basic structure he means a society's main political, social and economic institutions, and how they fit together into one unified system of social cooperation. Accepting the political conception of justice does not presuppose accepting any particular comprehensive religious, philosophical or moral doctrine. According to him, citizens do not accept the political conception of justice on any religious or moral authority. They accept the political conception of justice because it can serve as "the focus of an overlapping consensus" of a variety of comprehensive views citizens hold.[22]

Rawls' political conception of justice may be called a minimal moral value. I do not employ this characteristic "minimal" in a disparaging way. His concept of justice has a "higher" theoretical status than the minimal politico-moral values mentioned before. This means that his conception of justice is built upon these minimal politic-moral values. However, although Rawls presents a substantial conception of justice, ultimately, it is no more than a result of an overlapping consensus. From comprehensive worldviews there is more to say about justice but this "more" is excluded by Rawls from this consensus. Yet, this "more" does interest me in relationship to the central questions of this article.

### Formal, Minimal and Comprehensive Conceptions of Democracy

For the sake of clarity I want to distinguish between formal, minimal and comprehensive conceptions of democracy. The formal conception contains legal articles, rules and procedures or what Maritain calls the practical charter. The minimal conception of democracy contains politico-moral values as a result of a tacit overlapping consensus that underlies these rules and procedures or in Maritain's phrase: the moral charter underlies the practical charter. These moral values are

---

[21] See William A. Galston, *Liberal Purposes. Goods, Virtues, and Diversity in the Liberal State* (Cambridge: Cambridge University Press, 1991), pp. 301-04.
[22] John Rawls, *Political Liberalism* (New York: Columbia University Press, 1993), pp. 11-12, 97, 175.

called minimal because they are generally accepted (despite private worldviews citizens have). Moreover, citizens may interpret and elaborate these minimal moral values (by virtue of their private and comprehensive worldviews) into comprehensive conceptions of democracy to strengthen the formal conception or what Maritain calls theoretical justification.

Citizens may hold comprehensive conceptions of democracy because they are concerned about whether or not minimal politico-moral values are an adequate basis of a constitutional democracy to solve certain social and political problems. They may wonder whether, for instance, by defending the legal rights of speech, press, etc., a minimal conception of democracy has adequate legal instruments to resist racist or other discriminatory groups that strive for their ideas in accordance with formal democratic rules to change ultimately these rules. Or they may wonder whether it has adequate instruments to control the role of money in politics.

Lefort argues that substantial moral values, for instance human rights, are "generative principles" of a democratic society. He acknowledges that human rights are not fixed in democratic societies once and for all. Their content changes with time, new rights emerge and give rise to political debate. However, there is an awareness of human rights that underlies this debate and that leads to legal formulations of certain human rights. This debate is fragmented: it emerges from different worldviews, places and groups within society (labour unions, political parties, and other organizations).[23] Lefort defends the value of this debate as an expression of initiatives taken by groups seeking greater participation in various fields of society. He argues that a constitutional democracy can be revitalized only by a vital civil society: "[T]he establishment of a power of limited right, of such a kind that outside the political sphere ..., economic, legal, cultural, scientific and aesthetic spheres are circumscribed, each of which obeys its own norms."[24]

Rawls also acknowledges the existence of those substantial moral values of comprehensive worldviews but he fears their mutual competition at the same time. He wants to minimize their influence in public life to safeguard the "underlying basis of consensus": a rational consensus as a result of rational compromises that may be valued as correct.

I admit that Rawls' search for this consensus as a minimal basis of a constitutional democracy is a real challenge. However, these minimal politico-moral values are not the result of a consensus only, but they are also the conditions that enable citizens to elaborate them by virtue of their comprehensive worldviews. There is another challenge as well that Maritain discusses: How can the minimal conception of democracy be strengthened by comprehensive ideas? To clarify Maritain's significance for the contemporary democracy debate, I shall discuss the essentials of the theory of the American political philosopher Philip Selznick who discusses this question without lapsing in to moralism or utopism.

---

[23] *The Political Forms*, pp. 259-72.
[24] Ibid., pp. 279-81.

## Comprehensive Conceptions of Democracy

Selznick holds that the abstract idea of "consent of the governed" does not require democracy. There may be consent to a monarchy or a tyranny (for instance, Nazism). To avoid the danger of a tyrant, the *Declaration of Independence* of the United States couples "consent of the governed" with an affirmation of "inalienable rights." Moreover, the founders of the United States also coupled *consent* of the governed with *rule* by the people. Selznick holds that democracy is the self-preserving consent of the governed that maintains the liberties and institutions of a free people. At a minimum this concept of democracy requires freedom of speech and association, legitimate opposition, and legitimate elections. This means that consent must be revocable. Only then does consent of the people become sovereignty of the people.

Moreover, regarding these ingredients of democracy as a self-preserving consent of the governed, Selznick holds that the people cannot be considered as an aggregate of individuals but as a functioning community: "*The sovereignty of the people is established, confirmed, and exercised in and through community*. People act democratically not as isolated or self-sufficient units, but as bearers of a common culture, including a political structure of society."[25] This is consistent with Maritain's thesis that democracy should not be primarily understood as a form of government based upon political rights of individuals but as a form of community in which citizens employ their rights to serve their common political destination. Like Maritain, Selznick admits that democracy also nurtures and sustains diversity and individuality. Next, Selznick considers four principles of communal democracy.

The first principle is *the protection and integration of minorities*. Selznick argues that democracy cannot be equated with the formal or mathematical rule "the majority rules" because the sovereignty of the people is not the same as the sovereignty of the majority. The power of the majority can never be absolute because the rights of minorities to freedom of speech, association and opposition must be maintained.[26]

The second principle is *the moral primacy of the commonwealth over the state*. A government may be considered to be the agent of a preexisting community, not of hitherto dissociated individuals. This community is composed of many complex groups and relationships—economic, familial, religious, political—whose stability and vitality depend on the protection of fundamental rights. These rights are not only individual-centered but also group-centered. The idea of civil society answers this view of a socially differentiated society. Those social groups do not exist by the grace of the state nor are they organized by principles of the market. They employ their rights and liberties according to their own nature. Group-centered rights are vital ingredients of a communal democracy. Selznick holds: "They create an infrastructure for democracy."[27]

---

[25] Philip Selznick, *The Moral Commonwealth. Social Theory and the Promise of Community* (Berkeley: University of California Press, 1992), p. 502.
[26] Ibid., pp. 503-04.
[27] Ibid., p. 509.

The third one is *the responsibility of the government for communal well-being*. We have seen that the legal power of the government ought to be limited by the proper rights and liberties of civic associations. This does imply a limited government, not a minimal government, because the government has to promote justice. Even the strongest advocates of minimal government have recognized a role for the government in providing for public goods such as defence, public safety, education and sanitation. The modern state has to take responsibility for old age pensions, medical care, expanded education, housing, child care, employment policy, and the mitigation of poverty. This welfare policy is needed to help human beings fulfill their responsibilities, not to supplant them. While civic associations have an enduring worth, from the standpoint of the communities as well as individuals, the experience of oppression within these associations is often played down or overlooked. In fact many associations are undemocratic. According to Selznick, principles of communal democracy should be applied to civic associations as well as the state.[28]

The fourth and final principle is *the social basis of political participation*. Selznick argues that democracy is communication, and communication is education. The consent of the governed is creative, critical, and participatory. They combine participation in private associations with civic participation that they bind to public ends. Selznick argues that the political process should be open to direct participation by individuals. Moreover, every form of direct participation must be mediated by an infrastructure of association, interdependence, communication and moral education. Democracy cannot flourish if this infrastructure of civil society, i.e., the main sources of personal responsibility, are attenuated or lost.[29]

Although Selznick's argument is more sophisticated than Maritain's, like Maritain, he is arguing that a constitutional democracy should be considered as an integrated part of communal life.

## Civil Society as Infrastructure of Democracy

Like Maritain, Selznick argues that citizens may hold very different comprehensive conceptions of democracy. These conceptions are expressions of various worldviews and groups in civil society. This religious and socially differentiated society is called the infrastructure of a constitutional democracy. This means that formal and minimal conceptions of democracy (that may presuppose an aggregate of selfish human beings with their individual rights and interests) should be strengthened by legally indicated rights and liberties of citizens and their private associations that underlie the idea of communal life.

As I already discussed, all formal and minimal conceptions of democracy contain substantial ideas, but these conceptions are related to rights and interests of individuals and groups. They are not related explicitly to communal life. However,

---

[28] Ibid., pp. 510-21.
[29] Ibid., pp. 522-24.

citizens who are aware of being a part of a constitutional democracy as a community should not only pursue their own interests but also bear responsibility for the whole.

However, there are also many connections between the state and civil society. There is even a process of transformation of a relatively passive, apolitical civil society into a politically active one, which promotes not only private rights and interests of different groups but also different and competing conceptions of the common good.

Within contemporary Western societies social groups, political, social and economic elites struggle for control over the formation of the cultural, economic and political centres of society. This continuous struggle for control between state, the market and civil society may develop in two opposite directions. The first direction is the continuous expansion of civil society along with the expansion of democracy. This involves a greater participation of sectors of society in politics and economy. The second direction is either the victory of the state over society and economy in totalitarian countries or the victory of the market over politics and society.

In constitutional democracies the first direction is dominant. For this reason Lefort argues, like Selznick, that civil society is the infrastructure of a democratic state: political power in democracy should represent and make visible the social organization of civil society. However, there is always the power of the state to control society, like there is the power of the market to master society. Politics always tends to weaken existing semi-monopolistic social and economic centres of power. It may increase political and administrative power of the state over civil society in the name of public order, safety and justice.[30] An important challenge for constitutional democracies is: to create a common framework in which various comprehensive views of democracy and the common good can compete and give adequate support to a democratic government without undermining the very possibility of the system working.[31]

## Comprehensive Conceptions of Democracy for Justice

Answering this question Selznick combines, unlike Rawls, a procedural conception of justice with a substantial or "robust conception of justice". Like Michael Walzer[32], Selznick argues that justice is a principle that underlies communities and that should be worked out within communities to improve the quality of life: a just distribution of social goods should occur through and within differentiated communities. He does not agree with authors who interpret this principle as a minimal conception of justice: to mitigate oppression and to avoid destructive conflicts. On the contrary, Selznick argues: "The process of doing justice

---

[30] See S. N. Eisenstadt, "The Cultural Programme of Modernity and Democracy," in *Culture, Modernity and Revolution: Essays in Honour of Zygmunt Bauman* (New York: Routledge, 1996), pp. 35-36.
[31] Ibid., pp. 37-39.

stimulates moral and legal development. ... Justice affirms the moral worth of individuals; sustains autonomy and self-respect; domesticates authority; and establishes a framework for moral discourse on public matters."[33]

Selznick demonstrates that justice is a comprehensive concept. Its meaning cannot be captured by a single element, such as impartiality of procedural fairness, or by an abstract formula such as giving to each his due. If we minimize justice, we lose a great deal of its resonance and promise.

Selznick refers to Aristotle who argues that the purpose of every human being and community should strive for the desirable good life or what Selznick characterizes as moral well-being. He is aware of the fact that many contemporary philosophers have resisted this idea, mainly because it is incompatible with the doctrine that moral value is a reflex of will and an arbitrary choice. Moreover, there is concern that the notion of the good life commits us to specific conclusions as to what ends are worth having. However, like Alasdair MacIntyre, Selznick argues that the purpose of the good life does not necessarily specify means, ends or outcomes.[34] Citizens who hold various comprehensive conceptions of democracy can strive for this purpose by discussion and through conflict. In this way they give support to the quality of a democratic government.

Selznick does not present a blueprint of a just society or good life but he maintains that justice gives direction to human striving for individual and social well-being. This well-being is often called the common good. However, Selznick does neither interpret common good as the sum of individual goods, like libertarians often do, nor as the goods of the community as a whole, like socialists defended in former days. He argues that the common good is a normative idea that directs the process of a just distribution and redistribution of material and immaterial goods among individuals and groups participating in society.[35]

In the democratic debate on justice Maritain's own comprehensive ideas on democracy may be relevant, just like his theory of the common good. Like Selznick, Maritain argues that the purpose of a democratic state ought to be the common good of the entire nation, in which everyone has the economic right to labour and property, possesses civic and political rights, and cultural participatory rights.[36] As such the common good is the general goal or a normative characteristic of the political society: "[T]his good of the social body is a common good of human persons, as the social body itself is a whole made up of *human persons*." So, the common good refers to what is "*common to the whole and the parts*."[37]

---

[32] See Michael Walzer, *Spheres of Justice:. A Defense of Pluralism and Equality* (Oxford: Basil Blackwell, 1983).
[33] *The Moral Commonwealth*, pp. 430-431.
[34] Ibid., pp. 148-151. See Alasdair MacIntyre, *After Virtue: A Study in Moral Theory* (London: Duckworth, 1981), p. 164.
[35] *The Moral Commonwealth*, pp. 535-37.
[36] *Man and the State*, pp. 10, 20, 54.
[37] *Rights of Man*, pp. 94-96. See Maritain, *The Person and the Common Good* (Notre Dame, Indiana: University of Notre Dame Press, 1985), pp. 29-30, 47-89. See also Diana Caplin, "The Good Citizen and the Demands of Democracy: An Application of the Political Philosophy of Yves R. Simon," in *Freedom, Virtue, and the Common*

Like many authors, Maritain and Selznick are discussing democracy within the bounds of the nation state. How far is this national limitation still relevant in a world that is characterized by processes of internationalization and globalization? Finally, I shall discuss this question in relationship to the European Union.

## Globalization and Democracy

The French political philosopher Jean-Marie Guéhenno argues that the political significance of national states will fade away.[38] Solidarity within the bounds of territories will be replaced by global technological networks. Financial markets, economic developments, military operations and national authorities are already organized within supranational institutions. As a consequence the state will disappear, and the parliamentary democracy as well. For centuries the idea of democracy was connected with the idea of freedom: the right of a people to determine its own future, and the right of protection of everyone against abuse of power of the government or other institutions. This freedom is fading away. Moreover, we need to accept the end of the era of institutional power. Rather, institutional power has become much more widespread and complicated. Nowadays democratic freedom tends to maintain the rules or procedures for the functioning of a society that has no goal anymore.

However, in the last chapter of his book Guéhenno argues that we have to fight a "spiritual revolution": we have to redefine the relationships to our life world; we need moral debates on our relationship to the public square. In these debates people should be in search of new forms of solidarity based upon feelings of responsibility for their life world. These debates need to start from the grass roots or bottom up: by local democracies and self-defining communities. Through these debates politics may perhaps return.

Guéhenno is rethinking the process of democracy. His idea of democracy is not primarily formal but he starts with debates on comprehensive ideas of human responsibility and forms of solidarity. In that respect he is discussing humanitarian activities for the people in our neighbourhood and those in Third World countries who are suffering under poverty, economic arrears and violations of elementary human rights. He holds that many citizens try to find solutions for those problems through non-governmental organizations, rather than through politics.

Without disparaging the merits of non-governmental organizations I think we have to acknowledge that for the long term suffering people cannot be helped only by activities of humanity or charity. They need laws of justice, in particular legal instruments, for their protection. We need a new international legal and economic order to achieve this protection. However, we cannot achieve this new international order without the existing states. These states can be really democratic

---

*Good*, eds. Curtis L. Hancock and Anthony O. Simon (Notre Dame, Indiana: University of Notre Dame Press/American Maritain Association, 1995), pp. 293-306.

[38] Jean-Marie Guéhenno, *The End of the Nation State* (Minneapolis: University of Minnesota Press, 1995).

only if they also represent the needs of suffering people, and if they strive for their civic and economic rights and liberties, both nationally and internationally. Therefore, I hold that the state is neither irrelevant nor an absolute entity in the discussion on democracy, as I shall illustrate with the example of European Union.

## Democracy in the European Union

In many respects the European Union is a democratic miracle because it is based upon contracts of fifteen nation states under supervision of their national parliaments. The Union maintains certain political, civic and economic human rights, a European Court, and elections for the European parliament. On the other hand, the Union is characterized by democratic defects. The European policy is made by the European Commission, meetings of members of the national governments, committees of diplomats and other officials in bureaucratic networks. There is no European Constitution, no Constitutional Assembly and the European Parliament has limited competencies. It can neither control European commissioners nor ministers of national governments. However, the European politics of authority is limiting the competences of national governments and parliaments more and more. Although political borderlines between the member states have been relativized, feelings of cultural and national identity block the growth of a real constitutional democracy of the Union.

Regarding a minimal conception of democracy, a democratic European Union should meet at least three conditions. First, the Union should maintain a minimum level of civilization: the member states should pursue the maintenance of human rights and solve their conflicts without war. Second, the Union should promote political participation of citizens in democratic procedures and establish democratic institutions for an effective control of the policy of European commissioners in order to enforce social justice in a well-ordered European society and the good life of its citizens. Third, the Union should maintain a pluralist society: the ethnic, historic, lingual and worldview diversity of its citizens, and the rights and liberties of their private associations. For the sake of the central question of this article, I summarize these conditions into the following question: How do we strengthen the practical and moral charter of the European Union that is characterized by cultural and political diversity and that intends to promote a European *community*?

Discussing the European Union as a community we need to have an idea of communal life without nostalgic nationalist sentiments, moralistic arguments or utopian ideas. However, the idea of a community is not a given or a starting point, it is only an achievement—an achievement that John Dewey claims can be realized in and through democratic communal life only. Many European citizens and politicians have an instrumental conception of community: they regard a community as a set of social arrangements as a necessary burden and cooperate only for the sake of pursuing their private and national ends. We need, however, a constitutive conception of community: European citizens should conceive their identity as defined to some extent by the European community of which they are a part.[39]

From this constitutive conception of community Dewey holds: "The clear consciousness of a communal life, ... constitutes the idea of democracy."[40] Dewey argues "that democracy is not an alternative to other principles of associated life. It is the idea of community life itself."[41] For the European Union I claim the negative formulation of Dewey's thesis: Without the clear consciousness of a communal life the idea of an effective democracy cannot be constituted and practised.

In this connection the relevance of Maritain's theory is evident as far as he is discussing the *common ethos* of democracy. The clear consciousness of a communal life that constitutes the idea of democracy (Dewey) may be understood as the inner energy of both the secular faith and the socio-political morality to revitalize the practical charter. Moreover, citizens can try to strengthen this practical charter from their comprehensive ideas of a communal European life.

In short, a constitutional European democracy can only be revitalized by a vital European civil society as its infrastructure: national member states and socially and religiously differentiated societies. On the one hand, this infrastructure channels citizens' comprehensive social and political ideas. On the other hand, these ideas may converge by pursuing justice as a normative idea that transcends national borderlines.

---

[39] See Richard J. Bernstein, *Philosophical Profiles: Essays in a Pragmatic Mode* (Philadelphia: University of Pennsylvania Press, 1986), pp. 268-69.
[40] John Dewey, *The Public and Its Problems* (Denver, Colorado: Alan Swallow, 1957), p. 149.
[41] Ibid., p. 148.

# 7

## Acknowledging Ambiguity and Difference in Politics: A Christian Realist Challenge to Thomists

### *Jeanne M. Heffernan*

During the 1930s and 40s democracy faced powerful challenges from various quarters. Rival ideologies challenged the foundations of democratic politics most directly, but even sympathetic observers were critical of democratic governance. Perceiving a crisis in democratic theory, several prominent Christian intellectuals proposed new theoretical support for democracy. Among these, Reinhold Niebuhr and Yves R. Simon deserve renewed attention, for their work marks a critical contribution to democratic theory. Niebuhr and Simon, working from Protestant and Catholic traditions, respectively, drew upon widely divergent theological orientations which have at times produced opposing accounts of human nature and politics. From Niebuhr's perspective, Catholic thought was incapable of offering a principled, not merely pragmatic, defense of democratic politics. Yet, as I shall demonstrate, Simon's Thomism grounds a comprehensive philosophy of democratic government, answering Niebuhr's criticisms with a defense of democracy drawn from the tradition of Catholic natural law theory.

Niebuhr and Simon each attempted in his own way to illuminate "the essence of democracy" and provide it with "a more compelling justification" than liberalism could offer.[1] Yet, while Niebuhr and Simon commonly perceived liberalism as defective and undertook similar tasks in proposing an alternative foundation for democracy, and while each approached his task from a theologically informed perspective, the positions they articulate appear strikingly different. Just how fundamental and deep these differences are requires exploration, especially given Niebuhr's criticism of Catholic natural law theory as itself an inadequate philosophical foundation for democratic politics. Considering the challenges of

---

[1] Yves R. Simon, "Thomism and Democracy" in *Science, Philosophy and Religion, Second Symposium*, eds. Louis Finkelstein and Lyman Bryson (New York: The Conference on Science, Philosophy, and Religion in Their Relations to the Democratic Way of Life, Inc., 1942), vol. 2, p. 260; Reinhold Niebuhr, *The Children of Light and the Children of Darkness* (New York: Charles Scribner's Sons, 1944), p. xii.

contemporary pluralism, a close examination of Niebuhr's claim that the natural law tradition produces a rigid ethical system that lends itself to intolerant politics is in order.

### Clear-sighted Children of Light: Christian Realists

Reinhold Niebuhr's commitment to Christian Realism underlies his criticism of liberalism as a naively optimistic faith in man's moral progress and of natural law theory as a semi-Pelagian moral philosophy with anti-democratic implications. As Niebuhr articulates it, Christian Realism constitutes a theological orientation in the tradition of Augustine and the Reformers with certain key emphases, especially sin. A Christian Realist perspective—unlike its liberal Protestant cousins—attempts to recover Biblical insights on man's sinfulness and need for redemption. As Niebuhr puts it:

> The high estimate of the human stature implied in the concept of "image of God" stands in paradoxical juxtaposition to the low estimate of human virtue in Christian thought. Man is a sinner. His sin is defined as rebellion against God. The Christian estimate of human evil is so serious precisely because it places evil at the very centre of human personality: in the will.[2]

The root of sin resides within man himself, for man, whose essence is freedom, has the inclination to deny his creatureliness, his dependence upon God, and to claim divinity for himself and infallibility for his opinions; this, Niebuhr tells us, is "the very inclination which Christianity defines as original sin."[3]

Underscoring the problem of sin, Christian Realism reflects anew on the doctrine of original sin. The doctrine plays a critical role in Niebuhr's conception of man, as it draws together insights from revelation that are amply confirmed by experience. For Niebuhr, its significance lies in the fact that it expresses an existential and paradoxical truth: there is a "bias toward evil" in the human will which cannot be attributed to external factors, such as historical institutions or traditions. No, "the temptation to sin lies ... in the human situation itself." Man, created finite and free, recognizes that he transcends natural necessity on the one hand, but is limited on the other; this recognition evokes anxiety, and in his anxiety man attempts "to transmute his finiteness into infinity, his weakness into strength, his dependence into independence ... [T]he self lacks the faith and trust to subject itself to God. It seeks to establish itself independently. It seeks to find its life and thereby loses it."[4] Such is the sin of pride, which manifests itself in endless permutations, from overt violence to subtle manipulation.

The social effects of sin are as varied and pervasive as sin itself, for the temptation to selfishness and will-to-power is exaggerated in human collectives.[5] In Niebuhr's

---

[2] Niebuhr, *The Nature and Destiny of Man* (New York: Charles Scribner's Sons, 1941), vol. 1, p. 16.
[3] Ibid., vol. 1, p. 98.
[4] Ibid., vol. 1, p. 248, pp. 251-2.
[5] Niebuhr, *Moral Man and Immoral Society* (New York: Charles Scribner's Sons, 1932), pp. 48, 272.

estimation, the basic pattern of communal life reflects Augustine's description of the *civitas terrena*, which enjoys only a precarious peace. Conflict and domination disturb its concord, as competing factions vie for supremacy; partial and particular communities exalt their own purposes, arrogating to themselves undue authority and power. Within these communities, moreover, domination and injustice often prevail on account of a self-worshipping ruling caste. Thus, Niebuhr laments, "[M]an's collective, like his individual, life is involved in death through the very strategies by which life is maintained, against both external and internal peril."[6]

An adequate political philosophy pays heed to this fact. It reflects a sober assessment of the human situation and outlines a politics of modest ends and realistic means. As Niebuhr puts it, "To establish justice in a sinful world is the whole sad duty of the political order," which relies upon a combination of moral, rational, and coercive forces to avert anarchy and create a tolerable degree of justice and peace. To this end, political society must seek to achieve:

> The greatest possible equilibrium of power, the greatest possible number of centers of power, the greatest possible social check upon the administration of power, and the greatest possible inner moral check on human ambition, as well as the most effective use of forms of power in which consent and coercion are compounded.[7]

A democratic regime best approximates this balance of power, for democratic institutions "place checks upon the power of the ruler and administrator and thus prevent it from becoming vexatious," while allowing individuals and groups to reach "tentative and tolerable adjustments between their competing interests and … arrive at some common notions of justice which transcend all partial interests."[8] Niebuhr recommends a federal constitutional democracy of the Madisonian stripe, for it fragments power among different branches and levels of government and, in contemporary parlance, affords multiple points of access to organized interests, as well as to individual citizens equipped with voting rights. More than other regimes, this kind of system fosters a symbiotic relationship between freedom and order, inasmuch as it guarantees individual freedoms within the context of a legal order to which all are bound—legislator and executive no less than private citizen. Negatively, this splintering of power curbs the ability of any one person or group to exercise what Augustine calls the *libido dominandi*; in other words, it will "deflect, harness, and restrain self-interest, individual and collective, for the sake of the community."[9] Positively, it allows in the best case individual and collective centers of vitality to express their creativity without a premature foreclosure of possibilities

---

[6] Niebuhr, *Faith and History* (New York: Charles Scribner's Sons, 1949), pp. 221-22.
[7] Niebuhr, "The National Preaching Mission," *Radical Religion*, vol. 2 (Spring, 1937), p. 3; "Coercion, Self-Interest and Love" in *The Organizational Revolution*, ed. Kenneth E. Boulding (New York: Harper and Brothers, 1953), p. 242.
[8] Niebuhr, *The Children of Light and the Children of Darkness*, p. xii.
[9] Ibid., p. 41.

by the heavy hand of government. These structural features, Niebuhr observes, give rise to an ethos of openness and free inquiry, the *sine qua non* of a healthy political society. This ethos tempers the sinful tendency of the powerful to identify their partial interests with the common good and chastens each group to recognize the ideological taint in their own purposes. In short, democratic life requires and optimally fosters "a spirit of tolerant cooperation" among individuals and groups that neither moral cynics nor moral idealists can achieve: the former know no law beyond their own interest, while the latter recognize such a law but remain unconscious of the corruption tainting their own conception of it.[10] Such is the Christian Realist defense of democratic politics.

### Misguided Children of Light: Thomists

Unlike Christian Realism, according to Niebuhr, political Thomism and natural law theory cannot serve as a philosophical foundation for democracy. To understand Niebuhr's assessment of Catholic natural law theory, one must view it in light of his more general criticism of Catholic theology. For Niebuhr, the historic emphases of Catholic theology on either the problem of human finitude *vis-a-vis* an infinite God or of human ignorance *vis-a-vis* an omniscient God misses the more central issue recognized by Augustine and the Reformers: sinful pride, not simple finitude or ignorance, effects human alienation from God. While related to finitude and ignorance, pride is distinct from it; the former are not intrinsically sinful, the latter is. Man, as Niebuhr relates, becomes aware of his finitude and contingency. With this awareness comes the temptation for him to shore up his existential hold on life, to make secure the ground of his existence. In the process, he tries in vain to suppress awareness of mortality. If he succumbs to the temptation, he commits the sin of pride, the primal sin, so basic because it constitutes a willful rejection of God's created order. Once in sin, man will invariably assert himself over others, attempting to make men and the things of this world his existential foundation. From the sin of man's rebellion against God's order flows all other sin. Deceit, injustice, sexual lust—indeed, every manifestation of fallen nature—find its root in pride's rejection of human finitude and ignorance. We know that we are mortal, and we deny our mortality. We know that we do not know, and we pretend to omniscience. What leads us from one to the other in Niebuhr's Kierkegaardian view of sin is anxiety, the nervous apprehension of finitude in the absence of a trust in God's loving providence. But because man has an imperfect and inconsistent grasp of God's care, he is ever tempted to sin. Thus, original sin is a symbolic depiction of any given existential moment in which man is tempted to deny his dependence upon God and establish his own ontological order.

In light of this, it is not surprising that Niebuhr identifies an inadequate account of sin as the fundamental flaw of Catholic natural law theory. This stems in large

---

[10] Ibid., p. 152.

part from its understanding of original sin. As Niebuhr describes it, Thomistic doctrine holds that "the Fall robbed man of a *donum superadditum* but left him with a *pura naturalia*, which includes a capacity for natural justice." Until the "further gifts" are restored, man is subject to the natural limitations of his finite nature. Original sin, according to Niebuhr, is thus interpreted negatively: "It is the privation of something which does not belong to man essentially and, therefore, cannot be regarded as a corruption of his essential nature."[11] The fallen man, Niebuhr emphasizes, is basically an incomplete man who is made complete by the infusion of sacramental grace which nearly restores all of the supernatural virtues lost in the Fall. Thus in the estimate of Thomistic theology, Niebuhr concludes, "The Fall does not seriously impair man's capacity for natural justice."[12] Man is left with his reason and will essentially intact, however incapable he is of reaching the heights of perfection made possible by the supernatural gifts.

Niebuhr regards the Thomistic account of sin "semi-Pelagian,"[13] since it posits the essential freedom of the post-lapsarian will and the intactness of reason as an instrument of natural justice. This interpretation of original sin fails on two counts for Niebuhr. First, it underestimates the enduring noetic and moral effects of original sin. "The loss of man's original perfection," Niebuhr insists, "never leaves him with an untarnished though incomplete natural justice."[14] Rather, sin infects man's intellect and will, leaving him alienated from God and his fellows. His most basic sin, pride, reveals itself in so many ways as to discredit the Catholic notion of natural justice. Pride, or man's unwillingness to recognize his creatureliness and ultimate dependence upon God, insinuates itself into man's social relations; it prompts him to forget his finitude, deny the partiality of his perspective, and usurp the place of God in pronouncing final judgment on human actions. This, Niebuhr maintains, is the seed of "ideological taint" in human knowledge, and it affects every articulation of moral and political norms.

Catholic natural law theory fails to recognize this insidious taint and so fails "to understand the full seriousness of human sin or the full tragedy of human history."[15] Thus, it too simply affirms the possibility of identifying natural law precepts and deriving universally valid moral judgments therefrom. As Niebuhr explains, Catholicism attempted to systematize ethics, appropriating the Stoic conception of the natural law with its distinction between a relative and an absolute natural law. In so doing, the Church made rational norms of justice definitive for the Christian conception of virtue and vice. "The difficulty with this impressive structure of Catholic ethics, finally elaborated into a detailed casuistic application of general moral standards to every conceivable particular situation, is that it

---

[11] Niebuhr, *The Nature and Destiny of Man*, vol. 1, p. 248.
[12] Niebuhr, "Christian Faith and Natural Law," *Theology*, 40, no. 236 (February 1940), p. 87.
[13] Niebuhr, *The Nature and Destiny of Man*, vol. 1, p. 247.
[14] Niebuhr, "Christian Faith and Natural Law," p. 87.
[15] Niebuhr, *The Nature and Destiny of Man*, vol. 1, p. 148.

constantly insinuates religious absolutes into highly contingent and historical moral judgments." The tendency for Catholic thought to confuse ultimate religious perspectives and relative historical ones underlies "the fury and self-righteousness into which Catholicism is betrayed when it defends feudal types of civilization in contemporary history as in Spain for instance."[16]

Relatedly, Niebuhr specifically criticizes the anthropology underlying Jacques Maritain's definition of natural law in *The Rights of Man and Natural Law*. According to Maritain, "Natural law is the ensemble of things to do and not to do which follow therefrom in a *necessary* fashion and from the simple fact that man is man, nothing else being taken into account."[17] Niebuhr takes issue with Maritain's claim, noting:

> One of the facts about man as man is that his vitalities may be elaborated in indeterminate variety. That is the fruit of his freedom. Not all of these elaborations are equally wholesome and creative. But it is very difficult to derive "in a necessary fashion" the final rules of his individual and social existence. It is this indeterminateness and variety which makes analogies between the "laws of nature" in the exact sense of the words and laws of human nature, so great a source of confusion. It is man's nature to transcend nature and to elaborate his own historical existence in indeterminate degree.[18]

Catholic natural law ethics, moreover, fails to acknowledge the fact that the very men articulating natural law norms are themselves sinful and subject to the corrosive influence of self-interest. Thus, the male oligarchy, for instance, appealed to "natural laws" concerning the place of women in society to protect its hegemony against an emerging social movement. Far from revealing the eternal intentions of the Creator, natural law formulations more often reflect the particular biases of the age, introducing "contingent practical applications into the definition of the principle[s]."[19] Catholic natural law theory's "[u]ndue confidence in human reason, as the seat and source of natural law, makes this very concept of law into a vehicle of human sin. It gives the sanctity of universality to the peculiar conditions and unique circumstances in which reason operates in a particular historical moment." For example, Niebuhr maintains that the "social ethics of Aquinas embody the peculiarities and the contingent factors of a feudal-agrarian economy into a system of fixed socio-ethical principles,"[20] just as the specific content of the putatively natural laws of the eighteenth-century physiocrats justified the aspirations of the bourgeois classes.

The epistemological optimism—not to say arrogance—of Thomistic theology reinforces for Niebuhr the grounds upon which Catholic ecclesiology claims its

---

[16] Ibid., vol. 1, p. 221.
[17] Quoted in Niebuhr, *Children of Light*, pp. 77-78.
[18] Niebuhr, *Children of Light*, p. 78.
[19] Ibid., p. 72.
[20] Niebuhr, *The Nature and Destiny of Man*, vol. 1, p. 281.

uniqueness. Roman Catholicism arrogates to itself an "unconditioned possession of truth"[21] which destroys the Biblical paradox of the "having" and "not having" of the kingdom. In Niebuhr's estimation, the confidence with which Catholicism regards its own epistemological power undergirds the Church's "officially intolerant"[22] stance toward opposing opinions and the practice of other religions; hence the Church's favorable view in principle of religious establishment articulated in Leo XIII's *Immortale Dei* and its merely pragmatic acceptance of religious toleration as outlined by Frs. Ryan and Boland in *Catholic Principles of Politics*.[23] Catholicism, Niebuhr contends, assimilated Greek rationalism in its theology and subjected the individual to the universal rules of the natural law as the mind of the magisterium discerned them. In its articulation of these laws, the Church employed a rigid distinction between truth and error, thus obscuring the "ambiguous character of all knowledge" and engaging in a "sinful spiritual imperialism."[24]

Given its epistemological pretensions, Catholic natural law theory is particularly disturbing politically. It lends itself, Niebuhr insists, to the justification of anti-democratic politics, and it has been used in just this way by Catholic regimes. For instance, Niebuhr recalls, feudal aristocrats appealed to the Church's natural law-based prohibition of usury in order to prop up their position over against burgeoning commercial classes. This ostensibly universal principle was in fact time-bound and "could be maintained only as long as the dominant aristocratic class were borrowers rather than lenders of money. When the static wealth of the landowners yielded to the more dynamic wealth of the financiers and industrialists, the prohibition of usury vanished."[25] This example attests for Niebuhr to the danger of turning relative judgments into absolute principles. This has special significance in politics, since absolute principles are an inadequate, even dangerous, guide for the statesman who must navigate the "morally ambiguous"[26] waters of politics which require "the arbitration of conflicting interests and the choice of relative values required in an imperfect world."[27]

## A Thomistic Response

Reinhold Niebuhr's indictment of Catholic political thought includes four counts. First, Catholic political thought presupposes an overly optimistic anthropology that lacks self-critical perspective. Second, it relies on natural law ethics which itself tends to absolutize relative historical judgments. Third, the

---

[21] Ibid., vol. 2, p. 221.
[22] Ibid., vol. 2, p. 222.
[23] Niebuhr, *Children of Light*, p. 127. It is important to note that Niebuhr's criticism here preceded Vatican II's affirmation of religious freedom in its *Declaration on Religious Liberty*. Thus, in certain aspects, his critique is now dated, though the heart of his claims about the epistemological status of religious claims and moral and political norms still deserves attention.
[24] Niebuhr, *The Nature and Destiny of Man*, vol. 2, p. 224.
[25] Niebuhr, "Christian Faith and Natural Law," p. 89.
[26] Niebuhr, *Children of Light*, p. 73.
[27] Reinhold Niebuhr, *An Interpretation of Christian Ethics* (San Francisco: Harper and Row, 1935), pp. 144-45.

combined force of one and two make it incompatible with the compromise and contingency of political judgments in democratic politics. Fourth, it has been associated historically with the Church's negative view of democratic institutions and advocacy of absolutist regimes. The cumulative strength of Niebuhr's criticisms demands consideration and response. Upon reviewing the work of Yves R. Simon in light of Niebuhr's criticism, one finds ample evidence to suggest that mainstream twentieth-century Thomism offers a powerful rejoinder to Niebuhr and reveals significant points of convergence with Christian Realism.

First, a brief point with respect to the fourth claim above. In Niebuhr's estimation, the fact that the Catholic Church has deployed natural law arguments in the service of dubious religio-political ends reinforces his substantive criticism of Thomistic natural law theory. This claim will not receive much attention here.[28] Suffice it to say that Niebuhr can be criticized for making a "guilt by association" fallacy, since it does not follow that because an intellectual tradition—or some of its language or methods—has been appropriated for dubious purposes, the substance of that tradition is *ipso facto* dubious.

In any event, it is in response to Niebuhr's other criticisms that Yves Simon's work appears so fruitful. Considering the first indictment, the theological anthropology underlying Simon's political thought does not succumb to Niebuhr's criticism. A careful reading of Simon indicates that while his anthropology appears more positive than Niebuhr's, it is by no means sanguine. It is, arguably, realistic. And its realism, like Niebuhr's, derives from experience—Simon did encounter the fascist menace face-to-face—and Christian reflection on sin. Considering the possibility of a distinctively "Christian Humanism," Simon proposes that "Christian beliefs concerning original sin do not exclude the confident vision of man that humanism implies," seeming to confirm Niebuhr's criticism. But, Simon hastens to add:

> They do contain a warning against the myths of naturalistic optimism. The Christian knows how easily the confidence of the humanist deteriorates into a rejection of the supernatural order. Correspondingly the humanist is permanently tempted to see in Christian mysteries a threat to his exalted notion of man. The solution lies in a humanistic theory which places at the center of its universe the union of divine and human nature in Christ.[29]

Here, Simon, like Niebuhr, does justice to the dignity of man as the imago Dei while recognizing man's temptation to inflate his place in creation. In this regard, Simon can espouse both "ontological optimism" and "moral pessimism."[30]

---

[28] Part of the rationale behind this decision is the recognition that with the change of the Church's formal position on democracy and religious liberty, Niebuhr's criticism becomes dated. Attention is better spent on the substantive, and potentially perennially valid, criticism of natural law theory.

[29] Yves R. Simon, "Christian Humanism: A Way to World Order," in *From Disorder to World Order*, ed. John O. Riedl (Milwaukee, Wisconsin: Marquette University Press, 1956), p. 200.

[30] Ibid., p. 198; Yves R. Simon, *Philosophy of Democratic Government* (Notre Dame, Indiana: University of Notre Dame Press, 1993), pp. 80-81.

This ontological optimism, Niebuhr might respond, is itself dubious. Here, too, Simon offers a strong rejoinder and explains the conceptual apparatus Niebuhr rejects. In the Thomistic schema, two systems of gifts, supernatural and preternatural, mark the state of original innocence: the former enabled man to know and love God on a level of which created being is not naturally capable; the latter protected man from hardships to which nature subjects him. Original sin stripped these added perfections. Contrary to Niebuhr's interpretation of Thomism on this point, Simon underscores the serious effects of the Fall, as he emphasizes that the removal of the *superadditum* wounded nature itself, leaving two kinds of effects. The formal consequences are the wounds of nature, the "disquieting propensities" and "incapacities" that created man knew not.[31] The material consequences are natural conditions, preternaturally suspended in innocence, such as mortality, susceptibility to disease, fallibility in opinion, and the precariousness of virtue. Lest these Thomistic categories obscure the existential quality of Simon's anthropology, he testifies to the frailty of post-lapsarian human nature thus:

> All that is implied by moral pessimism is a profound feeling of the wretchedness of our condition; a perfectly sincere disposition to see evil wherever it shows itself, together with its frequency and its extent; will and resolution to knock down the protective screens which our fear and our laziness manufacture to spare us the sight of evil; a thorough sense of the immense difficulties which the accomplishment of good presents. One could say that pessimism is nothing but *depth of moral intelligence*. . . Optimists are men who believe that there are easy questions in the order of human action; men who believe that one can easily be good, become better, improve mankind's lot: they are the shallow minds, the idiots, of the moral order.[32]

Simon's ontological optimism did not yield a moral optimism; the fact that human nature did not suffer total corruption in the Fall does not imply a propensity for moral perfectibility in history.

Indeed, Simon underscores the difficulty of achieving virtue and the propensity to err in moral and intellectual judgments. His account of practical reasoning constitutes a rejoinder to Niebuhr's second claim that Thomistic natural law theorists place undue confidence in reason, devise a rigidly deductive scheme of ethics from general principles, and view the moral life as action in accordance with absolute principles. First, it should be noted that Simon's recognition of the difficulty of developing the intellectual virtues informs his own tone of epistemic humility, a far cry from the triumphalist neo-Thomism one might expect from Niebuhr's description. Simon insists that even "the most trifling questions, once examined, will always turn out to be incomparably more difficult than one could have forseen," and he scolds those blind to the challenges of the mind: "Only shallow minds

---

[31] Simon, "Christian Humanism," p. 196.
[32] Yves R. Simon, *Freedom and Community* (New York: Fordham University Press, 1968), pp. 177-78.

believe that there are such things as easy questions in the sciences, in philosophy, and history. Profound minds know that there are no easy questions."[33]

Not only does Simon perceive the challenge of intellectual life, he clearly acknowledges the difficulties involved in the moral life and has an account of prudence adequate to the complicated facts of moral decision-making. Like Niebuhr, Simon perceives the ambiguity of action; his account of practical knowledge reflects this sensitivity. Rather than a neat, let alone infallible, derivation from a universal principle, a practical judgment always risks error, as it always involves contingent conditions. It may conform to the factual state of affairs, or it may not. "In that sense a practical judgment always falls short of certainty inasmuch as any practical situation involves contingencies that defeat the most earnest endeavor to establish the conformity of our judgments to the factual state of things contingent… "[34] Even our best intentions may go awry. Thus, truth in practical knowledge denotes "a relation of conformity between a judgment or a proposition and the requirements of an honest will," not the logical certainty found in a catalogue of absolute principles concerning all matters of practical affairs; such certainty is illusory.

Moreover, for Simon a practical judgment proceeds from cognition and inclination. The moral agent rationally deliberates but finally settles on a course of action because of inclination. Deliberation does not cease because one has arrived at an airtight conclusion through rational deduction. In fact, Simon argues that deductive reasoning aids little in concrete decision-making, since the life of action involves so many contingencies. And "wherever the contingent is relevant to a decision, logical connection with ethical principles is either loose or purely and simply impossible . . . for prudence cannot determine the mean by derivation from general principles. To know what the right thing to do in this unique existential situation," Simon insists, "the prudent man relies on inclination."[35] The affective and non-logical character of the movement of the will in a practical judgment renders the practical judgment incommunicable. Just as the practical judgment fails of theoretical truth, it eludes full explanation. In this light, Simon counsels, "Adjustment to life, good sense, good judgment consists, to a large extent, in an ability to know where to stop in the indispensable quest for a certainty that indeed cannot be attained in the world of contingency in which our actions take place."[36] Simon's account of practical knowledge offers a powerful rejoinder to Niebuhr's criticism of Thomistic ethics.

Finally, with respect to Niebuhr's concern that Thomistic natural law theory yields anti-democratic political principles, Simon makes a compelling counter-argument, using a Thomistic framework to erect a philosophy of democratic governance. Simon's defense of democracy includes Niebuhrian insights into the

---

[33] Ibid., p. 178.
[34] Yves R. Simon, *Practical Knowledge* (New York: Fordham University Press, 1991), p. 12.
[35] Yves R. Simon, *Definition of Moral Virtue* (New York: Fordham University Press, 1986), pp. 116, 127.
[36] Simon, *Practical Knowledge*, pp. 12-13.

necessity of coercion and an equilibrium of power, but it is not fundamentally pragmatic. Rather, in the words of Jerome Kerwin, Simon offers a philosophical account "that shows democracy to be grounded firmly on rational principles."[37]

Simon justifies political authority as he does authority *per se*, that is, he argues that political authority originates not in human sinfulness, but in human plenitude. The essential function of authority is to choose the means to a given end when those means are not univocal. The essential function of political authority, then, is to direct the community to the common good when the means to that end are plural, a likely situation given human creativity and inventiveness. This function, Simon insists, "originates not in the defects of men and societies but in the nature of society."[38]

But what form would political authority take? Would it be anti-democratic? Simon's analysis of political authority in fact grounds his explicit defense of democracy. Simon espouses a "transmission" theory of government. According to the transmission theory, the first bearer of civil authority—given by God—is the people as a whole, the civil multitude. Circumstances warranting, the people can designate distinct governing personnel, that is, they can *transmit* their natural political authority to a governor or body of governors—the governing personnel may take many forms; what is essential is that it rule the people for the common good.

While the Thomistic tradition recognizes the validity of several forms of government, Simon maintains that there are significant resources in the tradition to support the democratic form. One finds the initial locus of this position in Aquinas himself, as he recognizes the people as the original bearer of political authority. Elaborating on Aquinas, Cajetan affirms that "the royal power, by natural law, resides primarily in the people, and from the people is transferred to the king; it resides first in a community," a position further expounded by Bellarmine and Suarez.[39] As Simon understands it, the natural law tradition recognizes that democracy is a natural institution, inasmuch as it can exist without any positive disposition. The move to a distinct governing personnel is a judgment about the common good.

Simon recognizes that in most cases such personnel will be necessary, and he contends that a strong natural law argument exists for a representative democracy over other forms of appointment. Borrowing Aquinas' distinction between political and despotic regimes, Simon argues that a representative democracy actualizes most effectively the political nature of a regime, since the governed have the institutional means of resistance to bad government readily at their disposal in the electoral process. And it is right that this means be available to all: "That the multitude in charge of selecting the governing personnel should comprise all citizens follows from the nature of political society. Other societies are built on the basis of

---

[37] Simon, *Philosophy of Democratic Government*, p. vii.
[38] Ibid., p. 33.
[39] Ibid., p. 164.

exclusive membership; not so the state, which is, by essence, the concern of all."[40] Not only ought the people retain this power as a guard against despotic governance—a good Niebuhrian measure—they ought to remain actively engaged in political decision-making at various levels of government, in accord with the principle of autonomy (subsidiarity), because this is what human plenitude requires.

Human plenitude, according to Simon, also requires various civil freedoms fully compatible with a natural law-based theory of democracy. Sharing Niebuhr's concern over the premature suppression of vitality, Simon affirms that government based on the people's deliberation demands freedom of expression, of the press, and of association, so as to discuss openly the means to the common good. Also wary of moralistic absolutism, Simon recommends that "civil government cannot afford to demand much along the line of ethical perfection; whenever it crusades indiscriminately, it destroys little evil and much good."[41] Likewise, Simon fears the heavy hand of the law in coercing moral behavior. While the state legitimately exercises this function, it ought prefer persuasion as an instrument; a strong democracy relies on the latter far more than the former.

## Conclusion

Simon thus proposes a theoretical defense of democracy largely compatible with Reinhold Niebuhr's, though it is grounded in the Thomistic natural law tradition. His understanding of human nature, sin, moral action, and political authority meets the challenges posed by Niebuhr's Christian Realist criticism and in so doing defies the conventional polarization of the two positions. In short, Simon's work reveals that a Thomistic anthropology and political vision yields a realistic view of man's situation, a theoretical framework to ground democratic government, and an account of practical reasoning compatible with the challenges of democratic citizenship in an age of pluralism.

---

[40] Ibid., p. 87.
[41] Ibid., p. 137.

# 8

# Kant's Contribution to the Idea of Democratic Pluralism

## John R. Goodreau

The literature comparing Kant and Maritain is minimal, especially with respect to their political philosophies. Yet Maritain's disagreement with Kant is clear enough; as McInerny puts it, "Maritain wrote [in *Principes d'une politique humaniste*, New York, 1944] of the false political emancipation and false conception of human rights which derive from the anthropocentrism of Rousseau and Kant based on the autonomy of the human person. One is free if he obeys only himself."[1] In *Man and the State*, Maritain writes that Kant and Rousseau reject any measure or regulation derived from the world of nature because regulations originating from the natural order of things would destroy the autonomy and supreme dignity of the human person.[2] But while it is certainly true that Kant does not derive his Categorical Imperative from an ontological standpoint, it is not entirely fair to say that Kant's practical philosophy is in no way objective.[3] The German Enlightenment was in no way a revolutionary movement. At least according to its basic structure, the German Enlightenment was faithful to tradition. Kant's practical project was precisely to save morality and religion from relativism; as he writes in a famous text from the "Preface" to the second edition of the first *Critique*, "I therefore had to annul *knowledge* in order to make room for *faith*."[4] Indeed, Maritain's position with respect to

---

[1] Ralph McInerny, *Art and Prudence: Studies in the Thought of Jacques Maritain* (Notre Dame, Indiana: University of Notre Dame Press, 1988), p. 79.
[2] Jacques Maritain, *Man and the State* (Washington, D.C.: The Catholic University of America Press, 1998), pp. 83-84.
[3] Kant's disagreement with Maritain would be essentially epistemological; for Kant reason is the only purely objective moral principle knowable by a finite rational being such as ourselves, and therefore the only possible ground of a principle that can be recognized by human persons as absolutely necessary. As Korsgaard points out, Kantian laws of autonomy are positive laws; moral laws exist because we legislate them. (Christine M. Korsgaard, *Creating the Kingdom of Ends* (Cambridge: Cambridge University Press, 1996), p. 66. For Kant, this is the necessary result of his critical epistemology. Maritain's disagreement with Kant concerns the proper object of a free will, the good as such, which is an ontological principle. For Maritain, Kant's transcendental freedom implicitly deprives the will of its very purpose. See, for example, James V. Schall, *Jacques Maritain: The Philosopher in Society* (Lanham, Maryland: Rowman & Littlefield Publishers, 1998), p. 130.

Kant would soften somewhat later in his career; Kant does derive his practical philosophy from an essential human nature, and were Kant alive today, he would appreciate the force of Maritain's critique. An attempt at such a reconciliation may be seen in the postwar Christian Democratic movement in Europe and Latin America, although Maritain believed they failed for the most part to prepare, through the necessary lengthy process of education, for an authentic Christian politics.[5]

Although the term "pluralism" occurs only once in Kant's published works,[6] Kant's political philosophy embodies the principles that Maritain includes under the term "pluralism" in *Man and the State*. In the *Anthropology from a Pragmatic Point of View* (1798) he contrasts pluralism, by which he means a state of mind in which the self understands that it is not the whole world, to egoism, by which he means solipsism.[7] The purpose of this paper will be to present some of Kant's arguments that prepare the way for the modern concept of a pluralist democratic state. Section one will present Kant's account of the distinction that must be made between juridical and ethical lawgiving. Section two will review the constitution of the state according to Kant, and the third section will consider Kant's view of the relationship between church and state.

I

Maritain describes "pluralism" as "an organic heterogeneity in the very structure of civil society."[8] A pluralist commonwealth is understood by Maritain to be one that gives the fullest measure of autonomy to the groupings that make it up; that is to say, a pluralist commonwealth is one that will diversify its own internal structure in accord with the typical claims of the various natures of the groups that comprise it.[9] It is opposed essentially to the twentieth-century totalitarian state.

Kant, too, is committed to a political structure that gives the fullest measure of autonomy to its members. His Universal Principle of Right, which is given in the "Introduction to the Doctrine of Right" of the *Metaphysics of Morals* (1797),

---

[4] Immanuel Kant, *Critique of Pure Reason*, trans. Werner S. Pluhar (Indianapolis, Indiana: Hackett, 1996), p. 31; AK 3:19.
[5] John DiJoseph, *Jacques Maritain and the Moral Foundation of Democracy* (Lanham, Maryland: Rowman & Littlefield Publishers, 1996), pp. 144-45.
[6] *Kants gesammelte Schriften*, Herausgegeben von der Königlich Preußischen Akademie der Wissenschaften. Volumes 1-9, 10, 11, 12, 13, floppy disk edition (Bonn: Institut für angewandte Kommunikation und Sprachforschung, 1988-94).
[7] Anthropology for Kant is, of course, a science that deals with the human being as phenomenon, and so the question as to whether I, as a thinking being, have any reason to assume that beside my own existence there exists a totality of other beings that I call a world and with whom I am in relation, is a metaphysical and not an anthropological question. Immanuel Kant, *Anthropology from a Pragmatic Point of View*, trans. Victor Lyle Dowdell (Carbondale, Illinois: Southern Illinois University Press, 1978), pp. 12-13; AK 7:130.
[8] Jacques Maritain, *True Humanism* (New York: Charles Scribner's Sons, 1938), p. 157. The same locution is used in his earlier work *Freedom in the Modern World*, trans. Richard O'Sullivan (New York: Charles Scribner's Sons, 1936), p. 61.
[9] Ibid., pp. 156-57.

exemplifies this principle; it states that "any action is right if it can coexist with everyone's freedom in accordance with a universal law, or if on its maxim the freedom of choice of each can coexist with everyone's freedom in accordance with a universal law."[10] "The Doctrine of Right" deals with the totality of laws for which an external lawgiving is possible,[11] while the second part of the *Metaphysics of Morals*, "The Doctrine of Virtue," deals with subjective principles of choice, or, in other words, internal lawgiving.[12] This distinction between external and internal lawgiving is the underpinning of a pluralist society; it is the distinction between civil law and morality, and indeed Maritain regards such a distinction as unavoidable in *Man and the State*.[13] As he writes in Chapter VI of that work, the sound application of the pluralist principle means that care must be taken not to impose by force of law rules of morality too heavy for the moral capacity of large groups of the population.[14]

In "The Doctrine of Right" Kant intends to provide a rational account for this distinction. That is to say, Kant systematically investigates the purely rational conditions, independent of experience, under which a community of empirically free subjects is possible. Freedom is defined by Kant in "The Doctrine of Right" as independence from being constrained by another's choice.[15] This is an empirical or outward freedom; it is not the transcendental freedom upon which morality depends. Nevertheless, it is clear that Kant's "Doctrine of Right" is a natural outgrowth of his critical practical philosophy. His definition of "Right" (*Recht*) as the sum of the conditions under which the choice of one can be united with the choice of another in accordance with a universal law of freedom[16] is the natural empirical corollary to the Categorical Imperative, especially in its articulation as the formula of autonomy, which states that the supreme condition of the will's conformity with universal practical reason is the idea that the will of every rational being is a will that legislates universal law. This, as everyone knows, leads to the concept of a Kingdom of Ends, which is a principle of transcendental freedom but which has its corresponding empirical principle in the Universal Principle of Right.

---

[10] Immanuel Kant, *The Metaphysics of Morals*, trans. Mary Gregor (Cambridge: Cambridge University Press, 1991), p. 56; AK 6:230.
[11] Ibid., p. 55; AK 6:229.
[12] As we shall see, the central point in the distinction between rights and virtues lies in the distinction between the two possible kinds of incentives. Leslie Arthur Mulholland, *Kant's System of Rights* (New York: Columbia University Press, 1990), p. 147.
[13] *Man and the State*, pp. 76-79, Maritain distinguishes between practical conclusions regarding the various rights possessed by man in his personal and social existence and the rational justification of these practical conclusions and rights. Maritain argues that practical conclusions regarding the various rights possessed by human beings in their personal and social existence required that the speculative/theoretical justification of those rights and the attendant moral and metaphysical certainties to which each individual subscribes must be put aside.
[14] Ibid., pp. 169-70.
[15] *Metaphysics of Morals*, p. 63; AK 6:237.
[16] Ibid., p. 56; AK 6:230.

Will is defined in the *Grounding for the Metaphysics of Morals* as a kind of causality belonging to living beings insofar as they are rational; freedom, then, would be the property of this causality that makes it effective independent of any determination by alien causes.[17] This is transcendental freedom, without which there is no morality, and although Kant believes that theoretical reason cannot demonstrate that freedom is a property of the will of all rational beings, he holds that it is a postulate of pure practical reason that must be assumed if the antinomy of practical reason is to be resolved, i.e., if there is to be a rational account of morality.[18] Perhaps more to the point, Kant holds that every being which cannot act in any way other than under the idea of freedom is for that very reason free from a practical point of view. Hence all moral laws, which are inseparably bound to the idea of freedom, are just as valid for such a being as they would be if speculative philosophy could demonstrate that the will of a rational being is indeed free. We cannot possibly think of a reason that consciously lets its judgments be determined by some alien cause; in such a case the subject would ascribe the determination of his judgment to some impulse instead of to his reason. We must, therefore, necessarily attribute to every rational being who has a will the *idea* of freedom. The will of a rational being can be a will of its own only under the idea of transcendental freedom.[19]

In the *Metaphysics of Morals*, the will is considered specifically in relation to the determining ground for action. Will is desire determined by reason. Choice is desire related to action. Insofar as will determines choice, it is practical reason. Will chooses the determining ground for action, or in less Kantian terminology, will chooses the reason to do something. Choice that can be determined by pure reason is called free choice; choice determined only by inclination (i.e., sensible

---

[17] Kant, Immanuel, *Grounding for the Metaphysics of Morals*, 2nd ed., trans. James W. Ellington (Indianapolis, Indiana: Hackett, 1981), p. 49.
[18] The antinomy of practical reason is as follows: The highest good is the synthesis of the concepts happiness and virtue (worthiness to be happy). Since the combination is not analytic, it must be thought as the connection of cause and effect, for it concerns a practical good, i.e., one that is possible through action. Either the desire for happiness is the motive to maxims of virtue, or the maxim of virtue is the efficient cause of happiness. The former is absolutely impossible because maxims which put the determining ground of the will in the desire for happiness (understood as the satisfaction of inclination) cannot be the ground of virtue. The latter is also impossible because practical connections of causes and effects in the world, as a determination of the will, is dependent on knowledge of natural laws and the capacity to make use of them and not moral intentions. Yet the furthering of the highest good is an *a priori* necessary object of our will. The resolution of this antinomy is to regard oneself as *noumenon*, as pure intelligence, existing without temporal determination, and thus as a being possessing transcendental freedom. When we regard ourselves as *noumenon* in an intelligible world it is not impossible that moral intention is a cause of happiness in the sensuous world, but this relation is indirect, mediated by an intelligible Author of nature. Hence the highest good, which is the union of virtue and happiness, is practically possible as the necessary highest end of a morally determined will. From this solution of the antinomy of practical reason it follows that in practical principles a natural and necessary connection between the consciousness of morality and the expectation of proportionate happiness as its consequence may be thought at least possible although it is by no means understood. Immanuel Kant, *Critique of Practical Reason*, trans. Lewis White Beck (New York: Macmillan, 1956), pp. 117-23; AK 5:113-19.
[19] *Grounding*, p. 50; AK 4:447-8.

impulse) is called animal choice. *Human* choice is a capacity for choice that can be *affected* but not *determined* by impulses, and is therefore not in itself pure (apart from an acquired aptitude of reason), but it can still be determined to actions by pure will. Freedom of choice is this independence from being *determined* by sensible impulses.[20] This does not mean that happiness can have no part in morality, Kant's point is that we must abstract from such considerations as soon as the Idea of duty supervenes. We are not expected to *renounce* our natural aim of attaining happiness as soon as the question of following our duty arises; as finite rational beings, this is impossible in any case. What is required is that we on no account make considerations of our happiness the condition of obeying the moral law.[21]

Moral laws, which are laws of freedom, are contrasted to laws of nature, which are laws of cause and effect. Laws of freedom directed merely to external actions are called juridical laws; they operate through coercion; one speaks of their legality. Laws that are the *determining grounds* of actions are ethical laws; one speaks of their morality. Juridical laws speak to freedom in the external use of choice; ethical laws speak to freedom in *both* the external and internal use of choice (insofar as choice is determined by laws of reason).[22]

Whether a law prescribes internal or external actions, and whether it prescribes them *a priori* by reason alone or by the choice of some other lawgiver, there are two elements involved, the law itself and an incentive. A law represents an action to be done as objectively necessary. An incentive subjectively connects a ground for determining choice to the action prescribed by the law, i.e., the incentive provides the will with a motive. The difference between ethics and legality lies in the motive. Ethical law makes an action a duty and at the same time makes this Idea (*Idee*) of duty itself the incentive.[23] Laws that do not include the incentive of duty and so admit an incentive other than the Idea of duty itself is *juridical*. Juridical laws draw

---

[20] *Metaphysics of Morals*, p. 42; AK 6:213.
[21] That Kant's moral theory excludes happiness is, of course, an old objection, and Kant speaks to it in his 1793 essay, *On the Common Saying: 'This May be True in Theory, but it does not Apply in Practice.'* In that essay, Kant responds to an earlier essay by Christian Garve, in which Garve interprets Kant as having asserted that adherence to the moral law, regardless of happiness, is the one and only ultimate end for man, and that it must be considered as the creator's unique intention. Kant's reply is that his theory is that the creator's unique intention is neither human morality in itself nor happiness in itself, but the highest good possible on earth, namely the union and harmony of both. Immanuel Kant, "On the Common Saying: 'This May be True in Theory, but it does not Apply in Practice," in *Kant's Political Writings*, ed. Hans Reiss and trans. H. B. Nisbet (Cambridge: Cambridge University Press, 1970), pp. 64-65; AK 8:279. As Kant tells us in the first *Critique*, in Section 2 of "The Canon of Pure Reason," the highest good is really an idea of reason since the sensible world holds no promise that any such systematic unity of ends can arise from the nature of things (A814). Yet a world in accordance with all moral laws is *possible* by means of the freedom of rational beings, and so we are obliged to strive towards it—the answer to the question what ought I to do? is necessarily do that through which I become worthy of happiness (A808-9). Can implies ought in this case, and therefore we are obliged to regard the idea of a moral world (which includes God and a future life (A811) as having objective reality, i.e., as referring to the sensible world viewed as a *corpus mysticum* of the rational beings in it insofar as the free will of each being is under moral laws in complete systematic unity with itself and with the freedom of every other (A808).
[22] *Metaphysics of Morals*, pp. 42-43; AK 6:214.
[23] Duty is the necessity of an action done out of respect for the law. *Grounding*, p. 13; AK 4:400.

their incentive from sensibly dependent determining grounds of choice, namely aversions. Conformity of an action with a law is called its *legality* irrespective of the incentive (it could be accidental); conformity of an action with a law when the Idea of duty arising from the law is the incentive is called its *morality*. Ethical lawgiving is that in which the incentive *cannot* be external (not even the external lawgiving of a divine will), since the incentive can only be the Idea of duty; this is what Kant means when he says a person is only subject to the law he gives himself.[24] In the end, one chooses to obey any law, be it Divine Law or the Categorical Imperative.[25] Juridical lawgiving is that in which the incentive can be external as well. Juridical laws have to do with rights and involve coercion; there is no coercion possible with respect to duties of virtue. Ethics may have specific duties in common with juridical law (Right), for example, in the precept that it is ethical to obey civil law generally, but it differs fundamentally in the kind of obligation.[26] For Kant, in one sense, namely from coercion, it is possible to "legislate morality." But in the moral sense, it is not possible to legislate morality precisely because morality is a good will, which is beyond the reach of juridical lawgiving.

II

Kant holds that there is only one innate human right, namely, external freedom, or independence from being constrained by another's choice. Freedom, insofar as it can coexist with the freedom of everyone else in accordance with a universal law

---

[24] In *Man and the State*, Maritain adduces a quote from the "Introduction to the Metaphysics of Morals" (AK 6:223) as follows: "A person is subject to no other laws than those which he (either alone or jointly with others) gives to himself." He goes on to say that this rationalist philosophy has built no solid foundations for the rights of the human person because it led men to conceive rights as escaping every objective measure and denying every limitation imposed upon the claims of the ego, which leads to the expression of the absolute independence of the human subject and to a so-called absolute right to unfold one's cherished possibilities at the expense of all other beings. (*Man and the State*, pp. 83-84).

This is certainly not Kant's intention. Although Kant does try to ground morality through *a priori* principles of pure reason, he does so precisely for the sake of providing an objective (in a rational sense) principle of morality. As he says in the *Grounding for the Metaphysics of Morals*, if a law is to be morally valid, it must carry with it absolute necessity, in other words, it must be purely objective (AK 4:389). In the passage Maritain cites, Kant is trying to articulate the concept of moral personhood. Kant defines a person as a free subject whose actions can be imputed to him; moral personality is the freedom of a rational being under moral laws. From this it follows that a person is subject to no laws other than those he chooses for himself. The point is that the individual subject must choose to obey the law whatever its origin; in this sense, a person is subject to no other laws than those which he gives to himself.

Moreover, the point of the Categorical Imperative is precisely to subordinate the subjective ego to an objective (in the rational sense) principle. For Kant, moral autonomy is the ability of the person to choose maxims independent of any subjective principle or determination of nature. The point is that our essential moral capacity is the ability to transcend the influence of the spatio-temporal empirical world. Although Kant derives his principle from *a priori* principles of reason, reason and freedom as well as moral feeling are taken by Kant to be essential qualities of human nature, and the object of a good will is always morality. These are points on which both the neo-Thomist and the neo-Kantian can agree.

[25] Korsgaard points out that this is an old Hobbesian thought (*Leviathan*, Part I Chapter 14), that nothing can be a law for me unless I am bound to obey it, and nothing can bind me to obey it unless I have a motive for obeying it. Kant goes one step farther than Hobbes, however, to say that nothing except my own will can make a law normative for me (*Creating the Kingdom of Ends*, p. 65).

[26] *Metaphysics of Morals*, pp. 45-47; AK 6:218-20.

(and so equality is included in the concept), is the only original right belonging to people by virtue of their humanity.[27] In Section II of Kant's essay *On the Common Saying: 'This may be True in Theory, but it does not Apply in Practice'* (1793), entitled "On the Relationship of Theory to Practice in Political Right (against Hobbes)," Kant examines the original constitution of the commonwealth.[28]

Kant argues that the contract establishing a civil constitution is of an exceptional nature in that it involves an absolute and primary duty in all external relationships among human beings (who cannot avoid each other) to regard their union as an end in itself in which all ought to share. Such a union is found only in a society insofar as it constitutes a civil state. The end of a civil state is to secure the right of persons under coercive public laws by which each can be given what is due him and is secured from attack by others.[29] This is the highest formal condition of all other external duties.[30] Kant defines the state as a union of persons under laws of right. Since all members of a state are united through their common interest in being in a rightful condition, the state is called a commonwealth.[31]

From the innate right of freedom it follows that the civil state is based on three *a priori* principles which define the only way a state can be established in accordance with pure rational principles of external human right. The first principle is that of the freedom of every member of society as a human being. The only conceivable government for persons who are capable of possessing rights is one in which everyone in the state, including its head, regards himself as authorized to protect the rights of the commonwealth by laws of the general will, but not to subject the commonwealth to his personal use at his own absolute pleasure. An individual cannot legislate for a commonwealth since in general the will of one person cannot decide anything for another without injustice. The second principle is that of the equality of each member of the commonwealth as a subject. This is an argument primarily against hereditary privilege. Each member of the commonwealth has rights of coercion in relation to all the other members except in relation to the head of state. In this context, the head of state is not strictly speaking a member of the commonwealth, but rather its creator or preserver; and, as such, the head of state alone is authorized to coerce others without being subject to any coercive law himself. The third principle is that of the independence of each member of a commonwealth as a co-legislator, i.e., as a citizen (although Kant does not grant

---

[27] Ibid., p. 63; AK 6:237.
[28] This essay predates by some four years "The Doctrine of Right" of the *Metaphysics of Morals* (1797), but it contains the same principles found in that work.
[29] Right, considered as the capacity for putting others under obligation, is divided into innate and acquired right. Natural Right rests only on *a priori* principles; positive (statutory) right proceeds from the will of a legislator. An innate right is one that belongs to everyone by nature, an acquired right requires some establishing act *Metaphysics of Morals*, p. 63; AK 6:237.
[30] Immanuel Kant, *Kant's Political Writings*, ed. Hans Reiss and trans. H. B. Nisbet (Cambridge: Cambridge University Press, 1970), pp. 73-74; AK 8:289-90.
[31] *Metaphysics of Morals*, p. 123; AK 6:311.

universal suffrage). That is to say, all rights depend on laws, and a public law is an act of a public will from which all right proceeds. Of course, unanimity of opinion is not to be expected, but the principle of being content with majority decision reached by the voters or their representatives must be accepted unanimously and embodied in a contract; this is the ultimate basis on which a civil constitution is established.[32]

The original contract is an idea of reason, which nevertheless has practical reality since it can oblige every legislator to frame laws in such a way that they could have been produced by the united will of the whole nation, and to regard each citizen as if he had consented within the general will.[33] This is the test of the rightfulness of every public law. As long as it is not self-contradictory to say that an entire people could agree to a particular law, no matter how painful it might seem, the law is in harmony with right. Happiness cannot be the basis of a generally valid principle because everyone has a different view as to what constitutes the empirical end of happiness; it is impossible to unite the will of everyone under such an empirical concept.

Every state contains three authorities in it, the sovereign authority in the person of the legislator, the executive authority in the person of the ruler (in conformity to law), and the judicial authority in the person of the judge.[34] The legislative authority can belong only to the united will of the people, and since all Right proceeds from it, it cannot do anyone wrong by its law. These three distinct authorities are the authority by which a state has its autonomy, i.e., the authority by which it forms and preserves itself in accordance with laws of freedom. A state's well-being, understood to be the condition in which its constitution conforms most fully to principles of Right, consists in the unity of these three authorities, and this condition of well-being is that condition which reason, by a categorical imperative, makes it obligatory for us to strive after.[35]

---

[32] *Kant's Political Writings*, pp. 74-79; AK 8: 290-6.
[33] Indeed, in the first edition of *The Critique of Pure Reason* (1781) we read (A 316) that a constitution (*Verfassung*) consisting of the greatest human freedom according to laws through which the freedom of each can coexist with the freedom of the others is a necessary idea; an idea that must lie at the foundation not only when first drafting a political constitution (*Staatsverfassung*), but in all law. The more legislation and government are established in harmony with this idea, Kant writes, the less would punishment (and coercion) be needed, and so Plato was right to hold that in the perfectly arranged government no punishment would be needed at all. And although such a perfect arrangement may never come about, it is right to hold this idea as an archetype in order to bring the legal organization of human beings ever closer to the greatest possible perfection. *Critique of Pure Reason*, p. 364; AK 4:201.
[34] *Metaphysics of Morals*, p. 125; AK 6:313. Maritain, of course, argues that the concept of sovereignty is a very troublesome one; he argues that if the term sovereignty is properly understood, it is nothing other than absolutism (*Man and the State*, p. 38). As such, it is necessarily opposed to the pluralist principle (*Ibid.*, p. 51). Maritain prefers to speak of *autonomy*; the body politic has a right to full autonomy internally with respect to itself and externally with respect to other bodies politic (*Ibid.*, p. 40). Of course we are free to say "sovereignty" when we really mean full autonomy (*Ibid.*, p. 49). At this point, it seems that what Kant has in mind when he refers to the sovereign authority of the legislative branch is autonomy. Kant does not speak of absolute freedom in the context of right; his principle is one of maximizing the freedom of individuals *consistent with the freedom of all other individuals*, be they persons or states. But when it comes to the problem of the people's redress against the government, Kant does come up against the problem that Maritain describes under the topic of sovereignty.
[35] *Metaphysics of Morals*, p. 129; AK 6:318. A categorical imperative represents an action as good in itself and hence as necessary in a will that conforms to reason as a principle of the will as opposed to inclination. *Grounding*, p. 25; AK 4:415.

The principle that the presently existing legislative authority ought to be obeyed, whatever its origin, is to be considered a holy and inviolable law, and from this principle follows the proposition that the head of a state has only rights against his subjects and no duties that he can be coerced to fulfill. Kant holds that a people cannot offer any resistance to the legislative head of a state that can be consistent with right, since a rightful condition is only possible through submission to its general legislative will. There is, therefore, no right to sedition, much less rebellion. The contradiction inherent in such actions is evident as soon as one asks who is to be the judge in this dispute between people and sovereign.[36] Kant holds that changes in the constitution, which may be necessary at times, can only be carried out through reform by the sovereign itself. No active resistance by the people combining at will to coerce the government to take a certain course of action is permitted, only negative resistance, a refusal of the people (in parliament) to accede to every demand the government puts forth as necessary for administering the state, is allowed.[37]

Nevertheless, Kant does hold that the people have inalienable rights with respect to the head of state. Citing Hobbes' declaration that the head of state has no contractual obligations towards the people, can do no injustice to a citizen, and can generally act towards the citizen as is pleases, Kant says that although the proposition in its general form is quite terrifying, it would be perfectly correct *if* injustice were taken to mean any injury which gave the injured party a *coercive* right against the head of state.[38] Kant is clearly trying to walk the tightrope here. He does not want to say that the members of the commonwealth have no rights with respect to the head of state but without the commonwealth there are no rights at all, and so its preservation must be the paramount concern. Sovereignty is a problem Kant wrestles with, and it is difficult to see the difference between the Hobbesian sovereign and the Kantian head of state.[39]

Ultimately, Kant depends on the good will of the sovereign authority. The non-resisting subject must be able to assume that his ruler's attitude is one of good will, and that any injustice suffered is the result of error or of ignorance on the part of the supreme authority as to certain consequences of the laws it has made. Therefore the citizen must be entitled to make public his opinion on whatever of the ruler's measures seem to him to constitute an injustice against the commonwealth. The freedom of the pen is the only safeguard of the rights of the

---

[36] *Metaphysics of Morals*, p. 131; AK 6:320.
[37] Ibid., p. 133; AK 6:321-2.
[38] Reiss and Nisbet, *Kant's Political Writings*, p. 84; AK 8:303-4.
[39] Mulholland argues that the essential difference between Hobbes and Kant is that Kant denies that the idea of a social contract is the basis of an obligation to submit to civil authority. For Kant the idea of the social contract supplies the idea of a general will uniting individuals who have the attributes of citizenship and does not include tacit or actual consent. According to Mulholland, Kant's treatment of the constitution as an application of his principle of innate right distinguishes it from a constitution based on the ideals of the social contract as expressed in classical contractual theory (*Kant's System of Rights*, pp. 346-47). This distinction is not always apparent in Kant's account, however.

people, and to try to deny the citizen this freedom means not only that the subject can claim no rights against the ruler, but that the ruler is prevented from gaining knowledge of matters which he would rectify himself if he knew of them. To encourage the head of state to fear that independent and public thought might cause political unrest, which Kant believes Hobbes has done, is tantamount to making the ruler distrust his own power and feel hatred towards the people.[40]

The general principle is this: Whatever a people cannot impose upon itself cannot be imposed upon it by the legislator. As an example, Kant argues that the state cannot enshrine a particular set of ecclesiastical doctrines into law on the grounds that such legislation prevents the further progress in knowledge of the people and the correcting of past mistakes. This is something they could not will for themselves since it frustrates the natural purpose of mankind.[41]

### III

Kant, of course, took a famous pledge not to discourse publicly on religion during the reign of Frederick William II, who did not share the liberal attitude of his predecessor, Frederick the Great, and who was offended by Kant's book *Religion Within the Limits of Reason Alone* (1793).[42] In that work, Kant calls for the establishment of an "ethical commonwealth." In a juridical commonwealth the general will sets up an external legal control of individual actions. But in an ethical commonwealth, the general will of the people cannot be regarded as legislative. In an ethical commonwealth, the purpose of legislation is to promote the morality of actions, which is something *inner* and not subject to public laws. But if ethical laws are thought of as emanating merely from the will of a superior being, they would be no different from juridical laws. Morality lies in the motive, which cannot be coercion; it must be the free duty of virtue. Ethical laws, which are known by pure practical reason, must be represented as also being divine commands, which means that there must be someone able to see into the innermost parts of the disposition of each individual *and* to see that each receives whatever his actions are

---

[40] Reiss and Nisbet, p. 85; AK 8:304. As Williams points out, Kant believes this point puts him at odds with Hobbes, whom he argues demands the uncritical allegiance of the citizens to their sovereign. The absolutely irreproachable power of the *Leviathan* is neither justified nor just, Howard Williams, *Kant's Political Philosophy* (Oxford: Basic Blackwell Publisher Limited, 1983), p. 150.

[41] Reiss and Nisbet, p. 85; AK 8:304-5. The idea that the state should sanction the establishment of a certain set of ecclesiastical doctrines is impossible. In *What is Enlightenment?*, Kant writes that a contract of this kind, concluded with a view to preventing the further enlightenment of mankind forever, is absolutely null and void even if ratified by the supreme power, by Imperial Diets and the most solemn peace treaties. This would be to put succeeding generations in a position where it would be impossible for them to extend and correct their knowledge, or to make any progress whatsoever in enlightenment, which would be a crime against human nature, *whose original destiny lies precisely in such progress*. (Reiss and Nisbet, p. 57; AK 8:38-9). Kant does not address the possibility of a supreme legislator who is *not* of good will; interestingly he rationalizes the French Revolution, which he admired, saying that the King had abandoned his sovereign power to the Third Estate (Ibid., p. 30).

[42] Kant published the letter from the King's Minister Woellner as well as his reply in the preface to *The Conflict of the Faculties* (1798). In a footnote he explains that he chose the words of his pledge carefully so as not to renounce his freedom to discourse on religion forever, but only during the reign of Friedrich Wilhelm II.

worth. This is the concept of God as the moral ruler of the world, and an ethical commonwealth can only be thought of as a people under divine commands, i.e., under laws of virtue.[43] The promotion of an ethical commonwealth is the proper role of religion, according to Kant.

Kant argues that only rational faith, which he calls pure religious faith, or moral faith, can be believed in and shared by everyone. This is because by pure religious faith he simply means the considering of the precepts of pure practical reason, which are objective, as divine commands. All religion consists in the fact that in all our duties we look upon God as the lawgiver. We may think of the divine legislative will as giving commands either through merely statutory laws or through purely moral laws. If we consider the divine commands as purely moral laws, each individual can know through his own reason the will of God which lies at the basis of his religion, namely, to act solely out of respect for the moral law. This is, for Kant, because the concept of God really arises from the consciousness of moral laws, which he thinks is innate, and from the need of reason to postulate a power which can bring about results conformable to them, i.e., happiness in accordance with virtue. The concept of a divine will determined according to pure moral laws alone allows us to think of one purely moral religion. But if we think of divine laws as merely statutory commands, knowledge of such laws is possible not through our own reason alone but only through revelation, which, whether it is given publicly or to each individual in secret, would have to be an historical and not a pure rational faith. Historical faith, which is grounded solely on empirical facts, is limited to the extent that it can promulgate itself and is subject to circumstances of time and place as well as the capacity of individuals to judge its veracity.[44]

Given Kant's understanding, it cannot be the case that a government can establish ethical laws, much less an ethical commonwealth. Religion concerns the inner disposition of the subject, which is beyond the reach of the state, and so religious pluralism is the only legitimate governmental stance. In his essay, *An Answer to the Question, What is Enlightenment?* (1784), Kant writes that "enlightenment" is man's emergence from his self-incurred inability to use one's own understanding without the guidance of another. This immaturity is self-incurred when its cause is not a lack of understanding, but rather a lack of courage and resolution to use it without the guidance of another. The motto of enlightenment is therefore: *Sapere aude*, "Dare to be wise." Have the courage to use your own understanding.[45]

---

[43] Immanuel Kant, *Religion Within the Limits of Reason Alone*, trans. Theodore M. Greene and Hoyt H. Hudson (La Salle, Illinois: Open Court Publishing Co., 1934), pp. 90-91; AK 6:98-9.
[44] Ibid., pp. 94-95: AK 6:102-4.
[45] Reiss and Nisbet, p. 54; AK 8:35. It is so convenient to be immature, Kant writes; I need not think so long as I can pay. If I have a book to provide me with understanding, a spiritual adviser to provide a conscience for me, a doctor

All that is needed for enlightenment of this kind is the freedom to make public use of one's reason in all matters. But some restrictions, instead of hindering enlightenment actually promote it, insofar as such restrictions are necessary to the preservation of civil society, without which there is no progress towards enlightenment. Kant makes a distinction between the public and *private* use of reason; the private use of reason is that of a person in his or her capacity of holding a particular civil post or office. In such cases, for example, in the case of a military officer, obedience is imperative if the well-being of the commonwealth is to be preserved. But insofar as this individual who acts as part of the establishment is considered as a member of a commonwealth, he or she may indeed argue. For example, it would be very harmful if an officer receiving orders from a superior were to openly question the order while on duty, but the officer cannot be reasonably banned from making observations as a man of learning concerning the errors in the military service and from submitting these observations to the public for judgment. The case is similar for the taxman and the clergyman. This Kant considers the *public* use of one's freedom, namely that use which anyone can make of it as a person of learning addressing the entire reading public.[46]

Here Kant gives a hint as to the means by which the people may correct the government. The test as to whether any particular measure can be agreed upon as a law for a people is to ask whether a people could well impose such a law upon itself. Each citizen, therefore, should be given a free hand as a scholar to comment publicly, i.e., in writing, on the inadequacies of current institutions. The established order would continue to exist until public insight into the nature of such matters had progressed to the point where by general consent (if not unanimously) a proposal could be submitted to the crown (the authorities). This would protect congregations who had, for example, agreed to alter their religious establishment in accordance with their own notions as to what higher insight is in such a way as to not to obstruct those who want things to remain the same. But it is absolutely impermissible to agree to a permanent religious constitution which no one can publicly question.[47]

Kant remarks that he has portrayed religious matters as the focal point of enlightenment because in the first place rulers have no interest in acting as guardians over the arts and sciences, and in the second place because religious immaturity is the most pernicious and dishonorable of all. But the head of state who favors freedom in the arts and sciences should also realize that there is no danger to his legislation if he allows his subjects to make *public* use of their reason and to put

---

to judge my diet for me, I need not make any effort at all. Thus it is difficult for each individual to work his way out of the immaturity that has become like a second nature. Dogmas and formulas are the ball and chain of his personal immaturity. Indeed, there is more chance of an entire public enlightening itself, in fact public enlightenment is almost inevitable if only the public concerned is left in freedom. (Ibid., pp. 54-55; AK 8:36).

[46] Ibid., pp. 55-56; AK 8:36-8.
[47] Ibid., pp. 57-58; AK 8:39-40.

before the public their thoughts on better ways of drawing up laws, even if this means criticism of current legislation. Kant cites his then current monarch, Frederick the Great, as an example of such an enlightened head of state. But only an enlightened ruler who also has on hand a well-disciplined and numerous army to guarantee public security would dare to say what no *republic* would dare to say - argue as much as you like about whatever you like, but obey! Kant's conclusion is that although a high degree of civil freedom seems advantageous to a people's intellectual freedom, it also sets up insuperable barriers to it in terms of a lack of public order. Hence a lesser degree of civil freedom gives intellectual freedom enough room to expand to its fullest extent. Once the human inclination and vocation to think freely has developed sufficiently it will eventually influence the principles of governments.[48]

## Conclusion

Kant's argument from pure practical reason aims at maximizing the freedom of the individual in the body politic as most conducive to the common good, which he understands as the maximizing of justice and public virtue. The concepts of tolerance, freedom, universal human reason and universal human rights which underlie the concept of pluralism embodied in the idea of modern democracy advocated by Maritain are to be found in Kant's political philosophy. Of course, Kant struggles with the problem of sovereignty, which, as Maritain argues in *Man and the State*, is hard to distinguish from absolutism when properly understood. Maritain might well charge the Kantian supreme authority with absolutism, but Maritain himself struggles with the problems of the means by which the people can effect a change in the regime. Maritain's strongest argument with respect to replacing the concept of sovereignty with the concept of autonomy is in the context of international relations, but Kant might well respond that even if governments were to renounce the idea of sovereignty in favor of autonomy within some international framework such as the United Nations,[49] we are still left with the problem of an infinite ascension in the hierarchy of subordination, for who is to decide a dispute between the United Nations and a member state? Maritain's answer is that only God is sovereign, while Kant would appeal to pure practical reason. But the German Enlightenment was in no way atheist or hedonistic; certainly Kant holds that the Idea of God is a necessary postulate of pure practical reason, and that we are obligated to promote the highest good in all our actions. Ultimately, we are left with good will; whether the principle is Maritain's or Kant's only individuals can choose to give their assent. Kant's project is to find a solution for the problem of moral relativism and to promote civil society based on the

---

[48] Ibid., p. 59; AK 8:41-2.
[49] Indeed, Kant calls for just such a solution in his discussion of Cosmopolitan Right, which this paper did not address. See, for example, *Metaphysics of Morals*, pp. 150-59; AK 6:343-53.

proper use of freedom, in this respect there is substantial agreement between Maritain and Kant. Given this common goal, and given the significant parallels in the way the two philosophers develop arguments supporting the concept of pluralism in the modern state, were they alive today, they would clearly find grounds for continued and fruitful dialogue.

# 9

# Liberalism and Legitimacy: An Indictment*

## *James Hanink*

Nations, Scripture says, are "as rust on scales." (Isaiah 40: 15) Should we say the same of states? In particular what of our own liberal state? We must look to our scales. How are we to weigh such a state?

In *Man and the State*, Jacques Maritain proposes a personalist criterion: "the State is for man."[1] This is the personalist test of a critical democrat. Neither the state nor the body politic, he insists, is absolutely sovereign. Both must honor natural law and the common good. Thus, he says, "[a]n unjust law, even if it expresses the will of the people, is not law."[2] So not every state, nor every regime, has a *right* to be obeyed. Maritain himself was a witness to state lawlessness. Indeed, his sometime colleague Emmanuel Mounier spoke of an established *dis*order.

But again what of our liberal state?

Has it brought an end to ideology? If not, is it still the best we can hope for? Or is it yet another established disorder?

If we follow Maritain we will reach our verdict by raising, and answering, a pair of his diagnostic questions.[3] First, what are the values of our liberal state? Second, how does this state act?

In putting the state on trial, philosophers have often dallied with utopianism. On occasion they have run to embrace it. But Maritain is a realist. At the same time, his is a Christian realism, so disputed questions become "complicated" by Christian simplicity. In any case I will urge, as a peasant of the megalopolis, a strategic debunking of our liberal order.

---

*David Arias and Carroll Kearley graciously commented on an earlier version of this essay.

[1] Jacques Maritain, *Man and the State* (Washington, D.C.: The Catholic University of America Press, 1998), p. 13.
[2] Ibid., p. 48.
[3] Jacques Maritain, *The Person and the Common Good* (Notre Dame, Indiana: University of Notre Dame Press, 1966), p. 90.

## Liberalism: An Established Disorder

To begin, we need to characterize "liberalism." In view of its semantic shifts—nay, shiftiness!—I will not attempt a final definition.[4]

The liberalism at issue is a political order that gives priority to liberty, that is, "negative freedom," in a procedural—and sometimes minimal—state. Such an order assumes an ethical pluralism and an atomistic understanding of human nature. Together these assumptions involve a "public philosophy" which Michael Sandel ably describes. We live, he notes, by:

> ...a certain version of liberal political theory. Its central idea is that government should be neutral toward the moral and religious views its citizens espouse. Since people disagree about the best way to live, government should not affirm in law any particular vision of the good life. Instead, it should provide a framework of rights that respects persons as free and independent selves, capable of choosing their own values and ends.[5]

Such liberalism is not without merit. It does profess to take rights seriously. Nor does it set out to play the tyrant. Yet virtue grows suspect. We see, for example, liberalism's boast and folly in the language of the 1992 *Planned Parenthood v. Casey* decision: "[A]t the heart of liberty is the right to define one's own concept of existence, of meaning, of the universe, and of the mystery of human life." (*Casey*, 505 U.S. at 851) Whether one's concept captures *what is*, however, has far more to do with one's true freedom. The Court's solipsism is a prison of the spirit.

*Liberal Values*

It is easy enough, so characterizing liberalism, to identify its chief value: individual autonomy. But we need to look more closely at the liberal individual. In practice, this individual is a consumer. The range of his or her consumption is impressive. It includes the ordinary consumer products: cars, condominiums, and casino chips. But it also includes extraordinary "consumerized" products, the booty of the new commodificationism: health care, education, and political voice—for starters.

Indeed, there is more. Human life itself is increasingly seen in terms of an investment. What is a human being worth? Why, it is worth what citizen-consumers have invested.

Consider, for example, Ronald Dworkin's maneuver in his book *Life's Dominion*.[6] Do we want a middle ground on life issues? Focus, he urges, on the inviolability of each human being. But there is a *caveat*. Inviolability is not so inviolable as we might think. Why not? Because its measure is a function of prior investment.

---

[4] Loren E. Lomasky traces the shifts in his "Classical Liberalism and Civil Society," prepared for the Ethikon Institute's *Alternative Conceptions of Civil Society Project* (in press). eds. Will Kymlicka and Simone Chambers (Princeton: Princeton University Press).

[5] Michael Sandel, *Democracy's Discontent: America in Search of a Public Philosophy* (Cambridge: Harvard University Press, 1996), p. 4.

[6] Ronald Dworkin, *Life's Dominion: An Argument about Abortion, Euthanasia, and Individual Freedom* (New York: Knopf, 1993).

In his fine analysis of *Life's Dominion*, Richard Stith identifies its calculative core.[7] What makes one killing worse than another? Dworkin answers that:

> [H]ow bad this is...depends on the stage of life in which it occurs, because the frustration is greater if it takes place after rather than before the person has made a significant personal investment in his own life, and less if it occurs after any investment has been substantially fulfilled, or as substantially fulfilled as is anyway likely.[8]

He proceeds apace to apply his principle.

If abortion makes us "uncomfortable," it is because ordinarily there has been some investment in this human being and there could be much more. If euthanasia troubles us, it is because ordinarily there has been a great investment in a human being, though there is little "return" that we can now expect. But if a healthy young person dies, Dworkin points out, our grief is palpable. We have made a huge investment and cannot realize our return.

Nor is there any gap between the liberalism of *Casey v. Planned Parenthood* and Dworkin's commodification of life. As Stith notes, Dworkin cites with approval the Court's declaration on liberty and private definition—whether of self, meaning, or the universe.[9]

To be sure, Ronald Dworkin is (only) a liberal theorist, not the liberal state. Yet his client is in the dock: the liberal order. By no means reluctantly, he helps us understand the liberal individual who dwells therein.

*Liberal Practice*

But now it is time to pursue our inquiry. Given its values and anthropology, how does the liberal state act? I want to address three arenas: its promoting of secularism, its fostering of self-deception, and its agnosticism about the goods of the person.

Let us begin with secularism. We are familiar, of course, with the argument that only the liberal state safeguards religious liberty and that restive believers are blinkered if they think otherwise.

This argument fails, and for two reasons.

First, *any* state that recognizes the dignity of conscience not only can but must respect religious liberty.

Second, there is evidence that it is not so much a regard for conscience as it is religious indifference, and even hostility, that motivates current liberalism. Recently, for example, liberal statists have lamented the Wisconsin Supreme Court's decision to uphold the use of public funds for parochial school tuition. In this vein, *The New York Times* editorializes that "[m]any church schools have religious indoctrination as a core purpose" and that vouchers "attack" institutions "essential ... for a democratic

---

[7] Richard Stith, "On Death and Dworkin: A Critique of His Theory of Inviolability," *Maryland Law Review* 56, no. 2 (1997).
[8] Dworkin, *Life's Dominion*, p. 88.
[9] Ibid., p. 175.

society."[10] Left unsaid is that such institutions, by their imposed silence, teach a secularism that threatens to undermine religious liberty. The power to tax easily becomes the power to destroy.

Such a secularism also denies anything like a Thomist understanding of the natural law. For if the natural law is a participation in the eternal law of God, as Maritain believed, the liberal curriculum already excludes it. The neglect might pretend to be benign. Its effects nonetheless are malignant, so much so that liberalism cannot but encourage self-deception.

How does it do so? Consider the reign of autonomy. Why maximize autonomy (of a sort), unless each person has an equal claim to be autonomous? But why suppose this equal claim unless each person is of equal worth? Yet liberalism cannot ground the equal worth of its citizens. To do so requires making the substantive case for human dignity that liberalism eschews. At most liberalism can resort to pragmatic artifice. Paying lip service to equal worth becomes a privileged rhetoric. As Walker Percy observes, we cannot both be "organisms" in the environment and enjoy an "intrinsic dignity" such that "the highest value to which a democratic society can be committed is the respect of the sacredness and worth of the individual."[11] That the liberal citizen believes, and is encouraged to believe, otherwise does not cure the contradiction.

There is however a logical consonance in liberalism's secularity and its self-deception. Both follow from the liberal's professed agnosticism about the goods of the human person. If we cannot, as a polity, have good reason to believe that harmony with God is a good, our political voice must be secular. If we cannot, as a polity, have reason to believe that human life is an intrinsic good, we cannot effectively challenge its commodification. If we cannot, as a polity, reasonably affirm that truth is a good essential to human flourishing, we cannot overcome self-deception. Note: such agnosticism introduces a morally vicious circle. If liberalism is agnostic about the goods of the person, then it cannot teach them to its citizens. Its only doctrine is a formal proceduralism. But the consequence of this silence is (at best) that its citizens drift into agnosticism—which in turn credentials the agnosticism of the liberal state. Yet even a bare procedural fairness calls for virtues which the state can only haltingly advance.

Perhaps the first casualty of this agnosticism is the intelligibility of choice. Emmanuel Mounier goes to the heart of the problem:

> [A] sort of philosophic myopia tends to see the center and pivot of freedom in the act of choice, whereas it lies in progressive liberation to choose the good … [a]nd if men today are becoming indifferent to freedom, may it not be that they no longer know what to do with freedom?[12]

---

[10] "Breaching the Church-State Wall," *The New York Times*, June 12, 1998, A22.

[11] Walker Percy, "The Delta Factor," in *The Message in the Bottle* (New York: Farrar, Straus and Giroux, 1954), p. 20.

[12] Emmanuel Mounier, *Personalism* (Notre Dame, Indiana: University of Notre Dame Press), 1952, p. 63.

To illustrate his verdict, American style, we need look no further than the classic Lincoln v. Douglas debates. Their shadow, as much as their light, still lies over the land.

Indeed, Stephen Douglas's appeal to choice—in defense of slavery—has become increasingly seductive. Consider a single example of his language:

> I am now speaking of rights under the Constitution. I am not speaking of the moral and religious right. I don't discuss the morals of the people of Missouri, but let them settle that for themselves...Let each State mind its own business, and let its neighbors alone—then Mr. Lincoln will find that this Republic can exist forever divided into free and slave States...[13]

Besides, Douglas hastens to add, such a stance gives business a boost and expedites foreign policy.

> Stand by that great principle, and then we can go on as we have done, increasing in wealth and in population, in power and all the elements of greatness until we shall be the admiration and the terror of the world.[14]

How that "great principle" bears on moral authority is an altogether different matter.

*Some Implications*

Even an initial characterizing of liberalism has introduced some of its implications. Highlighting its values and sketching its practice has identified others. But now there are further and critical implications to examine.

Liberalism undermines trust. Why trust a liberal state? Hindered by its own restrictions, it is doubtful whether its agents can muster the moral *gravitas* for ethical analysis. Why trust an order under whose tutelage self-interest trumps truth? In assessing Maritain's analysis of Machiavelli, James Schall makes a related observation. Deceit does not just corrupt the regime it informs; it numbs the conscience of citizens and produces a "lack of hope" in ethics.[15]

The family in contrast is a natural matrix of trust. Here we do well to note another liberal tendency: to slight the role of the family, not only in respect to trust but also as a social reality more basic than State. The state is for the family. While the state has its own good, it is instrumental to family life. John Finnis makes the point well:

> [T]he common good specific to the *civitas* as such—the public good—is not basic but, rather, instrumental to securing human goods which are basic (including other forms of community or association, especially domestic and religious associations) and none of which is in itself political.[16]

---

[13] *The Lincoln-Douglas Debates*, ed. Harold Holzer (New York: Harper Collins, 1993), pp. 310-11.
[14] Ibid., p. 311.
[15] James V. Schall, *Jacques Maritain: The Philosopher in Society* (Lanham, Maryland: Rowman & Littlefield, 1998), p. 5.
[16] John Finnis, "The Specifically Political Common Good in Aquinas," in *Natural Law & Moral Inquiry: Ethics, Metaphysics, and Politics in the Work of Germain Grisez*, ed. Robert P. George (Washington, D.C.: Georgetown University Press, 1998), p. 192.

Here Finnis follows St. Thomas's judgment that "Human beings are by nature more conjugal than political."[17]

Yet our liberal order feels increasingly free to itself define the family in a (supposedly) morally neutral fashion. The family however is neither morally neutral nor dependent on definitions which pretend to be so. The liberal state, though, does not limit itself to breaking its right relation to the family.

The liberal state also violates solidarity; it does so across a whole range of life issues. Here I take solidarity to affirm that the first measure of justice in a society is how it treats the most vulnerable. And the source of such a principle? We must look to the harms we suffer and to their healing if we are to keep our lives. But with solidarity "I" becomes "we." The harms that others suffer are my harms; others, in turn, bind up my wounds as their own.[18]

Suppose we apply such a standard to our own liberal order. More pointedly, we might focus on three issues widely debated under the rubric of a consistent ethics of life.

With respect to abortion, the Supreme Court in effect refuses to protect preborn human beings. It also affirms the legislation of particular states that requires citizens to publicly fund abortion. This contempt for solidarity with the "least little ones" recalls Chesterton's indictment of Carthage. "[T]he worshippers of Moloch," he notes, "were members of a mature and polished civilization ...".[19] Yet they chose "to invoke the blessings of heaven ... by throwing hundreds of their infants into a large furnace."[20] Across the centuries we might ask "only hundreds?"

With respect to euthanasia the Supreme Court finds that "the asserted 'right' to assistance in committing suicide is not a fundamental liberty interest protected by the due process clause." (*Washington v. Glucksberg*, No. 96-110) Yet the Court compliments the several states for their "serious, thoughtful examinations of physician-assisted suicide" and allows euthanasia when a particular state sanctions it. The Attorney General declines to block such a practice by using the Controlled Substances Act. Once more, the liberal disorder affirms due process but is unable, or unwilling, to affirm the good of life—even when it admits that suicide is "a serious public health problem, especially among persons in otherwise vulnerable groups." (*Washington v. Glucksberg*)

Consider, too, capital punishment. Procedural safeguards abound. In practice, they slow the pace of executions for capital crimes. But the liberal order cannot say that human life, as such, is a profound good. Substantive policy becomes a matter for legislative decision. But here popular resolution is especially dangerous. Part of what makes a murderer so vulnerable is the overwhelming outrage of the citizenry.

---

[17] *In Ethics* VIII.12 n.19 (1720).
[18] Christians speak of suffering with Christ. But how? St. Matthew's image of the Last Judgment answers this question with the test of solidarity (Matthew 25: 31-46). In a different key, John Paul II teaches that "the more that individuals are defenseless within a given society, the more they require the care and concern of others, and in particular the intervention of governmental authority" (*Centesimus Annus*, #10).
[19] Gilbert Keith Chesterton, *The Everlasting Man* (New York: Dodd, Mead & Co., 1926), p. 169.
[20] Ibid.

In our outrage we easily ignore or deny the ontological dignity of the person. Why did Mother Teresa plead for the lives of murderers? It was because she saw them as among "the poorest of the poor."

Might we now, reversing the usual scheme, turn to a contrast—and then a comparison? The death penalty, as Dr. Johnson put it, "concentrates" the mind.[21] It can also fix the wandering mind of the public. There is a particular felon, a scheduled hour, a designated place. A sentence moves toward fulfillment. For all of us there is time to reflect.

Contrast all this with the policy of nuclear deterrence in our liberal order. Weapons of mass destruction threaten whole cities and regions. Yet no particular criminal is targeted. Neither does a particular time nor place fix the wandering mind. Rather there is a pledge of destruction. In the ebb and flow of events, the deterrence policy induces periods of moral reflection; the nuclear displays of Pakistan and India do this much. But for the most part conscience becomes numbed. Doubtful excuses are accepted, and we domesticate our dissimulation.[22]

To be sure, liberalism has no special responsibility for nuclear deterrence. But ordinary responsibility is onerous enough. Our liberal order claims a sovereignty that trumps even the lives of the innocent. Our liberalism is incapable of affirming the principle that it is always wrong intentionally to kill the innocent.[23] How then can it recognize that it is always wrong to *threaten* to kill the innocent?

Having contrasted capital punishment and deterrence, we might compare deterrence and abortion, and chiefly on this note: we regret both but forego neither. Both are entrenched and supported by professional elites. Both win the consent of institutions and academic approbation. Indeed, the last implication of liberalism to identify is the net of complicity with which it entangles its citizens. Often the complicity is economic and obvious: public funds support abortion and deterrence—and the technical training that makes them possible. Sometimes the complicity is structural. Insofar as a military or political policy implicitly depends on nuclear deterrence that policy is itself compromised.[24] When professional standing depends on meeting the requirements of professional associations which legitimate attacks on human life, the professions themselves are compromised.

And what are we to say when the political order, whether state or party, disallows the effective participation of those who recognize substantive moral goods? Is our participation in that order compromised? Does our state, itself in disorder, often forfeit its right to obedience?

---

[21] See James Boswell, *Life of Johnson* (London: Oxford University Press, 1970), p. 849.
[22] Recall the letter of the Catholic Bishops of the United States *The Challenge of Peace: God's Promise and Our Response* (1983). We read therein that "it is not morally acceptable to intend to kill the innocent as part of a strategy of deterring nuclear war." (#178) Does our policy harbor such an intent? In a footnote, the then national security advisor William Clark, in a "helpful" letter, tells us it does not. *Nemo judex in causa sui.*
[23] Pope John Paul II, *The Gospel of Life* (New York: Random House, 1995), #57, pp. 100-3.
[24] We find a cogent argument for this thesis in John Finnis, Joseph M. Boyle, Jr., Germain Grisez, *Nuclear Deterrence, Morality and Realism* (New York: Oxford University Press, 1987), pp. 343-44.

## Realism v. Utopianism

Yes, I want to say, participating in the liberal disorder readily becomes morally compromising. Yes, our state together with the regime, often forfeits the right to obedience. But there is more. Unless we publicly contest state and regime, we jeopardize our democratic citizenship.

St. Thomas, after all, recognizes the possibility of forfeit and compromise—and in doing so follows St. Augustine. In his account of human law, Thomas notes that "the law can be rightly changed on account of the changed condition of man, to whom different things are expedient according to the difference of his condition," and appeals to Augustine's verdict:

> If the people have a sense of moderation and responsibility, and are most careful guardians of the commonweal, it is right to enact a law allowing such a people to choose their own magistrates ... But if, as time goes on, the same people become so corrupt as to sell their votes, and entrust the government to scoundrels and criminals; then the right of appointing their public officials is rightly forfeit to such a people, and the choice devolves to a few good men. [25]

There are, as we know, many ways of selling one's vote.

But we also know, perhaps better than Thomas, how hard it is to identify "a few good men" (or women) to whom the responsibility for the commonweal might safely devolve. Past searches have been troubled by a surfeit of self-ordained candidates. Worse still, candidates have seized power with the dismal result of a greater disorder than that which incited them. So even friends of my critique of liberalism might now ask that I cease and desist. Will not such a critique encourage a utopianism more dangerous than any liberal compromise? What distinguishes its conclusion from the manifestos of grim secular revolutionaries? And are not they the very ones who have often swept away the liberal order with rivers of blood, the blood of the innocent?

Such questions are sobering. They have great force in the United States, a government founded on an experiment in freedom. With an eye to this legacy, Roger Kimball—singling out the brothers Berrigan—asserts that "in a democracy illegality is not a justifiable brand of political opposition ..." [26] "[O]ne's country," he adds, "continues to exercise a legitimate claim on one's allegiance ... that cannot be disposed of in a fit of self-righteous bravado." [27]

James Schall, in exploring Maritain's analysis of Machiavelli, reminds us of a further point against a utopian posture. A healthy realism, he says, recognizes that in evil times it is "less and less clear what is and what is not an unjust action." [28] Why? One reason is that, in Maritain's words, "the application of moral rules immutable in

---

[25] *Summa Theological*, I-II, p. 97. a.1. Trans. the Fathers of the English Dominican Province. David Arias drew my attention to this passage.
[26] Roger Kimball, "The Politics of Delegitimation," in *The New Criterion* (March, 1998), p. 10.
[27] Ibid.
[28] Schall, *Jacques Maritain*, p. 16.

themselves takes lower and lower forms as the social environment declines."[29] Does not this suggest, then, that the liberal order might be (nearly) the best we can hope for?

Liberalism's corruption of its citizenry is to be feared. But in light of our failed search for leaders to replace it, our duty to democracy, and the limits of even immutable principles, we ought to err on the side of caution. Or so argues the anti-utopian. And does not St. Thomas himself agree? In *De Regno* he cites with favor the woman who prays that today's tyrant *not* die. After all, her prayers that earlier tyrants perish led only to their being replaced by still worse tyrants and finally to the very one for whom she now prays.[30] The principle is clear. Unmasking the regime might be wrong because what follows might be worse.

Maritain himself is well aware of this principle in his discussion of world government, the preface to which is his rejection of the bogus sovereignty of national states. In *Man and the State* he warns that a world government might show equal hubris and echo "the old utopia of universal Empire."[31] In our era, he thinks, "[t]he pursuit of an absolute World Superstate would be the pursuit of a democratic multinational Empire ... no better than the others."[32]

The foes of utopia, to be sure, have their own differences. But they share an historical sobriety. Roger Kimball looks back to the halcyon days of the New Left. James Schall sees the peril of political pietism. St. Thomas knows Roman history. Maritain lived through much of the bloodiest of centuries. We dare not ignore this collective warning. But what is it, chiefly, that we are to learn? The lesson, I think, is not that anti-utopianism exhausts political realism. Nor is the lesson of history that we must so fear the future as to anoint the present. It teaches, rather, that we must be wise as serpents if we would be guiless as doves. (Matthew 10: 16)

## Conclusion

But serpentine ways do not encoil contradictions. St. Thomas does not both support and oppose holding the state accountable, even to the point of revolution. Maritain does not both support and oppose unjust laws. It is the case, however, that right reason in acting issues in action. Gandhian "direct action" can be prudential. A slow process of legislative reform, despite judicial sabotage, can be prudential.[33] Yet neither is an adequate response to the liberal disorder. Even together they are not enough, though both belong to what Mounier called the dialectic of "integral action."[34]

There is, however, a third element—my listing is hardly exhaustive—of integral action which here I want to underscore. It expresses the chief guide to action that my analysis of the liberal disorder suggests. We ought to *speak openly and often* about the

---

[29] Ibid.
[30] Ptolemy of Lucca with portions attributed to Thomas Aquinas, *On the Government of Rulers: De Regimine Principum* trans. James M. Blythe (Philadelphia: University of Pennsylvania Press, 1997).
[31] Maritain, *Man and the State*, p. 204.
[32] Ibid.
[33] For a cogent discussion of judicial usurpation of politics, see Russell Hittinger's "A Crisis of Legitimacy," *First Things*, November 1996, pp. 25-29.

striated yet structural illegitimacy of the liberal disorder and, most immediately, its current managers.

A campaign of "unmasking" should first call attention to particular measures of the state that constitute unjust laws, even if they express the will of the citizenry. No measure which establishes or upholds abortion, infanticide, or euthanasia can promote the common good. Neither can any tax to fund such a measure. A policy that sanctions the killing of the innocent should be named for what it is: murder. More broadly still, Pope John XXIII held "if any government does not acknowledge the rights of man or violates them, it not only fails in its duty, but its orders completely lack juridical force."[35]

John Paul II's *Evangelium Vitae* advances its own "integral action" by identifying the effect of such "decrees" on democracies which maintain them:

> If, as a result of a tragic obscuring of the collective conscience, an attitude of skepticism were to succeed in bringing into question even the fundamental principles of the moral law, the democratic system itself would be shaken in its foundations, and would be reduced to a mere mechanism for regulating direct and opposing interests on a purely empirical basis.[36]

A "tragic obscuring," yes, and a tragic loss to democracy. But life is full of tragedy, is it not? Can a realist hope for anything better?

On John Paul's view, we must hope for more. He continues:

> Some might think that even this function, in the absence of anything better, should be valued for the sake of peace in society. While one acknowledges some element of truth in this ... without an objective moral grounding not even democracy is capable of ensuring a stable peace, especially since peace ... not built on the values of the dignity of every individual and of solidarity between all people frequently proves to be illusory.[37]

Here he realizes the precarity of civil order. He equally recognizes how a merely procedural democracy establishes disorder. In doing so he indicts a hollow democracy and exposes the last refuge of *Realpolitik*.

But what has happened to our friend, Jacques Maritain? What place does he have in a campaign to unmask the liberal disorder? Maritain would be the first to say that he thought and wrote within a tradition. Insofar as he draws us into the tradition of Christian political realism, we have not parted company with him. Still a pair of his critical insights comes readily to mind. They bring my reflections to a close.

Maritain addresses, in a pointed way, the civic character of personal responsibility. Again in *Man and the State*, he explores the idea of an international advisory council. It might work as a kind of a remote preparation for a new world order. One specific way it might serve the person in the shadow of the state is striking. He writes:

---

[34] Mounier, *Personalism*, p. 94.
[35] John XXIII, *Peace on Earth (Pacem in Terris)* (Boston: Daughters of St. Paul, 1963), §61.
[36] *The Gospel of Life*, #70.
[37] Ibid., #71.

> People know that sharing in an unjust war is homicide. They are told, on the other hand, that things have become so obscure and entangled that they lack competence to bear judgment on each particular case: am I bound, then, to share in what is *perhaps* a crime, because my government is a better judge than I on the matter, even if I were a German at the time of a Hitlerian war? [38]

Gordon Zahn's *In Solitary Witness* tells the story of Franz Jagerstatter, an Austrian peasant drafted into the army of the Reich. Jagerstatter's answer to Maritain's question was "no," and for this he was executed. [39] May peasants of the megalopolis, and their distinguished advisors, be as wise—cost what it may.

And Jacques Maritain's final insight? It insists, as does Jagerstatter's martyrdom, that we recognize the deepest truth of Christian realism. Like Jagerstatter the martyr, Maritain the philosopher would lead us to Mystery, the mystery of suffering. In *Man and the State* he reminds us that "[g]iven the human condition, the most significant synonym for *living together* is *suffering together*." [40] In the political realm the character of suffering becomes plain enough. "What sufferings indeed?" he asks, and immediately answers "[s]ufferings due to solidarity." [41] Out of death, life.

---

[38] Jacques Maritain, *Man and the State*, p. 215.
[39] Gordon Zahn, *In Solitary Witness* (Springfield, Illinois: Templegate, 1986), especially pp. 160-79.
[40] Jacques Maritain, *Man and the State*, p. 207.
[41] Ibid.

# III

# Natural Law Foundations for Liberalism

# 10

## Maritain, St. Thomas Aquinas, and the First Principles of the Natural Law

### *Gregory Doolan*

In *Man and the State* Jacques Maritain observes, "The only practical knowledge all men have naturally and infallibly in common as a self-evident principle, intellectually perceived by virtue of the concepts involved, is that we must do good and avoid evil."[1] Maritain maintains that Thomas Aquinas's natural law theory calls for an historical approach because, as he contends, man's knowledge of that law has been progressively shaped by his natural inclinations, providing over time for a richer understanding of the precepts of the natural law. However, while Thomas certainly acknowledges that most of the precepts prescribed by that law are not self-evident and must be deduced, he by no means limits the natural law to only *one* self-evident principle. Just as there are several such principles of the speculative intellect, Thomas argues, so too are there several of the practical—and these are what he calls the first precepts of the natural law. Thus, while Thomas might concur with Maritain that our understanding of the natural law involves some sort of historical development—he would *not* concur with the notion that our understanding of the most general precepts of that law are the result of such a development.

Maritain maintains that the historical development of the natural law has progressed in two ways: first as regards a movement away from a confused understanding of what he calls the "primordial regulations" of the natural law, and second as regards a dawning social awareness of the "further higher regulations" of that law by means of what he terms "a knowledge through inclination."[2]

For the natural law to be indeed natural, however, it must somehow be grounded in man's nature, which is to say that it must be grounded in some natural recognition of right from wrong. Thus, Thomas Aquinas observes that all men naturally know

---

[1] Jacques Maritain, *Man and the State* (Chicago: The University of Chicago Press, 1951), p. 90.
[2] Ibid., pp. 93-94.

what he terms "the universal principles of right" (*universalia iuris præcepta*).³ These universal principles, he explains, are found in the practical intellect, i.e., in the intellect as it is directed towards practical matters. Just as the speculative intellect argues about speculative matters, so the practical intellect does about practical ones. Thus, Thomas concludes that we must naturally have an understanding—not only of speculative principles—but of practical ones as well. And it is these principles that Thomas refers to as the universal principles of right.

This habit of first practical principles, he explains, is bestowed on us by nature.⁴ Nevertheless, it is not natural to man as if these principles were innate. Rather, Thomas explains, their existence is due partly to nature and partly to some extrinsic principle.⁵ To make this fact clear, he gives an example from the speculative first principle that *every whole is greater than its part*:

> For it is on account of the very nature of the intellectual soul that man, having grasped what a "whole" is and what a "part" is, should at once (*statim*) understand that every whole is greater than its part—and it is the same with the other [first principles]. But *what* a "whole" is and *what* a "part" is he cannot know except through the intelligible species which he has received from phantasms. And for this reason the Philosopher at the end of the *Posterior Analytics* shows that knowledge of principles comes to us from the senses.⁶

Thomas concludes that the first principles of the practical intellect are instilled in us in the same way. It is in this respect, then, that the habit of first principles is a natural one: because of man's natural *capacity* to acquire those principles. For this reason, the universal principles of right that man is obliged to know he also knows naturally. But what are these principles? Thomas begins by explaining that the first thing that falls under the apprehension of the intellect *simply* is *being* since this notion is included in everything that is apprehended. Consequently, the first principle of the *speculative* intellect is the principle of non-contradiction: that the same thing cannot be affirmed and denied at the same time. Now the *practical* intellect is directed towards action, thus the first thing that falls under the apprehension of the *practical* intellect is *being* considered under the aspect of *good* since every act is performed for some end which is desirable. Thus, Thomas explains that the first principle of the practical intellect states that *good is that which all things seek after*. And so, the first *precept* or command of the natural law is that *good*

---

³ Saint Thomas Aquinas, *Summa Theologiæ*, (henceforth ST) I-II, q. 76 a. 2. Thomas refers to these principles as the Ten Commandments in the *De Malo* (q. 3, a. 7, c.), not simply inasmuch as they are part of revelation but inasmuch as they are naturally known.
⁴ *ST*, I, q. 79, a. 12.
⁵ *ST*, I-II, q. 51, a. 1.
⁶ Ibid. Emphasis added. "Ex ipsa enim natura animae intellectualis, convenit homini quod statim, cognito quid est totum et quid est pars, cognoscat quod omne totum est maius sua parte; et simile est in ceteris. Sed quid sit totum, et quid sit pars, cognoscere non potest nisi per species intelligibiles a phantasmatibus acceptas. Et propter hoc Philosophus in fine *Post.* ostendit quod cognitio principiorum provenit nobis ex sensu" (Ottawa ed. 918b24-34).

*is to be done and pursued, and evil is to be avoided.*⁷ Just as all the first principles of the speculative intellect follow from the principle of non-contradiction, so the other first principles of the *practical* intellect (or first precepts of the natural law) follow from *this* first one—principles, Thomas explains, "which the practical intellect naturally apprehends as the good of man."⁸ And these other principles follow from the first, he notes, according to the order of man's natural inclinations.

As Thomas explains, man's most basic nature is as a substance; thus some of the precepts of the natural law follow from man's inclination to the good in accordance with his nature simply as a substance. Since each substance seeks to preserve its own being according to its nature, Thomas concludes that "according to this inclination, those things pertain to the natural law by which man's life is preserved, as do those things by which [what is] contrary [to man's life] are thwarted."⁹ Thomas next observes that it is also part of man's nature to be an animal. Inasmuch as he is one, then, he has inclinations that he shares in common with other animals. Thus, Thomas concludes that "those things are said to be part of the natural law 'which nature has taught to all animals,' such as sexual intercourse, education of children, and so forth."¹⁰ But man is more than simply an animal, he is a *rational* animal. So Thomas concludes that there is also in man an inclination to good which is according to the nature of his reason—which nature is proper to him. Thus, man has a natural inclination to know the truth about God and to live in society.¹¹ In discussing whether all the moral precepts of the Old Law are reducible to the ten precepts of the decalogue, Thomas later observes that the two principles *Thou shalt love the Lord thy God* and *Thou shalt love thy neighbor* are both self-evident, first general principles of the natural law—the former one through faith, but the latter through nature.¹²

In this way, while the precepts of the natural law are founded upon one common foundation, they are nonetheless many. Man is *obliged* to know the most general

---

⁷ *ST*, I-II, q. 94, a. 2.
⁸ Ibid. "Hoc est ergo primum praeceptum legis, quod bonum est faciendum et prosequendum, et malum vitandum. Et super hoc fundantur omnia alia praecepta legis naturae, ut scilicet omnia illa facienda vel vitanda pertineant ad praecepta legis naturae, quae ratio practica naturaliter apprehendit esse bona humana" (Ottawa ed. 1225b25-32).
⁹ Ibid. "Secundum igitur ordinem inclinationum naturalium est ordo praeceptorum legis naturae. Inest enim primo inclinatio homini ad bonum secundum naturam in qua communicat cum omnibus substantiis, prout scilicet quaelibet substantia appetit conservationem sui esse secundum suam naturam. Et secundum hanc inclinationem pertinent ad legem naturalerm ea per quae vita hominis conservatur, et contrarium impeditur" (Ottawa ed. 1225b39-49).
¹⁰ Ibid. "Secundo inest homini inclinatio ad aliqua magis specialia, secundum naturam in qua communicat cum ceteris animalibus. Et secundum hoc dicuntur ea esse de lege naturali 'quae natura omnia animalia docuit', ut est commixtio maris et feminae, et educatio liberorum, et similia" (Ottawa ed. 1225b50-1226a3).
¹¹ Ibid. "Tertio modo inest homini inclinatio ad bonum secundum naturam rationis, quae est sibi propria; sicut homo habet naturalem inclinationem ad hoc quod veritatem cognoscat de Deo, et ad hoc quod in societate vivat. Et secundum hoc, ad legem naturalem pertinent ea quae ad huiusmodi inclinationem spectant, utpote quod homo ignorantiam vitet, quod alios non offendat cum quibus debet conversari, et cetera huiusmodi quae ad hoc spectant" (Ottawa ed. 1226a3-a14). Thomas's implication is that these inclinations are self-evident first principles of the practical intellect.
¹² *ST*, I-II, q. 100, a. 3, obj. & ad 1.

precepts inasmuch as they are the universal principles of right, but he *naturally* knows them inasmuch as they are the first principles of the practical intellect. Consequently, knowledge of these precepts transcends time and culture. One cannot be ignorant of them, Thomas suggests, because these precepts of the natural law are *self-evident* to everyone.

Thomas identifies these self-evident precepts as one type of moral judgment. But not everything that belongs to the natural law is self-evident, some matters require more careful judgment regarding various circumstances. Thus Thomas identifies a second type of moral judgment as regards such matters that only the wise are competent to judge carefully. Finally, he identifies a third type of moral judgment as regards those matters that one cannot judge at all without assistance from Divine Instruction.[13]

What judgments, then, can be deemed to be so evident that *everyone* is able to approve or disapprove of them from the first principles? Is it possible because of historical or cultural influences, *e.g.*, for one not to know the basic moral precepts as outlined in the Ten Commandments? In discussing whether all the moral precepts of the Old Law belong to the natural law, Thomas gives examples of the three types of moral judgments just mentioned:

> All of the moral precepts [of the Old Law] necessarily belong to the natural law, but in different ways. For there are certain things that the natural reason of each and every man judges *instantly of its own accord* (*statim per se*) to be done or not to be done—*e.g.*, 'Honor thy father and thy mother'; and 'Thou shalt not kill'; 'Thou shalt not steal'. And such things belong to the nature law absolutely.—And, again, there are certain things that, with a more careful consideration of reason, are judged by wise men to be obligatory. And such things belong to the natural law, yet so that they need to be inculcated, the less wise being instructed by the more so: *e.g.*, 'Rise up before the hoary head, and honor the person of the aged man," and the like.— And, again, there are certain things the judgment of which human reason requires divine instruction, whereby we are taught about things concerning God: *e.g.*, 'Thou shalt not make to thyself a graven thing, nor the likeness of anything;' 'Thou shalt not take the name of the Lord thy God in vain.'[14]

Thomas later explains that the precepts contained in the Decalogue are referred as conclusions to the two self-evident principles *Thou shalt love the Lord thy God* and *Thou shalt love thy neighbor*, thus implying that they are not themselves self-

---

[13] *ST*, I-II, q. 100, a. 1.

[14] Ibid. Emphasis added. "Sic igitur patet quod cum moralia praecepta sint de his quae pertinent ad bonos mores, haec autem sunt quae rationi conveniunt, omne autem rationis humanae iudicium aliqualiter a naturali ratione derivatur; necesse est quod omnia praecepta moralia pertineant ad legem naturae, sed diversimode. Quaedam enim sunt quae statim per se ratio naturalis cuiuslibet hominis diiudicat esse facienda vel non facienda; sicut: 'Honora patrem tuum et matrem'; et 'Non occides; Non furtum facies'. Et huiusmodi sunt absolute de lege naturae. — Quaedam vero sunt quae subtiliori consideratione rationis a sapientibus iudicantur esse observanda. Et ista sic sunt de lege naturae, ut tamen indigeant disciplina, qua minores a sapientioribus instruantur, sicut illud: 'Coram cano capite consurge, et honora personam senis', et alia huiusmodi. — Quaedam vero sunt ad quae iudicanda ratio humana indiget instructione divina, per quam erudimur de divinis; sicut est illud : 'Non facies tibi sculptile neque omnem similitudinem; Non assumes nomen Dei tui in vanum' " (Ottawa ed. 1259b6-b32).

evident.[15] Nevertheless, he observes that "those precepts belong to the decalogue the knowledge of which man has through his very nature (*per seipsum*), from God— such precepts that can be known from general first principles immediately (*statim*) with but slight consideration."[16] This is why Thomas describes the precepts of the second tablet as being known by the intellect "instantly of its own accord,"[17] and elsewhere describes them as being "like self-evident first principles."[18]

Thomas thus thinks that all men naturally know that it is wrong to kill, to steal, to commit adultery, *etc.*[19] Unlike the first general precepts of the natural law, they are not strictly "self-evident." But unlike the precepts that must be 'inculcated' in all by wise men, these precepts are naturally and immediately acquired. Thus, just as with the speculative intellect—when one first understands the nature of a whole, *e.g.*, and that of a part he immediately recognizes that the whole is always greater—so too, Thomas suggests that, with the practical intellect, as soon as one recognizes the nature of a man and the nature of taking another's property or taking another's life, one recognizes of his own accord and at once that it is wrong to steal or to kill.

Given Thomas's discussion of the general precepts of the natural law, why then does Maritain insist that the only self-evident precept is that we must do good and avoid evil? The answer lies in certain epistemological differences between himself and Thomas. Maritain notes emphatically, ". . . let us stress that human reason does not discover the regulations of natural law in an abstract and theoretical manner, as a series of geometrical theorems. Nay more, *it does not discover them through the conceptual exercise of the intellect, or by way of rational knowledge.*"[20] How then does man discover the regulations of the natural law? Maritain's response: through *inclination*.

As we have seen, Thomas describes the precepts of the natural law as following according to the order of man's natural inclinations: his inclinations *qua* substance, *qua* animal, and *qua* rational. Maritain suggests that Thomas's teaching on this

---

[15] *ST*, I-II, q. 100, a. 3, obj. & ad 1.
[16] *ST*, I-II, q. 100, a. 3. Emphasis added. "Illa ergo praecepta ad decalogum pertinent, quorum notitiam homo habet per seipsum a Deo. Huiusmodi vero sunt illa quae statim ex principiis communibus primis cognosci possunt modica consideratione; et iterum illa quae statim ex fide divinitus infusa innotescunt" (Ottawa ed. 1261a24-30).
[17] *ST*, I-II, q. 100, a. 1.
[18] *ST*, II-II, q. 170, a. 2, obj. & ad 1 (Ottawa ed. 2259a4-7). Thomas makes this observation in an article examining whether the precepts of the virtues annexed to temperance are suitably given in the Divine law. The objector argues: "Praecepta enim decalogi, ut dictum est, sunt quaedam universalia principia totius legis divinae. Sed 'superbia est initium omnis peccati', ut dicitur *Eccli.* X. Ergo inter praecepta decalogi debuit aliquod poni prohibitivum superbiae" (Ottawa ed. 2258b1-6). To this objection, Thomas responds: "Dicendum quod superbia est initium peccati, sed latens in corde, cuius etiam inordinatio non perpenditur communiter ab omnibus. Unde eius prohibitio non debuit poni inter praecepta decalogi, quae sunt prima principia per se nota" (Ottawa ed. 2259a1-7). A variant text is listed as stating "quae sunt sicut prima principia per se nota" (emphasis added). This variation is more consistent with what Thomas says on this matter in other texts.
[19] *ST*, I-II, q. 100, a. 3.
[20] *Man and the State*, p. 91. Emphasis added.

matter has not been sufficiently understood. As he explains, when Thomas "says that human reason discovers the regulations of natural law through the guidance of inclinations of human nature, he means that the very mode or manner in which human reason knows natural law is not rational knowledge, but knowledge *through inclination*." [21]

But is Thomas really arguing this? Maritain grants that Thomas does not say as much, but he contends that this *is* Thomas's meaning.[22] But consider again Thomas's explanation for the foundation of the first precept of the natural law: it is rooted, he says, in the practical intellect's apprehension of *being*, in short, in the *concept of being*—a concept considered under the aspect of *good*. From this apprehension, then, is founded the first principle of the practical intellect from which we draw self-evident propositions of the natural law in the manner that the speculative intellect draws self-evident propositions from the principle of non-contradiction. Thomas would seem to be describing a foundation for the natural law that rests upon rational knowledge. What Maritain maintains, however, is that "The matter has been obscured somewhat because of the perpetual comparison that St. Thomas uses in these articles between the speculative and the practical intellect, and by reason of which he speaks of the propria principia of Natural law as 'quasi conclusiones principiorum communium.'"[23]

Maritain explains that—as opposed to the general principles of the natural law which Thomas describes as first principles, the *propria principia* or more specific precepts play a part that is *similar* to the conclusions of the speculative intellect—*but*, he emphasizes, that similarity should not be taken too literally. He argues that the specific precepts of the natural law (such as *Parricide is to be avoided* as opposed to *Murder is to be avoided*) are in fact *not* conclusions that are rationally deduced. How Maritain thinks they are arrived at we will consider in a moment; for now, let us grant his position regarding the specific precepts. But what about the *general* ones? Thomas's comparison between these two intellects is presented first and foremost to illustrate the similarities between the most general *first* principles of each. It is *this* similarity which is key; it is by *this* comparison that Thomas concludes it to be "evident that, as regards the general principles either of the speculative or of practical intellect, truth or rectitude is the same for all, and is equally known by all."[24] In short, Thomas concludes that these general, first principles—ones which Maritain calls the "primordial regulations"—are *self-evident*. They are not discovered by society over time, nor (*qua* general principles) are they even understood in a "less confused" manner over time, as Maritain suggests. Rather, as self-evident principles they are understood fully and clearly the moment the concepts involved

---

[21] Ibid.
[22] Ibid., n. 11.
[23] Ibid.
[24] *ST*, I-II, q. 94, a. 4. "Sic igitur patet quod quantum ad communia principia rationis sive speculativae sive practicae, est eadem veritas seu rectitudo apud omnes, et aequaliter nota" (Ottawa ed. 1227b31-b34).

are understood. And as Thomas shows, despite Maritain's claim to the contrary, these self-evident precepts of the natural law involve much more than simply the principle that man should do good and avoid evil.

Thus, by comparing the first principles of the practical intellect with those of the speculative, Thomas is able to illustrate the conceptual origins of the most general precepts of the natural law. But as we have seen, Maritain argues that the intellect does not discover these moral principles by means of a conceptual exercise of the intellect. Again, turning to Thomas's statements regarding inclination, Maritain maintains that such knowledge is attained through inclination. As Maritain notes, "That kind of knowledge is not clear knowledge through concepts and conceptual judgments;" what is it then? He goes on to explain, "it is obscure, unsystematic, vital knowledge by connaturality or congeniality, in which the intellect, in order to bear judgment, consults and listens to the inner melody that the vibrating strings of abiding tendencies make present in the subject."[25]

But how does this poetic discussion of "inner melody" and "vibrating strings" fit into the framework of a Thomistic epistemology? As regards natural cognition, Thomas describes only three acts of the intellect: simple apprehension whereby we form concepts; composition and division whereby we make judgments in light of those concepts; and reasoning whereby we draw conclusions from our conceptual judgments.[26] As regards the most general precepts of the natural law, Maritain maintains that our knowledge is not "clear knowledge through concepts and conceptual judgments." As we have seen, however, Thomas does not reach the same conclusion. He describes these general precepts as self-evident principles: which is precisely to say that they are judgments—judgments involving concepts. Maritain's interpretation of the role of inclination thus contradicts the Thomistic account. Nevertheless, he is correct to point out that Thomas cites man's inclinations as being the origin of this law. Where, then, does Thomas's discussion of inclination fit into his epistemology?

We have seen that Thomas describes three types of inclinations in man: substantial, animalistic, and rational. It is the third type of inclination that is proper to man *qua* man and, thus, most relevant to any discussion of the natural law—for as Thomas observes, other substances and animals do not partake of the natural law.[27] Since Thomas presents this discussion of inclination within the context of cognition, he seems to be referring simply to the capacity of the knowing faculty to receive knowledge. Thus, inasmuch as man *is* rational, whatsoever knowledge he receives, he is inclined to receive as a rational being—just as wax is inclined to receive a seal according to its nature as wax. What Thomas concludes is that the first principles of both the speculative and practical intellect are *necessarily* recognized insofar as man receives knowledge at all. Considered in this respect, Thomas's

---

[25] *Man and the State*, pp. 91-92.
[26] *ST*, I, q. 85, a. 5.
[27] *ST*, I-II, q. 91, a. 3, ad 3.

discussion of the similarities between the two intellects does not obscure his discussion of inclination, as Maritain claims. Just as man is inclined to know the self-evident principle that a whole is always greater than its part, so too is he inclined to know the self-evident precept that one should do evil to no man.[28] Thus, Thomas's discussion of inclination should be seen as one of man's inclining to recognize the self-evident principles of the natural law: in short, an inclination (contrary to Maritain's claim) to recognize self-evident, *conceptual* judgments.

These self-evident, conceptual judgments are what form the habit of first practical principles, also known as *synderesis*; and this habit, Thomas argues, can never be in error.[29] In other words, no one errs regarding these first principles.[30] Furthermore, Thomas continues, as synderesis is not learnt, neither can it be lost. Like the habit of the first principles of understanding, synderesis is caused immediately by the active intellect. Consequently, it is incorruptible, either directly or indirectly. As Thomas explains, the habit of first practical principles cannot be corrupted either by forgetfulness or deception.[31]

If we cannot err regarding the first precepts of the natural law, it might seem as though there should be no error regarding our actions. But as Maritain himself points out, "Montaigne maliciously remarked that, among certain peoples, incest and thievery were considered virtuous acts."[32] When the Canaanites sacrificed their children to Moloch, they did so in the belief that it was a good and pious act; and when Hindus practiced suttee—the ritual of burning a bride upon the death of her husband—they did so too. But nonetheless, these acts violated the precept of the natural law which forbids killing. Thomas explains that the answer to how man can commit such violations of the natural law despite the fact that he is possessed of unerring universal principles lies precisely in the nature of these principles *as* universal.

Reason, Thomas notes, directs all human acts according to a twofold knowledge: both universal and particular. When presented with a choice, the intellect confers about what should be done through the use of a syllogism, the conclusion of which is a judgment or choice made. While the precepts of the natural law are universal judgments, actions concern singulars: *viz.*, that *this* act should or should not be performed. Consequently, the conclusion of a practical syllogism is a particular proposition. But a particular proposition follows from a universal one only through the medium of another particular proposition. Thus, one rejects the sin of parricide by considering the universal proposition that it is wrong to kill one's father as well as the particular proposition that *this* man is one's father. "Hence," Thomas explains, "ignorance about either of these two [propositions] (*viz.* the universal principle

---

[28] *ST*, I-II, q. 100, a 3.
[29] *ST*, I-II, q. 91, a. 3, ad 3.
[30] *ST*, I, q. 79, a. 12, ad 3.
[31] *ST*, I-II, q. 53, a. 1.
[32] *Man and the State*, p. 90.

that is a rule of reason, or the particular circumstance) can cause an act of parricide."[33] Error can result, furthermore, when the practical intellect does not make a correct application of the universal principle to acts. Thus, Thomas explains that just as the speculative intellect can arrive at a false conclusion when it neglects to construct a syllogism according to the proper form of argumentation, so can the practical intellect arrive at a false conclusion in the same manner.[34]

Earlier we had granted Maritain's position that "those *propria principia* or specific precepts of Natural law are in no way conclusions rationally deduced ..."[35]— specific precepts like *Parricide is to be avoided*. But we see Thomas present here a model of the practical intellect reasoning syllogistically just as the speculative does. The significant difference between the two kinds of intellectual arguments would be the object: one concerning practical matters, the other speculative. Otherwise, Thomas suggests, the *mode* of understanding is the same. If we consider again the three acts of the intellect, man's understanding of the *propria principia* would *necessarily* involve a conceptual act since a precept is a judgment. And, since these specific precepts are not self-evident, they must be concluded from judgments that are; in short, they must be concluded from the first precepts, as Thomas observes. Again, when he speaks of inclination, he is referring to man's capacity to make conceptual judgments and to draw rational conclusions in these matters. There is no indication that the inclination that he describes is some non-rational mode of thought, nor is there any indication that he thinks our understanding of the specific moral precepts that follow from this inclination are as Maritain contends, "in *no way* rationally deduced."

Thus, in discussing the origin of moral error, Thomas notes that:

> We must say that as to the first general principles, the natural law is the same for all both as to rectitude and as to knowledge. But as to certain particulars *which are, as it were, conclusions of those general principles*, it is the same for all in most [cases], both as to rectitude and as to knowledge; yet in a few cases it can fail both as to rectitude ... and also as to knowledge, since some people have a perverted reason due to passion or due to evil habit or due to an evil disposition of nature; thus, as Julius Cæsar recounts in *The Gallic Wars*, formerly among the Germans theft was not considered wrong even though it is expressly contrary to the natural law.[36]

---

[33] *ST*, I-II, q. 76, a. 1. "Utriusque ergo ignorantia potest causare parricidii actum, scilicet et universalis principii, quod est quaedam regula rationis, et singularis circumstantiae" (Ottawa ed. 1131a2-6).
[34] Thomas Aquinas, *De Veritate*, q. 17, a. 2.
[35] *Man and the State*, p. 91.
[36] *ST*, I-II, q. 94, a. 4. Emphasis added. "Sic igitur dicendum est quod lex naturae quantum ad prima principia communia, est eadem apud omnes et secundum rectitudinem, et secundum notitiam. Sed quantum ad quaedam propria, quae sunt quasi conclusiones principiorum communium, est eadem apud omnes etiam ut in pluribus et secundum rectitudinem et secundum notitiam; sed ut in paucioribus potest deficere et quantum ad rectitudinem propter aliqua particularia impedimenta, sicut etiam naturae generabiles et corruptibiles deficiunt ut in paucioribus, propter impedimenta, et etiam quantum ad notitiam; et hoc propter hoc quod aliqui habent depravatam rationem ex passione, seu ex mala consuetudine, seu ex mala habitudine naturae; sicut apud Germanos olim latrocinium non reputabatur iniquum, cum tamen sit expresse contra legem naturae, ut refert Iulius Caesar in libro *De Bello Gallico*" (Ottawa ed. 1228a11-a32).

In this passage, Thomas acknowledges that cultural and historical circumstances *can* result in a certain ignorance regarding the natural law. When he notes that the ancient Germans did not consider theft to be wrong, however, Thomas is not suggesting that they were ignorant of the precept *Thou shalt not steal*. As we have seen, Thomas describes the precepts of the second tablet as being "like self-evident principles"—principles "which the natural reason of every man judges *instantly* of its own accord." Thus, the German acceptance of theft described by Cæsar was not an ignorance regarding the substance of the Seventh Commandment; rather, it was an ignorance that theft is wrong regarding certain details: *e.g.*, that it was wrong to steal from *these* tribes or from non-Germans, or even that such an act in regards to those people constituted theft at all. Such ignorance, therefore, is an error concerning the minor premise of a practical syllogism—in short, it is a deductive error.

The supposed pervasive cultural ignorance among the early Germans regarding the evil of theft, or that of Hindus regarding the practice of Suttee, is not simply the result of individual error, however. In the *Summa*, Thomas explains that as regards the more *specific* precepts of the natural law, "the natural law can be erased (*deleri*) from the hearts of man, either because of evil persuasions . . . or because of *vicious customs* and corrupt habits."[37] He seems to allow for such cultural influences in the *De Malo*, as well. There, Thomas notes that while ignorance generally signifies a privation of knowledge, "Sometimes ignorance is something opposed to knowledge, and that is said to be an ignorance from a perverse disposition, namely when someone has a habit of false principles and false opinions on account of which he is impeded from knowledge of the truth."[38]

Thus, Thomas shows that such violations of the natural law do not originate in an error as regards the most general precepts but as regards the *application* of those precepts—and that this error is, in part, a deductive one. When the Canaanites would sacrifice their children or when Hindus would burn their widows, they did so following certain false principles which custom and law had taught them, which is to say that they did so *believing* those principles to be true. As both Maritain and Thomas would conclude, their judgment had been corrupted. It is here that we see the possibility for what Maritain argues: *viz.*, an historical development of the understanding of the natural law.

As we have seen, Thomas describes three types of moral judgments concerning the precepts of the natural law. We have already considered the first type of judgments—*viz.*, those which are known to all men—and we have seen that it

---

[37] *ST*, I-II, q. 94, a. 6. Emphasis added. "Quantum vero ad alia praecepta secundaria, potest lex naturalis deleri de cordibus hominum, vel propter malas persuasiones, eo modo quo etiam in speculativis errores contingunt circa conclusiones necessarias; vel etiam propter pravas consuetudines et habitus corruptos, sicut apud quosdam non reputabantur latrocinia peccata; vel etiam vitia contra naturam, ut etiam Apostolus dicit, Ad Rom. I²⁴" (Ottawa ed. 1230a10-20).

[38] Thomas Aquinas, *De Malo* (henceforth DM), q. 3, a. 7. "Quandoque autem ignorantia est aliquid scientie contrarium, que dicitur ignorantia, peruerse dispositionis: puta cum aliquis habet habitum falsorum principiorum et falsarum opinionum, ex quibus impeditur a scientia ueritatis" (Leonine ed., vol. 23, p. 81, ll. 85-90).

consists of all of the moral precepts as enunciated in the second tablet of the Decalogue. These judgments are what Maritain refers to as the "primordial regulations of the natural law." Maritain notes of these precepts that "human reason has become aware [of them] in a less and less crepuscular, rough, and confused manner ... "[39] As we have also seen, however, Thomas describes certain of these precepts as *self-evident*; but self-evident propositions by definition are understood clearly and thoroughly the moment that their concepts are understood. Thus, contrary to Maritain's claim, it is impossible for there to be any development of understanding as regards this first type of judgments.

However, as regards the second type of moral judgment—*viz.*, those concerning matters that are discerned and inculcated by the wise—such judgments *do* admit of historical development. But such development would concern what Thomas refers to as the *propria principia* or more specific precepts of the natural law: such as that parricide is to be avoided. An historical development in this respect could involve such changes as a dawning social consciousness of the full implications of the first precepts of the natural law. To see how this could occur, we need to take a closer look at the erring conscience and how it can be corrected.

As we have already observed, when the Hindus burnt their widows, they did so in the belief that such acts are pious and good. In doing so, then, they were following their conscience. Now conscience, Thomas explains, directs human acts inasmuch as it applies universal precepts to particular actions. Consequently, conscience binds by the power of a precept.[40] Hence, Thomas concludes that one is bound by one's conscience no matter how false it may be—even if it contradicts the natural law.[41] As Thomas explains, "although that which an erroneous conscience dictates is not in harmony with God's law, nevertheless it is accepted by the mistaken person *as* the very law of God; for that reason (taking the thing in itself) if one departs from it, he departs from God's law even though it would be accidental that he does not depart from God's law."[42]

The Hindu whose conscience dictated that *All widows should be burned*, then, was bound by his conscience to do so. Nevertheless, while his conscience necessarily bound him, it did *not* necessarily excuse him from sin. The question whether an erring conscience excuses from sin concerns whether one's ignorance is voluntary or not. As Thomas explains, if conscience errs from an ignorance that is either willed directly or willed indirectly through negligence, then it does not excuse the will.[43] Accordingly, he concludes, "one who follows such a conscience and acts according to it acts contrary to God's law and sins mortally. For there was sin in the error itself since it happened through the person's ignorance of that which he

---

[39] *Man and the State*, p. 94.
[40] *De Veritate*, q. 17, a. 3.
[41] Ibid., q. 17, a. 4, *sed contra* 5.
[42] Ibid., q. 17, a. 4, ad 1. Emphasis added. "Ad primum igitur dicendum quod, quamvis id quod dictat erronea conscientia non sit consonum legi Dei tamen accipitur ab errante ut ipsa lex Dei, et ideo, per se loquendo si ab hoc recedat recedit a lege Dei quamvis per accidens sit quod a lege Dei non recedat" (Leonine ed. vol. 22.1, p. 526, ll. 190-95).

*ought* to have known."[44] Because of its specific nature, a precept such as *No widow should be burned* is not among the first principles of the practical intellect. Consequently, it is not self-evident. Nevertheless, simply because it is not a self-evident precept does not suggest that one is not obliged to know it.

The Hindu in this instance was culpable for his action regarding a *particular* judgment precisely because he was able to change his understanding of a universal one. Thus, while he had to abide by his conscience as long as it dictated that *All widows must be burned*, he was culpable for burning his brother's bride precisely because he could change his conscience. As Thomas explains, an erring conscience "does not oblige in every event. For something can happen, namely, a change of conscience, and, when such occurs, one is no longer bound."[45] Thus, when Thomas suggests that culture or historical circumstances can inculcate in a person a habit of false principles and opinions impeding him from a knowledge of truth, Thomas does *not* mean to say that that person is impeded absolutely so that he can *never* have knowledge of the truth. A false principle impedes knowledge inasmuch as the intellect does not admit of contraries. Hence, the Hindu who judged that *All widows should be burned* was impeded from the knowledge that *No widows should be burned* insofar as it is not possible for the intellect to affirm and deny the same thing at the same time.

However, if such erroneous judgments are removed, so too is the impediment to knowledge. The Hindu possessed of his false precept, then, was capable of learning that bride burning *is* a form of murder. Insofar as he was capable of making this judgment, so too was he capable of changing his conscience. And so too is an entire culture capable of changing *its* conscience. This is one example, then, of how an historical development of an understanding of the natural law can occur. And such realization, Thomas explains, is discerned and inculcated by the wise: not necessarily the wise absolutely speaking, but at least those wise enough to deduce the *propria principia* that follow from the first general precepts of the natural law. Such an historical development seems to be what Maritain describes as the kind that is "as regards the way in which [human reason] has become aware ... of [the natural law's] further, higher regulations."[46]

Thus, the second type of moral judgments that Thomas describes—those that are evident to the wise—would allow of an historical development. And, the third type of moral judgments would as well—*viz.*, those that can only be known by

---

[43] *ST*, I-II, q. 19, a. 6.
[44] *De Veritate*, q. 17, a. 4, ad 3. Emphasis added. "Ad tertium dicendum quod conscientia erronea errans in his quae sunt per se mala, dictat contraria legi Dei, sed tamen illa quae dictat dicit esse legem Dei, et ideo transgressor illius conscientiae efficitur quasi transgressor legis Dei, quamvis etiam conscientiam sequens et eam opere implens contra legem Dei faciens mortaliter peccet, quia in ipso errore peccatum erat cum contingeret per ignorantiam eius quod scire debebat" (22.1, p. 526, ll. 211-20).
[45] Ibid., q. 17, a. 4. "unde talis conscientia non obligat in omnem eventum, potest enim aliquid contingere, scilicet depositio conscientiae, quo contingente aliquis ulterius non ligatur" (vol. 22.2, p. 525, ll. 158-62). Cf. Ibid., ad 8.
[46] *Man and the State*, p. 94.

revelation. This is apparent if we simply consider the fact that the Jews received the Old Law from God whereas once they did not have it. But, again, the first type of judgments—those involving the first precepts of the natural law—can admit of *no* historical development whatsoever. It is true that the conclusions that follow from them and that stand as precepts in their own right can be developed, but if we are to argue as Thomas does that the first principles of the practical intellect are self-evident, then we must conclude that everyone who recognizes the concepts involved in those judgments recognizes the judgments themselves immediately. Thus, it is incorrect to conclude as Maritain does that "the knowledge of the primordial aspects of natural law was first expressed in *social patterns* rather than in personal judgments ... "[47] Social patterns might explain our developed understanding of the *specific* precepts of that law, but if our understanding of the natural law were not ultimately grounded in self-evident precepts—which is to say that if it were not ultimately grounded in self-evident "personal judgments"—then there could be no foundation for its expression in social patterns from the start.

Maritain maintains that Thomas's teaching on the natural law "should be understood in a much deeper and more precise fashion than is usual."[48] However, he does not present such an understanding in *Man and the State*; rather, he departs from that teaching on several essential points. Contrary to Thomas, Maritain maintains that only one precept of the natural law is self-evident: *viz.*, that man should do good and avoid evil. Thomas, however, enumerates several self-evident precepts. Contrary to Thomas, Maritain maintains that these first precepts are not conceptual judgments. Thomas, however, in describing them as self-evident principles, necessarily implies that they *are* conceptual judgments. Finally, contrary to Thomas, Maritain maintains that the more specific precepts that follow from these general ones are in no way rationally deduced. Thomas, however, leaves no room for the reader to conclude anything but that they *must* be deduced.

These departures from Thomas's teaching on the natural law are due principally to Maritain's interpretation of what is meant by the term "inclination". When Thomas speaks of man's inclinations in reference to the natural law, he does not mean by this term some sort of non-rational, non-conceptual mode of knowledge, as Maritain maintains; to the contrary, by inclination Thomas refers to nothing less than man's natural capacity to form concepts, make judgments, and deduce conclusions. It is precisely because man has this capacity to reason, Thomas explains, that he is capable of recognizing the natural law. Thus, Thomas's comparison between the speculative and practical intellect does not *obscure* matters, as Maritain claims; rather, it makes things all the more clear. Instead, it is Maritain's poetic interpretation of the natural law–with his discussion of "inner melodies" and "vibrating strings of abiding tendencies"–that, in the end, obscures Thomas's own theory by presenting it in a "less precise fashion than is usual."

---

[47] Ibid., p. 92. Emphasis added.
[48] Ibid., p. 91

# 11

## Liberal Democracy, Natural Law, and Jurisprudence: Thomistic Notes on an Irish Debate

### V. Bradley Lewis

Jacques Maritain is justly celebrated by Thomists for the role he played in the revival of Thomistic philosophy in the twentieth century. He is also famous for his attempt to reconcile Thomistic ideas about ethics and politics with modern liberal democracy.[1] The first of these achievements has borne rich fruit. One can entertain doubts about the second achievement, especially given Maritain's apparent optimism about the possibility of radical moral disagreement coexisting peacefully under the aegis of agreement about political institutions.[2] The liberal distinction between substance and procedure often has the effect of excluding and/or changing a great deal of non-liberal "substance" by subjecting it to liberal "procedure."[3] I will not be explicitly concerned here with Maritain's thought, but with events that would seem to challenge any optimism about the congruence of a politics grounded in the tradition of classical natural right and Thomistic natural law with modern liberal democracy. My purpose is not to contribute to that already large genre of literature, the dyspeptic Catholic critique of modernity, but rather to raise to consciousness some of the moral complexities of contemporary law and politics so to enable deeper reflection on our current situation.

---

[1] On Maritain's political legacy with respect to liberal democracy see Paul E. Sigmund, "Catholicism and Liberal Democracy," in *Catholicism and Liberalism: Contributions to American Public Philosophy*, eds. R. Bruce Douglass and David Hollenbach, (Cambridge: Cambridge University Press, 1994), 217-41, especially pp. 225-26; John P. Hittinger, "Jacques Maritain and Yves R. Simon's Use of Thomas Aquinas in Their Defense of Liberal Democracy," in *Thomas Aquinas and His Legacy*, ed. David M. Gallagher, (Washington, D.C.: The Catholic University of America Press, 1994), pp. 149-72; James V. Schall, *Jacques Maritain: The Philosopher in Society* (Lanham, Maryland: Rowman and Littlefield, 1998), chapter 6.

[2] There are passages in the fifth chapter of Maritain's *Man and the State* (Chicago: The University of Chicago Press, 1951) that are strikingly similar to John Rawls's notion of "overlapping consensus" in *Political Liberalism* (New York: Columbia University Press, 1993), Lecture IV.

[3] This is so much so that some liberal theorists have explicitly renounced the claim advanced by Rawls and others that a hallmark of liberalism is its neutrality with respect to conceptions of the good life. See especially the extraordinary paper by Stephen Macedo, "Transformative Constitutionalism and the Case of Religion: Defending the Moderate Hegemony of Liberalism," *Political Theory* 26 (1998), pp. 56-80, as well as his "Liberal Civic Education and Religious Fundamentalism: The Case of God v. John Rawls?" *Ethics* 105 (1995), pp. 468-96. Rawls's original argument for neutrality is in *A Theory of Justice* (Cambridge: Harvard University Press, 1971), chapter 7.

More specifically, this paper examines the efficacy of natural law argument in the public discourse and constitutional jurisprudence of modern liberal democracies by looking at the recent jurisprudence of the one jurisdiction in which natural law has been incorporated into actual decisions: Ireland.[4] The Irish case is noteworthy in itself and in the larger theoretical context mentioned above. It is also useful to examine in the context of the more parochial debate among American legal scholars and activists over the place of natural law in constitutional jurisprudence. The question surfaced in a very public way during the 1991 confirmation hearings of now Justice Clarence Thomas[5] and in the aftermath of a 1997 speech delivered by Justice Antonin Scalia in Rome, in which he seemed to advocate a form of legal positivism.[6] These events, as well as the exploration of moral questions in the courts themselves, have led to a continuing controversy over the role of natural law in public debate and constitutional adjudication.[7]

While there is a venerable tradition of constitutional scholarship that holds the American founding to have been informed by some version of natural law theory,[8] it is difficult to defend the thesis that American judges have ever deployed what one could plausibly call a natural law theory in deciding cases.[9] The American experience, then, is of limited value in assessing the possibility of a serious jurisprudence of natural law. The Irish case is a different matter, as we shall see below. Nevertheless, in May of 1995 the Irish Supreme Court issued an

---

[4] German judges and legal scholars flirted briefly with natural law theories after World War II. See Donald P. Kommers, *The Constitutional Jurisprudence of the Federal Republic of Germany* (Durham, North Carolina: Duke University Press, 1989), pp. 54-55, pp. 312-14.

[5] Thomas seemed to support recourse to some natural law ideas in constitutional interpretation in several articles and speeches: "Toward a 'Plain Reading' of the Constitution—The Declaration of Independence in Constitutional Interpretation," *Howard Law Journal* 30 (1987), pp. 983-95; "Why Black Americans Should Look to Conservative Policies," *Heritage Lectures* 119 (18 June 1987); "The Higher Law Background of the Privileges and Immunities Clause of the Fourteenth Amendment," *Harvard Journal of Law and Public Policy* 63 (1989), pp. 63-70. Thomas, of course, repudiated this view during his confirmation hearings.

[6] The speech is reprinted as "Of Democracy, Morality and the Majority," *Origins* 26 (27 June 1996), pp. 81, 83-90.

[7] See the exchange between Robert Bork, Hadley Arkes, Russell Hittinger, and William Bentley Ball in the March and May 1992 issues of *First Things* as well as the symposia published in the *Michigan Law Review* 90 (1992), *University of California, Davis Law Review* 26 (1993), *Southern California Interdisciplinary Law Journal* 4 (1995), and *Catholic Social Science Review* 1 (1996).

[8] Most famously, Edward S. Corwin, "The 'Higher Law' Background of American Constitutional Law," *Harvard Law Review* 42 (1928): pp. 149-85, 365-409. See also Thomas C. Grey, "Origins of the Unwritten Constitution: Fundamental Law in American Revolutionary Thought," *Stanford Law Review* 30 (1978), pp. 843-93 and more recently Michael P. Zuckert, *The Natural Rights Republic* (Notre Dame, Indiana: University of Notre Dame Press, 1996).

[9] Some of the early contract clause cases as well as those manifesting in the now defunct doctrine of economic substantive due process are often said to rest on natural law arguments, though in most cases they seem more directly grounded in historical interpretation. The standard view is evinced in, e.g., J.E. Nowak, R.D. Rotunda, and J.N. Young, *Constitutional Law*, 3d ed. (St. Paul: West, 1986), p. 331ff.; Lawrence H. Tribe, *American Constitutional Law*, 2d ed. (Minneola: Foundation Press, 1988), p. 560ff. Against it see Matthew J. Frank, *Against the Imperial Judiciary* (Lawrence, Kansas: University Press of Kansas, 1996); and Lane Sunderland, *Popular Government and the Supreme Court* (Lawrence, Kansas: University Press of Kansas, 1996). One confusing aspect of the scholarship is that "natural law" is often used as a label for values that the critics of whatever opinion is under consideration claim are extratextual. "Natural law," then, becomes an invidious label for whatever is *not* in the positive law. The greatest practitioner of this method of argument would seem to have been Justice Hugo Black, who frequently referred to views he opposed (views often grounded in history or tradition) as "natural law" (see, e.g., Black's dissents in *Adamson v. California* 332 U.S. 46 (1946), pp. 68-92 and In re Winship 397 U.S. 358 (1969), pp. 377-86) and has been followed—often unwittingly, I suspect—by many commentators.

extraordinary ruling that seemed decisively to reject natural law as an authority in its jurisprudence.[10] Before and after that ruling, Irish legal scholars, politicians, and pundits debated the role of natural law in Irish public life.

This Irish debate sheds light not only on the American case, but on the larger theoretical question of just what role natural law argument is likely to play in contemporary liberal democracies. To anticipate conclusions, I argue here first, that that role cannot be other than small in jurisprudence, and second, that that role is likely to be increasingly small in other areas of public life because of what one could call the cultural dynamic of liberalism. Pining after a jurisprudence of natural law, then, often looks like a desperate attempt to repair damage done to the culture at large in an arena not at all suited to the resolution of cultural questions.[11] However, I also want to suggest that the thoughtful reexamination of the tradition of natural law theory serves what may be a more important function in our present circumstances, that is, as part of an evaluative social science from the perspective of which contemporary cultural and political questions can be fruitfully assessed. In the first section, then, I sketch the sense in which Thomistic natural law suggests the outlines of an evaluative social science. In the second section, I want to discuss more fully the Irish case in light of natural law theory. Finally, in the third section I will suggest the conclusions of such an analysis and propose a few hypotheses and further questions.

## I

There is at least one immediate objection to the idea of a Thomistic social science, namely that there was no such thing as "social science" in the thirteenth century, and, of course, there was not. Why there was no such thing is itself instructive. The categories of medieval thought about 'social life' were still predominantly those of antiquity, and the horizon of such thought was political and not sub-political as it is in modern social science.[12] Indeed, modern social science is in the first instance the result of a rebellion against classical natural right within philosophy initiated by Machiavelli and Hobbes and later developed by Hume and Mill,[13] intended first to lower the goals of political life and second to reduce politics to the natural sciences. The modern social sciences aimed to replace natural right as the most important component of a science of human affairs.

By classical natural right, I mean, most basically, the theses first, that the soul should rule over the body; second, that the soul should itself be formed by the

---

[10] *In re Article 26 of the Constitution and the Regulation of Information (Services Outside the State for the Termination of Pregnancies) Bill 1995* [1995] 2 I.L.R.M. p. 81. Irish cases are conventionally cited by reference to either of the two major Irish law reports, the *Irish Law Report Monthly* (I.L.R.M.) and the *Irish Reports* (I.R.). Numbers before the abbreviations refer to the volume of the reports for that year.
[11] On this one might examine Justice Scalia's dissent in *Romer v. Evans* 517 U.S. 620 (1996), pp. 636-53.
[12] See, e.g., Aristotle *Nicomachean Ethics*, 1094a26-b15, 1095a14-17; cf. Aquinas, *In decem libros Ethicorum expositio* I, lect. 2, pp. 26-31.
[13] See, e.g., Niccolo Machiavelli, *The Prince*, ch. 15; Thomas Hobbes, *Leviathan*, ch. 15 (last three paragraphs); David Hume, *A Treatise of Human Nature*, Introduction; J. S. Mill, *A System of Logic*, book VI.

moral and intellectual virtues; and third, that this order should be the basis of the political order of society in both its recognition of claims to rule and in the norms that govern common life.[14] From within the tradition of classical natural right, the project of modern social science can be seen as, at best, the necessary preliminary collection of useful information,[15] and, at worst, unintelligible.[16] This is because classical natural right takes its stand from the perspective of the actor faced with the question of what action to take,[17] rather than from some external standpoint. It is a crucial characteristic of Aquinas's account of human affairs that it is not like modern moral theories, that is, a set of prescriptive rules about moral conduct separated from empirical descriptions of moral life. Natural law theory is not only evaluative, but also descriptive, thus combining two enterprises which modern thought characteristically separates: ethics and social science.[18] Aquinas himself provides the best illustrations of this.

What we first have to notice is that Aquinas's account of natural law is presented neither as a contribution to jurisprudence nor to political theory, nor can it be said to constitute a free-standing philosophical ethics.[19] Rather, it functions as a way of talking about the sense in which man's natural inclinations reveal a horizon to moral and political life[20] and the place of that horizon within the still-larger context of God's providential government of the universe.[21] What is most important about this account for our present purposes is that it holds the moral life to be present in human beings *potentially*

---

[14] This characterization is a drastic summary of the substance of classical political philosophy and it is also crucial that the classics recognized the impossibility of any perfect realization of such a scheme. For some important versions of the three theses see Plato *Gorgias* 464b-465d, 502e-503a, 504d, 506c-507a, 521d; *Laws* 631b-e, 650b, 689b, 690a-e, 697b-c, 705d, 713c-714b, 726a, 896c, 967d-968a; Aristotle *Politics* 1323a14-b36. The best synthetic discussion is Leo Strauss, *Natural Right and History* (Chicago: The University of Chicago Press, 1953), chapter 4.
[15] Aristotle *Nicomachean Ethics* 1181a12-b23.
[16] Compare Aquinas, *Summa Theologiae* 1-2.1.1 with B.F. Skinner, *Science and Human Behavior* (Glencoe, Illinois: The Free Press, 1965), pp. 36, 87-90.
[17] Aristotle, *Nicomachean Ethics* 1095a5-6, 1103b26-29, 1179a35-b4. Consider also *Politics* 1260b27-36, 1282b14-17, 1288b10-1289a25 and Aquinas, *In Libros Politicorum Aristotelis Expositio*, proemium.
[18] See Leo Strauss, "Political Philosophy and the Crisis of Our Time," in *The Post-Behavioral Era: Perspectives on Political Science*, eds. G.J. Graham and G.W. Carey (New York: David McKay Company, 1972), pp. 217-42 and the recent discussion in John M. Finnis, *Aquinas: Moral, Political, and Legal Theory* (Oxford: Oxford University Press, 1998), chapter 2. I have discussed this matter in more detail in "Modernity, Morality, and the Social Sciences: A Look at MacIntyre's Critique in Light of *Fides et Ratio*," *Communio* 26 (1999), pp. 104-21.
[19] On the place of natural law in Aquinas's overall understanding of ethics see E. A. Goerner, "On Thomistic Natural Law: The Bad Man's View of Thomistic Natural Right," *Political Theory* 7 (1979), pp. 101-22 and "Thomistic Natural Right: The Good Man's View of Thomistic Natural Law," *Political Theory* 11 (1983), pp. 393-418; and more recently Denis J.M. Bradley, *Aquinas on the Twofold Human Good: Reason and Human Happiness in Aquinas's Moral Science* (Washington, D.C.: Catholic University of America Press, 1997).
[20] The political character of the natural law is discussed more below. This aspect has been illuminated by Ernest Fortin, "Natural Law and Social Justice," *American Journal of Jurisprudence* 30 (1985), pp. 1-20.
[21] See Thomas W. Smith, "The Order of Presentation and the Order of Understanding in Aquinas's Account of Law," *The Review of Politics* 57 (1995), pp. 607-40, and Russell Hittinger, "*Veritatis Splendor* and the Theology of Natural Law," in *Veritatis Splendor and the Renewal of Moral Theology*, eds. J. A. DiNoia and Romanus Cessario (Chicago: Midwest Theological Forum, 1999), pp. 97-127.

and needs to be *brought* to completion.[22] The way we come to know the natural law is partly through reflection on our own actions,[23] and partly (probably mostly) by being taught—by our parents and by the habits and practices of our society.

More specifically, this education takes place, according to Aquinas, in four ways. First, we receive moral instruction from our parents.[24] Second, knowledge about the natural law comes from reflection on morality by the wise, who discover truths that were not known before (94.3, 5 ad3). Third, the natural law articulates itself in the positive law, through specification and through the punishment meted out to wrongdoers (95.1, 2; and cf. 92.2 ad4, 96.2 ad2). Finally, many learn about the natural law primarily from the church and its teaching of those elements of the divine law that contain parts of the natural law (91.4; 99.2; 100.1, 3). Taking all of these things together we can see them as a set of moral indicators about the general state of what we would now call a culture.

Talk about "cultures" may, at first blush, seem a bit odd in a Thomistic natural law context. The idea that culture is an important analytic category is usually associated with romanticism and the historicist attack on the very notion of natural right.[25] Part of the problem is linguistic. To speak of cultures suggests fuzzy and even morally suspect notions like "folk minds" or "blood knowledge," rightly brought into disrepute during the first half of the twentieth century. One need not have truck with such notions, however. Nor need it imply relativism or historicism. One only need acknowledge the obvious, that people living in different times and places have different habitual ways of pursuing the particular goods that make up the human good. A contemporary Thomistic Aristotelian, Alasdair MacIntyre, has discussed this in terms of what he calls "practices."[26] One can also see the term "culture" as a contemporary translation for the classical notion of regime (*politeia*). Leo Strauss defined the notion this way:

> Regime is the order, the form, which gives society its character. Regime is therefore a specific manner of life. Regime is the form of life as living together, the manner of living of society and in society, since this manner depends decisively on the predominance of human beings of a certain type, on the manifest domination of

---

[22] On the relationship between natural law and the human person as constituted by "dispositional properties" that must be realized, see Anthony J. Lisska, *Aquinas's Theory of Natural Law: An Analytic Reconstruction* (Oxford: Oxford University Press, 1996), chapter 4. While I am entirely in sympathy with Lisska's Aristotelian views on this point, it remains less than clear how much of this can be accounted for within the horizon of natural law as such.

[23] See Robert Sokolowski, "Knowing Natural Law," *Tijdschrift Voor Filosofie* 43 (1981), pp. 625-41; and Alasdair MacIntyre, "Plain Persons and Moral Philosophy: Rules, Virtues and Goods," *American Catholic Philosophical Quarterly* 66 (1992), pp. 3-19.

[24] *Summa Theologiae*, 1-2.95.1. Subsequent references to the *Prima secundae* in this section are given parenthetically in the text.

[25] One thinks in particular of Vico and Herder, as well as those who followed them. See the differing accounts in Leo Strauss, *Natural Right and History*, pp. 9-34; Hans-Georg Gadamer, *Truth and Method*, trans. J. Weinsheimer and D.G. Marshall (New York: Crossroad, 1989), pp. 173-264; Isaiah Berlin, *The Crooked Timber of Humanity* (Princeton: Princeton University Press, 1990), pp. 70-90.

[26] Alasdair MacIntyre, *After Virtue*, 2d ed. (Notre Dame, Indiana: University of Notre Dame Press, 1984), pp. 187-203.

society by human beings of a certain type. Regime means that whole, which we are today in the habit of viewing primarily in fragmentized form: regime means simultaneously the form of life of a society, its style of life, its moral taste, form of society, form of state, form of government, spirit of laws.[27]

The concept of regime was a central one in classical political philosophy.

While Aquinas takes for granted much that is in Aristotle's account of politics, his approach is sometimes different—or perhaps more accurately, differently accented.[28] While Aristotle is concerned to distinguish regimes in the service of answering the question "What is the best regime?", Aquinas is concerned to highlight features of all regimes in the service of his larger account of human action, itself part of a larger account of God's providential government of the cosmos. More central to Aquinas's account than regime is the more general concept of the common good (*bonum communae*). As a kind of law, the natural law has as its aim the common good and can itself be defined as the set of minimum necessary requirements for the efficacious pursuit of the common good by rational and political animals.[29]

As a minimum, however, the natural law is not sufficient for the operation of a political community (91.3). Human law is the specification of the general precepts of the natural law appropriate to particular political communities and is the province of legislators, the wise who have in their particular care the common good of the community (95.1 ad2). How are laws to be drawn up and who are the legislators? What claims to wisdom and rule are authoritative? An answer to questions like these points to the regime, which, while not discussed explicitly by Aquinas, must be a necessary component of his account.[30]

Aquinas's view is most clearly suggested by two discussions, one dealing with the distinction between the natural and human laws, the other dealing with the

---

[27] Leo Strauss, *What is Political Philosophy?* (Glencoe, Illinois: The Free Press, 1959), p. 34. Stephen G. Salkever has suggested "culture" as a more contemporary translation of *politeia* in *Finding the Mean: Theory and Practice in Aristotelian Political Philosophy* (Princeton: Princeton University Press, 1990), pp. 81-88.

[28] On some of the characteristic differences between Aristotle and Aquinas see Ernest L. Fortin, "Thomas Aquinas as Political Thinker," *Perspectives on Political Science* 26 (1997), pp. 92-96. With respect to natural law and Aristotle see Harry V. Jaffa, *Thomism and Aristotelianism* (Chicago: The University of Chicago Press, 1952) along with the papers by Goerner and Smith cited above in notes 19 and 21.

[29] This formulation is indebted to Alasdair MacIntyre, "Plain Persons and Moral Philosophy," and *Dependent Rational Animals: Why Human Beings Need the Virtues* (Chicago: Open Court, 1999), p. 111. That the precepts of the natural law, as precepts of law understood more generally, are directed to the common good (though this aspect is often overlooked) is stated in Aquinas's celebrated definition of law as "nothing else than an ordinance of reason for the common good, promulgated by him who has the care of the community" in *Summa theologiae* 1-2.90.4. While the language of "law" is one thing that differentiates Aquinas from Aristotle (a not inconsiderable point that cannot be discussed here), the *substance* of what Aquinas calls the natural law (*lex naturae*) as described above is quite similar to the account of natural right (*phusei dikaion*) given by Aristotle in *Nicomachean Ethics* 5.7. What the two accounts have in common—their suggestion of a natural basis to political life— is more important for my present purposes than their differences.

[30] That it was not an explicit subject of Aquinas's attention is a reminder that he was not concerned with constructing a free-standing account of politics, but rather with the role of law in his theologically contextualized account of the moral life. Had he completed his commentary of Aristotle's *Politics*, he would have had to treat regimes in detail.

notion of custom. The natural law urges on men two particular ends: knowing the truth about God and living in society (94.2). In a certain sense, the former, although more important, depends on the latter, since knowing requires that one achieve the sort of perfection one can only achieve in the society of others. Human beings cannot perfect themselves alone. The most common precepts of the natural law are general, and their specification must take into account a large number of particular circumstances. So one function of the human law is to provide the specification required by the natural law (91.3, 95.2, 97.1 ad1); another is to correct the failures of paternal instruction in the natural law through civil punishment (95.1).

Now given that the human law must specify the general precepts of the natural law in particular places and times, that specification must be appropriately tailored, and this Aquinas discusses in his treatment of custom (*consuetudo*).[31] Custom itself can have the force of law "promulgated in deed" rather than in word (97.3). It is important precisely because the same laws cannot apply to all men (95.2 ad3) given their peculiar circumstances, but should be tailored according to custom (95.3) and the decisions of different communities as communities (95.3). Of course, where judgment is involved the possibility of error exists and laws can be drawn up unjustly (96.4). Similarly the people themselves can become corrupt through bad habits (94.4, 6), though the most general principles cannot be effaced, even in the midst of great corruption (94.6).

The natural law, then, is instantiated in customs and in the human law in varying degrees. What the degree is depends on all four of the ways the natural law is taught, and all of these go into making up part of what is distinct about different cultures. The precepts of the natural law, then, must themselves be understood in a larger context that includes customs and mores and those institutions and practices that make up the classical notion of regime. Moreover, the efficacy of natural law argument is dependent on such contexts. I do not mean to imply anything like moral relativism or historicism, but rather the fact that people's willingness to listen to moral arguments is often crucially influenced by the formation of their opinions and characters and that these things are often a function of the type of society they live in, of the regime. Discussions of the natural law are often incoherent and advocacy of natural law arguments often falls on deaf ears in regimes that have developed on the basis of the rejection of natural right as is often the case in contemporary liberal democracies.

This suggests, albeit in a very general and inadequate way, the framework of an evaluative social science with both interpretive and nomological[32] elements. The great advantage of such a science is in its subtle dialectic between institutions,

---

[31] While *consuetudo* is the word Aquinas uses, the sense of the concept is also indicated in the authority he quotes in 97.3, St. Augustine (*Epistles*, 36.1 [*Patrologia Latina* 33, 136]), who writes of the *mos populi*, the "ways" or "mores" of the people. On the role of custom in Aquinas's understanding of political institutions see Mark C. Murphy, "Consent, Custom and the Common Good in Aquinas's Account of Political Authority," *The Review of Politics* 59 (1997), pp. 323-50.

[32] Understood to include the Aristotelian qualification "characteristically and for the most part," and not to imply the formal nomological-deductive model common in the philosophy of natural science. See Alasdair MacIntyre, *After Virtue*, chapter 8.

culture, and nature, where modern theories usually attempt to reduce human affairs to one of these dimensions. This account also suggests the necessary framework of natural law. I want now to turn to the instantiation of natural law in contemporary Irish political culture with particular reference to constitutional jurisprudence.

## II

The adoption of the Irish Constitution of 1937 (Bunreacht na hÉireann) represented an important moment in the history of Catholicism's relationship with liberalism. For most of the nineteenth century, the Church fought a pitched battle with liberalism, the documentation of which is available in a string of encyclical letters of which Pius IX's *Quanta cura* (1864) is only the most well-known. The pontificate of Leo XIII signaled some softening. In *Immortale Dei* (1885) Leo endorsed elements of liberal democracy including the protection of rights and freedoms rightly ordered, though he repeated earlier criticisms in *Libertas humana* (1888).[33] When Eamon de Valera oversaw the drafting of the 1937 Irish document, he incorporated a good bit of what Leo took to be acceptable as well as some of the social doctrines promulgated in *Rerum novarum* (1891) and Pius XI's *Quadragesimo anno* (1931) and went out of his way to secure the approval of the Holy See.[34] Since the articles dealing with religion did not officially establish the Roman Catholic Church, Pius XI was unwilling to endorse the document, though several years later Pius XII praised the Bunreacht na hÉireann for its foundation in natural law.[35] No constitution save the Austrian constitution of 1934 so thoroughly attempted to incorporate Catholic social and political thought into its provisions.

There are several features of the 1937 Constitution that indicate its debt to Catholic thought. The most straightforward evidence of this is contained in the extraordinary preamble:

> In the name of the Most Holy Trinity, from Whom is all authority and to Whom, as our final end, all actions both of men and States must be referred, We the people of Éire, Humbly acknowledging all our obligations to our Divine Lord, Jesus Christ, Who sustained our fathers through centuries of trial, Gratefully remembering their heroic and unremitting struggle to regain the rightful independence of our Nation, And seeking to promote the common good, with due observance of Prudence, Justice, and Charity, so that the dignity and freedom of the individual may be assured, true social order attained, the unity of our country restored, and concord established with other nations, Do hereby adopt, enact, and give ourselves this Constitution.

---

[33] Peter Steinfels, "The Failed Encounter: The Catholic Church and Liberalism in the Nineteenth Century," in *Catholicism and Liberalism*, pp. 19-44.
[34] See Ronan Fanning, "Mr. de Valera Drafts a Constitution" in *De Valera's Constitution and Ours*, ed. Brian Farrell (Dublin: Gill & Macmillan, 1988), pp. 33-45; Dermot Keogh, "The Irish Constitutional Revolution: An Analysis of the Making of the Constitution" in *The Constitution of Ireland: 1937-1987*, Frank Litton, editor, (Dublin: Institute of Public Administration, 1988), pp. 4-84; and The Earl of Longford and Thomas P. O'Neill, *Eamon de Valera* (Boston: Houghton Mifflin, 1971), pp. 295-96.
[35] "Ireland," weekly bulletin of the Department of External Affairs, No. 421, 13 October 1958, quoted in J. M. Kelly, *Fundamental Rights in the Irish Law and Constitution*, 2nd ed. (New York: Oceana, 1968), p. 64, n. 175.

Numerous other features of the constitution also suggest its decidedly less secular character, though one must acknowledge their "aspirational" qualities: all governmental powers are explicitly said to derive "under God, from the people" (6.1);[36] God is incorporated into the three oaths prescribed for the president, members of the Council of State, and judges (12.8, 31.4, 34.5.1); a 1983 amendment guarantees that the government will protect the right to life of the unborn (40.3.3); the constitution's guarantee of free speech is "subject to public order and morality," with blasphemous and indecent material explicitly denied protection; the family is recognized as the "natural primary and fundamental unit group of society, and as a moral institution possessing inalienable and imprescriptible rights, antecedent and superior to all positive law" (41.1.1); the state is pledged to endeavor "to ensure that mothers shall not be obliged by economic necessity to engage in labour to the neglect of their duties in the home" (41.2.2); the state pledges to "guard with special care the institution of marriage, on which the family is founded, and to protect it against attack" (41.3.1 through 41.3.2 originally contained a prohibition on divorce which was repealed by referendum in 1995.); the state "acknowledges that the primary and natural educator of the child is the family and guarantees to respect the inalienable right and duty of parents to provide, according to their means, for the religious and moral, intellectual, physical, and social education of their children" (42.1); the right to property is said to be a "natural right, antecedent to positive law," and held in virtue of man's "rational being" (43.1.1); the article guaranteeing religious freedom also says that "the state acknowledges that the homage of public worship is due to almighty God," pledging "to hold His Name in reverence, and shall respect and honor religion" (44.1). A non-justiciable provision commits the state to social policies that "promote the welfare of the whole people by securing and protecting as effectively as it may a social order in which justice and charity shall inform all the institutions of the national life," endorsing in principle the living wage, just distribution of resources, and to "safeguard with especial care the economic interests of the weaker sections of the community, and, where necessary, to contribute to the support of the infirm, the widow, the orphan, and the aged" (45). Somewhat more ambiguous is Art. 40.3, by which the state "guarantees in its laws to respect, and, as far as practicable, by its laws to defend and vindicate the personal rights of the citizen." Section 2 goes on to read:

> The state shall, *in particular*, by its laws protect as best it may from unjust attack and, in the case of injustice done, vindicate the life, person, good name, and property rights of every citizen" (emphasis added).

The open-ended "personal rights" in 40.3.1 and the "in particular" in subsection 2 have created a space for the discovery of unenumerated rights, the main area where natural law theory has been deployed by judges.

---

[36] In the next paragraph I cite the English text of the Bunreacht na hÉireann by article, section, and sometimes subsection.

Historians and legal scholars are in agreement that the Bunreacht na hÉireann is grounded in a natural law perspective on political morality.[37] What is more remarkable is that Irish courts have decided cases partly on the basis of claims about the content of natural law.[38] In 1965 the Irish High Court invoked "the Christian and democratic nature of the state" as justification for recognizing an "unspecified personal right" to bodily integrity.[39] Interestingly, the link between the "Christian and democratic nature of the state" and the unspecified personal right to bodily integrity was the High Court justice's appeal to John XXIII's encyclical letter, *Pacem in Terris*.[40] In another case, the issue of the severity of the offense of drunk driving was settled when the same judge took expert testimony from a moral theologian on the severity of drunk driving according to the natural law.[41]

The role of natural law was more explicitly and directly explored nine years later in a case dealing with the sale and importation of contraceptives. In that case the Irish Supreme Court vindicated a married woman's right to access to contraceptives that she claimed were necessary to prevent pregnancy that would pose a serious danger to her due to a heart condition. The court held that the law violated marital privacy and endangered the woman's life under articles 40.3.1 and 42. Justice Brian Walsh's opinion was remarkable first for the very narrow ground on which he invalidated the law in question, going so far as to suggest that in other circumstances the state could validly outlaw contraceptives, but that they just could not do it under these circumstances.[42] More importantly, Walsh used his opinion in the case to reflect, in almost anguished terms, about the role of natural law. First he acknowledged the place of natural law in the constitution, writing:

---

[37] Vincent Grogan, "The Constitution and the Natural Law," *Christus Rex* 8 (1954), pp. 201-18; Declan Costello. "The Natural Law and the Irish Constitution," *Studies* 45 (1956), pp. 403-14; Colum Gavan Duffy, "The Irish Constitution and Current Problems," *Christus Rex* 12 (1958), pp. 99-121; Seamus Henchy, "Precedent in the Irish Supreme Court," *Modern Law Review* 25 (1962), pp. 549-50, 557-58; Michael Bertram Crowe, "Human Rights, the Irish Constitution and the Courts," *Notre Dame Lawyer* 47 (1971), pp. 281-96; F.F.V.R. von Prondzynski, "Natural Law and the Constitution," *Dublin University Law Journal* 1 (1977), pp. 32-37; David Gwynn Morgan, *Constitutional Law of Ireland*, 2d ed. (Dublin: Round Hall Press, 1990), p. 30; Mary Redmond, "Fundamental Rights in the Irish Constitution," *Morality and the Law*, ed. Desmond M. Clarke (Dublin: Mercier/RTE, 1982), pp. 93-102; Enda McDonagh, "Philosophical-Theological Reflections on the Constitution," *The Constitution of Ireland: 1937-1987*, ed. Frank Litton (Dublin: Institute of Public Administration, 1988), pp. 192-205

[38] I have given a fuller account of this jurisprudence in "Natural Law in Irish Constitutional Jurisprudence," *Catholic Social Science Review* 2 (1997), pp. 171-82.

[39] *Ryan v. The Attorney General* [1965] I.R. 294. On this basis a number of other unspecified rights have been admitted, e.g., marital privacy (*McGee v. the Attorney General* [1974] I.R. 284), begetting of children (*Murray v. Ireland* [1985] I.R. 532), privacy in personal communications (*Kennedy v. Ireland* [1987] I.R. 587), earning a livelihood (*Murtagh Properties v. Cleary* [1972] I.R. 330), access to courts (*Macauley v. Minister for Posts and Telegraphs* [1966] I.R. 345), and fair procedures in government decisions (*Garvey v. Ireland* [1980] I.R. 75).

[40] *Ryan v. the Attorney General*, 313-14.

[41] *Conroy v. the Attorney General* [1965] I.R. 411, 419-420. This High Court judgment was sustained in the Supreme Court. The justice who wrote the opinion supported the High Court's view that the severity of the offense was a matter of natural law. Ibid., 78.

[42] *McGee v. the Attorney General* [1974] I.R. 284, , 308-14. Justice Walsh's caution has not been shared by others. The Irish parliament legalized the production and distribution of contraceptives albeit under careful regulation in 1979. Amendments to the law in 1985, 1992, and 1993 have abolished nearly all of the remaining restrictions.

Articles 41, 42 and 43 emphatically reject the theory that there are no rights without laws, no rights contrary to the law and no rights anterior to the law. They indicate that justice is placed above the law and acknowledge that natural rights, or human rights, are not created by law but that the Constitution confirms their existence and gives them protection.[43]

Justice Walsh later went on to reflect on the status of natural law more generally, suggesting some of the difficulties facing a judge in his position:

> The natural or human rights to which I have referred earlier in this judgment are part of what is generally called the natural law. There are many who argue that natural law may be regarded only as an ethical concept and as such is a re-affirmation of the ethical content of law in its ideal of justice. The natural law as a theological concept is the law of God promulgated by reason and is the ultimate governor of all the laws of men. In view of the acknowledgment of Christianity in the preamble and in view of the reference to God on Article 6 of the constitution, it must be accepted that the Constitution intended the natural human rights I have mentioned as being in the latter category rather than simply an acknowledgment of the ethical content of law in its ideal of justice. What exactly natural law is and what precisely it imports is a question which has exercised the minds of theologians for many centuries and on which they are not yet fully agreed. While the Constitution speaks of certain rights as being imprescriptible or inalienable, or being antecedent and superior to all positive law, it does not specify them.[44]

Notice the conundrum pointed to here: there is no denying, Walsh seems to say, the natural law basis of the constitution's protection of fundamental rights, yet there is nothing like a specific set of rights, nor criteria by which a judge might determine how to strike a balance in particular cases. If there were, then the judge would become with respect to the law a kind of casuist. But judges have no such training: they are neither philosophers nor theologians. This might be puzzling enough, but the problem is further complicated by the sociological reality of disagreement about fundamental moral questions:

> In a pluralist society such as ours, the Courts cannot as a matter of constitutional law be asked to choose between the differing views, where they exist, of experts on the interpretation by the different religious denominations of either the nature or extent of these natural rights as they are to be found in the natural law ... In this country it falls finally upon the judges to interpret the Constitution and in doing so to determine, where necessary, the rights which are superior or antecedent to positive law or which are imprescriptible or inalienable.[45]

Judges cannot determine the content of the natural law, Walsh seems to say, nor can they adjudicate disputes between different philosophers or theologians in different religions about the content of the natural law. Yet they must make

---

[43] Ibid., 310.
[44] Ibid., 317-18.
[45] Ibid., 318.

determinations in specific cases as to whether a right in question which is not specified in the constitution should be specified. But how?

Again Justice Walsh:

> In the performance of this difficult duty there are certain guidelines laid down in the Constitution for the judge. The very structure of the Articles dealing with fundamental rights clearly indicates that justice is not subordinate to the law. In particular, the terms of s. 3 of Article 40 expressly subordinate the law to justice. Both Aristotle and the Christian philosophers have regarded justice as the highest human virtue. The virtue of prudence was also esteemed by Aristotle as by the philosophers of the Christian world. But the great additional virtue introduced by Christianity was that of charity—not the charity which consists of giving to the deserving, for that is justice, but the charity which is also called mercy. According to the preamble, the people gave themselves the Constitution to promote the common good with due observance of prudence, justice and charity so that the dignity and freedom of the individual might be assured. The judges must, therefore, as best they can from their training and their experience interpret these rights in accordance with their ideas of prudence, justice, and charity.[46]

The constitutional hermeneutic of charity seems to emerge from the specifically Christian character of the constitution, though we can see that this too is subject to change. One final quote:

> It is natural that from time to time the prevailing ideas of these virtues may be conditioned by the passage of time; no interpretation of the Constitution is intended to be final for all time. It is given in the light of prevailing ideas and concepts.[47]

As evidence for this Walsh pointed to the Ninth Amendment of the U.S. Constitution.[48] While natural law has made appearances in several other Irish cases,[49] we need not examine them here, since Walsh's *McGee* opinion states the issue precisely. The internal conflicts of Walsh's *McGee* opinion become more clear when we turn to the academic debate in Ireland.

As we have seen, natural law was mainly treated as a source of unenumerated constitutional rights, the discovery of which was licensed by Art. 40.1.1 as interpreted in *Ryan's* case. This Article, then, plays a role analogous to that of the

---

[46] Ibid., 318-19.
[47] Ibid., 319.
[48] Justice Walsh later defended his views in several subsequent articles, though never again with the concentrated drama of the *McGee* judgment. See "The Judicial Power and the Protection of the Right to Privacy," *Dublin University Law Journal* 1 (1977), p. 3; "Existence and Meaning of Fundamental Rights in Ireland," *Human Rights Law Journal* 1 (1980), pp. 171-81; "The Constitution and Constitutional Rights" in *The Constitution of Ireland*, Frank Litton, editor, (Dublin: Institute of Public Administration, 1988), pp. 86-109.
[49] I discuss several of them in "Natural Law in Irish Constitutional Jurisprudence." The most important decisions are *Norris v. the Attorney General* [1984] I.R. 36; *The Attorney General (S.P.U.C.) v. Open Door Counselling Ltd.* [1988] I.R. 593; *Article 26 of the Constitution and the Regulation of Infirmation (Services Outside the State for the Termination of Pregnancies) Bill 1995* [1995] 2 I.L.R.M. 81 (This case will be further discussed below).

due process clause of the fourteenth amendment to the U.S. Constitution, and the American debate over constitutional law has loomed over the Irish. As early as 1961, some legal scholars expressed doubts about the natural law language in the Bunreacht na hÉireann. The late J.M. Kelly, considered one of the foremost authorities on the Irish constitution, wondered what the judicial significance of such language could be, suggesting that it amounted to no more than "the precept of loving justice and hating iniquity, of avoiding evil and doing good."[50] Such discussions became even more pointed following the courts' rulings in *Ryan*, *McGee*, and other cases where the natural law provisions were interpreted. Some commentators objected to the philosophical basis of natural law theory, taking particular aim at the equivocity of the term "nature" and the lack of any universally acceptable version of natural law theory.[51] Others have attacked it as providing a ready cloak for illicit judicial activism. The most prominent of this latter group is Gerard Hogan of Trinity College Dublin. Hogan has generally advocated what American legal scholars used to call "strict constructionism," writing that:

> ... if important constitutional decisions are based on what amounts to a subjective interpretation of an amorphous higher law this will ultimately lead to a lack of respect for the judicial process. Judicial decisions will be perceived as resting on personal whim and the pragmatic subjective judgment. This is why the natural law or higher law approach must be viewed with reserve.[52]

Interestingly, Hogan is one of the first Irish scholars to try and bring American constitutional theory to bear on the dilemmas faced by Irish judges. In a detailed critique of the *Ryan* decision, he commends the work of both Robert Bork and John Hart Ely, even going so far as to compare *Ryan* to the U.S. Supreme Court's infamous decision in *Lochner v. New York*.[53] He similarly criticizes Walsh's *McGee*

---

[50] *Fundamental Rights in the Irish Law and Constitution*, 2d ed. (New York: Oceana, 1968; 1st ed. 1961), p. 69. Kelly did not question the idea that natural law could supply a basis for opposing patently unjust legislation, though he did not expect such a thing to happen much (pp. 67, 71) and speculated that a legislature willing to pass really unjust laws would not be stopped by judges (pp. 71, 73). Declan Costello, later president of the High Court, reviewed the first edition of Kelly's book and defended the natural law basis of the constitution's list of rights and argued that it would make the guarantees more effective in practice. See *Studies* 51 (1962), pp. 201-203.

[51] The most consistent such critic has been Desmond M. Clarke, a philosopher at University College Cork. See "Natural Law and Dynamics of the Will," *Philosophical Studies* 27 (1980), pp. 40-54; "Moral Disagreement," in *Morality and Law*, ed. D.M. Clarke (Dublin: Mercier/RTE, 1982), pp. 10-19; "The Role of Natural Law in Irish Constitutional Law," *The Irish Jurist* 17 (1982), pp. 187-220; and "Natural Law and Constitutional Consistency" in *Justice and Legal Theory in Ireland*, ed. G. Quinn, A. Ingram, and S. Livingstone (Dublin: Oak Tree Press, 1995), pp. 22-36. Philosophically, Clarke has attacked natural law as committing the naturalistic fallacy and failing to supply judgments on which most people can agree. From a jurisprudential standpoint he writes: "The promised determinacy and objectivity of natural law is an unintended camouflage for judicial indiscretion, poor judgment, unreasonable or unreasoned decisions and, at least in principle, the subversion of democratically enacted laws in deference to the subjective views of members of the judiciary" ("The Role of Natural Law," p. 219).

[52] "Constitutional Interpretation" in *The Constitution of Ireland: 1937-1987*, ed. Frank Litton (Dublin: Institute of Public Administration, 1988), pp. 173-91, 181. Hogan concluded that "Of all the methods surveyed, the approach that seeks to construe the Constitution from within its corners and upholds only those guarantees protected either expressly or by necessary implication is the one which may best satisfy this test" (p. 188). What complicates matters is, of course, that natural rights *are* expressly referred to in the constitution, a fact discussed more below.

opinion as "practically tantamount to an open invitation to the judiciary to become latter-day philosopher-kings via the guise of constitutional adjudication."[54] Hogan concludes by suggesting that since there is no "precise, objective" standard for evaluating unenumerated rights claims, judges should refrain from accepting them absent support from constitutional provisions other than Art. 40.3, even suggesting that amending the constitution may be the only solution.[55]

Natural law jurisprudence has also had its defenders. Among the most prominent is Richard Humphreys of University College Dublin, whose work specifically criticizes Hogan. Humphreys' central point is that natural rights are mentioned in the text of the Bunreacht na hÉireann, making them a "positivistic fact."[56] Moreover, Humphreys, like Costello, believes that the natural law basis makes the rights provisions stronger than they otherwise would be.[57] Humphreys is critical of the theological aspect given natural law by Justice Walsh arguing that the theory implicit in the constitution must be "effectively a secular one."[58] In interpreting the content of natural rights Humphreys suggests that Irish judges look to international law, particularly to American constitutional law and the jurisprudence of the European Court of Human Rights.[59] Irish legal scholars, then, have argued both for strict constructionism and natural law. One position that has not gained much enthusiasm is the intentionalism favored by many American conservatives.[60]

Up to this point the discussion had largely been academic and was concerned first and foremost with the issue of constitutional hermeneutics and the discovery and protection of unenumerated rights. In late 1992 this would change, and the issue of

---

[53] 198 U.S. 45 (1905). This is the case in which the court invalidated a law intended to protect bakery workers on the basis of *laissez-faire* economic theory.
[54] "Unenumerated Personal Rights: *Ryan's* Case Re-Evaluated," *The Irish Jurist* 25-27 (n.s.) (1990-92), pp. 95-116, 110.
[55] Ibid., pp. 115-16.
[56] "Constitutional Interpretation," *Dublin University Law Journal* 15 (1993): pp. 59-77, 70. See also "Interpreting Natural Rights," *The Irish Jurist* 28-30 (n.s.) (1993-95), pp. 221-30, 222, where Humphreys writes: "One can like it or not, but the existence of God and natural law are given constitutional facts ... what is significant is that the judge who is asked to interpret the Constitution must set his or her skepticism about natural rights aside. ... For the purpose of any practical exercise in constitutional interpretation, natural rights exist because the Constitution says they do." The point has also been made by Declan Costello, "The Irish Judge as Law-Maker" in *Constitutional Adjudication in European Community and National Law: Essays for the Hon. Mr. Justice T.F. O'Higgins*, D. Curtin and D. O'Keeffe, editors, (Dublin: Butterworths, 1992), pp. 159-67: "A judge may be a legal positivist and have no use for natural law concepts, but if the Constitution (as it does) explicitly recognizes the existence of rights anterior to positive law these jurisprudential views must yield to the clear conclusions which are to be drawn from the construction of the constitutional text" (p. 161).
[57] Indeed, he thinks this is the case regardless of whether there is anything like natural law, writing that "if natural rights are a fiction, they are a necessary fiction" ("Interpreting Natural Rights," pp. 224-25).
[58] "Constitutional Interpretation," pp. 69-70, 77. The reason is this: "Indeed to give any legal force to the Constitution's somewhat rhetorical pronouncements on the deity would introduce a note of divisiveness if not indeed provincialism into the debate, a result which is not warranted by the text" (. 69). It seems difficult to argue this given that the first words of the Constitution are "In the Name of the Most Holy Trinity ..."
[59] "Constitutional Interpretation," pp. 72-75; "Interpreting Natural Rights," p. 230. See also Clarke, "The Role of Natural Law," p. 218.
[60] See Hogan, "Constitutional Interpretation," p. 176; Humphreys, "Constitutional Interpretation," pp. 63-64. What Hogan admires in Bork is his attack on judicial activism, not his theory of "original understanding," which he says very little about.

the natural law basis of the constitution would be thrust to the center of public debate. Here parallels to the American experience are obvious, for the issue that reoriented the debate was abortion. Abortion has been prohibited by statute in Ireland since the mid-nineteenth century, and even before the eighth amendment to the constitution was ratified in 1983 Irish judges considered unborn life protected by Art. 40.3.2.[61] The amendment seemed to end the question until a 1992 case, *The Attorney General v. X*,[62] opened up the issue. The case concerned a fourteen-year-old girl raped and pregnant by a family friend. After she said that she would commit suicide rather than carry the pregnancy to term, her parents decided to take her to England for an abortion. An injunction, however, prevented her travel on grounds of the constitutional mandate to protect unborn life. The girl, whose identity was shielded by the initial "X," pleaded that this was a violation of her liberty, and her family stressed her earlier talk of suicide. The Supreme Court agreed, holding that "if it is established as a matter of probability that there is a real and substantial risk to the life, as distinct from the health, of the mother, which can only be avoided by the termination of her pregnancy, such termination is permissible."[63]

While this holding relieved the intense political tension of the *X* case, it left much else in doubt. The courts had earlier ruled that even the dissemination of information about procuring foreign abortions was unconstitutional, and the *X* ruling suggested that in similar cases the right to travel abroad for an unconstitutional abortion had to be allowed. The government's response, after much controversy, was to propose three constitutional amendments for referenda: first, a new wording to the prohibition on abortion specifically allowing for abortion in cases of threats to the life of the mother; second, that the abortion prohibition could not infringe the right to travel outside the state; and third, that it could not preclude the dissemination of information about constitutionally permissible abortions. The first amendment was defeated, while those relating to travel and information were approved. The information provision required enabling legislation, which was approved three years later in 1995. The Regulation of Information (Services Outside the State for Termination of Pregnancies) Act, 1995 was narrowly drawn, and before signing it then President Mary Robinson referred it to the Supreme Court for review under Art. 26 of the Constitution, which allows referrals of legislation in cases where the constitutionality of the law is questioned. If the court approves the law, it can never be challenged on such grounds again.

The court assigned two counsels to argue against the law, one representing the interests of women and one representing the interests of the unborn. The former counsel opposed the law as too restrictive. The latter took the bold strategy of

---

[61] See the dicta in *Ryan v. the Attorney General* [1965] I.R. 294, 314; *McGee v. the Attorney General* [1974] I.R. 284, 312; and *G. v. An Bord Uchtála* [1980] I.R. 32, 69. On the subject of the right to life in Irish constitutional law more generally see Ann Sherlock, "The Right to Life of the Unborn and the Irish Constitution," *The Irish Jurist* 24 (n.s.) (1989), pp. 13-50.
[62] [1992] I.R. 1.
[63] Ibid., 54-55.

arguing that it was invalid in so far as it contravened the natural law in permitting any direct abortions at all. Moreover, he argued that the *X* case itself was wrongly decided for the same reason.⁶⁴ The Supreme Court rejected these arguments explicitly, writing first, that the constitution enshrined the principle of popular sovereignty limited only by the express provisions of the constitution, all of which are subject to amendment,⁶⁵ second, that their understanding of the values in the constitution was conditioned by historical development,⁶⁶ and third, interpreting their own past decisions, that "The Courts, as they were bound to, recognized the Constitution as the fundamental law of the State to which all organs were subject and at no stage recognized the provisions of the natural law as superior to the Constitution."⁶⁷ Thus the justices seemed to end the Irish experiment with natural law jurisprudence.

Reaction to the court's judgment in Ireland was strong on all sides. In the weeks before the court announced its judgment, one strand of public debate identified natural law with the Catholic Church's traditionally strong hold over Irish life and urged the court to reject it for that reason. After the decision was announced, this sentiment was given prominent voice in a lead editorial by the *Irish Times*, the principal voice of elite opinion.⁶⁸ Shortly before the ruling an *Irish Times* columnist wrote what many of the new Irish elite already thought, that natural law is an instrument of ecclesiastical control at variance with liberal democracy.⁶⁹

Between the three referenda and the Supreme Court's *Abortion Information* ruling, another debate broke out among scholars. Judge Roderick O'Hanlon of the High Court (and a former professor at University College Dublin) argued that the referenda were themselves of doubtful constitutional validity since they conflicted with the right to life of the unborn guaranteed by Art. 40.3.3, that is, he argued for a doctrine of what has been called unconstitutional constitutional amendments.⁷⁰ Given the place of natural law in the structure of the Bunreacht na

---

⁶⁴ The lawyer assigned to represent the interests of the unborn, Peter Kelly, lectured the court for three hours, pressing into service discussions of natural law in Aristotle, Cicero, Aquinas, and Martin Luther King, Jr. *The Irish Times*, 5 April 1995, City Edition.
⁶⁵ *In re Art. 26 of the Constitution and the Regulation of Information (Services Outside the State for Termination of Pregnancies) Bill 1995* [1995] 2 I.L.R.M. 81, 102-04.
⁶⁶ Ibid., 104-08.
⁶⁷ Ibid., 107.
⁶⁸ *The Irish Times*, 13 May 1995, page 15. Denis Coghlan, the *Times's* chief political correspondent, in an infelicitous metaphor, wrote that the ruling "cut away the umbilical cord of Catholic control inherent in the concept of natural law" (page 7), concluding that the "closure of the 'natural law' door, with its inherent threat of Catholic control and of a paternalistic/theocratic society, represents the most important step forward" (*ibid.*).
⁶⁹ "... although the idea of the natural law originated with pre-Christian Greeks and was developed by Cicero, the pagan pre-Christian Roman philosopher, it has become essentially a Catholic instrument. The natural law doctrine is the device whereby Catholic teaching is infused into the fundamentals of our basic law in a way that undermines claims to pluralism in this state." Vincent Browne, "Will the country be run under natural law?" *Irish Times*, 26 April 1995, p. 14.
⁷⁰ See Walter F. Murphy, "An Ordering of Constitutional Values," *Southern California Law Review* 53 (1980), pp. 703-60; and "Consent and Constitutional Change" in *Human Rights and Constitutional Change: Essays in Honour of Brian Walsh*, James O'Reilly, editor, (Dublin: Round Hall Press, 1992), pp. 123-46.

hÉireann, O'Hanlon argued that "no law could be enacted, no amendment of the Constitution could lawfully be adopted, and no judicial decision could lawfully be given, which conflicted with the natural law."[71] O'Hanlon's argument was answered by scholars who saw in it primarily antidemocratic sectarianism.[72] For them, the Irish Constitution was primarily a document securing a liberal democratic politics for a dynamic modern society, just emerging from its ecclesiastically dominated childhood.[73] Since this latest controversy, the secularization of Irish public life has accelerated. Open public demonstrations in support of abortion rights, a phenomenon unthinkable as late as the early 1990s, have taken place in Dublin and public discussion of amending the constitution to remove its 'sectarian' language and provisions is common.[74]

### III

While the last word has by no means been spoken in this debate,[75] a few things are clear. There is no question that the constitution was written by men whose basic political attitudes included a kind of natural law theory, that is, the one they learned from either the Jesuits or Christian Brothers in school (most likely in the old and unsatisfactory manual tradition). That theory made sense of the constitution and the political order in such a way that it did not often need to be made explicit. When judges were faced with claims that were made on the basis of individual rights unspecified by the constitutional text, as they were beginning in the mid-1960s and increasingly in the 1970s and 1980s, they naturally turned to what they understood to be the natural law for guidance. That understanding was doubtless vague and abstract, as reflected in the opinions judges produced. Moreover, these rights cases were being decided at precisely the time that the cultural instantiation of the natural law in Ireland began to change.

If one recalls the four ways that natural law is spread throughout society in Aquinas's account as summarized in section I above, one can see in every case that those factors are becoming increasingly attenuated in contemporary Ireland. First, the role of parents in the moral formation of children has become complicated by

---

[71] "Natural Rights and the Irish Constitution," *Irish Law Times and Solicitor's Journal* 11 (January 1993), pp. 8-11, 10.
[72] See Tim Murphy, "Democracy, Natural Law and the Irish Constitution," *Irish Law Times* 11 (April 1993), pp. 81-83; Roderick J. O'Hanlon, "The Judiciary and the Moral Law," *Irish Law Times* 11 (June 1993), pp. 129-32; and Desmond M. Clarke, "The Constitution and Natural Law: A Reply to Mr Justice O'Hanlon," *Irish Law Times* 11 (August 1993), pp. 177-80.
[73] An interesting study could be made of the replacement of England by the Church as the oppressive force from which Ireland must free itself in the rhetoric of Irish nationalism.
[74] In July of 1996 a commission charged with recommending amendments to the constitution released its report. The recommendations, many of which would remove Catholic elements of the document, are discussed at length in Francis X. Beytagh, *Constitutionalism in Contemporary Ireland* (Dublin: Round Hall/ Sweet and Maxwell, 1997), chapter 5.
[75] See, e.g., Gerard Quinn, "Legal Change, Natural Law and the Authority of Courts," *Doctrine and Life* 45 (1995), pp. 97-118 with responses in the same issue; Ruth Cannon, "Matters of Irish Constitutional Debate: Originalism, Democracy and Natural Law," *Irish Student Law Review* 5 (1995), pp. 22-38; Rory O'Connell, "Natural Law: Alive and Kicking? A Look at the Constitutional Morality of Sexual Privacy in Ireland," *Ratio Juris* 9 (1996), pp. 258-82; Adrian F. Twomey, "The Death of Natural Law?" *Irish Law Times* 13 (November 1995), pp. 270-73; and, most interesting of all, G.F. Whyte, "Natural Law and the Constitution," *Irish Law Times* 14 (January 1996), pp. 8-12.

the increasing penetration of Irish life by first the British and more recently the global mass media. This process has been promoted by the integration of Ireland into both the European Union and the global economic order. Second, the increasing democratization of Irish life has decreased the influence of traditional elites (the "wise" in Aquinas's account) and replaced it by the influence of public opinion and media elites. Third, the influence of the law on the formation of public morality has been radically altered, especially with respect to the decriminalization of moral offenses. Finally, the influence of the church as a teacher of the natural law has been attenuated by all of the factors just mentioned (secularization for short) and in an even more concentrated form by the infamous pedophilia scandals which have drastically eroded the Irish Church's moral authority in recent years.

Under the circumstances it is difficult for many to see the judicial use of natural law as anything other than the willful imposition of traditionalist values on a population in the process of throwing off just those values. This, I think, explains Justice Walsh's anguished meditation in the *McGee* case and the surrender of natural law by the Supreme Court in the *Regulation of Information* case. It also seems significant that the public (as distinct from the academic) debate over natural law really began only after abortion opponents appealed to natural law against the X judgment and the referenda and legislation that followed. There was no popular resistance to the idea when it was used exclusively as a means of defending unenumerated personal rights of citizens.

Two hypotheses are suggested on the basis of the preceding account. First, natural law can serve little if any role in constitutional jurisprudence absent important cultural conditions that legitimate such judgments understood in both theological and political (i.e., with reference to the regime) contexts. Detached from such contexts, natural law theory used in jurisprudence tends to undermine the legitimacy of the judiciary and of natural law itself.[76] Second, this has already happened in significant ways in Ireland. Perhaps it is also worth mentioning that according to the latest census upwards of 90 per cent of the population of the Irish Republic is Roman Catholic. The pluralism that Irish intellectuals discuss is not the pluralism of different sects (except when one takes into consideration the still separated north), but the pluralism of Catholicism and secularism. In all of this Ireland has arrived late at the conditions of modernity that characterize the public life of other liberal democracies in North America and Western Europe. The quickness of the change allows one to witness the process as a whole in a striking way.

This does not, of course, mean that the natural law is inoperative or in danger of being completely effaced. This is impossible since the most important precepts of the natural law are the very conditions of political association. Nevertheless, the substantive end towards which the natural law is directed, the common good, is

---

[76] Even Aquinas seems to recommend a limited role for judges in these matters. See Russell Hittinger, "The Natural Law in the Positive Laws: A Legislative or Adjudicative Issue?" *The Review of Politics* 55 (1993), pp. 5-34.

greatly attenuated in contemporary liberal democratic nation states both because of their size and their proceduralist claims.[77] Moreover, the efficacy of moral and political arguments based on natural right and natural law face two other obstacles in modern liberal democracies: first the popular (and political) culture dominated by a mass media that is, to say the very least, uninterested in substantive moral argument and unwilling to recognize as authoritative anything that conflicts with its sense of public opinion as determined by the latest techniques of market research; and second, the authority of modern science in its rejection of any notion of natural teleology.[78] Both of these obstacles point back to the original context of classical natural right and suggest the most important task for those who identify themselves with this tradition. That task is the disciplined recovery of the original premises of natural right as well as those of its early modern opponents, sustained inquiry into the context of natural right with respect to regime and teleology, and the honest application of these researches to our own culture and institutions. The execution of these tasks would entail the construction of a social science that is the modern analogue of Aristotle's philosophy of human affairs, which is to say, the recovery of political philosophy "in its own full dignity."[79]

---

[77] This attenuation has been recognized by a number of critics of liberalism, though understood in different ways. Alasdair MacIntyre has argued that the modern state, as a political form, is inconsistent with the pursuit of the common good in "Politics, Philosophy and the Common Good," in *The MacIntyre Reader*, ed. Kelvin Knight, (Notre Dame, Indiana: University of Notre Dame Press, 1998), pp. 235-52 and *Dependent Rational Animals*, chapter 11. Alternatively, John Finnis has argued for the instrumentality of the "political common good," in "Is Natural Law Theory Compatible with Limited Government?" in *Natural Law, Liberalism, and Morality*, ed. Robert P. George (Oxford: Clarendon Press, 1996), pp. 1-26. Unlike MacIntyre, Finnis holds this instrumentality of the common good not to be a character of the modern nation state as such, but as a fundamental principle of political association, based on his reading of church documents and of Aquinas. See Finnis's *Aquinas: Moral, Political, and Legal Theory*, chapter 7.

[78] There are, of course, versions of natural law theory that claim not to be based on natural teleology, most notably that of John Finnis. The adequacy of that theory is a large and important topic that cannot be treated here. Nevertheless, the least one can say is that (1) the status of the theory as natural law is controversial, and (2) its rhetorical success in public debate does not appear substantially greater than that of the more traditional teleological accounts.

[79] Cf. John Paul II, *Fides et Ratio*, § 6.

# 12

## Denying What We Can't Not Know

### J. Budziszewski

To know the natural moral law is one of the easiest things in the world; to get the theory of it right is one of the hardest. We can get an idea just how hard this is by considering a few remarks of Jacques Maritain, who in my opinion did get it largely right. In the famous chapter on natural rights in *Man and the State*, Maritain observes that people often make the mistake of thinking the natural law is like a *written* law which we can know and survey all at once. But that is not at all how it really is, he explained. In reality, most of it has to be learned. The only thing we all know from the beginning is that good is to be grasped and evil avoided. All the rest of our knowledge comes to us gradually, from inclination and reasoning about the matters presented to us for decision.

For example, a newborn already "knows," not by reflection but by inclination, that there is a big difference between things to be grasped, like Mama's breast, and things to be avoided, like loud noises—but the newborn certainly does not know that murdering a man is among the things to be avoided. He does not even know that killing a man is different than killing an animal. Aquinas, surprisingly, agrees. He would ask: How could the baby know, when he has no conception of the meanings of "man," "animal," "murder," or "killing"? His mind has not yet been stocked with concepts; the raw materials necessary to frame the proposition "Murdering a man is wrong" or "Killing a man is different than killing an animal" are just not available to him. Not in the same way, but in a similar way, thinks Maritain, the human race must pass from lesser knowledge of the natural moral law to greater knowledge of the natural moral law. It will never occur to a person that genocide is wrong until he has heard of genocide; it will never occur to him that it is wrong to mix the human and chimpanzee genomes until he has learned what a genome is.

I began by saying that to know the natural moral law is one of the easiest things in the world, but that to get the theory of it right is one of the hardest. Now the reason Maritain's remarks make such a good illustration of my point is that ironically, his correction of *one* theoretical misunderstanding has itself been widely misunderstood, or perhaps embodies a misunderstanding. He wants to emphasize that the natural moral law is not like a written law—very well, but we take that idea too far. When ordinary people in our culture tell us that questions of right and wrong are terribly difficult, that they cannot find any blacks and whites, that all the world is shades of gray, we are all too ready to take them at their word—we are all too ready to assume that they are just as ignorant as they say they are. If Tom asks the doctor to administer a killing drug to Grandma we assume that Tom really doesn't know that euthanasia is wrong; if Martha takes the life of her unborn daughter we assume that she really doesn't know that abortion is wrong. By contrast with Aquinas, who declared that the general principles of the natural law are the same for all not only as to rectitude but as to knowledge—that is, that they are not only right for all, but also *known* to all—we suppose that although the general principles of the natural law are right for all, they are known to fewer and fewer. The former doctrine, "Right for all and known to all," is the teaching of natural law: both ontologically and epistemologically assertive. The latter doctrine, "Right for all but *not* known to all," is mere moral realism: ontologically assertive, but epistemologically timid.

Maritain's intention was to be not a mere moral realist, but a true natural law theorist like Aquinas. Take the natural law against murder. On the one hand both thinkers taught that if you haven't learned the meaning of "murdering a man," you won't know that murdering a man is wrong; but on the other hand both thinkers taught that if you *have* learned the meaning of "murdering a man," you *can't not* know that murdering a man is wrong. The knowledge of the concepts (for Aquinas) or the asking of the right question (for Maritain) is connatural with the knowledge of the precept. It is in *this* sense that the general principles of the natural moral law are not only right for all, but also known to all. They are known to all who know the concepts which are needed to frame them as propositions—or, in Maritain, who know the questions to which they can be given as answers—and that means, mind you, that they are known to every normal adult.

Reproach me not, my fellow scholars, with those ancient Germans who, according to Julius Caesar, did not know that robbing was wrong. They have become the stock example of mere moral realism. Yes, I know Aquinas mentions them. But in another place he declares that the wrong of taking what belongs to another is one of those general principles that everyone knows. If this is true, it follows that the ancient Germans must have known it too. Is Aquinas contradicting himself? No, he is merely speaking imprecisely. The problem with the Germans was not that they did not know that robbing was wrong. The problem was that they did not recognize that raiding another tribe was robbery. They hadn't connected the dots.

But is it plausible that the general principles of the natural moral law are the same for all not only as to rectitude but also as to knowledge? That would mean people do know much more than they seem to know, much more than they even claim to know. Can it be? Can it be that the hoodlum who seems to lack remorse for blowing away the video rental clerk knows that he did wrong? Can it be that the woman who seems to lack remorse for laying her child in the razor talons of the abortionist knows that she did wrong? Can it be that the abortionist himself, who murders a dozen and then takes his wife to dinner and a show—can it be that even he knows he did wrong?

Yes, it can. The guilt of abortion, for example, is an open secret among practitioners and advocates of the abomination. That is why Naomi Wolf has recently been so roundly criticized by her fellow feminists. Like them, Miss Wolf is pro-abortion. The difference is that she has let the cat out of the bag. For years, she says, feminists have been pretending not to know that the fetus is a baby, but really they do know. For years they have been pretending not to know that abortion is murder, but really they know that too. She forthrightly declares that abortion is real sin that incurs real guilt and requires real atonement, and that she and her comrades have known it all along. The only problem is that Miss Wolf does not carry her reasoning to its conclusion. She wants women to go on aborting, but proposes that they hold candlelight vigils at abortion facilities afterward to show their sorrow.

So they really do know. And if they do, it changes everything. For what I am suggesting is that most of what we call moral ignorance is not ignorance at all, but denial. The problem is not that we don't know right from wrong, but that we rationalize and pretend that we don't.

Neglect of the phenomenon of denial has led to a series of embarrassments for the theory of natural law. The most obvious is that we find it harder to defend the doctrine of natural law than we ought to. Opponents say things like this: "You say there are moral principles which are not only right for all, but known to all. If your theory were true, then I would know them. I don't, therefore your theory is wrong." We take such deniers too seriously. Instead we ought to call their bluff. We ought to reply, "You're lying. Perhaps to yourself, more than to us, but you're lying. You know the wrong of murder, the wrong of rape, the wrong of dishonoring parents as well as we do. You only think you don't." And we ought to show how much better the hypothesis of denial accounts for the data of the inner life than the hypothesis of genuine ignorance does. What kind of data? Well, a denier does not admit to remorse, because he does not admit he has done wrong. But the gorge of suppressed remorse rises in him despite his efforts to hold it down, and this can be observed. Alas for Freud, who knew of the repression of libido but not about the repression of conscience. Some who deny their remorse find it impossible to be serious about anything, because even a moment of gravity might be enough to wake the tormenting harpies. Others suffer suicidal depressions on the anniversaries of their misdeeds—a phenomenon well known to crisis pregnancy counselors. Some even become ethical philosophers and devote all their energies to rationalizing what the rest of the world calls sin. But I suppose we know nothing about that.

A second embarrassment to which the neglect of the phenomenon of denial leads us is that it leaves us unable to make sense of the precise kind of moral confusion the people of our time suffer, or say they suffer. Consider this tissue of contradictions: Most who call abortion wrong call it killing. Most who call it killing say it kills a baby. Most who call it killing a baby decline to prohibit it altogether. Most who decline to prohibit it think it should be restricted. More and more people favor restrictions. Yet greater and greater numbers of people have had or have been involved in abortions. Or consider this one: most adults are worried about teenage sex. Yet rather than telling kids to wait until marriage, most tell kids to wait until they are "older," as we are. Most say that premarital sex between consenting adults is a normal expression of natural desires. Yet hardly any are comfortable telling anyone, especially their own children, how many people they have slept with themselves. Or consider this one: accessories to suicide often write about the act; they produce page after page to show why it is right. Yet a large part of what they write about is guilt. Author George E. Delury, jailed for poisoning and suffocating his wife, says in his written account of the affair that his guilt feelings were so strong they were "almost physical."

Isn't all this confusion fishy? As to the first example, if abortion kills a baby then it ought to be banned to everyone; why allow it? But if it doesn't kill a baby it is hard to see why we should be uneasy about it at all; why restrict it? We restrict what we allow because we know it is wrong but don't want to give it up; we feed our hearts scraps in hopes of hushing them, as cooks quiet their kitchen puppies. As to the second example, sexual promiscuity has exactly the same bad consequences among adults as it has among teenagers. But if it is just an innocent pleasure, then why not talk it up? Swinging is no longer a novelty; the sexual revolution is now gray with age. If shame persists, the only possible explanation is that guilt persists as well. And the third example speaks for itself. Delury calls the very strength of his feelings a proof that they did not express "moral" guilt, merely the "dissonance" resulting from violation of an instinctual block inherited from our primate ancestors. We might paraphrase his theory, "the stronger the guilt, the less it matters."

A third embarrassment to which neglect of the phenomenon of denial has led is an inability to explain the sheer dynamism of wickedness—for the fact that we aren't gently wafted into the abyss but violently propel ourselves into it. Sometimes people think that suppressed moral knowledge is the same as *weakened* moral knowledge with weakened power over behavior. On the contrary, pressing down one's conscience doesn't make it weak any more than pressing down a wildcat makes it docile. It only makes it violent. One woman I know about had an abortion to punish her husband for unfaithfulness. By the time she became pregnant again she was finished punishing him, yet she aborted a second time. Her reason? "I wanted to be able to hate myself more for what I did to the first baby." Outraged conscience revenged itself by driving her to repeat the sin. You see? The suppression of moral knowledge we cannot help but have doesn't just weaken our resistance to doing wrong; it hurls us into wrong. When the conscience of an individual or a society becomes corrupted, the result is less like the erosion of an earthen dike so that it fails to hold the water back, than like the compression of a powerful spring so that it buckles savagely to the side.

By the way, this power of suppressed conscience to revenge itself is one of the reasons that when a culture turns aside from the narrow path it so swiftly gets worse and worse. The reason it plummets so quickly lies not in the weakness of conscience but in its strength, not in its shapelessness but in its shape. I spoke a moment ago of propelling ourselves into the abyss. The propulsive force is even greater in a culture like our own, for people here have more to hold down than in some places. After all, our country once had a Christian culture. Consequently, the people of our generation must hold down not only the present knowledge of natural law, but the troubling memory of special revelation. The more there is to suppress, the more monumental the energies that must be expended to hold it down, and the more violent and disruptive the side effects.

Allow me to consider these side effects. Guilt is different from guilty feelings. The knowledge of guilt always produces certain objective needs, which demand satisfaction irrespective of the state of the feelings. These needs include confession, atonement, reconciliation, and justification. Now when guilt is acknowledged, the guilty deed can be repented so that these four needs can be genuinely satisfied. But when the guilty knowledge is suppressed, they can only be displaced. That is what generates the impulse to further wrong. Taking the four needs one by one, let's see how this happens.

*The need to confess arises from transgression against what we know, at some level, to be truth.* I have already commented on the tendency of accessories to suicide to write about their acts. Besides George Delury, who killed his wife, we may mention Timothy E. Quill, who prescribed lethal pills for his patient, and Andrew Solomon, who participated in the death of his mother. Solomon, for instance, writes in *The New Yorker* that "the act of speaking or writing about your involvement is, inevitably, a plea for absolution." Many readers will remember the full-page signature advertisements feminists took out in the early days of the abortion movement, telling the world that they had killed their own unborn children. At first it seems baffling that the sacrament of confession can be inverted to serve the ends of advocacy. Only by recognizing the power of suppressed conscience can this paradox be understood.

*The need to atone arises from the knowledge of a debt that must somehow be paid.* One would think such knowledge would always lead directly to repentance, but the counselors whom I have interviewed tell a different story. This is where the story fits that I told a few minutes ago—the story of the woman who aborted a second time so that she could hate herself more for aborting the first time. It was the effort to atone without repenting that drove her to do it again.

*The need for reconciliation arises from the fact that guilt cuts us off from God and man.* Without repentance, intimacy must be simulated precisely by sharing with others in the guilty act. Andrew Solomon says that he, his brothers, and his father are united by the "weird legacy" of their implication in his mother's death, and quotes a nurse who participated in her own mother's death as telling him, "I know some people will have trouble with my saying this but it was the most intimate time I've ever had with anyone." And no wonder. Violation of a basic human bond is so terrible that the burdened conscience must instantly establish an abnormal one to compensate; the very gravity of the transgression invests the new bond with a sense of profound significance. Naturally some will find it attractive. The reconciliation need has a public dimension, too. Isolated from the community of moral judgment, transgressors strive to gather a substitute around themselves. They don't sin privately; they recruit. The more ambitious among them go further. Refusing to go to the mountain, they require the mountain to come to them: society must be transformed so that it no longer stands in awful judgment. So it is that they change the laws, infiltrate the schools, and create intrusive social-welfare bureaucracies.

*Finally we come to the need for justification, which requires more detailed attention.* Unhooked from justice, justification becomes rationalization, which is a more dangerous game than it seems. The problem is that the ordinances written on the heart all hang together. They depend on each other in such a way that we cannot suppress one except by rearranging all the others. Think, for example, what is necessary to rationalize abortion. Because we can't not know that it is wrong to deliberately kill human beings, there are only four options. We must deny that the act is deliberate, deny that it kills, deny that its victims are human, or deny that wrong must not be done. The last option is literally nonsense. That something must not be done is what it means for it to be wrong; to deny that wrong may not be done is merely to say "wrong is not wrong," or "what must not be done may be done." The first option is hardly promising either. Abortion does not just happen; it must be performed. Its proponents not only admit there is a "choice," they boast of it. As to the second option, if it was ever promising, it is no longer. Millions of women have viewed sonograms of their babies kicking, sucking their thumbs, and turning somersaults; whatever these little ones are, they are busily alive. Even most feminists have given up calling the baby a "blood clot" or describing abortion as the "extraction of menses."

The only option even barely left is number three: to deny the humanity of the victims. It is at this point that the machinery slips out of control. For the only way to make option three work is to ignore biological nature, which tells us that from conception onward the child is as human as you or me (does anyone imagine that a dog is growing in there?)—and invent another criterion of humanity, one that makes it a matter of degree. Some of us must turn out more human, others less. This is a dicey business even for abortionists. It hardly needs to be said that no one has been able to come up with a criterion that makes babies in the womb less human but leaves everyone else as he was; the teeth of the moral gears are too finely set for that. The less fully human must yield to the interests of the more fully human; all that remains is to sort us all out.

Do we protest that the progression is too extreme? That people are not that logical? Ah, but they are; they are only logical slowly. The implication which they do not grasp today they may grasp in thirty years; if they do not grasp it even then, their children will grasp it. It is happening already. Look around.

So conscience has its revenge. We can't not know the preciousness of human life—therefore, if we tell ourselves that humanity is a matter of degree, we can't help holding those who are more human more precious than those who are less. The urge to rationalize abortion drives us inexorably to a system of moral castes more pitiless than anything the East has devised. Of course we can fiddle with the grading criteria: consciousness, self-awareness, and contribution to society have been proposed; racial purity has been tried. No such tinkering avails to change the character of our deeds. If we will a caste system, then we shall have one; if we will that some shall have their way, then in time there shall be a nobility of Those Who Have Their Way. All that our fiddling with the criteria achieves is a rearrangement of the castes.

Now what does all this imply for those of us whose vocation is to search for wisdom about these matters and teach it to others? What it implies, I think, is that most of our efforts at moral persuasion proceed backwards. If it is really true that the problem of human wrongdoing is more volitional than cognitive—if it is really true that it has more to do with the state of our will than with the state of our knowledge—if it is really true that most defenses of moral evil reflect self-deception rather than real intellectual difficulties—then our main task is not to teach people things they really don't know, but to remove the mask from their self-deceptions and bring to the surface what they know already.

We know that the mask can be stripped in private conversation. A young man proclaimed to a colleague that morality is relative, that we don't even know that murder is really wrong. My colleague asked him "Are you at this moment in any real doubt about murder being wrong for everyone?" After a long uncomfortable silence the young man simply admitted that he wasn't.

And we know that the mask can be stripped in the classroom. A student confessed to me one day that my lecture about Aristotle had frightened him, and I saw that he was trembling. All the old pagan's talk about virtue had made him realize, he said, that he had not led a virtuous life.

The task before us is to find out how to strip the mask, not just in private conversation and in the classroom, but in the academy and in the public square. In a decadent age, this seems to be our vocation. We are called to a political science that assumes the moral law which no one else avouches and asks the questions which everyone thinks but no one speaks. We are called to a public moral apologetics that connects the dots of our nation's moral consciousness and reminds people, absurdly, of what they know already. We are called to a civic rhetoric that dissipates smokescreens and disperses self-deceptions.

There is no such political science, public apologetics, or civic rhetoric today. We are a stunted generation, and the task of founding them is too high for us. Nevertheless, if we neglect it the next generation will be even shorter. So let us try.

# 13

## Different Music – the Same Keyboard: Obscene Art/Pornography and the First Amendment Debate

*John G. Trapani, Jr.*

"... *different music is played on this same keyboard, either in harmony or in discord with human dignity."*

### Introduction

The tension between pornography and offensive works of art, on the one hand, and freedom of expression and the right of public access to another's ideas, on the other hand, frame much of the First Amendment debate. From Serrano's "Piss-Christ" to Gangsta Rap lyrics; from Mapplethorpe's homo-erotic photography to Scorsese's film "The Last Temptation of Christ;" from Larry Flint's *Hustler* magazine to the internet porn industry, the questions loom large: "where should a society draw the line concerning pornography and obscene art without violating the First Amendment rights of free expression and of public access to it?" And "is the aesthetic and moral offense that might arise from one's encounter with pornography or certain pieces of art or art forms (themselves regarded as value-neutral) merely a matter of the variables of personal taste, where the risk of offense is simply the price we pay for preserving the fundamental right of free expression in a democratic society?"

In his book, *The Time of Our Lives*,[1] Mortimer Adler offers an important distinction that can provide a valuable insight in this discussion. There are, he says, essentially three levels of practical reasoning in the ethical order: the level of universal principles, the level of general rules, and the level of concrete decisions. Adler's claim is that whatever measure of certitude there is to be found in ethics occurs on the level of universal principles. General rules have less certainty since their assertions are only generally, not universally, applied. In decisions made in the concrete or existential order, there is often little certitude to be found: the best that one can hope for in a specific case is that a decision be a principled one, i.e., based upon reasoning derived from universal principles and supported by virtue.

---

[1] Mortimer J. Adler, *The Time of Our Lives* (New York: Fordham University Press, 1996), pp. 188-200.

This paper will begin by exploring the basic categories involved in the First Amendment debate, namely: a) the virtue of art and the variability of taste, and b) human nature and the foundations of human rights and human society; it will conclude by reflecting on the three levels of ethical reasoning and by asking whether they can be successfully applied to aesthetic judgments and the issue of free speech. Or, to say the same thing in another way by borrowing a metaphor from Jacques Maritain, we will ask whether the one keyboard of universal principles can be legitimately used to play the different music of specific cases … as long as they remain in harmony with human dignity.

### The Virtue of Art and the Variability of Taste

The uses of the English word "art" obscure a subtle distinction that was known to the Ancients. In Book VI of his *Nichomachean Ethics*, Aristotle identifies five intellectual virtues, dividing them into two groups: three are grouped in the speculative order and two in the practical order. The two practical virtues are differentiated by two distinguishable spheres of action, the one called *praxis* or *agibilia* ("doing"), the other *poiesis* or *factibilia* ("making"). These two spheres of action are themselves usually identified in English as "ethics" and "art." The intellectual virtue proper to each of these is rendered, respectively, *phronesis* (practical wisdom or prudence) in ethics, and *techne* (art or skill) in art. Thus, the term "art" is used in two related but subtly distinguishable ways: art as a work-producing activity, and art as a virtue or perfectible skill of this human activity. The possible confusion that can result when these two uses are not clearly distinguished becomes apparent when expressed in this analogy: prudence is to ethics as art is to art.

The value of this distinction is that it helps us to differentiate between the way a child might build a tree house (a making activity), as opposed to the way a skilled carpenter might do it (craftsmanship); they both engage in a work-producing activity while only the carpenter has the art of carpentry, the skill which seeks the good of the object made. When applied to the fine arts, we can observe the difference between one piece of music composition that is poorly executed and a second composition that is crafted with consummate skill. In this way we can distinguish, in principle, good art from bad art: both compositions are forms or pieces of art as products of a work-making activity, but the one is the result of a degree of competence or skill which the other does not possess. Although this distinction is perhaps more easily discernible in carpentry than in music, it is a valid distinction nonetheless.

Reflection upon Jacques Maritain's signature use of the term "Poetry" as a form of intuition that is a gift which the creative, fine artist either does or does not have (and which passes from the artist to the work of art itself when the artist does have it) takes us further and helps to solidify the idea that a good work of art has an additional intrinsic quality (beyond the three traditional objective criteria of beauty: integrity, proportion, and radiance) which other works do not possess. By noting that all of these qualities *reside in the work of art itself*, we can understand something about the foundation for both the objective evaluation of works of art, on the one hand, and the subjective variability of individual taste on the other. Thus, while it may be true that "*degustibus non est disputantum*" (taste is not disputable), it is also true that not all works of art are created equal — some indeed are better and more praiseworthy than others. In this way too, we can understand that the expression "beauty is in the eyes of the beholder" may be true in the limited sense of referring to individual, subjective taste (equivalent to saying that "I like what I like"), but certainly not true concerning the universal, objective criteria or principles involved in the critical evaluations about good art. The fact that there can be debate about the specifics of these criteria or principles should not lead us to the illogical conclusion that they therefore do not exist.

Moreover, in the concrete or existential order of judgments about specific works of art, truth and certainty are often as equally elusive and difficult to discern as judgments concerning concrete actions in the ethical order. And yet, as noted earlier, Mortimer Adler makes clear that this is precisely the best that can be hoped for. In saying this however, we should not be faint-hearted; to lack the precision of empirical verification on the level of concrete judgments in either the aesthetic or ethical orders does not mean that we have gained no truth or insight at all. Rather, we have gained the measure of wisdom that the subject matter allows; Aristotle himself observed long ago that we ought not expect greater certainty than a particular subject matter permits.[2]

From the above discussion, the following conclusions emerge:

1) that objective criteria for the evaluation of good art do exist, even if the articulation of those criteria is incomplete, imprecise, and evolving;

2) that these criteria may be both disputable in themselves and disputable on the existential level concerning their application to specific works of art;

3) that this fact of disputability and possible controversy should *not* lead anyone to the erroneous conclusion that the objective criteria of good art or a good work of art therefore do not exist;[3]

4) that the evaluation of these criteria involves expertise and knowledge commensurate with and proportioned to the particular art-medium and to the exercise of the intellectual virtue itself (i.e., just as the prudent person is the one qualified to make good moral judgment, so the artful or skillful person is the one who is more qualified to make sound judgments of artistic excellence);

5) that, as a result, judgments about good art are not simply a matter of the subjective determinants of personal taste, popular appeal, economic value, or political correctness;

---

[2] Aristotle, *Nicomachean Ethics*, Bk. I,3, trans. W. D. Ross, "Our discussion will be adequate if it has as much clearness as the subject-matter admits of, for precision is not to be sought for alike in all discussions, any more than in all the products of the crafts."

[3] Mortimer J. Adler makes the identical point concerning the moral order and the difficulty of relating universal principles to concrete decision-making; cf. his *Intellect* (New York: Macmillan, 1990), p. 160.

6) that, however much these influencing factors of personal taste may operate in the concrete social order, they are nonetheless extraneous to the objective quality of the work itself—fashions, trends, movements, and the appeals of popular taste may come and go, but the work of art, like the farmer-in-the-dell's cheese, "stands alone;"

7) that, as a result of the above considerations, the attraction and appeal of certain so-called pieces of art may be due to factors that have nothing to do with their artistic merit — from sensual or erotic attraction to shock value and a perverse delight in the scandalous, the reasons for their appeal may be legion but, considered in themselves, those things have nothing to do with true aesthetic merit or value; and

8) that, finally, judgments about artistic quality or merit should not be confused with judgments about freedom of expression. The former concerns judgments about the objective qualities that reside in a work of art and which are a result of the artist's virtue (bad art is still art, it's just poorly executed or has nothing to say), while the latter concerns the conflict that arises between the rights of the individual (for "free" self-expression) and the rights of a good society to protect itself from harm or detriment.

The discussion of this last point can be clarified by an example. It is one thing to render a negative judgment concerning the artistic merits of Serrano's "Piss-Christ," and it is quite another thing to assess and evaluate its social/cultural impact vis-a-vis the First Amendment. These are two distinct questions and they should be dealt with separately. Concerning judgments about aesthetic merit, we must remember to distinguish "an art work" from "a *good* work of art." Moreover, our judgments must be freed from the unassailable sanctimony of "artistic freedom" or "poetic license," which concludes that *all* art is automatically the result of superior, noteworthy human achievement. The truth to the contrary, however, is that when we dress up vulgarity as "serious art," we elevate it to a status that it does not deserve all the while that we insulate it from legitimate criticism. It is a myopia created by the aesthetic equivalent of the classic fable of the "King's New Clothes." The outcome is that, while pornography has been lawfully limited when a social community argues against the harm and offense that it creates within the community itself, crude vulgarity masquerading as art is euphemistically disguised and thus inoculated against the possibility of deserved criticism. And yet, the reality of the work is and remains what it is … or, as farmers here in the Mid-West are known to say: "you can call it 'organic fertilizer,' … but it's still manure!"

Beyond these insights, however, the second question still remains: what is the social impact of pornography and obscene or offensive art on society? Do artists have any moral or social responsibilities to society, or is their "artistic license" a free pass for them to do with impunity whatever it is they wish? Furthermore, does a society have any moral or social responsibility to protect its citizens by imposing restrictions on either artists or their work, and if so, do these restrictions then become violations of the artists' right of free speech? To answer these questions, we must reflect upon the basic principles of human nature, and the foundations of human rights and human society.

## Human Nature, And the Foundations of Human Rights and Human Society

The artist or pornographer is first and foremost a human person, situated essentially and existentially within all of the categories that define the members of the human family. Existentially, Maritain rightly observes that the person is not only a member of a social community or nation, he or she is also a member of a political society or body politic which is a work of human intelligence and design.[4] As such, just as an individual aims at an ultimate end (viz., a good life) so too the state must aim at some end. In *Man and the State*, Maritain asks: "What is the final aim and most essential task of the body politic or political society?" Not "... the material convenience of scattered individuals, each absorbed in his own well-being and in enriching himself." Rather, the aim of society ought to be the betterment of "... the conditions of human life itself, or to procure the common good of the multitude."[5] But what exactly is the common good, and how are human rights determined? The answer to this question is important for society since, without a secure, factually objective answer to it, any hope of grounding society upon true, universal social principles is lost.

The answer to this question is found in our common, shared human nature. Natural desires or needs are fulfilled by real goods; since these natural desires are the same for everyone, what is really good for one person is thus really good for everyone. In this way, real goods are common goods, and common goods are what everyone has a right to, i.e., they are universal human rights.[6]

The notion, "human nature," should not be understood as some simplistic, static, fixed and predetermined pattern. Rather, "human nature is constituted by all the potentialities that are the species-specific properties common to all members of the human species."[7] This definition, while allowing for our nurtural differences, also takes into account the depths of human mystery which result in the difficulty of establishing any complete or definitive listing of these common, shared human goods or rights. Our understanding of the dynamics of human nature is highly complex, often obscure, and continually expanding and revising as all of the relevant sciences contribute new knowledge. The acknowledgment of these epistemological limitations, however, should not lead us to the error of concluding that there is no such thing as a common human nature and universal, inalienable human rights.

---

[4] Jacques Maritain, *Man and the State* (Chicago: The University of Chicago Press, 1951), pp. 2-3.
[5] Ibid., p. 54.
[6] Cf. Mortimer J. Adler, *Aristotle For Everybody: Difficult Thought Made Easy* (New York: Bantam Books, 1978), pp. 78-85.
[7] Mortimer J. Adler, "Human Nature," *Ten Philosophical Mistakes* (New York: Macmillan, 1985), p. 161.

In *Man and the State*, Maritain asserts that, despite the advantages and disadvantages of individual and cultural pluralism, democracy is the only form of governance that can safeguard these human rights. Moreover, as a Christian philosopher, he recognizes that human nature is a sinful nature, fallen yet redeemed, and as such, since the end of the state is the realization of the common human good, achieved by attaining a "civilized life ... which is ensured by ... political rights, civil virtues, and the cultivation of the mind," we can then see that it "cannot conceivably succeed ... without the impact of Christianity on the political life of [humankind] and the penetration of the Gospel inspiration in the substance of the body politic."[8] In this regard, there are two Maritains, so to speak: the political theory of "Maritain the Christian Philosopher" affirms the highest principles concerning our human spiritual nature and the ideal of human society whose end is the same in the political realm as the ideal of human nature is in the moral or ethical realm: namely, human goodness and perfection. On the other hand, "Maritain the Political Realist" also recognizes "that the flesh is weak" and that it "would be nonsense to require perfection and impeccability from anyone who seeks justice."[9] This is certainly true in a non-Christian pluralist society as we observe it in America today.

It is in this context that Maritain identifies the intersection of what he calls the two "ultimate ends" of human life, the one temporal, the other eternal.[10] The first occurs in the social order and concerns the terrestrial common good, while the second occurs in the metaphysical order and concerns the transcendent common good. Wisely, Maritain shows that individual ethics ought to take account of the former while aiming at the latter; political ethics, on the other hand, ought to take account of the latter while aiming at the former. All of these distinctions will be valuable when reflecting on the problems found in a pluralist society, particularly the First Amendment debate.

## Conclusion: Different Music ... the Same Keyboard

The problems of pornography and obscene or offensive art, though related, are really quite distinct. First, the problem of pornography or smut involves the examination of our human sexual nature. Our ethical principles concerning human sexuality are rooted in our understanding of human nature and natural law, which themselves are subject to revision due to our ever-increasing knowledge. It is now generally agreed, for example, that sexual relations are not for the purpose of propagation alone; conjugal intimacy is also a symbol and expression of love as well as a means to solidify and intensify the very union that is its origin. But what of erotica, where some may find the "naughty" and the "dirty" to be arousing and pleasurable, while others may not? What part do the erotic energies of the libido play

---

[8] *Man and the State*, pp. 54-55.
[9] Ibid., p. 61.
[10] Cf., p. 62.

in human nature? Are they always simply the same as inordinate, immoral lust, even when considered inside of a marriage relationship where there might be the mutual consent of, and enjoyment by, both partners? What part of our individual responses to sexuality is the result of nurture rather than nature? Does erotica always and necessarily conflict with the call to the fulfillment of our higher spiritual nature?

The answers to these questions are neither simple nor clear; differing opinions abound, even within Christian circles. Although there is general agreement among both academics and ordinary citizens that deceptive, dishonest or non-consensual sex or erotica, or that which harms or coerces another against his or her will, is morally unacceptable, the same condemnation cannot be unilaterally directed against honest, consensual, non-coercive sexual activity (including erotica) between married couples or among single, emotionally healthy, mutually consenting adults.[11] Thus the question concerning pornography or erotica and the First Amendment finds its difficult resolution about specific cases wrapped up in both theoretical and practical judgments: theoretical judgments about our human sexual nature and nurture, and an individual's rights of free expression and access; and practical judgments which concern a society's right to restrict or prohibit expression of or access to certain things in order to protect its members from the unacceptable harm or detriment caused by some against others in that community (either as participants, consumers, or citizens).

The problem of offensive or obscene art is similar but different. First, the art work may be sexually offensive or not. The reason or source of the offense, objectionable to some but not to others, is, however surprising this may seem, irrelevant. In the end, in all cases that concern artistic merit, each work must be judged for its own intrinsic aesthetic value, as discussed earlier. Thus, on the one hand, qualitatively good art may be scandalous to some (nudity in painting, for example), while, on the other hand, simply calling something "art" does not automatically make it qualitatively good nor require that it be taken seriously. The skunk by any other name still smells as bad.

Moreover, it is one thing to have difficulty in making judgments about the acceptability or unacceptability of either pornography or offensive art vis-a-vis the sensibilities of individual taste and the demands of moral principles; but it is another thing to consider those difficulties that concern pornography/offensive art and the rights and common goods of a society as a whole. Together, these issues comprise the intersection of two conflicting but equally legitimate human rights—the right of individuals to freely express themselves and consume what they wish versus the right of a society to protect itself and its constituents from harm.

Maritain's discussion of natural law offers some insight to this problem. On the one hand, he tells us that we should not expect that positive law (the body of customary or statue law which is in force in a given social group) will ever perfectly

---

[11] For an argument justifying the latter, see *The Times of Our Lives*, pp. 325-28.

mirror natural law. There are too many variables in any pluralist, democratic society, and natural law still leaves the specific details of positive law undetermined. On the other hand, it is through the work of human reason that the specific determinations of positive law are worked out, and ideally, they should be related to, and an extension of, natural law in much the same way that the general rules of ethics are related to, and derived from, universal principles. However, just as the general rules have less certitude than the universal principles, so too is positive law related to the natural law. Thus it is easier for a pluralist culture to see the value and importance of preserving universal human freedoms, including the freedom of expression, than it is for these same people of good will to agree on the specific application of these universal human rights in positive laws. The successes or failures of human reason result in a variety of laws down through history, with truth, as the correction of history's imperfection, emerging slowly and gradually.[12]

Maritain acknowledges this difficulty. Some human rights, he says, are absolutely inalienable, while others, like free speech, are "inalienable only substantially." That is to say that, in the existential order (what Maritain calls the order of exercise) many of these inalienable rights may be "liable to limitation." In every case, however, whatever limitations are prescribed, they must be assessed by reflecting upon the relation between the positive law itself, on the one hand, and the human rights and common good affirmed by the natural law, on the other. It is in this way that Maritain distinguishes between the possession of a right and its exercise. The former may be inalienable, but the latter is not. This distinction is one that Maritain considers to be "of serious importance," since it "enables us to explain the limitations that can be justly imposed upon the assertion of certain rights under certain circumstances...."[13]

Taken at face value, it would appear that this last distinction *should* be successfully employed in restricting the social and moral harm and offense created by pornography and obscene or offensive art. Two problems, however, stand in the way of such a victory. The first is that we are reminded again of the evolution of our understanding of human nature and human desire. The "what," the "how," and the "how often" of human sexuality, both individually and culturally, defy clear answers. This imprecision inhibits a pluralist society's ability to adjudicate or legislate restrictions. In response, some may argue that this difficulty is but a case of our inability to distinguish between rights and limitations that are "clear in themselves" versus those that may or may not be "clear to us." This difficulty should not be taken lightly; indeed, Maritain writes: "... in natural law there is immutability as regards ... the law itself ... but progress and relativity as regards human awareness of it."[14] It is in the concrete application of the various human rights to specific cases of law, not a disagreement over the rights themselves, that we find the source of so much confusion and conflict in our culture today. Thus

---

[12] Cf. *Man and the State*, p. 99.
[13] Ibid.
[14] Ibid., p. 103.

our second problem: our tendency to absolutize certain rights at one time in history may blind us from seeing other rights which might "counterbalance" or otherwise conflict with them at another time. In a pluralist society, this type of conflict is as unavoidable as it is inherent in the nature of democracy.

Moreover, we cannot place too much stress, Maritain says, on the fact that these human rights are not the privilege of any particular school of thought. It is only normal that, in the unfolding of human history, as new awareness emerges, rights will conflict. "What creates irreducible differences and antagonisms among [humankind] is ... the determination of the *scale of values* that governs the exercise ... of these rights. Here we are confronted with the clash between incompatible political philosophies."[15] Among all persons of good will, living peaceably within the same society, their individual judgments about individual cases are filtered through the lens of their differing value systems and political philosophies. "It is by virtue of the hierarchy of values to which we thus subscribe," Maritain writes, "that we determine the way in which [human rights], economic and social as well as individual, should, in our eyes, pass into the realm of existence."[16] Maritain identifies three prototypes of these competing political philosophies: 1) there are those who are the "advocates of a liberal-individualistic type of society," and who emphasize personal goods and individual liberty over the common goods of society; 2) there are those who are the "advocates of a communistic type of society," and who emphasize the common goods of a collective society over those of the individual; and 3) there are those who are the "advocates of a personalist type of society," and who emphasize that the common goods of humanity should be used at the service of the moral and spiritual goods of individuals and the community, and vice versa.[17]

Maritain declares himself to be unequivocally in favor of the third of these political philosophies, recognizing as he does that we ought to be aiming at the things of heaven while attending to the things on earth. Our own society, by contrast, seems to be clearly of the first type, as romanticized by the image of the western cowboy, and defiantly expressed in the lyrics to the song "My Way," which Frank Sinatra so proudly professed as our "true" National Anthem.

What becomes clear from this whole discussion is that the ethical, aesthetic, and social/legal conundrum created by the debate about pornography, obscene art, and the First Amendment is a direct result of both 1) the liberal, consumer-oriented value system which drives our American culture and is in many respects at odds with human goodness and dignity; and 2) our inability to understand adequately the relation between the objective certitude of universal principles, and the relative lack of it in judging concrete or specific cases, whether it be in morality or, as we have explored them in this paper, in works of art, erotica, human rights,

---

[15] Ibid., p. 106 [emphasis added].
[16] Ibid., pp. 106-107.
[17] Cf., p. 107.

and civil law. With the first, we are challenged: challenged to rededicate ourselves to the work of ensuring that the laws of our society are in accord with a true understanding of our human, spiritual nature from which we discern our natural human needs, our common real goods, our inalienable human rights, and our true human dignity. With the second, we perhaps desire more clarity and certitude than we should; unfortunately, most people desire the simplicity of black-and-white answers and are not comfortable with the ambiguity that results from and is required by subtle philosophical distinctions which demand that we exercise our thinking differently when understanding universal principles as opposed to applying those principles clearly in concrete cases.

It is in the application of these universal principles to the contingencies and uncertainties of individual cases that is something like what Maritain has in mind when, to return to our modified adaptation of Maritain's metaphor quoted at the beginning of this paper, he writes that we are "... dealing with the tonality, the specific key, by virtue of which different music is played on this same keyboard, *either in harmony or in discord with human dignity.*"[18] It is this final caveat concerning human dignity, and by extension, human sanctity, that is the secret to both the understanding of Maritain's thought and the resolution of the First Amendment debate.

---

[18] Ibid. [emphasis added].

# IV

# Maritain and the Church in the Modern World

# 14

## The Cooperation of Church and State: Maritain's Argument from the Unity of the Person

*John P. Hittinger*

*The root requirement for a sound mutual cooperation between Church and the body politic is not the unity of a religio-political body, as the respublica Christiana of the Middle Ages was, but the very unity of the human person, simultaneously a member of the body politic and of the Church, if he freely adheres to her.*[1]

On December 8, 1965 the curtain closed on a great religious event of the twentieth century, the Second Vatican Council. Culminating decades of initiatives for renewal, the Council reappropriated and refashioned its fundamental message, or "deposit of faith," in order to bear it more effective witness in the modern world. It was to unleash ferment, doubt, and hesitations within the Catholic Church for decades to come. On that closing day, in the still of a winter afternoon in Rome, perhaps an eye of a storm, a slightly stooped octogenarian approached Pope Paul VI and received from him a message from the Council Fathers to "Men of thought and science." It was a poignant moment for both men, since Paul VI once had referred to Jacques Maritain as his mentor. The message was brief. It offered encouragement and admiration for the great duty and responsibility of intellectual inquiry and its long search. "Our paths could not fail to cross," the Council Fathers wrote to the intellectuals of the world. And indeed Jacques Maritain was just the man at "the crossroads"—a man engaged with many of the great intellectual and practical issues of the century in science and philosophy, politics and ethics, art and religion. But he too was a man of deep faith, whose conversion to Catholicism was a great story in its own right.[2] So the Council Fathers also offered, "without dazzling brilliance," the light of "our mysterious lamp which is faith." This faith, they said, is a "great friend of intelligence," and

---
[1] Jacques Maritain, *Man and the State* (Chicago: The University of Chicago Press, 1951), p. 160.
[2] See Raissa Maritain, *We have Been Friends Together and Adventures in Grace: The Memoirs of Raissa Maritain*, trans. Julie Kernan (Garden City, New York: Image Books, Doubleday, 1961); and Raissa Maritain, ed. *Leon Bloy, Pilgrim of the Absolute* (New York: Pantheon Books, 1947).

they foresaw the possibility of a deep understanding and cooperation between science and faith. They only asked that one does not "stand in the way of this important meeting." Some thirty years later Pope John Paul II would single out Maritain again as an exemplary philosopher whose life and work had exhibited the boldness of reason combined with the illumination of faith.[3]

So too do we find in Maritain's life and work an exemplary account of the relation of Church and State. As a citizen of the world, engaged with the United Nations (UNESCO), and as a French ex-patriot in American Universities such as Princeton, Notre Dame and Chicago, Maritain was at the crossroads of new opportunities for Church-State relations. Here too did he often argue that the Church is a great friend of freedom, calling for new era of cooperation, and asking that obscurantists not stand in the way of such historic meetings. If faith and science have paths which cannot fail to cross, so too must the Church and State. Historically, the relation of Church and State is one of the major motifs of history.[4] As early as the 1930s Maritain had begun to unveil his account of the new era for Church-State relations that he named "New Christendom." It would involve the recognition of a new historic climate in which the permanent principles would be applied in new creative ways. *Man and the State* reiterates this theme, and often refers back to the groundbreaking work of his previous publications[5] (*The Things that are not Caesar's* and *Integral Humanism*). It anticipates the great work of Vatican II in this area, and it finds its fulfillment in Maritain's poorly received book *The Peasant of the Garonne*, published in 1966 but written within a month after that poignant meeting between him and Pope Paul VI.[6]

In this paper I wish to sketch Maritain's understanding of Church and State as developed in *Man and the State*; then take a brief look at the understanding of Vatican II on the role of the Church in the Modern World; and finally consider Maritain's attempt in *The Peasant of the Garonne* to interpret the meaning of Vatican II in light of the new relation of Church and State that he had previously articulated.

## *Man and the State* and the Reconciliation of Liberty and Religion

In 1949, Jacques Maritain delivered six lectures at the University of Chicago under the auspices of the Charles R. Walgreen Foundation for the Study of American Institutions. Maritain had high praise for the American constitution, describing it as "an outstanding lay Christian document tinged with the philosophy of the day."[7]

---

[3] Pope John Paul II, *Fides et Ratio: On the Relationship between Faith and Reason* (Boston: Daughters of St. Paul, 1998), #74.
[4] See Luigi Sturzo, *Church and State*, trans. Barbara Barclay Carter (Notre Dame, Indiana: University of Notre Dame Press, 1962).
[5] See Jacques Maritain, *The Things That are not Caesar's*, trans. J. F. Scanlan (London: Sheed and Ward, 1939) and Jacques Maritain, *Integral Humanism*, trans. Joseph W. Evans (Notre Dame, Indiana: University of Notre Dame Press, 1973).
[6] Jacques Maritain, *The Peasant of the Garonne: An Old Layman Questions Himself about the Present Time*, trans. Michael Cuddihy and Elizabeth Hughes (New York: Holt, Rinehart and Winston, 1968). On the controversy caused by this book see Brooke W. Smith, *Jacques Maritain: Antimodern or Ultramodern?* (New York: Elsevier, 1976).
[7] *Man and the State*, p. 183.

The American political tradition he saw as a viable example of a tradition built upon a sharp distinction between Church and State combined with their actual cooperation: "The spirit and inspiration of this great political Christian document is basically repugnant to the idea of making human society stand aloof from God and from any religious faith." He sought to avoid two extremes which had plagued Europe: on the one hand, the practice of a form of civil intolerance which made non-Christians or non-Catholics second-class citizens; on the other hand, the behavior of those who sought to marginalize the Church by isolating it from the activities of modern society. The former extreme could take the form of maintaining clerical privilege and keeping up a façade of the Christian state. Maritain saw in this the effect of increased bitterness and misunderstanding, as well the encouragement of Pharisaical citizens. The latter extreme could take the form of indifference to religious affairs, or the historicist claim that the principles of prior ages are irrelevant and religion has no place at all in the modern world. Maritain finds the golden mean through a distinction between the fundamental principles, imperishable principles, and the conditions for application, historic conditions which call for analogous explication and application. That is, he does not merely say that the historic conditions are less than perfect and require a prudential application and approximation, but that the very historic climate of the modern age, different as it is from the sacral age of the medieval time, requires a different analogous understanding of the principles at work. Thus he is neither a historicist on matter of principle nor an absolutist on the question of proper understanding of the relationship between Church and State.

Maritain bases his account of Church and State on the notion of degrees or orders of human achievement and flourishing. The common good civil life is "an ultimate end" but in a certain order, that is, the order of temporal achievement. It is an end "worthy in itself." In his first chapter Maritain derives from the Greek sense of the polis an account of the dignity of the political order. The common good of the body politic is constituted by justice and friendship, a form of association that "tends toward a really human and freely achieved communion. It lives on the devotion of human persons and their gift of themselves."[8] The common good includes economic and political infrastructure but most of all "the sociological integration of all the civic conscience, political virtues and sense of law and freedom, of all the activity, material prosperity and spiritual riches of unconsciously operating hereditary wisdom, of moral rectitude, justice, friendship, happiness, virtue and heroism in the individual lives of the members of the body politic." It is important to note that Maritain distinguishes the "state" from the "body politic" the former being the instrument of the body politic to administer justice and good order. Thus the very notion of Church and State must recall this distinction during the discussion of their relations and cooperation, for the church finds a place within

---

[8] Ibid., p. 10.

the notion of the body politic with its various associations and heritage. So the common good of the political society must include "an intrinsic though indirect ordination to something which transcends it." It is subordinate to a higher good because there is in human nature a higher aspiration. The seeds of such transcendence are to be found in natural human aspirations to "spiritual goods" such as truth, justice, and beauty which lead one beyond nation or state. The state can claim no sovereignty over the life of the mind. The political common good cannot be closed in on itself; nor should the state attempt to curb the impulse to truth and beauty, such is the basis for civil liberties for freedom of thought and expression. For the ancients, this aspiration was embodied in the philosopher who existed beyond the city, and who was even beyond that religion which was poetical or civil in nature. But the philosopher embraced a true philosophical religion, a rational or metaphysical religion.

The human person transcends the state and the body politic through "what is supra-temporal." Maritain recognizes a capacity for transcendence in all, not just the few, and that capacity finds an ultimate perfection in religion. From a Christian perspective the absolute ultimate end lies in the supernatural order, union with God through grace. But he is careful to explain each principle and each step of his argument from the standpoint of both the believer and the unbeliever. There will be an "unavoidable mutual misapprehension" between the two,[9] but nevertheless a philosophical case can be made for the notion of "sharp distinction and actual cooperation."

Maritain develops three general principles which he says are "imperishable" or true always and everywhere, but they require historic conditioning in their application. The three general principles are: (1) the freedom of the Church to teach and preach and worship; (2) the superiority of the Church – that is, of the spiritual – over the body politic and the State; and (3) the necessary cooperation between the Church and the body politic and the State. He elaborates and defends each one in turn.

Maritain presents a variety of reasons for freedom of religion. It follows from his overall account of the transcendence of the human person. The perfections of intellect and will which characterize the full development of the human person have a terminus beyond political life in "supra-temporal goods" which "constitute the moral heritage of mankind, the spiritual common good of civilization or the community of minds."[10] We can call this metaphysical ground for freedom of religion. Maritain also gives a more direct political argument. On the basis of freedom of association the freedom of religion or Church can be derived. Churches are one of the primary intermediate groups to which the human person is a member and derives much benefit; society as well derives such benefit. So too can we appeal

---
[9] Ibid., p. 186.
[10] Ibid., p. 150.

to freedom of conscience, which Maritain calls "the most basic and inalienable of all the human rights." For the believer, on the other hand, there is a more profound basis for freedom of the Church. The Church is understood to be a superior society by virtue of its supernatural character. It derives from the mandate to preach the Gospel given by Jesus.

The second principle, concerning the superiority of the Church, derives from a historical, as well as a theological claim. Prior to the arrival of Christianity the political society would make divine claims for itself or for its ruler. The very distinction between Church and State is made possible by Christianity and the admonition to "Render to Caesar what is Caesar's and to God what is God's." As Maritain so eloquently puts it "the terrestrial and national frameworks in which the spiritual was confined have been shattered." The superiority of the spiritual is manifest in the very distinction – i.e., God is greater than Caesar.[11] And yet Maritain points out, following Leo XIII, the de-divinizing of the State does not harm the state. The State is "autonomous" within its own order. The Church makes no claim for direct rule over temporal affairs on this account.

Finally, for the third principle, perhaps most controversial, is an argument based upon the benefit of the Church to society. All the Church asks is freedom – in return much will be rendered to the State in terms of moral influence. Of course it is now the very influence on morality that many resent. But the argument from the unity of the human person is brought in precisely at this point. It would be unnatural for the Church and State to ignore each other because it would amount to splitting the person in two halves – for the sake of the integrity of the person there must be cooperation between Church and State. Determining what kind of cooperation is needed requires us to consider the historic climate in which we now live in contrast to the climate of an earlier era.

Maritain's unique breakthrough on the topic of Church and State, and I might add an anticipation of the position adopted by Vatican II, derives from his account of history. Maritain proposes that we approach the issue in light of the "climate or constellation of existential conditions" dealing with juridical, social political and intellectual factors that define a given era. The application of the principles in each era calls for a different mode of application. That is, Maritain does not see the historical conditions as so many limits to a prudential application, which in more favorable conditions would allow for a greater achievement. Rather the new era requires an analogous application. The conservatives, if you will, do not grasp the historical climate or opportunities for a new style of Christian witness and a new style of Church-State relations. They are abstract absolutists with respect to the principles, but have a univocal grasp of what they mean or entail. For their position would entail a denial of equal civil rights to the non-believer and it would ultimately

---

[11] "The pagan City, which claimed to be the absolute whole of the human being, absorbed the spiritual in the temporal power and at the same time apotheosised the State. Its ultimate worship of the Emperors was the sure consequence of an infallible internal logic." *The Things that are not Caesar's*, p. 1.

entail a form of violence against them. The liberals, if you will, declare that the principles have now become obsolete and fall into historicism. Their problem stems from an equivocal understanding of the principles. It entails indifferentism and perhaps the aggressive attack on religion in the public square that we witness today. It is part of Maritain's life-long philosophical and theological project to confront the modern world from the standpoint of the Thomistic tradition and to extend the basic principles to the problems of the day. He wishes to embrace the advances of the modern world but by purifying the errors of its philosophy and first principles.

Maritain's understanding of the modern era centers on a distinction between the "sacral" versus the "lay" state. The distinction is most fully articulated in *Integral Humanism*, and it is the centerpiece of Maritain's understanding of the achievement of Vatican II as explained in *The Peasant of the Garonne*, to be examined below. Maritain describes the medieval era as characterized by a distinction between the two powers, temporal and spiritual, but a unification of the two through the use of faith for the unity of the body politic. Religious creed was used as the basis for unity in the body politic, so a rupture in belief was seen as a rupture in the body politic. The heretic therefore was seen as threat to the political order. The methods of the inquisition served both the Church and the State; the State could use it as an instrument for state unity; the Church could use the temporal power as a means for its goals. The temporal therefore was subordinated to the spiritual as a means or an instrument for a spiritual end.[12] The medieval era was also characterized by what Maritain calls "fortitude in the service of justice" as its public ideal. The public servant aimed at the embodiment of a noble ideal. With the fragmentation of the religious unity of the state by way of the reformation, the "Baroque era" attempted to refund the unity of the state through the absolutism of the ruler whose faith would guarantee the unity of the spiritual and political order. Maritain views this as a halfway house, unworkable in the long run. The true modern era is described as a lay state whose two guiding principles are the differentiation and autonomy of the temporal sphere, from economics to politics and the public ideal of the conquest of freedom and human dignity. The unity of the state could no longer be grounded in a spiritual and religious unity, so it must be based upon a temporal goal as such. The notion of human dignity and the use of temporal power to empower or liberate human beings from bondage to nature or oppressive rule became the public ideal. The autonomy of the secular affairs Maritain says is a rightful unfolding of the very distinction of the affairs of God and Caesar. The new climate therefore requires the analogous application of the imperishable principles. The entailments are as follows. The state is no longer viewed as the "secular arm" of the church. The state is "autonomous and independent" within its own sphere.[13] Second, the equality of all members of the temporal society is

---

[12] See *Integral Humanism*, pp. 142ff.; see also Jacques Maritain, *On the Philosophy of History* (New York: Charles Scribner's Sons, 1957), pp. 111-14.
[13] Ibid., p. 161.

recognized as a fundamental tenant. The holding of office or the enjoyment of the civil rights is the same for all. Third, the Church and State both recognize the importance of "inner forces" as a preferred mode over coercion. Faith cannot be imposed by force, but neither can political persuasion or other fundamentals of belief. This leads to the highlighting of conscience as the great key to the new era. Freedom of conscience entails freedom of inquiry and freedom of expression.

In these new conditions Maritain sees a great new era for the relation of Church and State, traced back to the unity of the person. There are three aspects to the argument. First, the person is characterized by a unity or integrity – and although living in various orders with various pursuits, he has one conscience. The person is simultaneously a member of the body politic and a member of the Church. Hence "he would be cut in two if his temporal membership were cut off from his spiritual membership."[14] The wholeness of the person should incline us towards cooperation rather than antagonism. Second, the religious pursuit is essential to the "pursuit of happiness." Therefore the common good of society, which includes the flourishing of its members, cannot but be favorable towards the religious pursuit. Third, through the influence on conscience "Christian truths and incentives" would pass into the sphere of temporal existence and thereby assist the democratic state in rousing the "inner strength and spiritual stronghold of democracy."[15] The religious beliefs and practices will have a "leavening effect." They should uplift morality and sensitive moral conscience. The civil rights movement of the 1960s would be an example that Maritain has in mind. Maritain anticipates the communitarian critique of liberal philosophy – the attempt to develop a neutral, thin theory of the reason for the political society is impossible or weak. The pluralism of religious belief can be turned to the state's advantage if the various religious traditions can agree on concrete practical principles, but provide a more full-bodied understanding and defense of the principles at a higher level. The educational efforts of the Church are very important for the well being of the political society.[16] The students could see "the entire convictions" and personal inspiration behind their principles of government and social practice and embrace them more deeply. For this reason Maritain says that the isolation or separation of Church and State would "simply spell suicide."

The very distinction between Church and State grants to the Church her new found influence. She stands for universality and for the higher supratemporal good to which the human person aspires. The superiority of the Church is therefore not the basis for the use of coercive methods or for the dictation of public policy, but it should operate through the springs of conscience and persuasion. In a poignant passage Maritain says, "A superior agent is not confined or shut up within itself. It radiates. It stimulates the inner forces and energies of other agents – even autonomous in their own peculiar spheres – whose place is less high in the scale of

---

[14] Ibid., p. 176.
[15] Ibid.
[16] Ibid., pp. 121-22.

being. Superiority implies a penetrating and vivifying influence. The very token of the superiority of the Church is the moral power with which she vitally influence, penetrates and quickens, as a spiritual leaven, temporal existence and the inner energies of nature, so as to carry them to a higher and more perfect level in their own order."[17] So the autonomy of the temporal sphere is recognized and even celebrated, and the influence of the Church is to stimulate within the very political order its own proper excellence and achievement of its own proper end. It requires a distinct metaphysical conception, analogous to the relation of nature and grace – that grace does not destroy but rather builds upon and perfects nature.[18] Maritain's prophetic term for the new relation of Church and State, from the standpoint of the Church, is called the "sanctification of secular life." The temporal itself bears within itself the mark of the divine, a *quid divinum*.[19]

The Church therefore seeks to persuade and to revive the inner energies within the human person, within conscience. It thus forever forswears the use of coercive power. Rather, the Church now asks for freedom, the freedom to pursue its spiritual mission. No special privilege is required, just an acknowledgement that the temporal common good of the state is advanced by granting to the Church her freedom. It is a temporal good for the reasons mentioned above, the essential component of the pursuit of happiness and the leavening effect of Christian conscience within society at large. This constitutes an in-principled argument against state coercion for religious purposes. In addition there are prudential reasons for limiting even the legitimate secular reasons for morality as mediated through religion. Maritain explains the Thomistic adage that law should be proportionate to the capacity of the people. Thus not every moral standard will be legislated in full force.[20]

The actual cooperation should go beyond the negative freedom of the Church to be allowed to pursue her mission to preach the gospel. Maritain says that the state should ask the Church to do more in domains where she can assist – such as welfare and education. The state can help remove obstacles and "open the doors" for the Church to assist the "social and moral work of the nation, to provide people with a leisure worthy of human dignity, and to develop within them the sense of liberty and fraternity."[21]

At the end of the day Maritain understands that there will always be an ultimate misapprehension between the believer and the non-believer. But he thinks that the task is now clear. The influence of the Church on liberty is for the good; she has

---

[17] Ibid., pp. 164-65.
[18] See the book by Maritain's theological mentor, Charles Cardinal Journet, *The Meaning of Grace*, trans. A. V. Littledale (Princeton: Scepter Press, 1996).
[19] This notion of the *quid divinum* or the divine something that can be discovered at the heart of all secular work was brought to my attention by Fr. Bob Connor, of the Prelature of Opus Dei; he made reference to an important sermon by Mgr. Escrivá entitled "Passionately Loving the World," in Josemaria Escrivá, *Conversations with Mgr Escrivá De Balaguer* (Dublin: Scepter, 1968). Also see his *Friends of God* (Dublin: Scepter, 1981). An elaboration can be found in Jose Luis Illanes, *On the Theology of Work* (Dublin: Four Courts Press, 1982).
[20] *Man and the State*, pp. 167-71.
[21] Ibid., p. 179.

forsworn the use of coercion for religious purposes. The blind forces, which have attacked religion in the name of freedom and the dignity of the person, must now drop their mask and appear, as they are – opponents of liberty and human dignity. Their anti-religious animus, their virulent secularism, now becomes the sole reason for attacking and excluding religion. Maritain has traced our way through the Tocquevillian dilemma: "Where then are we? Men of religion fight against freedom, and lovers of liberty attack religion; noble and generous spirits praise slavery, while low servile minds preach independence; honest and enlightened citizens are the enemies of all progress, while men without patriotism or morals make themselves the apostles of civilization and enlightenment!"[22] And one hundred years later Maritain claims in his *Man and the State:* "Present times, however miserable they are, have the wherewithal to elate those who love the Church and love freedom. . . . The cause of freedom and the cause of the Church are one in the defense of man."[23]

## Vatican II on "The Church in the Modern World"

Considered one of the four great documents of Vatican II, "The Church in the Modern World" outlined a new emphasis and new strategy for the role of the Church.[24] Seeking to read "the signs of the times" the Council Fathers traced out many positive developments of the modern world, as well as the frustrated aspirations of the modern world. It emphasizes the dignity of the human person and depths of conscience. But one must also notice its Augustinian thread of the dark side, the sinfulness of man, as the ultimate reason for the frustrations and failures of such noble aspirations. Thus it argues that religion, Christianity, the Church, have an important role to play in the development of the modern world. Its new emphasis will involve the laity and their special role in the modern world. But throughout, the essential distinction between Church and State is recalled and reaffirmed. "The Church and the political community in their own fields are autonomous and independent from each other."[25] And following the position of Maritain the council fathers also emphasize the need for cooperation based upon the unity of the human person; both are devoted to the good of the "same man." Both must therefore foster sounder cooperation between themselves for the good of all. Autonomy therefore does not entail separation or antagonism.

In one of the key sections the council addresses itself to the objection whether "a closer bond between human activity and religion will work against the independence of men, of societies, or of the sciences." In order to properly answer

---

[22] Alexis de Tocqueville, *Democracy in America*, trans. George Lawrence, ed. J. P. Mayer (New York: Harper Collins, 1988), p. 17.
[23] *Man and the State*, p. 187; "Here [Vatican II] is accomplished the great reversal of virtue of which it is no longer the human which take charge of defending the divine, but the divine which offers itself to defend the human." *The Peasant of the Garonne*, p. 4.
[24] *Pastoral Constitution on the Church in the Modern World (Gaudium et Spes)* (Boston: Daughters of St. Paul, 1965); subsequent references will be to section numbers of "GS."
[25] GS, #76.

that fear various meanings of autonomy are explored. The proper meaning of autonomy comports with the Christian notion of creation:

> If by the autonomy of earthly affairs we mean that created things and societies themselves enjoy their own laws and values which must be gradually deciphered, put to use, and regulated by men, then it is entirely right to demand that autonomy. Such is not merely required by modern man, but harmonizes also with the will of the Creator. For by the very circumstance of their having been created, all things are endowed with their own stability, truth, goodness, proper laws and order. Man must respect these as he isolates them by the appropriate methods of the individual sciences or arts.[26]

Politics and economics therefore have their own proper autonomy – i.e., their own fundamental laws and intelligibility. The political community achieves its proper differentiation from the religious association, the Church or any other religious association. Political life has its proper excellence; its own proper dynamism; and its own proper role to play in the development of human beings. But by this same token, the political sphere is not the ultimate; it must not claim the mantle of religion for itself. It is not divine. One manner of claiming divinity or ultimacy for itself would be through self-sufficiency. That is if the State recognizes no power higher than itself, then it will verge towards idolatry of its own proper purpose and thereby distort it. Thus the council fathers rightly describe the "false" sense of autonomy:

> But if the expression, the independence of temporal affairs, is taken to mean that created things do not depend on God, and that man can use them without any reference to their Creator, anyone who acknowledges God will see how false such a meaning is. For without the Creator the creature would disappear. For their part, however, all believers of whatever religion always hear His revealing voice in the discourse of creatures. When God is forgotten, however, the creature itself grows unintelligible.[27]

Echoing the Thomistic notion of the *exitus et reditus*, the coming forth from God and the return of creatures to God, the council fathers point out that the origin and end of human life transcend the political order, for which a due reverence and respect must be acknowledged.[28] In fact, a great theme of this council is that the denial of this higher origin and destiny leads to the very assault upon human dignity with which the modern world is so concerned. The loss of the Creator entails the loss of the creature. The Church is therefore a "sign and safeguard of the transcendent character of the human person."[29] By fostering and elevating all that

---

[26] GS, #36.
[27] Ibid.
[28] "Only God is great. God alone is the beginning and end. God alone is the source of your authority and the foundation of your laws." Paul VI, "To the Guardians of Temporal Power: Message to Heads of State," appendix, p. 246. See GS #13: "Often refusing to acknowledge God as his beginning, man has disrupted also his proper relationship to his own ultimate goal as well as his whole relationship toward himself and others and all created things."
[29] GS, # 76

is true, good and beautiful, the Church has a great role to play in developing the modern world and the temporal and political community. It must be said that she uses her own proper methods – "the ways and means proper to the Gospel" which are different from those of the earthly city. In her turn the Church asks for freedom "to preach the faith, to teach her social doctrine." In his Message to Heads of State, Paul VI said "She asks of you only liberty."[30] The Church does not threaten temporal order but rather, "heals everything human of its fatal emptiness, transfigures it and fills it with hope, truth and beauty."[31]

This role becomes especially pronounced in light of the Augustinian theme of human weakness with its need for healing; this theme is taken up into the Thomistic idea of grace perfecting nature and elevating from within. It is the very autonomy of the temporal that is respected here – the ministrations of the Church are for the sake of the proper development of the political, the temporal, and the human as such. From the very outset of the document the Council fathers refer to the problem of evil: the Church wishes to help the modern world finds the fulfillment of its quest for dignity and freedom. But they must realize that this world is divided by sin.[32] It is an illusion to think that a genuine or total emancipation of mankind will be brought about without an acknowledgement of the deeper root of human failure.[33] It is anthropocentric humanism, premised upon this false sense of autonomy, which thinks that the world can sustain meaning without any reference to the divine, indeed, the modern temptation is to believe that the world lacks meaning only to be filled in by human creativity.[34] But the Council Fathers press the question: "What is this sense of sorrow, of evil, of death, which continues to exist despite so much progress? What purpose have these victories purchased at so high a cost?" Is it not apparent that human beings struggle with evil and find themselves almost unable to deal with it?[35] Sin obscures the very light of conscience.[36] Good human energies are distorted by pride and self love: "constantly imperiled by man's pride and deranged self-love, [they] must be purified and perfected."[37] The purification and perfection of the natural activity and disposition is a task assigned to the lay people. This is a great achievement of the council. The Church will fulfill this mission, this benefit to the earthly city, not by assuming temporal power or by using the means proper to the earthly city such as coercion

---

[30] "To the Guardians of Temporal Power: Message to Heads of State," appendix, p. 246.
[31] Ibid.
[32] GS, #2.
[33] Ibid., #10.
[34] Ibid.
[35] "Human life, whether individual or collective, shows itself to be a dramatic struggle between good and evil, between light and darkness. Indeed, man finds that by himself he is incapable of battling the assaults of evil successfully, so that everyone feels as though he is bound by chains. But the Lord Himself came to free and strengthen man, renewing him inwardly and casting out that prince of this world (*John* 12:31) who held him in the bondage of sin. For sin has diminished man, blocking his path to fulfillment." Ibid., #13.
[36] Ibid., #16.
[37] Ibid., #37.

or political power. Rather through the very means proper to the Gospel, through the inspiration of conscience and through a sacramental approach. It is through the lay people because of their unity of life. It is the same person who is a member of the Church and who is also a member of the political community. The burden of unity falls upon the individual person, the individual Christian, who is a member of both societies. Vatican II is known for its lack of anathemas and condemnations, taking a new approach to modernity no longer in terms of a syllabus of errors or condemnation of mistakes, but "to carry forward the work of Christ under the lead of the befriending Spirit."[38] And thus one of the few errors condemned is that on the part of Christians who divorce their own earthly affairs from their religious life: "This split between the faith which many profess and their daily lives deserves to be counted among the more serious errors of our age."[39] A Christian may not claim a warrant to neglect or to shirk their earthly duties because of a concern with the otherworldly. In fact such a Christian "jeopardizes his eternal salvation." The council fathers call for Christian laymen to gather into a "vital synthesis with religious values" all their earthly activities – humane, domestic, professional, social and technical enterprises. Indeed "secularity" is the very mark of the layman – "secular duties and activities belong properly to laymen" and they should work according to the "laws proper to each discipline" and yet seek to inscribe the divine law into the very life of the earthly city – by way of their own conscientious action.[40] The very secular work of the layman accomplishes both a religious mission and a temporal mission, to the benefit of both:

> Even by their secular activity they must aid one another to greater holiness of life, so that the world may be filled with the spirit of Christ and may the more effectively attain its destiny in justice, in love and in peace. The laity enjoys a principle role in the universal fulfillment of this task. Therefore, by their competence in secular disciplines and by their activity, interiorly raised up by grace, let them work earnestly in order that created goods through human labor, technical skill and civil culture may serve the utility of all men according to the plan of the creator and the light of his word . . . Thus, through the members of the Church, will Christ increasingly illuminate the whole of human society with his saving light.[41]

It is part of the universal call to holiness that the layman receives such an important new emphasis according to Vatican II. No longer is the notion of holiness to be reserved for the priests, the religious. And yet the layman is not called to holiness by a secondary imitation of the religious by a flight from the world or by an explicitly ecclesiastical mission; rather it is through unity of life, unity of religious devotion

---

[38] Ibid., #3.
[39] Ibid., #43.
[40] "Lumen Gentium," in Austin Flannery, ed. *Vatican Council II: The Conciliar and Postconciliar Documents*, vol. 1 (Northport, New York: Costello, 1998).
[41] Ibid., #36; on the positive meaning of "secularity" for the laity see Pope John Paul II, *The Lay Members of Christ's Faithful People* (Boston: Daughters of St. Paul, 1988) sections 9, 15, 17.

and professional energy, the former illuminating and purifying the latter, that the layman achieves holiness of life. It may be called a sanctification of the world, a sanctification of the temporal order itself, in terms of the proper finalities and autonomy of the temporal order itself. For good reason then did Paul VI remark in his message to rulers that the freedom of the Church will first of all benefit "your peoples" since the Church "forms for you loyal citizens, friends of social peace and progress." A sharp distinction is drawn between the proper orders of Church and State; yet a vital cooperation is recognized, for the benefit of each. Also for good reason, did Paul VI acknowledge Jacques Maritain at the end of the council by presenting him with his Message to Men of Thought and Science. Paul VI rightly indicated that the Vatican Council was in some ways the fulfillment of the life-long work of Maritain. Indeed, in his own closing remarks, Paul VI spoke about the religious significance of the Council turning upon a proper understanding of the "whole man."[42] And yet within a few months of that historic occasion, Jacques Maritain published what many took as a bitter attack upon the very work and promise of the council. *The Peasant of the Garonne*, significantly subtitled, "An Old Layman Questions Himself about the Present Time," does not in any way retract or attack his life-long aspiration and work for a "new Christendom." Indeed this book amplifies it and hones it. It is Maritain's cry of the heart; it is a very personal book for which any careful reader can discern beneath the bitterness of its surface, a rich, a sweet, a highly personal testimony of hope.

### *The Peasant of the Garonne:* Maritain's Last Word, Bitter or Sweet?

The impact of the new council went far beyond what anyone had anticipated. The effects have led some to question whether the council should have been called at all, and others who say that it did not go far enough and further changes are necessary. We still live in the chaos and confusion. But in 1967, Maritain saw the root principle of the excess and wrote this book, *Peasant of the Garonne*, designating a man who would not hesitate to call a "spade a spade." Maritain offers his book as a corrective, a rebuke to both extremes; he attempts to stabilize the core meanings of the council in light of history, spirituality, and philosophy.[43] Maritain wrote *Peasant* less than a year after the close of the council. Its relevance now more than thirty years after is astounding. John Paul II has accomplished the corrections and he has stabilized the core

---

[42] He said "Etiam ut nos hominem, hominem verum, *hominem integrum* penitus noscamus, Deum ipsam antea cognoscamus necesse est." Or "In order to know our humanity, true man, the whole man, it is necessary to know God." Emphasis added. See Maritain's use of this term in *Peasant*, p. 4.

[43] Pope Paul VI also made such attempts on the theological front with his post-conciliar writings, especially see Pope Paul VI, *On the Mystery of Faith* (Boston: Daughters of St. Paul, 1966); Pope Paul VI, *On Saints Peter and Paul* (Boston: Daughters of St. Paul, 1967); Pope Paul VI, *The Credo of the People of God* (Boston: Daughters of St. Paul, 1968). See also Candido Pozo, *The Credo of the People of God: A Theological Commentary*, trans. Mark A. Pilon (Chicago: Franciscan Herald Press, 1980).

meanings much in the vein traced by Maritain in *Peasant*. But much still waits to be discovered. Its call for renewal is still waiting to be discovered. To cover some of the scope of *Peasant*, I plan to explore two themes: first, the achievement of Vatican II, especially the key role of the laity in fulfilling the promise of the new age; second, the difference between the false and true renewal, namely what went wrong after the council and the intellectual and spiritual basis for the true appreciation and fulfillment of the promise of Vatican II.

## The Achievement of Vatican II

Maritain opens the book with a chapter entitled "Thanksgiving." He reminds the reader that the council was primarily pastoral and not doctrinal and that it met a historic task requiring "progress in evangelical awareness and attitudes of the heart," rather than the definition of dogma. This pastoral nature has itself been distorted and has become a rationale for abandoning doctrine or changing doctrines. As Maritain wryly notes, the council did in fact devote two documents to dogmatic constitutions; and further, he says that the dogmas have been defined once and for all, and new developments simply make explicit and complete old ones.

He outlines the great achievements – freedom and human dignity, especially freedom of conscience and religion; a new approach to non-Catholics, both Christian and non-Christian, especially the Jewish people; an affirmation of the value, beauty and dignity of the world; the universal call to holiness, especially of the laity. Each of these great achievements is subject to distortion. Each must be separated from an ideology which preys upon the truth and obscures the great opportunity for a new age. Indeed, the progressive interpretation of these items, both within and outside of the Church, conjures up a heady brew of liberalism, ecumenism, secularism, and laicism, the very things which many Catholics have found an enemy, the things that are wrong with modernity. Briefly stated here is what Maritain understands by these achievements: by liberalism, authentic liberalism, as Maritain sought to defend in *Man and the State*, he means the recognition of the "true idea of freedom" and a deeper appreciation of the dignity of the person and human rights. It also mean the recognition of religious freedom and the sanctity of conscience. By ecumenism, he celebrates friendship with non-Catholics, Christian and non-Christian. It especially means the elimination of anti-Semitism. By secularism, Maritain understands the very Thomistic principle of the "value, beauty, and dignity of world" and a corresponding temporal mission of the Christian. And finally, the emphasis upon the laity means that all are called to perfection of charity and the wisdom of the Holy Spirit, all are called to instill the spirit of the gospel in the temporal order.

These four achievements constitute a massive shift—in Church-State relations in particular. It is the end of an era, and the beginning of a new age. The council fulfills the great project which Maritain began with *Integral Humanism* and continued with *Man and the State*. Indeed, it is a fulfillment of a project initiated by his fellow Frenchman Alexis de Tocqueville, to whom we referred above: "Here is accomplished the great reversal of virtue of which it is no longer the human which takes charge of defending the divine, but the divine which offers itself to defend the human." The overarching achievement concerns an epochal change: "every vestige of the Holy Empire is today liquidated; we have definitively emerged from the sacral age and the baroque age." It is an era that requires of the church only freedom — freedom to preach the truth and act with charity. The Church's temporal mission is "reaffirmed under the sign of freedom" with a right to intervene not "ratione peccati"[44] to repress evil, but "ratione boni perficiendi"–"to quicken and prod and assist from above and without trespassing on the autonomy of the temporal."

The great achievements of Vatican II are best brought to focus in the temporal mission of the laity. Maritain elaborates upon the fundamental distinction of the two ends of human history that he made in *Man and the State*. It involves the differentiation of the temporal and the eternal ends of the human person. And this requires a proper understanding of the meaning of the autonomy of the temporal or secular. For as Maritain has long insisted, "we must distinguish in order to unite." The two ends, and their corresponding two missions, are complementary and interactive.

The very distinction between a "relative ultimate end" and an "absolute ultimate end" does present some initial confusions. In *The Peasant of the Garonne* Maritain draws a distinction between the "natural end" or "relatively final end" and a "supernatural end" which is the "absolutely final end." The kingdom of God is beyond history and requires a radical transfiguration of the natural. The natural end engages man in history and constitutes the progress of the temporal or secular order. The Christian engages this secular end in his "temporal mission" as a Christian. The supernatural end engages the Christian in history but as pointing to another world. This constitutes the proper mission of the Church, or the "spiritual mission" of the Christian. Now as we shall see, the two are very much interconnected and bound to each other. But the distinctions must be kept.

What is the specific end of secular progress? Maritain combines ancient and modern philosophy in his description of human purpose in this world. He describes it as a "triple and progressive expansion and conquest of man." The triple end comprises, first, the mastery of nature; this means we can affirm "loftiest ambition of modern science" and exercise control over the physical world and aim at elimination of servitude and subjection to another and the "violence of instrumentality." Maritain also speaks of action toward the goal of eliminating hunger, poverty, war, and injustice. The triple end also includes the development of self-perfecting spiritual activities such as knowledge and art and ethical achievement. Finally, it includes the development of the "manifest potentialities of human nature." It is part and parcel of the ontosophic truth to affirm the goodness

---

[44] On the notion of the *ratione peccati*, see Maritain's *The Things That are not Caesar's*, pp. 128-30.

of the structures and these ends of temporal society. Christians are called to fully participate in these human purposes and help to bring them to perfection.

Although he mentions Descartes, Maritain's position must be distinguished from the modern attempt of mastery of nature for a number of reasons.[45] To begin with, Maritain sets forth a three-point program for this relatively final end, the natural end or purpose of human history. It is not reducible to mastery alone, but is balanced by moral and cultural achievement. In addition, Maritain says that the goal cannot be attained once and for all, it is an unending path to be approached asymptotically. But more can be said—Maritain reminds us of the fact of death. The aspiration of enduring good is rendered futile by death.[46] Maritain in another context speaks about the natural aspiration for immortality and the transnatural aspiration for complete salvation which cannot be a result of natural development.[47] Finally Maritain points to the mystery of evil: the development of evil alongside that of good, and in the practical order the very real futility of individual moral striving. The Thomistic adage concerning grace perfecting nature takes on an additional Augustinian dimension. Society requires "the stimulus and elevation which Christianity naturally brings to the activities of nature in its own sphere."[48] Maritain chastises the modernists because they neglect the role of the cross and asceticism. They forget that we need the life of grace and prayer to make "natural energies more pure and upright in the very order of nature," that is, nature must be healed by grace. Readers of *Gaudium et Spes* often neglect the striking passages on sin in the middle of its description of the Christian's temporal mission, as we noted above. The temporal mission requires a spiritual mission for the reason of sin. Laymen must receive doctrinal and spiritual formation to be ready to go forth in the temporal mission. But so formed the Christian laity can enter deeply into the struggles and anguish of modern world and work for the progress in its own order, fully respecting its autonomy.

### Towards Authentic Renewal

At Vatican II the council fathers acknowledged an opportune time for renewal. Maritain ratified this view and he characterized our era as one of "immense spiritual ferment" and "religious aspiration" and as an era harboring a "nostalgia for the gospel, a passion for the absolute, a fervent presentiment of the liberty, the breadth and variety of the ways of God, a whole hearted longing for the perfection of charity."[49] Catholics, and indeed all Christians, have been presented with a

---

[45] See Richard Kennington, "Descartes and Mastery of Nature" in *Organism, Medicine and Metaphysics: Essays in Honor of Hans Jonas*, ed. S. F. Spicker (Dordrecht: D. Reidel, 1978), pp. 221-33; compare Jacques Maritain, *Three Reformers: Luther, Descartes, Rousseau* (New York: Charles Scribner's Sons, 1929), and Jacques Maritain, *The Dream of Descartes*, trans. Mabelle L. Andison (London: Editions Poetry London, 1946).
[46] *Peasant*, pp. 202-03.
[47] "The Immortality of the Soul," in *The Range of Reason* (New York: Charles Scribner's Sons, 1968), pp. 51-65.
[48] Ibid., p. 42.
[49] Ibid., p. 5.

wonderful opportunity for living lives that "bear witness to the love of Jesus for all men and to the generosity of God's spirit." So what is gone wrong? Why are Catholics in such disarray? Why the quibbling and bitter divisions? Indeed why the "immanent apostasy" and desperate forms of witness among contemporary Catholics who thus seem to save but a "dying Christianity for the modern world"? Why the uncertainty and lack of confidence in the "Catholic moment"?[50]

The deepest source of the crisis is a religious one, a spiritual one. It traces back to a pendulum which has swung from a "masked manicheism" characteristic of the Church prior to the council to the post-counciliar mistake of "kneeling before the world." The one called forth the other. Both extremes rest upon a fundamental error concerning the value of the world and temporal affairs. It turns on a "misunderstanding with a bitter fruit" concerning the distinction between the "mystical" and the "ontosophic" meaning of the "world." The mystical truth concerning the world is a practical truth, lived out by the saints. The ontosophic truth concerning the world is a speculative truth, affirmed by both theologians and philosophers. The practical truth lived by the saints is a contempt for the world deriving from their boundless love for God. St. Paul refers to the world as a dung hill in comparison with Christ and the knowledge of God. The world is seen as an obstacle to God insofar as the world is in sin and refuses God. The world hates God; it persecutes Christ and his followers. The saints, overwhelmed by their love of God, struggle against the world, exercise self-denial, and show contempt for the world. This is the mystical truth of contempt for the world. The ontosophic truth, a truth of theology and philosophy, reason and revelation, affirms the goodness of the world. The world has natural structures which are intelligible and natural ends which are good. This is the speculative truth. Grace builds upon and perfects does not destroy nature. The dangerous misunderstanding lies in making the practical truth a speculative one, or vice versa.

Centuries prior to the council the church came to misunderstand the mystical truth. The "dung hill" was extended to the world itself and "a masked Manicheism was thus superimposed on the Christian faith without ruining it."[51] It was a pastoral failure, not a doctrinal one, by which Manicheeism was "spread inwardly, in the form of purely moralistic prohibitions, injunctions to flight, habits of fear, disciplines of denial in which love had no part, and which led the soul to starvation and sickliness, and to a torturing sense of impotence."[52] The moral took precedent over the theological; flight from sin, precedence over charity. Human initiative, and refusal to sin, obscured the divine initiative of love and grace. In addition to this mistaken contempt for the world, Christians prior to the council were well

---

[50] See Ralph McInerny, *What Went Wrong with Vatican II: The Catholic Crisis Explained* (Manchester, New Hampshire: Sophia Institute Press, 1998), and Ralph M. Wiltgen, *The Rhine Flows into the Tiber: The Unknown Council* (New York: Hawthorne Books, 1967).
[51] *Peasant*, p. 46.
[52] Ibid., p. 48.

aware of the growing hostility of modern civilization to Christianity and thus formed a defensive reaction and inferiority complex. Further, there was generally poor doctrinal formation. Thus at the time of the council there was present an "enormous weight of frustration and disillusionment and resentment" which burst out into the open on the occasion of *aggiornamento*, or "updating." The pendulum swung from masked manichesim to frenzied modernism. For the theologians it was to mean a love for the latest trends and a love for the ephemeral. The spiritual teaching affirmed the goodness of the world, but failed to mention the other world, the cross, and the demands of sanctity. The temporal mission of the layman was mistaken for the mission of the Church as a whole. Such a position of kneeling before the world amounted to a complete temporalization of Christianity, an absorption of the kingdom of God by the temporal mission of the world. The prayer for the kingdom of God was mistaken for a dream of a "glorious parousia of collective man." This describes the present day activists well enough — either the liberation theologians or the radical feminists, among others, who demand that the Church embrace latest trends of the day. Of course, for the average churchgoer in the West the crisis persists in many confusions about the great achievements of Vatican II: concerning the role of the laity, who must now assume a position in the sacristy; concerning the affirmation of the world which has come to signify middle-class achievement and consumerism; concerning the ecumenical opening of the council which has come to mean little more than religious or doctrinal indifference and the ascendancy of the affective over cognitive religious education; and the hard-won emphasis upon the freedom and dignity of the human person which has come to the refusal of strict moral demands in the name of free conscience.

The great vision of Christian renewal of temporal structures, the true activation of the temporal mission of the lay Christian, requires a preparation in the order of philosophy and spirituality. It requires "a great and patient work of revitalizing in the order of intelligence and the order of spirituality."[53] We can but briefly outline the tasks ahead which Maritain calls the "true new fire" of renewal: ecumenical dialogue, the liberation of intelligence, and the sources of spiritual renewal in contemplation and liturgy. In these chapters Maritain illustrates and deepens the positions of *Man and the State*; he shows the inner depth behind the formulae. In *Man and the State* Maritain suggested that different points of view on the Church-State are often derived from different understandings of "Church." For an unbeliever the Church is but a sociological or natural phenomenon; for the believer the Church is a society representing a reality of a higher order. Misapprehension is inevitable; but if one wishes to do justice to the issue it is incumbent upon both sides to make the best understanding as the other understands itself. Maritain provides a unique opening to the post-conciliar understanding of the Church and its self-understanding in a new age for Church-State relations.

---

[53] Ibid., p. 53.

The claim for a new age for Church-State relations begins with an inner renewal, according to Maritain. It shall take a new attitude. The new attitude respects the dignity of the person; the Catholic is called to love the person as a person and not simply as a potential convert to the faith. In addition to the theme of a new attitude towards those of a different faith, Maritain returns to a theme found in *Man and the State*: the possibility of practical cooperation in a divided world.[54] Maritain is still confident about the possibility of practical cooperation in a divided world because of a convergence upon the notion of human rights. He always conceded that such an agreement was a minimum one, open to many ambiguities and ultimate differences. But such an agreement upon a "democratic charter" was necessary for political peace. Yet he is now more insistent that we not be led to an opposite extreme of "ignoring the imprescriptible rights of the speculative order—in other words of truth itself, which is superior to every human interest." As we cooperate more frequently on a practical level, truth will be served only if we are willing to actually "strengthen the edges of opposite convictions which divide us." In other words true ecumenical dialogue is vital to the secure peace and the deeper understanding of human rights. Maritain cites a marvelous line from Jean Cocteau concerning dialogue: "We must have a tough mind and a tender heart." To which Cocteau adds "the world is full of dried up hearts and flabby minds." Maritain also elaborates the various new approaches opened by Vatican Council II for Christian approaches to non-Catholics and unbelievers. Direct conversion is no longer the only mode nor the first mode of engagement with men and women of diverse creeds. Of particular note is the importance of the sphere of action, all the works of mercy and the efforts to develop social, economic and cultural advancement for all people. And yet Maritain is not a utopian in his praise for these efforts. He recognizes the limits of achievement in this area. And most of all he says that the renewal requires contemplative love and prayer.

The work of speculative reason is necessary for the proper understanding of the goodness of nature, the "ontosophic" truth of the world which was lost by many prior to the council and confused with a practical truth after the council. Maritain's philosophical efforts must be traced back to his metaphysical approaches to the world, especially his notion of the intuition of being.[55] Maritain fears that the emphasis upon efficacy and pragmatism has obscured the fundamental principles of philosophy. In an age of increasing influence of technology, the love of truth, the superior value of truth will have a liberating effect. Men look for substitutes in myths and fables because science itself is unable to answer the deeper personal

---

[54] *Man and the State*, pp. 76-80, 108-114; *Peasant*, pp. 64-70. The original speech which Maritain gave to UNESCO on the topic of practical cooperation and the UN Declaration of Human Rights may be found in Jacques Maritain, *The Range of Reason* (New York: Charles Scribner's Sons, 1968), pp. 180ff.
[55] See *Peasant*, pp. 99-101, 132-35; see also John P. Hittinger, "The Intuition of Being: Metaphysics or Poetry?" in *Jacques Maritain: The Man and His Metaphysics*, ed. John F. X. Knasas (Notre Dame, Indiana: American Maritain Association/University of Notre Dame Press, 1988), pp. 71-82.

questions about man, God and the world. Science will try to extrapolate from science to create fables and myths to answer these questions. Maritain was critical of Teilhard de Chardin because he viewed his efforts as an extrapolation, a poetic myth of science, covering over the deeper yearning for a true philosophical approach to the big issues. Also he criticizes the forms of contemporary philosophy because they bracket the question of being. As forms of epistemological idealism they trap the thinker within his own mind and never experience the relish of true being.

The most important point has to do with faith and reason. The relation of faith and reason is emblematic of the relation between Church and State. The issue of faith and reason brings the issue to a very personal dimension, not only a sociological or political one. And the resolution on the level of the person, the concrete thinker, provides clues to the larger political issue. It is as if Maritain would have us reverse the Socratic ploy to see the soul through the city; on this issue of Church and State it may be better to view the city through the soul.

Maritain's argument for the cooperation of faith and reason proceeds as follows. There is a distinction between philosophy and theology but not a separation. First, a philosopher is a human being with a set of beliefs about man, God and the world. These cannot be "locked up in a strong box." It is natural for these beliefs to influence the philosophy of the concrete person. Reason verges into the domain of faith because it has questions to ask of faith. It is not uncommon for the very spark of philosophy to derive from theological considerations, as for example with the ancient Greeks.[56] It also has a desire to discover the internal order of truth and finds an attraction to the higher domain.[57] Finally the very quest for wisdom impels us to seek a higher perspective. For its part faith may seek to enter the domain of reason. It is a superior light which elevates reason in its own order. As Maritain said in *Man and the State* – a superior agent is not shut up within itself; it radiates and stimulates from within the very activity of reason or nature. This issue cannot be understood without a proper understanding of nature and grace.[58] Faith can assist reason in being more alert to its own internal limits – such as overcoming allurements and irrational dreams of ideology.[59] If the person refuses to allow faith and reason to speak to each other in his own heart and mind then distortions occur in both domains. From the side of faith it is the distortion of "fideism" to allow faith to become separated from the intellectual life of the person. Faith would lie "like a stone at the bottom of a pond, no longer vitally received by a living being."[60] Skepticism and or indifference is bound to occur, undermining faith from within on a popular level. And as for the intellectuals, pastoral values and

---

[56] See Josef Pieper, *Leisure: The Basis of Culture*, trans. Gerald Malsbary (South Bend, Indiana: Saint Augustine's Press, 1998), pp. 117-134.
[57] See Pope John Paul II, *Fides et Ratio*.
[58] See Charles Journet, *The Meaning of Grace*.
[59] On the need for theology to prevent overall distortions in education, see John P. Hittinger, "Newman, Theology and Crisis of Liberal Education." *Journal of Interdisciplinary Studies* 11, no. 1/2 (1999), pp. 61-82.
[60] *Peasant*, p. 94; also pp. 144-45.

efficacy become the supreme rule, not truth itself. But faith is held as mystery of truth, inviting a humble penetration of the truth. The dynamic of "pastoral" gives rise to historicism and a constant reinterpretation of faith in light of the times. Vatican Council II called for the reinterpretation of the signs of the times in light of the enduring truths of faith and philosophy. The distortion from the side of reason concerns its own self-discipline and a refusal to generate ideology and myths of reason. Modern intellectuals tend to enclose themselves within a rational self-sufficiency which did not characterize ancient philosophy with its sense of enduring wonder and the position of the metaxy between beasts and gods. The ever-recurring temptation of science is the one first initiated so well by Lucretius – the poeticizing of the mechanisms of the world. Edward Wilson consciously invokes this same muse.[61] The great questions of meaning about man, God and the world must lie beyond the scope of science. But science will make its poetic attempt, often doing bad theology rather than doing none at all. As Maritain says, the bad money chases out the good. The great hunger of the soul goes unfed. What is needed is an attention to the very intrinsic order of human intelligence, not the indiscriminate mixing together. Here again is the very rationale for reason's forays into faith – to better appreciate the internal ordering of truth and to complete its aspiration for wisdom.

This relationship of faith and reason is emblematic of the relationship between Church and State. It is the nodal point for the cooperation for church and state. The elevating influence of faith must primarily come through the person, in conscience and mind, not through external law.[62] Indeed it may well be that the different understandings of Church and State relations tracks the fate of faith and theology in higher education.[63] On the basis of the unity of the person, and the need for a dynamic unity in the cognitive life of the person, faith will either be engaged or it will become unhinged. Surely it is not a good thing for the polity to have a proliferation of cults and enthusiasms smacking of servitude and irrationality. So too does the state exercise its own self-discipline by refusing ideologies which divinize itself or the make the fashions of the time the height of wisdom itself. The distinction between the things of Caesar and the things of God, State and Church, rest upon this proper and salutary relationship between faith and reason.

The final point from the *Peasant* which develops the argument from the unity of the person sketched out in *Man and the State* concerns the very life of the Church itself and the new understanding of the role of the laity, the primary agents and the locus for the cooperation between Church and State. Maritain celebrates the achievement of Vatican II in putting forward the mystery of the Church as a great themes for its reflections. As he said in *Man and the State*, there is an inevitable misapprehension between the believer and the unbeliever because of their different approaches to the reality and nature of the Church. If one wishes to understand the agent as he understands

---

[61] Edward O. Wilson, *Consilience - The Unity of Knowledge* (New York: Alfred A. Knopf, Inc., 1998), and Edward O. Wilson, "Resuming the Enlightenment Quest," *The Wilson Quarterly* 22, no. 1 (1998), pp. 16-27.
[62] See Tocqueville, *Democracy in America*, "On the use which Americans make of associations in civil life," especially p. 515.
[63] See James Tunstead Burtchaell, "The Decline and Fall of the Christian College." *First Things*, April 1991, pp. 16-30.

himself, then the document *Lumen gentium* is a very important text for all those who are concerned about the relation between Church and State. Maritain briefly points out that the council emphasized the mystery of the Church; it is more than a sociological phenomenon or a set of external laws and institutions. Perhaps that is all that the unbeliever can see. But there is in addition a historic reality, a unity of being and life across time. There is memory and voice. The recent statements by John Paul II make sense only within such a context or frame of understanding. He can apologize for what various personnel of the Church have done, all the while maintaining the integrity and holiness of the Church.[64] In terms resonating with Solzhenitsyn, Maritain quotes his own mentor Cardinal Journet who said that the line of good and evil, of Christ and Belial, passes through the heart of each believer.[65] The emphasis upon the phrase "People of God" adds the historic dimension of the Church, its presence in the world as a pilgrim. And it thus follows the emphasis upon the laity to be sent out into the midst of the world. No longer would the Church seek separation from the world but be in the midst of the world in service to the world. The cooperation between Church and state is actively sought out by the believer, not in the mode of conversion, but as a witness through the very service to the world. As we saw above, Maritain distinguishes the two missions of the believer – a spiritual mission and a temporal mission. The spiritual mission is the work proper of the Church – transforming the world spiritually for the ultimate end. But in addition members of the Church have a mission to transform the temporal world with a view to the good of the world itself. Here again we face a potential divide with extremes at both ends. There is a divide between the spiritual and the temporal missions, or vocations, of the lay Christian. The separation between the two is an unnatural gash or cleavage which must be remedied first of all. How is this to be done? Maritain outlines the philosophical basis for this. The two vocations are distinct but not separate. It is the unity of the person which must forge their integration. For the concrete person is not a "laborer of the world with a certain portion of his being, and a member of the church with another portion: it is a member of the Church who is the laborer of the world, sent to the land of the things which are Caesar's."[66] And the unity of the person is achieved as follows: the object of the work is the temporal vocation; the manner or mode in which the work is done is the spiritual vocation. The object of the work is to do the temporal task well – whatever portion of the secular work for which one has responsibility. The effects of the cooperation are salutary for the body politic. "Such a work needs to be vivified, for without the strengthening of Christ's grace our nature is too weak to

---

[64] See "The Church, Holy and Penitent," *Peasant*, pp. 185-89; and for a much greater elaboration, see Jacques Maritain, *On the Church of Christ*, trans. Joseph W. Evans (Notre Dame, Indiana: University of Notre Dame Press, 1973).
[65] *Peasant*, pp. 188-189; cf. Alexandr Solzhenitsyn, *The Gulag Archipelago: Two*, trans. Thomas P. Whitney (New York: Harper & Row, 1975), p. 615; see Jacques Maritain, *On the Philosophy of History*, pp. 128-30.
[66] *Peasant*, p. 208.

carry it out."⁶⁷ It is precisely through religious inspiration that we have some hope for overcoming internal weakness and restraint of evil. Justice without love is inhuman; friendship must add to justice. The polity itself needs the ministrations of charity for which the Church is a primary agent. The spirit of the work will reflect the Christian's devotion to God and charity of life. The "radiance of the gospel" will shine through the daily task itself. The grace of religion will penetrate and transform the natural activity itself and perfect it within its own order. Maritain thus comes to apply the basic principles of St. Thomas Aquinas, on nature and grace, to the great issue of the day – the vital cooperation of Church and State in the new age of freedom.

## Conclusion

Maritain prepared the way for a new approach to Church and State relations. In the groundwork he laid in earlier works and in *Man and the State* we find a clear mature formulation of the position. In *The Peasant of the Garonne* we find its final elaboration in light of the definitive achievement of Vatican II: "In truth, every vestige of the Holy Empire is today liquidated; we have definitely emerged from the sacral age and the baroque age. After sixteen centuries which it would be shameful to slander or repudiate, but which have completed their death agony and whose grave defects were incontestable, a new age begins."⁶⁸ Maritain has given us a fulfillment of Tocqueville's deepest wish. The lover of liberty and the lover of God are one and the same. And with a further echo of Tocqueville, Maritain believes that the new approach will be advanced not by large mass programs or political deals, but through intermediate groups, which Maritain affectionately calls "Little Flocks." Only in the small flocks can the relentless pressures of technology and "massification" be resisted. In the small associations of men and women devoted to the inner tasks of renewal will the promise of the new age be at last fulfilled. As Maritain was fond of saying, the prospects for a "new Christendom" may not be for tomorrow or the day after tomorrow. But it is a concrete historical ideal worth our devotion. And the life of the spirit and efforts of renewal, exemplified by Maritain and his wife, will be a testimony for centuries to come.

---

⁶⁷ Ibid., p. 204; see also p. 226.
⁶⁸ *Peasant*, p. 4

# 15

## Maritain's "Integral Humanism" and Catholic Social Teaching

### Joseph M. de Torre

"Culture must cultivate man and each man along the extension of an *integral and full-fledged humanism*, through which *the whole man and all men* are promoted *in the fullness of every human dimension*. Culture's essential purpose is that of promoting the being of man, and of providing him with the goods needed for the development of his individual and social being." John Paul II "In the Work of Culture God has Made an Alliance with Man." Rio de Janeiro, 1 July 1980

For a fair and faithful assessment of Maritain's ground-breaking socio-political thought in his two major works, viz. *Integral Humanism* (1936) and *Man and the State* (1951), it is indispensable to evaluate them in the full context of his other related works, both before and after them.[1] The major criticisms against Maritain related to *Integral Humanism* and *Man and the State*, such as those of Joseph Desclausais, Louis Salleron (both 1936), Julio Alleinvielle (1945-48), and A. Massineo, S.J. (1956), were largely flawed by their failure to contextualize Maritain, which was precisely done by the trenchant defenses of Maritain by Etienne Borne, M. D. Chenu, Etienne Gilson, Olivier Lacombe, Charles Journet, Reginald Garrigou-Lagrange, Alcide De Gasperi, Cornelio Fabro, and Adriano Gallia, among others.[2] However, it is the contention of this paper that the decisive key for the

---

[1] *Three Reformers: Luther, Descartes, Rousseau*, New York: Scribners, 1929; *Freedom in the Modern World*, trans. Richard O'Sullivan (New York: Charles Scribner's Sons, 1936); *The Things That Are Not Caesar's*, trans. J. F. Scanlan (London: Sheed and Ward, 1939); *Ransoming the Time* (New York: Charles Scribner's Sons, 1941); *The Rights of Man and Natural Law*, trans. Doris C. Anson (New York: Charles Scribner's Sons, 1943); *The Dream of Descartes*, trans. Mabelle L. Andison (London: Editions Poetry London, 1946); *Christianity and Democracy*, trans. Doris C. Anson (New York: Scribner's, 1950); *An Essay on Christian Philosophy*, trans. Edward H. Flannery (New York: Philosophical Library, 1955); *On the Philosophy of History* (New York: Scribners, 1957); *Reflections on America* (New York: Scribner's, 1958); *Scholasticism and Politics*, trans. Mortimer J. Adler (New York: Image Books, 1960); *The Person and the Common Good*, trans. John J. Fitzgerald (Notre Dame, Indiana: University of Notre Dame Press, 1966); *The Peasant of the Garonne: An Old Layman Questions Himself About the Present Time*, trans. Michael Cuddihy and Elizabeth Hughes (New York: Holt, Rinehart and Winston, 1968).

[2] For accounts of the criticisms and controversies see Joseph Amato, *Mounier and Maritain* (University, Alabama: The University of Alabama Press, 1975); Brooke W. Smith, *Jacques Maritain: Antimodern or Ultramodern?* (New York: Elsevier Scientific Publishing, 1976); Bernard Doering, *Jacques Maritain and the French Catholic Intellectuals*, (Notre Dame, Indiana: University of Notre Dame Press, 1983); see also review of Doering by John P. Hittinger, in *This World*, no. 5 (Summer/Spring 1983), pp. 164-68.

interpretation of those two books is the development of the social doctrine of the Church, especially starting from John XXIII's *Mater et Magistra* (1961) and *Pacem in Terris* (1963) and Vatican II's *Gaudium et Spes* (1965), going through Paul VI's *Ecclesiam Suam* (1964), *Populorum Progressio* (1967), *Humanae Vitae* (1968), and *Evangelii Nuntiandi* (1975), and culminating in John Paul II's monumental output, starting right from his first encyclical, *Redemptor Hominis* (1979). Maritain's notion of "integral humanism" has played a pivotal role in the development of this social teaching. It is the purpose of this paper to give a brief indication of the connections between Maritain ground-breaking work in political philosophy and the subsequent teachings of Catholic pontiffs, especially Pope John Paul II.

Ever since Leo XIII's *Rerum Novarum* (1891), the social teaching of the Church (sometimes called "doctrine" when focusing on principles, and "teaching" when applying those principles to specific existential areas), has been gradually taking more and more precise shape around the dignity of the human person (human rights), the centrality of the traditional family, and the meaning and purpose of the civil community. It is through this teaching that the Church intends to act as a leaven in secular society, inculturating herself in every national or regional culture without identifying herself with any of them in their temporality and pluralism, but remaining a transcendent and illuminating force, in order to build a "civilization of love" (Paul VI) from within, or a *consecratio mundi* (John XXIII). In May 1981 John Paul II had prepared a speech to commemorate the 90th anniversary of *Rerum Novarum*, but he was unable to deliver it due to the attempt on his life. It was nevertheless published, and in it he managed to put the social teaching of the Church in a nutshell:

> This social teaching is born in the light of the Word of God and of the authentic Magisterium, from the presence of Christians within the changing situations of the world, in contact with the challenges that come from them. Its object is and always remains the sacred dignity of man, the image of God, and the protection of his inalienable rights; its purpose, the realization of its justice understood *as the advancement and complete liberation of the human person in his earthly and transcendent dimension;* its foundation, the truth about human nature itself, a truth *learned from reason and illuminated by Revelation;* its propelling power, love as the Gospel commandment and norm of action.

John Paul's description could well serve as précis of the animating vision of Maritain's *Man and the State*. Maritain developed this vision for Catholic social and political philosophy through the dark events of World War II. And indeed, the present urgency of the task was stated by John Paul in his message commemorating the 50th Anniversary of World War II in Europe (8 May 1995). After emphasizing the obligation never to forget that tragedy, he describes what led to it and what followed after it: "The world, and Europe in particular, headed towards that enormous catastrophe because they had lost the moral strength needed to oppose everything that was pushing them into the maelstrom of war. For totalitarianism destroys fundamental human freedoms and tramples upon human rights." Further he said that the policies and ideologies that led to the war, premised upon the failure to understand "that a society worthy of the person is not built by destroying the person, by repression and discrimination" have not at all disappeared. Thus he urges that "This lesson of the Second World War has not yet been learned completely and in all quarters. And yet it remains and must stand as a warning for the next millennium."

John Paul II serves as a sentinel in the tradition of Maritain; he continues Maritain's efforts to build the intellectual basis for a personalist theory of democracy, or an "integral humanism." Maritain was developing his thought in the historical context of the rise of the totalitarian ideologies of Fascism, Nazism and Communism, destructive of human rights and of the family, as well as of a democracy of freedom and responsibility toward the common good. When he published *Integral Humanism*, those ideologies were already at work politically, and about to unleash the Second World War with the fanaticism of a racial and nationalistic imperialism. The "integral humanism" proposed by Maritain in 1936 aspired to lead the human person towards a full development under the "primacy of the spiritual" that would eventually be fulfilled in Christ, as he himself, together with his beloved wife Raissa and her sister Vera, and in interaction with Fr. Clérissac, Peguy, Léon Bloy and others had personally experienced, particularly after his baptism in 1906 and the beginning of his Thomistic studies in 1910. Through the latter he discovered a Christian anthropology which could become a cultural bridge for all persons in a free society. His book *Christianity and Democracy* was published in 1943 "in homage to the French people" during their suffering. At the end of the war, the "cold war" broke out due to the fact that only the first two of those ideologies had been defeated, but not the third one: Marxist-Leninist Communism grew in its imperialistic designs and its suppression of human rights, in spite of the United Nations Universal Declaration of Human Rights in 1948. Maritain's involvement in this historic Document is also well known. In *Man and the State* he made a bold attempt to formulate a "secular democratic faith" accepted by all in a free society as a body of self-evident or at least certainly demonstrable truths prior and transcendent to, and assumed by any legal constitution: "For a society of free men implies basic tenets which are at the core of its very existence. A genuine democracy implies a fundamental agreement between minds and wills on the bases of life in common; it is aware of itself and of its principles, and it must be capable of defending and promoting its own conception of social and political life: *it must bear within itself a common human creed, the creed of freedom.*" Indeed Maritain sought to articulate the moral strength of a democratic creed precisely to counter the very premises that weakened the west in its encounter with totalitarianism. Bourgeois liberalism is unable to defend freedom in a coherent philosophy of government and public life; thus "Just as it had no real *common good*, it had no real *common thought* - no brains of its own, but a neutral, empty skull clad with mirrors: no wonder that before the second world war, in countries that Fascist, racist, or communist propaganda was to disturb or to corrupt, it had become a society without any idea of itself and without faith in itself, without any *common faith* which could enable it to resist disintegration." The practical faith articulated by Maritain was first of all "a merely practical one, not a theoretical or dogmatic one." People of a democratic society with different "even opposite metaphysical or religious outlooks, can converge, not by virtue of any identity of doctrine, but by virtue of an analogical similitude in practical principles, toward the same practical conclusions, and can share in the same practical secular faith, provided that they similarly revere, perhaps for quite diverse reasons, truth and intelligence, human dignity, freedom, brotherly love, and the absolute value of moral good." And yet it is of vital importance that a theoretical account be given and that it be true, for the temptation to skepticism is one of the "most alarming symptoms of the crisis of our civilization."[3] Thus he says that education is "the primary means to foster common secular faith in the democratic charter." And he insists that such education cannot be neutral or cut off from the "philosophical or religious traditions and schools of thought" which have contributed to the formation of the nation.[4]

Maritain was painstakingly trying to advocate what the present Pope has called a "public philosophy" for a converging dialogue with the world as proposed by the social teaching of the Church, chiefly presented in the above cited documents of the magisterium. The accusations of pragmatism, secularism, naturalism, liberalism, idealism, nihilism, ultraspiritualism, Marxism and other niceties were first vigorously refuted by those who knew him better, as mentioned earlier. And his ideas gradually became part of the nucleus of the social teaching of the Church in the specific framework of the reality of culture, a world culture, a "public philosophy" enlivened by a Christian anthropology answering the ultimate questions about the human person and the human community.

The two Popes of Vatican II, and the latter's *Gaudium et Spes* took up this question of culture and the social Gospel. Pope John XXIII, showing his openness to the world, not to "conform" to it (cf. Rom 12:2) but to evangelize it by inculturating the Gospel, significantly addressed his encyclical *Pacem in Terris* (1963) not just to Catholics but "to all men of good will." Then Paul VI, after issuing his first encyclical, *Ecclesiam Suam* (1964) on the dialogue of the Church with the world, addressed the United Nations in October 1965 as from a contemporary Areopagus, with the language of a "public philosophy" committed to universal truth. That very same year, the closest spiritual and intellectual friend of Maritain's, Fr. Charles Journet, was made a Cardinal in January, and in September, just before Paul VI's trip to New York to address the UN, the Pope received Maritain in Castel Gandolfo. And on December 8, at the close of Vatican II with the full-blooded Christocentric humanism expounded in Gaudium et Spes, the Pope addressed the

---

[3] *Man and the State*, p. 84.
[4] *Man and the State*, pp. 119-21.

Council's "Message to Seekers of Truth" to Jacques Maritain.[5] But the decisive moment came with the publication of the encyclical *Populorum Progressio* in 1967 in which Paul VI makes two explicit references to Maritain, one of them to *Integral Humanism*, both in its French and English versions. The same Pope went back to the idea of an inculturated Gospel through an integral humanism in his Apostolic Exhortation *Evangelii Nuntiandi* of 1975.

And then came John Paul II, who placed the whole question of culture at the center of his Pontificate, first in his first encyclical *Redemptor Hominis* of 1979; then in his address to the UN in October that year; and then in his programmatic Address of 2 June 1980 to the United Nations Educational, Scientific and Cultural Organization (UNESCO), counter-pointing it with his insistence on the centrality of the Church's social teaching as the heart of evangelization. This entire "public philosophy" and "integral humanism" was particularly hammered out in the series of addresses to "people of culture" or "builders of society" and of a "civilization of love," that is to scientists, philosophers, artists, diplomats, public officials, industrialists and so forth.

In Rio de Janeiro on 1 July 1980, just a month after his UNESCO Address: "In the Work of Culture God has Made an Alliance with Man" John Paul II uses the term "integral humanism" to explain that it is through culture that the work of Christian in democratic society best takes shape. "Culture must cultivate man and each man along the extension of an *integral and full-fledged humanism*, through which *the whole man and all men* are promoted *in the fullness of every human dimension*." Freedom must be understood in a more substantive sense than mere freedom of choice. The freedom which Christian democracy seeks to promote above all is what "St. Augustine called *libertas maior*, namely freedom in its full development, freedom in a morally adult state, capable of autonomous choices in regard to the temptations coming from every form of disorderly love of self. *The integral culture* includes the moral formation, the education in virtues of individual, social and religious life."

According to John Paul II education has a decisive role to play in this effort, especially higher education. In addressing Professors and Students at the Cathedral of Cologne, on 18 November 1980 and addressing university teachers at Bologna 18 April 1982 John Paul II warned against the dehumanizing effects of reductionistic schemes extrapolating from science. Preserving and developing a wholistic account of human beings pertains to "the university community [which must] convincingly demonstrate this necessity by presenting the fascination of that *integral humanism* which has always inspired the ideals and which for sure responds at all times to so many secret expectations of our contemporaries." In that same year, in his November visit to Spain, he gave two Addresses along this line,

---

[5] See Pope Paul VI, *Closing Speeches, Vatican Council II* (Boston: Daughters of St Paul, 1965); see new translation in the appendix, p. 245.

one at Salamanca and the other at Madrid. Then, at the University of Fribourg, 13 June 1984, "Science is free if it allows itself to be determined by truth." A crisis arises in scientific cultures by virtue of the fact that "science is not in a position to respond to the questions of its own meaning. And today's crisis is to a great extent a crisis of the ideology of scientism, which persists in affirming the self-sufficiency of the scientific project as if by itself it could satisfy all the essential questions which man asks himself." A great task for culture and the defense of freedom is occasioned by a sense of the very limits and partiality of science. The positive task is that of "the integration of knowledge, in the sense of a synthesis in which the imposing accumulation of scientific findings would discover its meaning in the framework of an *integral vision of man and the universe*, of the *ordo rerum*." This dialogue, indeed confrontation of science and culture, is "indispensable for laying the foundations of an *integral humanism*." Again, to Men of Culture, on 15 May 1988 in Lima ("Cultural development both in inculturating the faith and in the world of work and enterprise") John Paul said that the Church seeks to support "a *true integral humanism* which elevates man's dignity to his true and unrenounceable dimension of son of God."

Finally, To Men of Culture, Mexico City, 12 May 1990 John Paul harkens back to Paul VI closing remarks of the council: "This unrenounceable vocation of service to man - *to the whole man and to all men* - is that which moves the Church to address her call to the Mexican intellectuals - beginning with the Catholic intellectuals - that opening new spaces to participation and creativity they may not spare any effort to reach the completion of the work of integration - proper to true science - which will lay the foundations of *an authentic integral humanism* which incarnates the higher values of culture and of Mexican history."[6] It is the great task of culture to secure and elaborate on the basic notion of human dignity. John Paul himself elaborates upon the Vatican Council in the Constitution *Gaudium et Spes*, regarding the mystery of Christ in relation to man which sought to unfold and specify the meaning of human dignity in three respects: the notion of the person, the human capacity to love, and the human capacity for work. Indeed these may serve as the three great themes of John Paul's prodigious output of writings and speeches on social and political doctrine. John Paul looks to the teaching of Vatican II as the basis for his teaching.

The fathers of Vatican II root the dignity of the person in Christ as he who "fully reveals man to himself and manifests to him his most exalted vocation" because he has "in a certain sense *united himself to every man*. He has worked with human hands, has thought with a human mind, has acted with a human will, has loved with a human heart" (GS, 22). The person must attempt to integrate "all realities which make up his existence in a harmonious synthesis of life, oriented towards an ultimate meaning, which is the most sublime expression of love' *(ibid)*. The notion of "integral humanism" designates the goal of such a synthesis or personal and cultural integration.

---

[6] This reference to integral humanism echoes "integrum humanum," appendix, p. 250.

The second aspect of human dignity pertains to the capacity to love. "By loving, one discovers that the profound capacity to give oneself elevates the person and enlightens him interiorly. In fact, love is a dazzling appeal to go out of oneself and to transcend oneself." Thus Pope John Paul speaks of developing "*the civilization of love*," which is a "very attractive goal and, at the same time, demanding." As mentioned above, John Paul adopted the term "the civilization of love" from Pope Paul VI, who in turn derived it from Maritain's notion of integral humanism.

As for the third aspect, work, it is "one of the great themes of culture, particularly in our time." John Paul seeks to overcome the ancient separation between work and culture. "Looking at the past, it is interesting to recall the scarce value that in classical antiquity was given to labor as part of culture. In fact, leisure and work were often regarded as antithetical. In the cultural panorama, even in our days human labor does not always appear as a means of personal fulfillment. But from the angle of faith, the perspective becomes larger to the extent that it renders human activity a means of sanctification and an experience of union with God." The problem of human labor and work occupied a central portion of Maritain's work; he briefly mentions in *Man and the State* the issues of labor and work as the most urgent problem of the day.[7] But again it is in his great work *Integral Humanism* that Maritain most fully developed the idea of work and the transformation of the modern regime through a new approach to work and labor. This in part has served as the basis for the later developments of John XXIII, Paul VI, and John Paul II.[8]

Maritain served as an innovator who sometimes incurred the hostility and criticism of many of his fellow Catholics. But now in the light of subsequent developments in Catholic social teaching following Vatican II and the great torrent of writings and travels by John Paul II we can truly say that Maritain's notion of "integral humanism" has served to open a great stream of social political doctrine. Indeed many years ago Maritain, in a moment of self reflection called himself above all a "spring finder":

> What am I, I asked myself then. A professor? I think not; I taught by necessity. A writer? Perhaps. A philosopher? I hope so. But also a kind of romantic of justice too prompt to imagine to himself, at each combat entered into, that justice and truth will have their day among men. And also perhaps a kind of spring-finder who presses his ear to the ground in order to hear the sound of hidden springs, and of invisible germinations.[9]

We may well say that Maritain's great works *Integral Humanism* and *Man and the State* did indeed discover the "sound of hidden springs and of invisible germinations" whose fruits are only now being seen.

---

[7] *Man and the State*, p. 104.
[8] Jacques Maritain, *Integral Humanism*, trans. Joseph W. Evans (Notre Dame, Indiana: University of Notre Dame Press, 1973), pp. 184-91, 228-40.
[9] Jacques Maritain, *Notebooks* (Albany, New York: Magi Books, 1964), p. 3.

# 16

## Christian Humility and Democratic Citizenry: St. Augustine and Jacques Maritain

*Deborah Wallace Ruddy*

### Introduction

Jacques Maritain believed that a solid and secure democracy would be animated by Gospel values. In *Man and the State* he describes this belief in the mutually reinforcing relationship between Christianity and democracy:

> The more the body politic were imbued with Christian convictions and aware of the religious faith which inspires it, the more deeply it would adhere to the secular faith in the democratic character; for as a matter of fact, the latter has taken shape in human history as a result of the Gospel inspiration awakening the "naturally Christian" potentialities of common secular consciousness, even among the diversity of spiritual lineages and schools of thought opposed to each other, and sometimes warped by a vitiated ideology.[1]

Unfortunately, those today who join Maritain in claiming that Christian convictions strengthen democratic values rarely consider the prominent role of humility in the Christian tradition. Throughout the history of Christianity, humility has been central to the understanding of Christian discipleship. However, in an age psychologically attuned to the problem of low self-esteem and in a culture fixated on self-promotion, humility has become an unpopular, if not forgotten, virtue. Once regarded as *the* Christian attribute, found in an authentic sense of creaturehood, an acknowledgment of one's need for God, and a total abandonment to the will of God, humility is now looked upon by many as a weakness or character flaw.[2] Humility goes against a deeply imbedded impulse in our culture to overcome

---

[1] Jacques Maritain, *Man and the State* (Chicago: The University of Chicago Press, 1951), p. 113.
[2] The following is a sampling of authors who discuss the marginal condition of humility in modern society, in today's Christian community, and in contemporary scholarship in religious ethics: Matthew Baasten, "Humility and Modern Ethics" *Reformed Review* Spring 38 (1985), p. 3; Roberta C. Bondi, "Humility: A Meditation on An Ancient Virtue For Modern Christians," *Quarterly Review* (1983); John Casey, *Pagan Virtue: An Essay in Ethics*, (Oxford: Clarendon Press, 1990), pp. 199-200, 211; Brian E. Daley, S.J., "To Be More Like Christ: The Background and Implications of 'Three Kinds of Humility,'" *Studies in the Spirituality of Jesuits* 27 (1995); James F. Keenan,

or simply deny the frailty, imperfection, and incompletion of our lives. Moreover, in our image-conscious, control-oriented world, it is often associated with passivity and a fawning deference to those in power.

Even within Christianity, concerns about humility have been raised in the latter half of this century. For example, in the Roman Catholic church, since the Second Vatican Council (1962-65), the world-affirming and liberating dimensions of Christian spirituality have been emphasized more than the earlier other-worldly and ascetical elements.[3] Attention is given to the power of our human capacities and each person's responsibility for shaping his or her identity and social context. Those on the margins of society and of the church are encouraged to stand up and be counted while those in subservient positions are urged to confront the structures of domination. However, these essential Christian values tend to be placed in opposition to humility, which is regarded, at best, as a private, ascetical disposition and, at worst, as an attitude of weak passivity. Amidst contemporary efforts to identify and cultivate the apostolic and empowering aspects of discipleship, humility has been relegated to the periphery of Christian life and is often seen as a hindrance to social justice.

My aim in this paper is to draw upon St. Augustine's theology in order to retrieve the distinctively Christian roots and social applications of humility. Augustine is exceptional among the Christian Fathers of both East and West in highlighting Christ's humility as the hallmark of Christianity, utterly different from the moral values of antiquity.[4] Through the teachings of Augustine, I will examine how this frequently dismissed virtue can be reappropriated in contemporary Christian life, even Christian political life. First I will briefly consider some contemporary concerns and criticisms of humility. Next, I will outline the Christological basis for Augustine's understanding of this Christian disposition. Then, based on this theological understanding of humility, I will show some of the political and social implications of Augustinian humility. Finally, I will consider how a true embodiment of humility among Christian citizens today could help advance Maritain's vision of a "personalist" democracy that fosters the "spirit of the Gospel."[5] This will bring into focus how Christian humility can be constructive for the task of education within a democracy, particularly a democracy in a pluralistic

---

*Virtues for Ordinary Christians* (Kansas City, Missouri: Sheed and Ward, 1996), pp. 70-71; Alexander Schmemann, *Great Lent* (Crestwood, New York: St. Vladimir's Seminary Press, 1974), pp. 18-21; Nancy Snow, "Humility," *The Journal of Value Inquiry* 29 (1995), pp. 203-16; John M. Templeton, *The Humble Approach: Scientists Discover God* (New York: The Seabury Press, 1981).
[3] See *Pastoral Constitution on the Church in the Modern World (Gaudium et Spes)* (Boston: Daughters of St. Paul, 1965), in eds. David J. O'Brien and Thomas A. Shannon, *Catholic Social Thought: The Documentary Heritage* (Maryknoll, NY: Orbis Books, 1992), pp. 191-195; National Conference of Catholic Bishops, *Catholic Social Teaching and the U.S. Economy* (Washington, D.C.: United States Catholic Conference, 1984).
[4] D. J. MacQueen, "*Contemptus Dei*: St. Augustine on the Disorder of Pride in Society, and Its Remedies," *Recherches Augustiniennes* 9 (1973), pp. 237-59, 280.
[5] Maritain, *Man and the State*, p. 179.

society. The link between Christian humility and democratic citizenry, then, is found specifically in Maritain's insistence that education, both in academia and more broadly within public discourse, is crucial to a more Christian culture and civilization. For Maritain, the political task is essentially "a task of civilization and culture."[6]

## Contemporary Views of Humility

In a society increasingly shaped by "the triumph of the therapeutic,"[7] humility evokes images of a self-deprecating person with little sense of his or her own self-worth. Thus, the modern person links humility with a polite modesty, or, more negatively, with cowardice. At the social level, humility is associated with a world-renouncing mentality that produces inaction and a retreat from serious engagement in the struggle, so essential to democracy, for justice and the common good.

One source of this challenge to humility comes from many contemporary feminists who voice concern that traditional Christian virtues, such as humility, can impede women's struggle for self-realization, and discourage a healthy egoism.[8] Many Christian feminists associate humility with submission to a male-dominated culture and church, which expect women to give of themselves in ways that compromise their own integrity.[9] In her now classic article, "The Human Situation: A Feminine View,"[10] Valerie Saiving Goldstein argues that traditional Christian exhortations to self-sacrifice serve to correct the *male* temptation to pride but are less applicable to the moral problems that most women face. For women, Goldstein argues, the primary temptation is failing to develop a centered self.[11] This discussion has led feminists to ask whether upholding humility as a central virtue favors a male-oriented approach to virtue and perpetuates a patriarchal framework for ethics.[12]

Offering a perspective somewhat unique in relation to many feminist scholars, Roberta Bondi takes up the task of seeking to recover humility from its long-standing misapplications, particularly in reference to women. For Bondi, the true humility found in the life and work of the early monastics inspires a reconsideration of this ancient virtue for modern times. Similar to the aims of this paper, Bondi seeks to re-present Christian humility and reclaim it for men and women in the modern context. She acknowledges the challenge of recovering this humility and

---

[6] Maritain, *The Rights of Man and Natural Law* (New York: Gordian Press, 1971), p. 44.
[7] Phillip Rieff, *The Triumph of the Therapeutic* (Chicago: The University of Chicago Press, 1966).
[8] Valerie Saiving Goldstein, "The Human Situation: A Feminine View," *Journal of Religion* 40 (1960), pp. 100-12; Anne E. Patrick, *Liberating Conscience: Feminist Explorations in Catholic Moral Theology* (New York: Continuum, 1996); Judith Plaskow, *Sex, Sin and Grace* (Lanham, Maryland: University Press of America, 1980).
[9] Roberta Bondi, *To Love As God Loves: Conversations with the Early Church* (Philadelphia: Fortress, 1987), pp. 46-56; Karen Jo Torjesen, *When Women Were Priests: Women's Leadership in the Early Church and the Scandal of their Subordination in the Rise of Christianity* (San Francisco: Harper, 1993).
[10] Valerie Saiving Goldstein, "The Human Situation: A Feminine View," *The Journal of Religion*, 40 (1960), pp. 100-12.
[11] Ibid., p. 109.
[12] Anne Patrick, "Narrative and The Social Dynamics of Virtue," in *Changing Values and Virtues*, eds. Dietmar Mieth and Jacques Pohier (Edinburgh: T. & T. Clark, 1987), pp. 77-78.

seeks to understand the negative associations it has acquired. Noting how humility has often been misapplied, she writes:

> Across the many centuries of the Christian era up to the modern world when women have been exhorted to be humble, humility included as one of its components being obedient to their husbands, fathers, brothers, and/or priests. Humility has been a shorthand word for recognizing and accepting an inferior position in the world. Sometimes it has included accepting that other people had a right to buy or sell them ... The real difficulty is not so much that women have been taught to serve but that service seems to demand loss of self. The very phrase, "selfless love" raises the specter of a woman without any needs, desires, or even personality of her own.[13]

Women, as we have seen, have been encouraged to adopt a type of false humility whereby they serve others at the expense of their true selves. They often compromise their own talents and freedom in submitting to others. Bondi points to the manipulative uses of humility which amount to a false humility. For example, self-sacrifice can be a ploy to induce guilt and put another person in one's debt. She writes:

> Unfortunately, so many of us have been so victimized by this pattern of relating to people at home, in church, and at work that both the words "self-sacrifice" and "humility" fill us with horror. One result is that to talk with any meaning of the humility or self-sacrifice of Christ has become nearly impossible to a good many people. But the "you take the only good chair" way of dealing with others is manipulation, not humility. It is a gross perversion of Christianity, and it needs to be recognized for what it is. Real humility brings freedom and love to its recipients, not guilt and resentment.[14]

Christian humility, Bondi argues, has nothing to do with such low self-esteem and somber self-accusation. The early monastics, for example, found in humility the grounds for building relationships free from the demands of image-making as well as the cultural norms of dominance and subservience. Humility does not suggest that a woman sacrifice the core of who she is to be wholly committed to others. "Being a doormat," Bondi argues, "is not being humble, nor is giving up the self in order to serve the needs, desires, and whims of another person who is not God."[15] Rather, a woman's devotion to others must flow out of her core identity which is found in her relationship to God—a relationship that makes possible a love that is fundamentally joyful, relational, and life-giving.

One of Augustine's great insights, beautifully illustrated in the *Confessions*, is that knowledge of self is inextricably linked to knowledge of God. True self-knowledge is found only in relationship to the divine. Augustine writes: "For what

---

[13] Bondi, *To Love as God Loves*, pp. 43-44.
[14] Ibid., p. 45.
[15] Ibid., p. 54.

I know of myself I know because you grant me light, and what I do not know of myself, I do not know until such time as my darkness becomes 'like noonday' before your face (Isa. 58:10)."[16] Paradoxically, leaving behind the illusory self, that is, the self that functions as its own *principium*, leads to the discovery of one's true identity in God. Before God, the true self, which readily gives of self to others, come to the surface.

Insofar as a person withholds his or her talents and human capabilities from others, false humility (a manifestation of pride) is at work. Exaggerated self-disparagement and a cowering detachment from others are distortions of Christian humility, even if they are all too frequently adopted in Christian attempts to live humbly. However, Christian humility, at its uncommon best, emerges from the free decision to give of oneself to God and others. In other words, humility has an expansive and liberating quality that frees a person from the fears of the ego and awakens a person to the fullest expression of human dignity.

And so, as we consider humility today it is important to distinguish Christian humility from false humility: to discern the difference between manipulative self-abnegation or coerced self-sacrifice, on the one hand, and a true giving of self to others modeled on the *kenosis* or outpouring of Christ's love, on the other.

### Augustine's Understanding of Humility

Writing in Latin-speaking North Africa at the end of the fourth century and the beginning of the fifth, Augustine consistently presents humility as a central notion for understanding Christ and the Christian way of life. Among the Church Fathers, Augustine is noted for insisting most strongly upon humility's centrality for Christian discipleship.[17] The theological basis for Augustine's doctrine of humility is in his Christology for he derives his understanding of humility from the Gospel narratives of the life, death, and resurrection of Jesus Christ.[18] Augustine upholds Christ as the archetype of Christian humility so that a truly compelling, transforming, and comprehensive account of this virtue must derive from an understanding of Christ who grounds and animates true humility. Augustine's wonder at the "humble God" (*humilis deus*)[19] of Jesus Christ reverberates throughout his works. In Jesus Christ, the Incarnate Word, divine love is revealed "in the form of a servant" (Phil 2:7). The self-emptying (*kenosis*) of the Word—the divine descent into human history—is the paradigmatic form and source of humility in Christian

---

[16] Augustine, *Confessions,* 10.5.7, trans. Henry Chadwick (Oxford: Oxford University Press, 1991), pp. 182-83.
[17] Clement of Alexandria, Origen, Gregory of Nyssa, Basil, Hilary of Poitiers, Ambrose, John Chrysostom all upheld Christ as the model of humility. But P. Adnès observes that Augustine is most insistent about this theme: "Mais c'est peut-être chez Augustin que le thème prend le plus de relief. Docteur et maître de l'humilité, le Christ l'est non seulement par ses paroles et sa doctrine, mais par ses actes et son exemple: 'Magister humilitatis verbo et exemplo.'" "Humilité," *Dictionnaire de spiritualité* 7 (1969), pp. 1153-54.
[18] *Enarrationes in Psalmos,* 31.2.18: "Via humilitatis huius aliunde manat; a Christo venit. Haec via ab illo est, qui cum esset altus, humilis venit." *Corpus Christianorum, Series Latina* (Turnhout: Brepols, 1981), vol. 38, p. 239.
[19] *De catechizandis rudibus,* 4.8.

discipleship.[20] Christian humility is thus more than a virtue that God urges upon us. It is the very way God's Word comes to us and invites us to pattern our lives.[21] The way of humility, then, is primarily God's way. Only by extension is it our way, insofar as we imitate the divine through Christian discipleship.

According to Augustine, one way to understand Christ's humility, is to see it in opposition to pride, the root of human sin expressed in the desire to substitute the self for God and dominate over others.[22] Augustine's use of the word *superbia*, often translated as "pride," means something more serious than what is generally conveyed by "pride" in the modern context where pride is regarded as boastfulness or at best, self-assuredness and confidence. Deriving his understanding of pride principally from the biblical doctrine of creation, and deeply influenced by the text of Ecclesiasticus (Sirach 10:13), Augustine writes: "'The beginning of all sin is pride; and 'The beginning of the pride of man is to fall off from God.'[23] It has been written, it is sure, it is true."[24] For Augustine, the vice of pride always entails, at its root, an offense or revolt against God. It does not have a strictly anthropocentric sphere of reference as it tends to in contemporary parlance.

In the *City of God*, Augustine discusses this fall of the human race as originating inwardly in the pride of the corrupted will:

> It was in secret that the first human beings began to be evil; and the result was that they slipped into open disobedience. For they would not have arrived at the evil act if an evil will had not preceded it. Now could anything but pride have been the start of the evil will? For 'pride is the start of every kind of sin' (Eccles. 10:13). And what is pride except a longing for a perverse kind of exaltation?[25]

Pride is the original sin: it was through pride that the first human parents fell from harmony with God and passed on to their descendants a need for the restoration of friendship with God. In the passage above, Augustine claims that this first sin originates not principally from the body but from the will. It begins in a failure to accept creatureliness. Instead of seeking to be like God according to God's will, the proud person wills to achieve God-like status on his or her own terms.[26]

Augustine views the dichotomy between pride and humility not principally in ethical terms but in ontological ones because pride offends the very structure of reality and humility abides by it. Pride and humility represent two fundamentally different responses to the givenness of created reality. Augustine believes that there

---

[20] *Serm.* 92.2; *Serm.* 68.
[21] Augustine often discusses humility in connection with the exhortation of Matthew's Gospel: "Learn from me; for I am gentle and humble of heart." (11:29); see *Confessions* 7.9.14; *Tractates on the Gospel of St. John* 25.18; *City of God* 14:13.
[22] Augustine and other Fathers (Basil, John Chrysostom, Dorotheus of Gaza) considered pride as the central vice.
[23] *Ecclesiaticus* 10:13 is first quoted in *De musica* 6.13.40.
[24] *Tractates on the Gospel of John*, 25.15 trans. J.W. Rettig, p. 253.
[25] Augustine, *The City of God*, 14.13, trans. Henry Bettenson (New York: Penguin Classics, 1984), p. 571.
[26] Marthinus Versfeld, "The notions of pride and imitation in St. Augustine," *South African Journal of Philosophy* 2.4 (1983), p. 180.

is truth and purpose in created reality, but it is not a purpose that *we* create. God alone gives purpose, meaning, and direction to the world. Humility, then, involves a submission: neither a submission to something of one's own creation, nor to an arbitrary set of rules, but, a submission to reality. This reality is designed with a definite orientation to goodness, a goodness modeled upon the goodness of God the Creator. Augustine teaches that ordered love (*ordo amoris*)[27] reflects the ordering of creation by the Creator. God is loved first above all other beings and in this love of God flows a proper love of self, neighbor, and lesser things, in that order.[28]

Augustine sees pride as the most nefarious of the vices because it can be present even when one appears to be doing good. Long before Nietzsche set out to reveal the pride hidden under the cloak of humility, Augustine warned his fellow African Christians about false humility for actions that seem humble often can be the most deeply arrogant. Knowing that when a person doing good begins to crave praise and honor, appearances can become more valued than the good deed, he warns: "We must be fearful of all the other vices in sin, but pride we have to fear even when we do right. We mustn't let our desire for praise cost us the things we do that are worthy of praise."[29]

Robert Markus points out that another feature of Augustine's notion of pride involves a retreat into privacy, at the expense of giving oneself to others and ultimately to God.[30] Pride can move from more overt expressions of dominance to a more concealed closing of the heart. Pursuing individual interest before the good of others turns the self in upon itself. Pride, then, has a depersonalizing and isolating effect in that one loves others not for what they are but for how they meet one's desires. In this underappreciated dimension of pride there is a movement of separation successively from God, oneself, and others. Markus explains:

> At first [pride] is identified with taking pleasure in the wrong things, pleasing oneself rather than God; in the second stage, this is refined: pride is here seen in taking pleasure in God's good things, but as if one had proprietary rights to them; finally, whittling it down to its most insidious form, he will present pride as the desire for privacy at the expense of sharing. Here is the opposition we found in the *De Genesi ad litteram* between the shared, the social, and the private, the last and most hidden refuge of pride. The subtlest temptation is that of the retreat into self, the fear "of belonging to another, or to others, or to God."[31]

The depersonalizing effect of pride is demonstrated in the first four books of the *Confessions* where Augustine, while being very sociable, does not mention any friends

---

[27] *City of God*, 15.22, p. 636.
[28] *Sermon* 336.2 in Augustine, *Sermons*, trans. Edmund Hill, ed. John E. Rotelle *The Works of Saint Augustine: A Translation for the 21st Century* (Brooklyn, New York: New City Press, 1990), part 3, vol. 9, p. 267. All other references to the sermons are from this edition.
[29] *Letters of Saint Augustine*, trans. John Leinenweber (Tarrytown, New York: Triumph Books, 1992), p. 101.
[30] R. A. Markus, "*De civitate dei*: Pride and the Common Good," *Augustine "Second Founder of the Faith"* (New York: Peter Lang, 1990), pp. 245-59.
[31] Ibid., p. 250.

by name, let alone the name of his mistress of fourteen years! Augustine even finds that he is a "stranger" to himself insofar as he is estranged from God.[32]

Relying on their own audacious drive for self-sufficiency, the proud stand alone and become their own *principium*. The Stoics, for example, ascribed virtue to themselves rather than acknowledging God as the source of all virtue and goodness.[33] Scorning the pride of the Manichaeans, Augustine remarks, "The trouble is that they want to be light not in the Lord but in themselves."[34] In the *City of God*, Augustine explains how pride can advance from a rejection of creatureliness to a lust for power and domination over others: "[P]ride is a perverted imitation of God. For pride hates a fellowship of equality under God, and seeks to impose its own dominion on fellow men, in place of God's rule."[35] The isolation and distortion of pride objectifies others who become the victims of a self-inflated ego. Here Augustine shows the interdependence of love of God and the love of neighbor for the rejection of one automatically entails a rejection of the other.

Having emphasized the fall from God through pride, Augustine turns to the remedy of Christ, "the humble God."[36] In an act of humility, Christ "came down" to us. Out of love, he shares in our creatureliness and reverses our rejection of creatureliness. He shows the scandal of our own pride and makes possible our restoration.[37] In *On the Catechising of the Uninstructed*, Augustine marvels at Christ's humility as the "counteracting remedy" to our pride:

> [T]he same Lord Jesus Christ, God-man, is both a manifestation of divine love towards us, and an example of human humility with us, to the end that our great swelling might be cured by a greater counteracting remedy. For here is a great misery, proud man! But there is greater mercy, a humble God![38]

Here Augustine points to the antitheses between pride/humility and illness/cure, as well as an antithesis of movement. The movement of the Incarnation "towards us" from superiority to inferiority is the reverse of the movement of human pride "away from God" from inferiority to superiority.

At a crucial moment in the *Confessions* Augustine sees the egoism of the Neoplatonists as *the reason* for their disdain toward the Incarnation. Stressing the contrast between Christ's *humilitas* and the Platonists' *superbia*, he asks: "Where was the charity which builds on the foundation of humility which is Christ Jesus?

---

[32] Perhaps one contemporary manifestation of this prideful depersonalization and withdrawal from others is the pervasive social and political apathy. In the United States, this is evidenced in the disheartening turnouts at the polls, the membership decline in voluntary associations, the growing mistrust of politicians, and the overall cynicism toward social and political engagement.
[33] *Letter* 155.2;4;6.
[34] *Confessions*, 8.10.22, Chadwick, p. 148.
[35] *City of God*, 19.12, Bettenson, pp. 868-69.
[36] Augustine, *On the Catechising of the Uninstructed*, 4.8, trans. S. D. F. Salmond, in *Nicene and Post-Nicene Fathers*, vol. 3, p. 287.
[37] Augustine, *Sermon* 50.8, vol. 2.
[38] Augustine, *On the Catechising of the Uninstructed*, 4.8.

When would the Platonist books teach me that?"[39] Here, Christ's humility is placed at the forefront of this tension between Greek philosophy and Christianity.

In Augustine's own conversion, Christ's humility plays a pivotal role in overcoming his pride for in contemplating "the humble God" he finds his love radically reoriented. In the final stages of his conversion, Augustine does not come to God by way of an intellectual insight or a moral breakthrough. Rather, the drama of divine lowliness evokes Augustine's surrender in faith. With awe he writes about the transforming power of humility made manifest in the Incarnation: "They [i.e., humble Christians] see at their feet divinity become weak by his sharing in our 'coat of skin' (Gen. 3:21). In their weariness they fall prostrate before this divine weakness which raises and lifts them up."[40]

As he reflects upon the mystery of the Incarnation and the Cross, Augustine insists that humility stands as the most fundamental disposition necessary for all who seek to follow in Christ's footsteps. In a famous letter to Dioscorus, a young Greek scholar, Augustine upholds humility as the condition and foundation for Christian living:

> To [Christ] ... I wish you to submit with complete devotion, and to construct no other way for yourself of grasping and holding the truth than the way constructed by Him who, as God, saw how faltering were our steps. This way is first humility, second humility, third humility, and however often you should ask me I would say the same, not because there are no other precepts to be explained, but if humility does not precede and accompany and follow every good work we do, and if it is not set before us to look upon, and beside us to lean upon, and behind us to fence us in, pride will wrest from our hand any good deed we do while we are in the very act of taking pleasure in it.[41]

Here Augustine applies his rhetorical skill to uphold humility as the beginning, middle, and end of Christian discipleship. He insists that humility is more than a virtue or an antidote to pride. It is the fundamental Christian orientation which prepares the way for all other Christian virtues.

At its most basic level, humility requires an honesty about our proper place in the divine ordering of creation. It does not insist upon self-degradation but true self-knowledge. Rather than being a mask for pride, true humility guards against pride and its many forms of self-aggrandizement. Humility holds in check the perverse human tendency to "play God."[42] It begins with a surrender to God's primacy and an acceptance of our creaturely dependence on God's grace. As humility deepens it entails a confession of sin (disordered love) which violates the created order, and reveals our need for God's grace. Finally, in freeing us from egocentricity, humility brings joy in the discovery of the true value of ourselves and others in God.

---

[39] Augustine, *Confessions*, 7.20.26, Chadwick, p. 130.
[40] Ibid., 7.18.24, Chadwick, p. 128.
[41] Augustine, "Letter 118," trans. Wilfrid Parsons, in *The Fathers of the Church*, vol. 18 (New York: The Fathers of the Church, Inc., 1953), p. 282.
[42] Augustine, *Sermon* 137.4, vol. 4, p. 374.

From this stance of truthfulness we can grow in a readiness to love as God loves: to give wholly of ourselves in love to others. Augustine's vision of Christ's humility as the distinctive mode and character of Christian loving highlights how such love has a sacrificial character requiring a free giving of self without the expectation of something in return. Integral to humility is the transformation of egocentric love into theocentric love which turns grasping, exploitative, and possessive impulses into an authentic love of self and a true solidarity with others for the sake of God.[43] This teaching on humility comes from one of Augustine's favorite passage from St. Paul: " … though he was in the form of God, [he] did not regard equality with God as something to be exploited, but emptied himself, taking the form of a slave, being born in human likeness" (Phil. 2:6-7).[44] Consequently, humility has a radically social dimension whereby it finds expression in service to others and in radical self-giving modeled on the *kenosis* or outpouring of the divine Word.

Augustine regularly links together humility and Christian love (*caritas*). Preaching in 413, he explains to his congregation that Christ's humility is the essential source and foundation of the Christian's own self-giving:

> Learn from him [Christ], because he is meek and humble of heart. Dig in yourself this foundation of humility, and you will eventually reach the pinnacle of charity.[45]

For Augustine, humility makes true Christian love possible for it is the soil out of which charity grows.[46]

Moreover, Christ is the standard by which we distinguish true humility from false humility. Preaching on Matthew 11:25-27 near the end of his life, Augustine says:

> You won't become humble unless you look at the one who became humble for your sake. Learn from Christ what you won't learn from man; in him is to be found the standard of humility (*norma humilitatis*). Those who measure up to him are first formed in humility, in order to be eventually honored with high nobility.[47]

Humble self-giving modeled on the humble Christ requires physical and active love of others. Humility calls for a readiness to place oneself wholly at the service of others, as Christ demonstrates in the washing of his disciples' feet. Humbling himself before them, Christ demonstrates that his love is concrete, tangible, and unafraid to touch the unwashed parts of humanity, literally and figuratively:

> We have learned, brothers, humbleness from an Exalted One; let us, humble in our turn, do what the Exalted One did humbly. Great is this commendation of humility! And the brothers do this to one another, and indeed by very visible activity, when

---

[43] Augustine, *Sermon* 250.5, vol. 7, p. 181.
[44] NRSV.
[45] *Sermon* 69.4, vol. 3, p. 237.
[46] Augustine, *The Trinity*, 4.2, trans. Edmund Hill, ed. John E. Rotelle *The Works of Saint Augustine: A Translation fot the 21st Century* (Brooklyn, New York: New City Press, 1990) part 1, vol. 5, p. 153.
[47] Augustine, *Sermon* 126.11: *"Disce a Christo, quod non discis ab homine: in illo est norma humilitatis; ad hunc qui accedit, prius in ipsa humilitate formatur, ut in exaltatione decoretur"*; see *Sermon* 68.11, vol. 3, p. 230.

they receive one another in hospitality. For among very many there is the habitual practice of this humility, even as regards the act by which it is exhibited and seen ... it is much better and indisputably truer that it should also be done by the hands; and let the Christian not disdain to do what Christ did. For when the body is bent to the brother's feet, the affection of humility itself either is stirred in the very heart or if it was already there, is strengthened ... by washing the feet of his already washed and cleansed disciples, the Lord signified, on account of the human affections in which we are involved on earth, that, however much progress we have made in the attainment of justice, we may know that we are not without sin; and he now and again washes by interceding for us when we pray that the Father who is in heaven forgive us our debts as we forgive our debtors.[48]

In this act of foot washing, Christ reveals our ongoing need for the cleansing forgiveness that his hands perpetually extend to each one of us. By his own actions, he sets a high standard for the *practice* of humility. Reflecting upon this scene in John's Gospel, Augustine does not limit the meaning of this action to a spiritual attitude of humility but describes the healing touch of humility that is shown with the hands.

In our own concrete self-offering to one another, we become Christ's presence in the world. The humility of Christ is repeated time and again in the flesh through such active self-giving. Humility, in this context, is not simply a pure unmerited gift, but a gift that, paradoxically, needs to be cultivated. In humble service, in literally kneeling before the feet of our brothers and sisters, the self is not destroyed in servile abasement but reconstituted and perfected through a participation in the divine pattern of loving.

In sum, Augustinian love shaped by humility begins with an awareness of creatureliness and a trusting reliance upon God's grace. This orients a person outward toward others in love and service. Pride, in contrast, begins with a rejection of creatureliness and the attempt to be self-sufficient. This orients a person inward, away from God and neighbor.

### Humility in Augustine's Political Thought

Augustine's belief that Christ is the foundation of humility has practical consequences and directly affects his ideas about the Christian disciple's relationship to the world. Augustine believed that the Christian is never fully a citizen of this world but is rather a "pilgrim" detached from those temporal concerns which prioritize the enjoyment of life, material possessions, and status. In the *City of God*, for instance, Augustine writes: "[H]umility is ... especially enjoined on the City of God during the time of its pilgrimage in this world."[49] The basic orientation of a Christian is to long for the true homeland that is the City of God. This "pilgrim" consciousness could curb some of the self-idolatry and materialism that can be so enervating in political life today. But is the "heavenly longing" so integral

---
[48] *Tractates on the Gospel of John*, 58.4.
[49] Augustine, *City of God*, 14:13, trans. Henry Bettenson, p. 573.

to Augustine's understanding of humility the type of longing that implies a contempt of the world and an isolation from social injustice? Does Augustine's promotion of humility among Christian citizens ultimately mean that Christians should be decent citizens, and just accept society as it is?[50]

In his own time, Augustine recognized social inequalities as wrong, but the sheer weight of classical culture and politics and the endless cycle of human sinfulness seemed so increasingly intractable that he did not imagine that significant transformation in the temporal sphere was possible. Furthermore, Augustine gave priority to interior disposition over the more "external" roles played in society. These factors led him to deem it better to be the slave of a human master than the slave to lust for domination.[51] In the *City of God*, he writes: "As for this mortal life, which ends after a few days' course, what does it matter under whose rule a man lives, being so soon to die, provided that the rulers do not force him to impious and wicked acts?"[52] Thus while acknowledging social injustices, Augustine did not expect a radical reformation of these structures of domination. Today after certain forms of slavery and oppression, though certainly not all, have been overcome, we are inevitably led to question Augustine's skepticism about social change.[53]

Despite Augustine's increasingly low expectations for lasting transformation in this world, his teaching on the actual practice of humility offers a helpful counterweight to those who would absent themselves from concrete engagement with the world. In his sermons and in the *City of God*, however, Augustine also stresses the active and communal dimension of humility which offsets this skepticism and resignation about social change. The sermons, in particular, as we will see, appeal to Christ's deeds and inner attitude to develop the Christian way of life. Augustine points out that a humble attitude liberates us from despairing when our ideals are not fully realized, for humility fosters a willingness to face up to the needs of our human situation and our radical dependence on God. Christ's humility points toward realism and away from an idealism that so easily collapses into despair and defeatism. With an honest awareness of the sinful human condition and a ready trust in God's mercy, humble self-knowledge paves the way for more sustained work in the world. True self-knowledge, which is a basic form of humility, ushers in the more active and mature dimension of humility that calls for a total giving of oneself in love of neighbor.

---

[50] Hannah Arendt, *Love and St. Augustine* (Chicago: The University of Chicago Press, 1996). Many scholars, Hannah Arendt most notably, have held that Augustine's political thought implies that Christians ought to remove themselves from the messiness of the world's political complexities.

[51] Augustine, *City of God*, 19.15: "And obviously it is a happier lot to be slave to a human being than to a lust; and, in fact, the most pitiless domination that devastates the hearts of men, is that exercised by this very lust for domination, to mention no others. However, in that order of peace in which men are subordinate to other men, humility is as salutary for the servants as pride is harmful to the masters. And yet by nature, in the condition in which God created man, no man is the slave either of man or of sin," Bettenson, p. 875.

[52] Augustine, *City of God*, 5.17, Bettenson, p. 205.

[53] Eugene TeSelle, "Towards an Augustinian Politics," *Journal of Religious Ethics*, p. 93.

In a homily on the works of mercy, Augustine refers to this *practice* of humility as "the humility of lending a helping hand."[54] He challenges the wealthy of his day to consider how humility requires more than giving from a distance to assist the material needs of the poor. One must give personally with one's own hands:[55]

> What's called for, you see, is not only the kindness of lavishing assistance, but also the humility of lending a helping hand. I don't know how it is, my brothers and sisters, but the spirit of the person who actually hands something to a poor man experiences a kind of sympathy with common humanity and infirmity, when the hand of the one who has is actually placed in the hand of the one who is in need. Although the one is giving, the other receiving, the one being attended to and the one attending are being joined in a real relationship. You see, it isn't calamity that really unites us but humanity.[56]

Here humility revealed by the Incarnate God calls for direct service and relationship with those in need. Humility is not the friendly condescension of the wealthy allaying their consciences. Rather, humility cuts through class differences by joining people in their common humanity, overturning the conventional patterns of human relating both in Augustine's time and our own. As Christ becomes a neighbor to us in humility, we become neighbors to one another. Humility teaches that we are in solidarity with one another as members of his one Body. From the outside, a rich person bending down to help someone who is poor can suggest a disparity in worth or dignity, but humility frees a person to see through such distortions; both are indebted to God who gives salvation out of love not merit.

Moreover, Augustine points out that a humble attitude liberates us from despairing when our ideals are not fully realized, for there is a willingness to face up to the needs of our human situation and our radical dependence on God. In a homily on the Gospel of John 14:16 ("I am the way, the truth, and the life."), Augustine explains:

> To keep, however, to the middle way, the true, straight road, threading its way, as it were, between the left hand of despair and the right hand of presumption, would be extremely difficult for us, unless Christ had said I am the way ... Christ the way is the humble Christ; Christ the truth and the life is Christ exalted and God. If you walk along the humble Christ, you will arrive at the exalted Christ; if in your sickly health and debility you do not spurn the humble one, you will abide in perfect health and strength with the exalted one. What else, after all, was the reason for Christ's humility, but your debility?[57]

Christ's humility, then, is the way out of despair and defeatism. With an honest acceptance of the human condition and a ready trust in God's mercy, humility paves the way for a moral and spiritual regeneration.

---

[54] *Sermon* 250.5, vol. 7, p. 182.
[55] Ibid., note 23, p. 184.
[56] Ibid., p. 182.
[57] *Sermon* 142.1, vol. 4, p. 413.

In the *City of God*, Augustine makes the point that the humble do not presume to know who is in the City of God. Those we consider our most reprehensible enemies may be future citizens of the City of God, for the two cities, of God and of man, are interwoven and intermixed until the separation at the last judgment. Thus, the logic of the two cities necessitates a refusal to pre-empt God's judgment. It calls for an openness to others, a Christian universality and egalitarianism which come from a concern for the destiny of every person, even those who seem unlikely citizens of the City of God. This eschatological outlook leads Augustine to point out that the church must bear in mind that among its pagan accusers "are hidden her future citizens; and when confronted with them she must not think it a fruitless task to *bear with their hostility* until she finds them confessing the faith."[58] Christians, then, ought not to dismiss their accusers but to persist with engagement and be alert to truth when it appears where it is least expected.[59] After all, according to Augustine's theological anthropology, no sinner is ever wholly cut off from the truth; no misconceptions or immorality are ever wasted. God uses our wanderings, even our sin, to further our conversion.[60] Furthermore, dialogue with those who do not share our convictions can be enriching and strengthening to our own grasp of the Christian tradition which is always incomplete. In the *City of God*, Augustine explains:

> For we can see that many matters of importance to the Catholic faith are canvassed by the feverish restlessness of heretics, and the result is that they are more carefully examined, more clearly understood, and more earnestly propounded, with a view to defending them against heretical attack, and thus an argument aroused by an adversary turns out to be an opportunity for instruction.[61]

This dialogue with the "other" is possible because Augustine understands that there is a gap between his own apprehension of the Christian tradition and the truth of the Christian tradition: the former is partial, the latter is absolute.[62] We must humbly accept that our grasp of the truth is always in need of further revision. And yet confidence in the tradition, not in one's own superiority, can allow for a certain dogmatic confidence about our beliefs and their importance for others.

In his article, "Pluralism, Otherness, and The Augustinian Tradition," Charles Mathewes refers to Augustine as the "master of engagement."[63] Mathewes argues that Augustine's theology responds to pluralism and otherness by highlighting anthropologically how the sinful self is other to itself and, theologically, God is "the absolute other."[64] Conversion is the process of ongoing struggle toward internal

---

[58] Augustine, *City of God* 1:35, Bettenson, p. 45, (emphasis mine).
[59] Augustine upholds the humble, crucified Christ as the most stark example of truth found where it is least expected.
[60] Augustine, *Confessions* 5.8.14, Chadwick, p. 81.
[61] Augustine, *City of God* 16.2, Bettenson, p. 650.
[62] Charles T. Mathewes, "Pluralism, Otherness and The Augustinian Tradition," *Modern Theology* 14:1 (January 1990), p. 101.
[63] Ibid., p. 82.
[64] Ibid., p. 88.

integrity where a person comes to understand "the self as always already in dialogue with, and 'possessed' by, another—namely, God."[65] Because the self is "anchored in the activity and presence of a 'radical' other, namely, the divine,"[66] selfhood is a necessarily communal discovery. This "otherness" which is central to the self is an ongoing reality as Mathewes explains:

> The Augustinian tradition is particularly suited to pluralism because it affirms a conversionist theology, a theology which understands that the love of God is at best only partially and provisionally appropriated in any human life, even though it is the key to every such life. Thus no one is wholly separated from the love of God, just as no one is wholly conformed to it.[67]

Thus humility brings us to recognize our partial apprehension of truth and our need for a deeper understanding. However, humility is always correlated with a confidence in the solidity of the truth that has essentially grasped us. Mathewes writes:

> Confidence and humility go hand in hand, as one has both confidence in the truth of one's claims, and humility about one's understanding of those same claims, even as one is making them. One engages other people with both the conviction that your message is one of genuine importance to them, and the recognition that through the engagement with them you will yourself learn from them, further deepen your own understanding.[68]

This illuminating application of Augustine's understanding of humility points to the Gospel's insistence that a Christian be open to the "stranger" for the good news is directed to "an estranged world."[69]

Given the situation of pluralism today, Augustine's teaching can be instructive. He urges Christians to acknowledge that God's redemptive power is not limited to the church or to an exclusive relationship with God; it essentially includes those who are "other." Each person is somehow integral to our life's deeper purpose and destiny. More specifically, the Augustinian tradition challenges us to see pluralism as an opportunity to dialogue and to deepen our conversion.[70]

## Augustinian Humility Applied to Maritain's Democratic Citizenry

Maritain was surely more inclined than Augustine to look at how human efforts can transform the world and advance what he called, a "socio-temporal realization of Gospel truths."[71] Nonetheless, Augustine's theologically rooted understanding of humility can be a valuable resource for Christians who hope, as Maritain did, that the "leaven of the Gospel"[72] would awaken citizens of a democracy to what is

---

[65] Ibid., p. 93.
[66] Ibid., p. 99.
[67] Ibid., p. 88.
[68] Ibid., p. 102.
[69] Ibid., p. 100.
[70] Ibid., p. 106.
[71] Maritain, *Man and the State*, p. 179.
[72] Ibid., p. 159.

"deep and lasting" in their humanity.[73] Contrary to many secular ethicists, Maritain maintained that the consciousness of the "Christian social" task is inseparable from the consciousness of the "Christian spiritual" task.[74] While Maritain acknowledged that natural ethics could establish important truths and provide helpful intellectual tools, he ultimately described natural ethics as "dangerously incomplete."[75] Similar to Augustine, he insisted that "theological truths are indispensable for the full constitution of ethics and the object of morals is only adequately known in the light of these truths."[76] Moreover, Maritain held that the "work of education, the taming of the irrational to reason, and developing the moral virtues, must constantly be pursued within the political body."[77]

In relating Christian humility to democratic citizenry, I will focus specifically on Maritain's claim in *Education at the Crossroads*, that education and substantive public discussion are crucial to the political task of "awakening" what is deepest in humanity. Maritain believed that teachers and scholars play a central role in the formation of democratic citizens. Building upon this notion, I will offer some suggestions as to how a humble Christian citizen, particularly a humble Christian scholar, would educate and communicate with others and advance democratic principles. To illustrate these points, I will note how Maritain's own principles and style as a political philosopher offer a powerful example of how humility can have a radical effect upon the exchange and advancement of ideas in a pluralistic setting.

In *Man and the State*, Maritain observed: "people are ordinarily distracted from their most capital aspirations and interests, as a people, by each one's everyday business and suffering."[78] Among such a tired and distracted people it is tempting to rally support for an idea through sheer propaganda and manipulative forms of advertising.[79] However, the real work of education must seek to convey the truth in a way that respects the dignity and God-given vocation of each individual. We must avoid the cheap "sound bite" and refrain from appeal to raw emotion if we hope for responsible participation in democratic forms of self-government.

Before considering how humility could be embodied in the work of a Christian educator, I would like to recall the way Augustine's understanding of pride and humility emerges out of an understanding of how we stand before truth. It is in pride that a person comes to think "I have a special claim on truth." The truth is then something "I possess," something "I own and distribute to others" in a classroom or at a conference. Augustine's understanding of Christian humility is based on an acknowledgment of the incompleteness of the self before truth. Marked

---

[73] Ibid., p. 137.
[74] Ibid., p. 229.
[75] Jacques Maritain, *Science and Wisdom*, trans. Bernard Wall (New York: Charles Scribner's Sons, 1940), p. 165.
[76] Ibid., p. 165 cited in Charles A. Fecher, *The Philosophy of Jacques Maritain* (Westminster, Maryland: Newman Press, 1953), p. 193.
[77] Maritain, *The Rights of Man and Natural Law*, p. 56.
[78] Maritain, *Man and the State*, p. 137.
[79] Ibid., p. 137.

by sin, we are never absolutely immune from distorted views and practices.

Pride, according to Augustine, is the principal source of our blindness to truth. Pride infiltrates our discourse when we find ourselves needing to be the center of conversation and insist on being understood before we understand others. As teachers we may seek adulation from students and exploit their dependence on our approval. As scholars we may refuse to acknowledge our dependence on peer review and correction.

Pride even leads us to invest so much meaning in our own words that we allow our words to substitute for a real living out of the truth. Are the truths we teach in the classroom or expound in an article, the same truths that we seek to embody in our day-to-day lives? In his own teaching, Maritain insisted that the task of bringing people from false beliefs to true beliefs entails more than philosophical and theological arguments. It requires concrete deeds and signs, a true witness that is vital and visible.[80] In *The Range of Reason*, Maritain writes:

> Things being as they are, it seems clear that the wisest reasonings and the most eloquent demonstrations and the best managed organizations are definitely not enough for the [people] of this time. [People] today need *signs*. They need deeds ... The faith must be an actual faith, practical and living. To believe in God must mean to live in such a manner that life could not possibly be lived if God did not exist. Then the earthly hope in the Gospel can become the quickening force of temporal history.[81]

At a basic level, humility involves an attitude toward scholarship which invites people to share in a truth that is infinitely shareable: a truth that is a gift, not a possession. The practice of Augustinian humility would then involve a readiness to learn from all people and even to expect that those outside our circle may have something to teach us. Augustine himself demonstrated this practice by incorporating Neoplatonic philosophy into his understanding of Christianity. Furthermore, he knew that Christianity needed philosophical resources and the human sciences to deal with the practical questions of politics and morality. In the *City of God*, for instance, he drew upon the wisdom of Cicero to formulate the proper relationship between Christians and the political order.

The humble Christian scholar would see all people as worthy of respect, even those making counter-claims to his or her own position. One would, as Augustine said: "bear with their hostility"[82] and strive for unity wherever it can be achieved. Humble citizens would recognize that they are not God; they are not all knowing, but they depend on others to enrich their understanding of truth. The humble scholar would not dismiss his or her most hardened opponents or blithely accept the fact that many have no voice in the public sphere. Maritain himself demonstrated a genuine openness to the world in its otherness. His efforts not to dismiss others but to see the element of truth in each philosophical

---

[80] Jacques Maritain, *The Range of Reason* (New York: Charles Scribner's Sons, 1968), p. 117.
[81] Ibid.
[82] Augustine, *City of God*, 1:35, Bettenson, p. 45.

system led his biographer Charles A. Fecher to explain that "there are probably few books that he would burn."[83] Maritain believed that philosophy is essentially a social task that requires the collaborative efforts of people from every nation and time. Thus he brought the wisdom of earlier masters (particularly Aquinas) as well as the insights of his wide-ranging contemporaries into his grappling with the most pressing problems of his day.

Maritain also accepted the slowness of human response in his efforts to establish world-wide unity about basic moral principles. He always guarded against the authoritarian imposition of ideas and an arbitrary dogmatism. In contributing to the United Nations Declaration of Universal Human Rights in 1948 he advocated practical agreement among nations locked in ideological differences. He recognized that minimal agreement was better than no agreement, given the horrors of the Second World War. Nonetheless, while advocating a practical response to pluralism, Maritain always held out hope for a deeper unity among diverse peoples based on our shared human capacity to reason and seek the truth. He never wanted politics to be reduced to questions of practical efficiency. Thus, in expressing his own reasons for human rights, Maritain sought to encourage a true pluralism whereby people of differing ideological positions would bring the full substance of their convictions into public discourse.[84]

Maritain's keen intellect and authentic humility enabled him to have an influence that extended well beyond the Catholic world. He taught at leading non-Catholic institutions—Columbia, Princeton, and the University of Chicago—and he attracted the interest of prominent Protestants, Jews, and secular philosophers throughout the world. Though widely recognized and successful, he graciously shunned public flattery and honors—even declining Pope Paul VI's offer of the cardinalate.

Part of humility, then, is a willingness to be self-critical and to place one's ideas before others for rigorous scrutiny as a way of being accountable and cognizant of our need for collaboration.[85] Humility fosters genuine inquiry, and a readiness to give someone yet another chance, to look again at an argument with an openness to being enlightened and perhaps corrected. But one may wonder whether this emphasis on humility fosters a style of discourse that is too "soft." Does the practice of humility compromise the standards of rigor? Does it smooth over the sharpness of our genuine disagreements? Does it hinder real intellectual challenge and confrontation? I think the answer is no. Humility gives a Christian educator the opportunity to exercise true courage. When the ego is not at stake in weighing various

---

[83] *The Philosophy of Jacques Maritain*, p. 196.
[84] Maritain, "On the Philosophy of Human Rights," in *Human Rights: Comments and Interpretations*, ed. UNESCO (New York: Columbia University Press, 1949), p. 72.
[85] Brian Daley's paper, "The Pursuit of Excellence and the 'Ordinary Manner': Humility and the Jesuit University" delivered at Georgetown University in February, 1996, has been enormously helpful to me in its exploration of the impact that a Chistologically shaped humility could have upon the academic community.

ideas, truth can be more readily identified and, in some cases, all the more unsettling, challenging, and confrontational. Because the humble place truth over self-congratulation, flattery, and worldly honors, they allow the truth to destabilize the constructions they use to possess the truth. For instance, in 1926 after Pope Pius XI's condemnation of the strongly nationalistic group *Action française*, led by Charles Maurras, Maritain admitted his mistaken sympathy for this movement and confessed his culpable negligence in failing to discern its true political purpose. Lastly, humble Christian scholars, such as Jacques Maritain, do not simply look within themselves but rely on dialogue with others and ultimately on the revelation of God for the full unfolding of truth. Maritain's consistent reliance on prayer throughout his life witnessed to his belief in humble dependence on God to promote the good.

## Conclusion

In this paper I have drawn upon Augustine's understanding of humility to show how Christian citizens who cultivate a humble style of discourse, as Maritain did, could be a corrective to the pride that is not only counter-productive, but detrimental to basic democratic principles. In particular, the task of education in shaping democratic citizens is severely hampered by the predominance of pride in academic circles.

Christian humility is not proposed as a central Christian disposition only *because* it can enrich democratic education and public discourse, however. Rather, Christian humility is central because it is indispensable to human fulfillment made possible by the truth of the "humble God," (*humilis deus*)[86] Jesus Christ. It is this most profound religious truth at the heart of humility that ultimately brings success to our social and political tasks. While Christian humility is one element in a wider vision of Christian service and political engagement, it is crucial to the renewal and revitalization of education and public discourse which will advance a true democracy.

---

[86] Augustine, *On the Catechising of the Uninstructed*, 4.8.

# 17

# Maritain's Contribution to the Development of the Magisterium on Means

### *Nicholas C. Lund-Molfese*

### Introduction

This paper has three parts.¹ First, I examine Maritain's treatment of the "problem of means." Second, I canvass statements of the *Magisterium on means*, giving particular attention to recent developments in the Church's teaching on war and capital punishment. Finally, I apply the work of Maritain, in light of the recent statements of the *Magisterium on means*, to an actual case so that the richness of Maritain's analysis might be demonstrated.

### Maritain's Problem of Means

Maritain addresses the problem of means at length in at least four of his published works. For Maritain, the problem of means is "the basic problem in political philosophy."² His earliest treatment of this topic appears to have been in "Religion and Culture," which was published in 1930.³ Therein, Maritain explains the particular context in which the problem of means arises: "The Church and Catholicism are essentially supernatural, supra-cultural things whose end is eternal life;" however, "Christian civilization and the Catholic cultural world remain a civilization and a world whose specific end . . . is in itself of the temporal order." The Church must not be "confused with any civilization whatsoever."⁴ The spiritual and the temporal orders can never be treated as identical, but just as pernicious an error is to believe that they are antithetical. It is within this context of the relationship of the spiritual order to the temporal order that the problem of means arises.

---

[1] This article was improved by the editorial assistance of Dina C. Barron.
[2] Jacques Maritain, *Man and the State* (Chicago: The University of Chicago Press, 1951), p. 54.
[3] Unless otherwise noted, the dates of publication for Maritain's works are taken from *The Collected Works of Jacques Maritain* VII (Notre Dame, Indiana: University of Notre Dame Press, 1995), pp. xxii-xxviii.
[4] Jacques Maritain, "Religion and Culture," trans. J. F. Scanlon, *Essays in Order* (New York: Macmillan Co., 1931), p. 35.

Maritain seeks to elucidate his point by drawing a scholastic distinction. There are two different ways in which an instrument can be considered: "in its own peculiar causality and [in] its instrumental causality."[5] The temporal order considered in its own causality has its own peculiar goods to safeguard. From this perspective the "decisive issue is victory or defeat" and we ought to wish greatly for victory for "it has biological importance": it may be a matter of life and death. However, insofar as the temporal order is considered in its instrumental causality,

> ... the temporal acts precisely as the instrument of the spiritual ... [and] the decisive issue is not victory in the battle, but the way in which the battle is fought and the weapons employed. Weapons of light! Of truth, loyalty, justice, innocence, let our weapons be unsullied! We shall be beaten, that goes without saying, historians and politicians are right in warning us. But it is impossible to be beaten; when the stake is not biological but spiritual, defeat or victory with unsullied weapons is always a victory.[6]

Therefore, temporal means, in the process of seeking success on this earth, must not impose on the means of the intemporal "for that would be an outrageous prevarication." Rather, temporal means must be "subject to the law of the spirit."[7] Thus far the matter is relatively straightforward. It is good to desire success on the temporal level and to take measures to secure such success; however, the means one uses to achieve success on the temporal realm are subject to the law of the spirit. Such means cannot involve lies, betrayal, injustice, or corruption,[8] that is to say, they cannot be evil in themselves. We must not do evil that good may come of it.

Maritain further asserts that even among temporal means which are "good in themselves, legitimate and normal," there is an "order" or "hierarchy."[9] This hierarchy is based on the degree to which a given temporal mean is instrumentalized to the spiritual order:

> There is the labor of the soldier, ... the ploughman [sic], the ... politician, the poet, the philosopher, there are the works of us Christians of the common herd, the works of the saints; there are the works of the saints with a mission to discharge such as ... St. Louis, and the works of saints exempt from any such mission ... What a weight of glory for the temporal was the history of the patriarchs and the long preparation for the Incarnation![10]

Maritain calls "rich temporal means" those so implicated in the work of the spirit that they "of their own nature postulate a certain degree of temporal success." Such means are "the particular means of this world ... in truth ... they fall within the domain of the Prince of this world. Our duty is to wrest them from him."[11] For example, due to Divine Providence, Moses' mother's plan of safeguarding her

---

[5] Ibid., p. 44.
[6] Ibid., my emphasis.
[7] Ibid., p. 45.
[8] This is the inverse of the list that Maritain gives in "Religion and Culture," p. 44.
[9] Ibid., p. 45.
[10] Ibid.

child by putting him in a basket and placing the basket among the reeds on the bank of the Nile River was going to be successful.[12]

In contrast, the poor temporal means "are the peculiar temporal means of the spirit ... The Cross is in them. The less burdened they are by matter, the more destitute, the less visible– the more efficacious they are."[13] The poor temporal means are not ordered for tangible success but rather "participate in the efficacy of the spirit."[14] As examples of poor temporal means, Maritain cites the writings of Aquinas, the discourses of Plato and Aristotle, and the singing of Homer and King David. According to Maritain, the full listing of the hierarchy of means, from highest to lowest is: pure spiritual means directed toward eternity; spiritual means directed toward the material world; and temporal means as already discussed.[15]

Maritain's most extensive treatment of the problem of means is contained in *Freedom in the Modern World*[16], published in 1933. Therein he states that, while "the purity and sincerity of an attempt to renew the temporal order on Christian principles excludes all ways and means that are not sincere and pure,"[17] it does not rule out victory, even temporal victory. A Christian revolution can succeed through the power of faith, for, Maritain reminds us "if faith is able to move mountains, is it powerless to shift the mighty from their seats?"[18] In addition to faith, even those who operate out of the perspective of the spiritual order may use a "measure of coercion."[19] In this context Maritain mentions several of the traditional criteria for resistance to a tyrannical government, but always in reserved terms. For example, only after first mentioning the possibility of "passive resistance" does he go on to condone the use of "armed and open force." Further, he immediately qualifies his position with the parenthetical phrase "by way of defensive action."[20] Maritain, after commenting on this tradition that allows, in certain well-defined cases, "opposing by violence, even to the shedding of blood,"[21] then goes on to question the relevance of that tradition and of the traditional criteria to the situations we face in the modern era:

> The question raised by the conditions of the temporal order in our time does not concern the action of a tyrant laying a city to waste by cruelty ... The question that confronts our time has to do with a universal state of depression and disorder ... In the political and social struggle that is the eternal lot of human society ... has the Christian ethic nothing else to offer to those who are engaged in temporal strife than abstract advice to moderate and limit in accordance with the

---

[11] Ibid., page 46.
[12] See *Exodus* 2:1-10. This is my example. Maritain himself refers to the successful reign of St. Louis. A somewhat different division and definition of means is given by Maritain in *Freedom in the Modern World*, trans. Richard O'Sullivan (New York; Charles Scribner's Sons, 1936), p. 133.
[13] *Religion and Culture*, pp. 46-47.
[14] Ibid., p. 47.
[15] Jacques Maritain, *Freedom in the Modern World*, pp. 185-86.
[16] Ibid.
[17] Ibid., p. 152.
[18] Ibid.
[19] Ibid., p. 153.
[20] Ibid.
[21] Ibid., p. 154.

rules of reason and of divine law the use of coercive force? ... If it really is so, is there not an inevitable conflict between the demands of Christian ethics and of temporal success ... Is the Christian soul doomed to defeat if it remains loyal; to infidelity if it declares for success? Or as an alternative, to perpetual inaction?[22]

Maritain's reply to these pointed questions is that they are the product not of a Christian but of a Manichean outlook. The Christian believes in Divine Providence and knows that, even though the work of the Spirit is often thwarted, it makes constant progress in time.[23] The Manichean's division of spirit and matter, of spiritual truths from the necessities of state, led in time to a:

> ... pharasaical spirituality [which] relied on political forces to do the work that its scruples forbade it to do ... In this way the actions of States as well as the conduct of wars and conspiracies, revolutions, acts of violence and the rest came to be the work of a tiny group of men who sacrificed their virtue on the altar of public welfare in much the same way that prostitutes sacrifice their honor to maintain the peace of families.[24]

In contrast, Maritain argues that the state should "not make sin one of its instruments" since "justice is of greater value than force in the conservation of the state."[25]

Still, what are Christians to do when they are members of a state that has made many sins its instruments? What are Christians to do when they find themselves locked in a struggle with the state on one or more matters of fundamental importance? Maritain, sounding like a contemporary commentator on the American political scene, surveys the tools that are commonly used in political struggles such as the "mobilization of all the devils of the human heart" and of the need to appeal to victim's demands for expiation, pride of race, and of class.

> "But bold and fearless falsehood, falsehood sure of itself, fast as the pillars of Hercules ... becomes the power par excellence that is demanded for the manufacture of political opinion. The whole people shall be nurtured on fable and steeped in imposture; that they shall be taught to call good evil and evil good."[26]

These are means which Christians will be sorely tempted to use if they believe the sole means available to them is secular warfare.[27] Fortunately, Maritain's purpose is to show us that not only are other means available, but they are more

---

[22] Ibid., pp. 154-56.
[23] Ibid., pp. 156-57.
[24] Ibid., p. 158. Maritain compares this situation to "the pious Jewish housewife who employs a goi servant so that the housework may be done on the Sabbath." To those unfamiliar with Maritain's work, it should be pointed out that by this comment he intended nothing disrespectful of the Jewish faith.
[25] Ibid., p. 160.
[26] Ibid., p. 161.
[27] In the course of his discussion, Maritain asks: "Are the arms of moral reconstruction the only arms he [a Christian] is at liberty to use?" (Ibid., p. 167) Maritain never directly answers this question although he does state, earlier on the same page, that "means of warfare, though not in themselves the most important, are nonetheless necessary. The history of mankind does not in fact dispense with these means." Still, the question of whether a Christian may do as history has done is left open.

effective and more powerful than the tools of sin. First, he explodes the myth that there is a conflict between the claims of ethics and those of temporal success.[28] He argues that the organic means of moral reconstruction, which he is proposing, have "more potency in promoting historical change than the ways of war."[29] Pure means are a kind of laboring to give birth: a bringing into being, "in the very center of the existing temporal regime, the institutions proper to a new order of things."[30]

As an example of the spiritual means of warfare, Maritain examines the practice and teachings of Gandhi. Unlike some Catholics of his generation (and ours), Maritain, while finding great value in Gandhi's doctrine of Satyagraha, is by no means romantically uncritical of it, stating that it "needs rectification on essential points."[31] Among the problems Maritain finds is that "Gandhi has no sense of state."[32] Maritain could not accept Gandhi's absolute rejection of the use of force by the state. In this Maritain finds an "escape to angelism which carried to its extreme limit involves … the rejection of the Incarnation."[33] In contradistinction to Gandhi, Maritain affirms the real difference between violence and force; the common good may call for the use of force against those who attack truth, even though violence should not be used to impose truth on others.[34]

A true doctrine of force, Maritain explains, will consider force as a power of the soul, as the moral virtue of fortitude. Fortitude, the virtue which inclines and steadies the will to do justice, come what may, admits of two principle aspects or manifestations. There is the fortitude that attacks and the fortitude that endures. The former is a "force of coercion" and "a force that inflicts suffering on others" while the latter is "the force of patience" and the "force that endures the infliction of suffering on oneself."[35] According to Maritain:

> … courage in endurance corresponds to the principle act of the virtue of fortitude and is characteristic of the "bravest of the brave." Such endurance derives its strength from something that possesses the greatest power of resistance in the world of nature, from the paradox of a nothing which is also a universe, the invisible power of human personality.[36]

The force of coercion "aims at the destruction of one evil by way of another evil"[37] and thus evil passes back and forth like a game of tag between the two parties. In contrast, the force of endurance is a force of "patience" and "voluntary suffering" which can "annihilate … evil by accepting and dissolving it in love."[38] Maritain

---

[28] Ibid., p. 166.
[29] Ibid., pp. 166-7.
[30] Ibid., pp. 164-7.
[31] Thus John DiJoseph's comment on page 119 of *Jacques Maritain and the Moral Foundation of Democracy* (Lanham, Maryland: Rowman & Littlefield, 1996) that Maritain's "solution to political conflict was to wholeheartedly adopt the techniques of creative nonviolence as developed in India by Mahatma Gandhi" seems overstated.
[32] Jacques Maritain, *Freedom in the Modern World*, p. 169.
[33] Ibid., p. 170.
[34] Ibid., p. 171.
[35] Ibid., pp. 172-73.
[36] Ibid., p. 174.
[37] Ibid., p. 175.

again qualifies his comments by noting that there is still an essential role to be played by coercive force.

> Even in relation to spiritual ends [coercive force] and material means may be used, within the limits of justice. Even St. Augustine in the end admitted that against the destruction wrought by heretics the Church might appeal to the material power of the secular arm. The Church ... is entitled in her own sphere to exercise a certain measure of coercion.[39]

Maritain goes so far as to say:

> Apart from the fact that the systematic refusal to render military service, such as is practiced by Conscientious Objectors, is based on an ideology that is shallow and steeped in illusion, it is also of no real effect against the evil of warfare and might well endanger the safety of the community in a case where a just war had to be waged.[40]

One would have thought that Maritain had made himself sufficiently clear on this point; however, some had apparently confused his treatment of the problem of means with the advocacy of pacifism. In August of 1934, a mere year after the French publication of *Freedom in the Modern World*, Maritain gave a series of six lectures at the Summer School of the University of Santander. Those lectures were later published as *True Humanism*.[41] Therein Maritain returns again to the problem of means, not to change what had gone before, but "only ... to remove certain misunderstandings."[42] He explains that "some people have thought that I condemned as impure in themselves, i.e., as intrinsically evil, means not evil in themselves, but of an inferior degree."[43] Again he confirms that the physical means of war, including "violence," "terror," and the "use of all the means of destruction" can be just if all of the relevant theological conditions for their use are met.[44]

Maritain's principle concern is with those who confuse "pharasaical purism" with the doctrine of the purification of means. They urge an abandonment of writing because "modern publicity is impure" or recommend that persons stop voting because the political process is corrupt. Such an attitude is directly counter to the program that Maritain is laboring to develop. The means one uses should, as near as possible, correspond to the end one is trying to achieve. The doctrine of means

> ... does not so much insist on the rejection of the use of certain means as on the positive will to raise up means not only good in general, but truly proportionate to their end, truly bearing on them the stamp and imprint of their end: means in which that sanctity and sanctification of the secular ... are incarnate.[45]

---

[38] Ibid., p. 176.
[39] Ibid., p. 177.
[40] Ibid., p. 180. Maritain wrote this some thirty-two years before Vatican II's *Gaudium et Spes* (Par. 79) declared that "it seems right that laws make humane provisions for the case of those who for reasons of conscience refuse to bear arms, provided, however, that they agree to serve the human community in some other way."
[41] Jacques Maritain, *True Humanism*, trans. Margot Adamson (London: Geoffrey Bles, 1938).
[42] Ibid., p. 240.
[43] Ibid., p. 241.
[44] Ibid.
[45] Ibid., pp. 244-45.

Maritain holds that a Christian may use force when absolutely necessary but that this turn of events will naturally be considered regrettable to the Christian as it runs contrary to the spirit of the ways of God.[46] Maritain returns for the final time to the problem of means in his Charles R. Walgreen Foundation lectures which he delivered in December of 1949, and which were later published as *Man and the State* in 1951.[47] While Maritain largely reiterates arguments I have already discussed, he does add several important points of clarification. Means are the basic problem of political philosophy because they are "the end itself in the very process of coming into existence."[48] Means are not extrinsic but intrinsic to the end achieved; therefore, it is simply impossible to achieve an intrinsically good end through the use of intrinsically evil means. The problem of means is uniquely important to democracy since the particular ends of democracy are justice and freedom. For a democracy to use means that are intrinsically destructive of these ends would be, literally, suicidal.[49]

### The Magisterium on Means

Several subsequent statements of the *Magisterium* bear a strong resemblance to Maritain's doctrine of the hierarchy of means. Strikingly, these statements utilize almost the exact same language as Maritain did. A textual search of all the major documents of the *Magisterium* since 1959 revealed five significant documents which utilize "means" in the same way that Maritain did.[50]

Pope John XXIII issued his encyclical *Pacem in Terris*[51] in 1963. Therein he implicitly confirms Maritain's hierarchy of means in regards to distributive justice, that is to say, in regards to a government's treatment of its people. The Pope states that:

> A civil authority which uses as its only or its chief means either threats and fear of punishment or promises of rewards cannot effectively move men to promote the common good of all. Even if it did so move them, this would be altogether opposed to their dignity as men, endowed with reason and free will. As authority rests chiefly on moral force, it follows that civil authority must appeal primarily to the conscience of individual citizens, that is, to each one's duty to collaborate readily for the common good of all.[52]

Obviously the encyclical is not condemning all use of incentives or punishments by government. The concern evidenced is for those civil authorities who have inverted the order of the hierarchy of means. Instead of using treats and fear of

---

[46] Ibid., p. 246.
[47] Jacques Maritain, *Man and the State* (Chicago: The University of Chicago Press, 1951).
[48] Ibid., p. 55.
[49] Ibid., p. 60.
[50] This search was performed using *Church Documents: Conciliar and Post-Conciliar*, Fifth edition (Boston: Pauline Software, 1997). The search yielded 1727 usage's of the term "means." An examination of these passages revealed that only five of the passages contain usages of "means" in the same sense as found in Maritain's discussion of the "problem of means."
[51] John XXIII, *Pacem in Terris*, (Peace on Earth), April 11, 1963. Citations taken from *Church Documents: Conciliar and Post-Conciliar*, Fifth edition (Boston: Pauline Software, 1997).
[52] Ibid., par. 48.

punishment as a last resort, they are being used as the first method, as the "only or chief means." The hierarchy of means for distributive justice requires that governments, first and foremost, use those means most in conformity with the dignity of the person and only resort to lesser means when absolutely necessary.

*Gaudium et Spes*, Vatican II's Pastoral Constitution on the Church in the Modern World,[53] issued on December 7, 1965, strongly echoes Maritain's treatment of the problem of means in "Religion and Culture." Just as in "Religion and Culture," *Gaudium et Spes* prefaces its discussion of means with a description of the relationship between the political community and the Church.

> It is very important ... that there be a correct notion of the relationship between the political community and the Church, and a clear distinction between the tasks which Christians undertake ... The Church, by reason of her role and competence, is not identified in any way with the political community nor bound to any political system ... The Church and the political community in their own fields are autonomous and independent from each other. Yet both, under different titles, are devoted to the personal and social vocation of the same men. [54]

The Constitution then goes on to distinguish the "ways and means proper to the Gospel" from the "means proper to the earthly city." Both the supernatural and the temporal are "closely linked" and the "Church herself makes use of temporal things insofar as her own mission requires it;" however, she uses only those temporal means which are in "accord with the Gospel."[55] The document goes on to implicitly recognize a hierarchy of temporal means in saying that governments "cannot be denied the right to legitimate defense once every means of peaceful settlement has been exhausted."[56] In other words, military defense, even when legitimate, should not be the first, but the last, of the temporal means used. The document also calls on people to "find means for resolving our disputes in a manner more worthy of man."[57] Again, the existence of a hierarchy of means is assumed. In the Constitution's description of the hierarchy, just as in Maritain's discussion, means are ranked in order of their conformity to the dignity of the human person.[58]

In 1986 the Sacred Congregation for the Doctrine of the Faith issued *Libertatis Conscientia*,[59] an "Instruction on Christian Freedom and Liberation." This document explicitly addressed the issue of the morality of means and, once again, there

---

[53] Vatican II, *Gaudium et Spes*, (Pastoral Constitution on the Church in the Modern World), December 7, 1965. Citations taken from *Church Documents: Conciliar and Post-Conciliar*, Fifth edition (Boston: Pauline Software, 1997).
[54] Ibid., par. 76.
[55] Ibid.
[56] Ibid., par. 79.
[57] Ibid., par. 81.
[58] I believe it is fair, for my purposes and given the context of the language, to equate the two phrases "worthy of man" and "dignity of the human person."
[59] *Libertatis Conscientia*, (Instruction on Christian Freedom and Liberation) Sacred Congregation for the Doctrine of the Faith, March 22, 1996. Citations taken from *Church Documents: Conciliar and Post-Conciliar*, Fifth edition (Boston: Pauline Software, 1997).

are strong similarities with Maritain's discussion. The document unequivocally states that "the means of action must be in conformity with human dignity ... There can be no true liberation if from the beginning the rights of freedom are not respected."[60] This is so because, as Maritain said in *Man and the State*, the means are "the end itself in the very process of coming into existence."[61] It is simply nonsensical to attempt to bring about freedom through slavery. Therefore:

> the fight against injustice is meaningless unless it is waged with a view to establishing a new social and political order in conformity with the demands of justice. Justice must already mark each stage of the establishment of this new order. There is a morality of means.[62]

The principle of "the morality of means" not only rules out false means, means which are absolutely incompatible with the end sought, but also requires respect for the hierarchy of means. Thus the instruction goes on to insist that it is only as "a last resort," in the case of "putting an end to an obvious and prolonged tyranny which is gravely damaging the fundamental rights of individuals and the common good," that the recourse to armed struggle is justifiable. It is only in the most extreme cases that the resort to the most extreme means is justified. "Passive resistance" is a preferable means in that it "shows a way more conformable to moral principles and [has] no less likelihood of success."[63]

Finally, and most persuasively, are the strong statements on the morality of means in both the *Catechism of the Catholic Church* and *Evangelium Vitae*. *Evangelium Vitae*,[64] issued by Pope John Paul II on March 25, 1995, promulgated a new level of clear and direct teaching on the problem of means. John Paul II notes as "signs of hope" the favoring of nonviolent means over war in public opinion and the "growing public opposition to the death penalty." He also observes that "modern society has the means of effectively suppressing crime by rendering criminals harmless without definitively denying them the chance to reform."[65]

It is not that the death penalty and war are impermissible means or means which are intrinsically evil. Rather, the Pope is concerned to enunciate the principle that all persons have a moral duty to act in accord with the hierarchy of means. Thus the state, in administering punishment, "ought not go to the extreme of executing the offender except in cases of absolute necessity: in other words, when it would not be possible to otherwise defend society."[66] The *Catechism of the Catholic Church* (revised) teaches that:

---

[60] Ibid., par. 76.
[61] Maritain, *Man and the State*, p. 55.
[62] *Libertatis Conscientia*, (Instruction on Christian Freedom and Liberation), par. 78. Cf. *Document of the Third General Conference of the Latin-American Episcopate at Puebla*, pars. 533-534. Cf. John Paul II, *Homily at Drogheda*, September 30, 1997: A.A.S. 71 (1979), pars. 1076-1085.
[63] Ibid., par. 79.
[64] John Paul II, *Evangelium Vitae*, (The Gospel of Life), March 25, 1995. Citations taken from *Church Documents: Conciliar and Post-Conciliar*, Fifth edition (Boston: Pauline Software, 1997).
[65] Ibid., par. 17.
[66] Ibid., par. 56.

the church does not exclude recourse to the death penalty, if this is the only possible way of effectively defending human lives against the unjust aggressor. If, however, nonlethal means are sufficient to defend and protect people's safety from the aggressor, authority will limit itself to such means, as these are more in keeping with the concrete conditions of the common good and more in conformity with the dignity of the human person.[67]

Again, conformity to the hierarchy of means is not optional but morally required as some means are more in conformity with the end, the dignity of the human person and the preservation of life, than others.

Did Maritain directly influence the development of the *Magisterium's* teaching on means or is it merely that both the *Magisterium* and Maritain were drawing from the same deep well of the Catholic Tradition and thus independently reasoned to the same understanding on the question of means? Only a proper historical study of the intellectual influences on the Counsel Fathers and John Paul II could definitively answer this question. What is clear is that Maritain's doctrine of means is more relevant today than when he first formulated it back in 1930, and it is still ahead of its time. The *Magisterium* appears to be in the early stages of adopting a doctrine of means that parallels the work of Maritain. By reading the *Magisterium's* teaching on means in light of Maritain's doctrine of the hierarchy of means one has a rich and powerful tool for moral analysis.

## Application of the Hierarchy of Means

Maritain's hierarchy of means can be considered as one way of practically applying the principle of double effect; however, Maritain has raised the principle to a higher level. Instead of describing the quandary in a minimalist way, Maritain describes it in the richest way possible. The traditional principle of double effect is based primarily on the formulation given by Aquinas in the Summa *Theologica*.[68] As Aquinas, in the course of answering the question, "Is it ever lawful to kill a man in self-defense," explains it:

> [N]othing hinders one act from having two effects, only one of which is intended, while the other is beside the intention. Now moral acts take their species according to what is intended and not according to what is beside the intention ... Accordingly the act of self defense may have two different effects, one of saving one's life, the other is the slaying of the aggressor. Therefore this act, since one's intention is to save one's own life, is not unlawful ... and yet, though proceeding from a good intention, an act may be rendered unlawful, if it be out of proportion to the end.[69]

---

[67] *Catechism of the Catholic Church* (Revised), par. 2267.
[68] Thomas Aquinas, *Summa Theologica*, II-II, Q. 64, Art. 7, trans. Fathers of the English Dominican Province (Westminster, Maryland: Christian Classics, 1981), p. 1465.
[69] Ibid.

The degree to which Maritain has enriched the tradition with the addition of the hierarchy of means becomes apparent if we apply both methods to a hypothetical case. This evening, after I return to my hotel room, I am robbed. The robber, after realizing that I have nothing to steal (being that I am a lowly assistant professor), decides to kill me in his frustration and anger. I cry out for help. Several of you assume that I am a practitioner of primal scream therapy and therefore do nothing. As the criminal reaches for his weapon to shoot me, a police officer who heard me bursts into my hotel room. The officer attempts to get the criminal to voluntarily disarm but, when that fails, he shoots and mortally wounds my assailant.

The traditional double effect analysis would include the following points. The intention of the police officer is to save my life or simply to preserve life. This is the effect that the officer intends by shooting the robber. Assuming that the officer is virtuous, while he foresees the possibility, he does not intend the death of my attacker. The death of the robber is a foreseen but unintended consequence of the officer's performance of his duty. The lethal force the officer uses is not disproportionate given that the thief appears ready to take my life immediately if not stopped by the police officer. So concludes the traditional analysis. The application of Maritain's doctrine of the hierarchy of means deepens and enriches the analysis. The police officer's actions, as just described, are indeed a permissible means, but a regrettable one. There is no pleasure in these means for the Christian, however necessary the circumstances might be. For the Christian police officer, or any officer who affirms the existence of God, Maritain holds out previous steps on the hierarchy of means that can be applied, and, by their very application, these steps shape and purify the intention of the officer, even in those cases where he must use lethal means. The first means would be spiritual directed toward the eternal. The Christian police officer should pray, and even fast, that persons will turn away from sin and toward God. The officer does this out of Christian charity, out of love for those who otherwise might become criminals. The officer thereby develops in himself an active love and concern for the souls of those who might give in to temptation. Like Christ, he attempts to pray hardest for and love most those who are most deeply mired in sin and crime. The second means would also be spiritual but directed toward the temporal. The officer might pray, and perhaps even fast, for the reduction of violent crime and for the reform of those persons he has arrested. He would ask God for the courage and self-control to carry out his appointed tasks with integrity. He might also pray for success in his task of preserving the lives of all those persons he will encounter that day, criminal and victim alike. Third, the officer would utilize temporal means, but in accordance with the hierarchy proper to them. When the officer is confronted with a situation in which it is his duty to act to preserve human life, he would first use those temporal means most in conformity with human dignity. Depending on the circumstances, he might first try to reason with the perpetrator and appeal to the criminal's better self, the criminal's sense of justice or virtue. If that fails, and if the situation allows, the officer might then point out to the criminal that it is in the criminal's self-interest to cooperate and surrender. Finally, if all of the above means fail, the office may be duty bound to use force; however, this use of force would still conform to the hierarchy of means insofar as some means of force are more, and others less, appropriate to the officers stated end: the preservation of human life. The officer would first threaten to use force by displaying his weapon or firing a warning shot. In the most desperate situations, the officer might have to apply those means least in conformity with his stated end of preserving human life: lethal force. Still, our virtuous officer would have diligently trained to be an expert in the use of his weapon. By this training he makes it more likely that, if he needs to use lethal force, he will be able to do so in a manner most likely to preserve human life. The officer will have the skill to more fully actualize his intention to preserve life: he will be able to "shoot to wound," rather than kill, the criminal.

As our virtuous officer has diligently respected the hierarchy of means, even though he is forced by circumstances to resort to the least means, even then he acts in a matter different than an officer who starts with the least means and ignores the existence of the hierarchy. Our virtuous officer will find it easier to remember his intended end, the preservation of life, and not slip into the vice of vengeance by intending the death of the criminal. Thus the hierarchy of means safeguards and purifies the intention of the officer, protecting him from moral corruption even when he must use the least means which also carry with them the greatest moral temptations. Also, even when using the least of means, the officer who has diligently applied the hierarchy will have the virtue to force even such lowly means to better conform with human dignity and his intended end, the preservation of human life.

Skeptical? Do any such police officers exist? They do. One of my students, a devoted, humble Catholic, who, although not knowing their name, had faithfully applied the hierarchy of means to his police work for many years. A man with a deeply developed respect for life, he complimented the image of my son's ultrasound, which I keep on my office wall next to a photo of my son after birth, saying: "You know professor, that is a great message against abortion." This officer, I'll call him John, was responding to a routine call with two fellow officers when they were ambushed in a bar. The call was staged so that the officers might be killed. The attacker was a special forces trained member of a foreign government who had developed a grudge against the local police. All three officers were immediately hit upon entering the establishment. John perceived where the shooting was coming from and, cocking the hammer of his weapon back, he pointed it at their attacker, who was only a few feet away. Providentially, their assailant's weapon had permanently jammed, saving all three of their lives. John became aware that both of his coworkers were seriously wounded, conceivably dead. Neither was moving. John felt the side of his head and it was covered in blood. He believed he had been struck in the head, perhaps mortally.[70]

---

[70] In fact, he had been struck in the shoulder and a piece of flesh from his shoulder had been blown onto the side of his head. Miraculously, all three officers survived the attack.

The temptation to take the law in his own hands must have been enormous, but instead John acted on his intention to preserve life. The attacker, in an intentionally suicidal move, grabbed the barrel of John's gun and pulled it against his head. He was trying to discharge John's gun into his head. As would be expected, the jerking motion released the hammer, but in the split second before it would have struck and fired the bullet into the criminal's head, John slipped his thumb between the hammer and the firing pin, stopping the gun from discharging, while causing himself considerable pain.

For his heroism, John was never rewarded in any way. In fact, after recovering and returning to active duty, he overheard his immediate supervisor telling another officer that John was an "idiot" for letting the criminal live when every officer knew that what John should have done was finish the lawbreaker off. John's ultimate reward is surely awaiting him in the life to come; however, even in the temporal realm, we can see the rewards available to those persons who diligently apply the hierarchy of means. John was able to resist moral corruption even when forced to use the least of means and, even while using such means, he was able use them in such a way as to dramatically affirm the dignity and the value of human life. John embodies Maritain's doctrine of the hierarchy of means. He does not so much reject the use of certain means, but rather exercises his will to raise up means which are "not only good in general, but truly proportionate to their end, truly bearing on them the stamp and imprint of their end: means in which that sanctity and sanctification of the secular … are incarnate."[71]

---

[71] Maritain, *True Humanism*, pp. 244-45.

# V

# Appendix:
# Pope Paul VI
# Discourse and Messages at the Close of Vatican II

Editor's Note: Pope Paul VI was deeply influenced by Jacques Maritain and honored him by presenting his "Message to Men of Thought and Science" to Maritain at the end of the Vatican Council. In turn, Maritain cited Paul VI's "Message to Heads of State" and his closing "Discourse" as providing the clues for proper interpretation of Vatican II.[1] Maritain believed that the Council signaled the end of the "sacral age" and the beginning of a new age whose dominant motif shall be the "goodness and humanity of God our Father" (Tit 3.4). He refers to Paul VI's use of the term "hominem integrum" (the whole man, or human beings in their full integrity) in the "Discourse" at the final session of Vatican II. In addition he states that the world shall see a great reversal in so far as the great task shall no longer be that the human Church must defend the divine, but rather the Church in her divine mission shall be the defender of the human. And citing Pope Paul VI's "Message to Heads of State," Maritain says that in this new age all the Church now asks is for liberty. These messages and this discourse contain some subtle turns of phrase upon which turn the future of the Church and its approach to modern world. A delicate balance is struck between the respect for the integrity and autonomy of secular affairs and the important role of religion in the influence of worldly affairs and the transcendence of the Church's aim. In the "Discourse," Paul VI explains how to understand the deepened respect for secular, human affairs in light of the central religious significance of the council. The translations done in 1965 sometimes distort or obscure some of the important phrases and ideas and they are not readily available. So we provide for the record fresh translations of these key statements.

---

[1] Jacques Maritain, *The Peasant of the Garonne: An Old Layman Questions Himself about the Present Time*, trans. Michael Cuddihy and Elizabeth Hughes (New York: Holt, Rinehart and Winston, 1968), p. 4.

Jacques Maritain receives "Message to Men of Thought and Science" from Pope Paul VI at the close of Vatican Council II, 8 December, 1965

## To Seekers of Truth: Message to Men of Thought and Science[1]

A very special greeting to you, seekers of truth, to you, men of thought and science, explorers of man, of the universe, and of history, to all of you who are pilgrims on the pathway to the light and also to those who have stopped along the way, worn out and disappointed by an empty search.

Why a special greeting to you? Because all of us here, Bishops, Fathers of the Council, long to hear the truth. What has our effort been during these last four years, if not a keener search for a deeper meaning of the message of truth entrusted to the Church, an effort at more perfect docility to the Spirit of Truth?

Surely our paths were bound to cross. Your road is ours. Your pathways are never foreign to ours. We are the friends of your calling as seekers, the brethren of your weariness, the admirers of your achievements, and, if need be, the consolers of your discouragements and your failures.

For you therefore, we have this message, too: continue to search, without ever tiring, nor ever despairing of the truth. Remember the word of one of your great friends, Saint Augustine: "Let us seek with the desire to find, and let us find with a desire to seek even more." Happy are those, who, possessing the truth, seek it more earnestly in order to renew it, to deepen it, to give it to others. Happy are those who, having not found it, advance toward it with a sincere heart: may they search for the light of tomorrow with the light of today, until the light is at its fullest.

But do not forget this: if thinking is a great thing, thinking is first of all a duty; woe to whoever willingly shuts his eyes to the light! Thinking is also a responsibility: woe to those who darken the spirit by the thousand tricks that degrade it, that inflate it with pride, that deceive it, that deform it. What other fundamental principle is there for men of science if not to make every effort to think rightly?

For this purpose, without disturbing your progress, without bedazzling your vision, we come to offer you the light of our mysterious lamp: faith. He who confided it to us is the supreme Master of thought, he whose humble disciples we are, the only one who said and who could have said "I am the light of the world; I am the way, and the truth, and the life."

This word applies to you. Never perhaps, thank God, has there been so clear a possibility as today of such a profound accord between true science and true faith, mutual servants of the same single truth. Do not stand in the way of such a fruitful meeting! Have confidence in faith, the great friend of intelligence! Enlighten yourselves in its light in order to grasp the truth, the whole truth. Such is the wish, the encouragement, and the hope that we, the Fathers of the whole world gathered in council in Rome express to you before we disband.

---

[1] December 8, 1965. *Acta Apostolicae Sedis* 58 (1966), pp. 10-11, trans. Richard Lemp and John P. Hittinger.

### To the Guardians of Temporal Power: Message to Heads of State[1]

At this solemn moment, we, the Fathers of the twenty-first ecumenical council of the Catholic Church, at the point of disbanding after four years of work and prayer, in full consciousness of our mission towards humanity, address ourselves with respect and confidence to those who hold in their hands the destiny of humankind on earth, to all the guardians of temporal power.

We publicly proclaim: we honor your authority and your sovereignty; we respect your office; we recognize your just laws; we esteem those who make them and those who apply them. But we must speak a sacred and inviolable truth: God alone is great. God alone is the beginning and the end of all things. God alone is the source of your authority and the foundation of your laws.

It is upon you that the task falls to be on this earth the promoters of order and peace among men. But do not forget: it is God, the true and living God, who is the Father of men. And it is Christ, his eternal Son, who came to tell us that and to teach us that we are all brothers. It is he who is the great artisan of order and peace on earth, for it is he who guides human history and who alone can incline hearts to renounce those evil passions that engender war and misfortune. It is he who blesses the bread of humanity, who sanctifies its work and its suffering, who gives it joys you cannot impart and who gives it comfort in sorrows you cannot console.

In the midst of your terrestrial and temporal city, he mysteriously builds his spiritual and eternal city, his Church. And what does she ask of you, this Church, after nearly two thousand years of all kinds of vicissitudes in its relations with you, the Powers of the Earth; what does she ask of you today? As we said in one of the major texts of this council: she only asks you for freedom, the freedom to believe and to preach her faith, the freedom to love her God and to serve Him, the freedom to flourish and to bear her message of life to men. Do not be afraid of this: she is in the image of her Master, whose mysterious action does not transgress on your prerogatives, but heals everything human of its fatal emptiness, transfigures it, and fills that emptiness with hope, truth, and beauty.

Let Christ exercise this purifying action on society! Do not crucify Him again: it would be sacrilege, for He is the Son of God; it would be suicide, for He is the Son of Man. Allow us, His humble ministers, to spread everywhere unfettered the "good news" of the Gospel of peace on which we have meditated during this council. Your peoples will be the first beneficiaries of it, for the Church will form loyal citizens for you, friends of social peace and of progress.

On this solemn day when she closes the sessions of her twenty-first ecumenical council, the Church offers you through our voice her friendship, her services, her spiritual and moral energies. She addresses to you all her message of salvation and benediction. Welcome it, as she offers it to you, with a joyous and sincere heart and bear it to all your peoples!

---

[1] December 8, 1965. *Acta Apostolicae Sedis* 58 (1966), pp. 11-12, trans. Richard Lemp and John P. Hittinger.

## On the Religious Significance of Vatican II:
## Discourse at the Last General Session of Vatican II[1]

Venerable Brothers,

Today we bring to a close the Second Vatican Ecumenical Council, and we bring it to a close while it is still very strong and vigorous. This is what your presence here in great numbers shows, the orderly arrangement of this assembly reveals, the formal conclusion of the council's work confirms, and the harmony of mind and will proclaims. And while some questions raised during the council's deliberations are not yet suitably resolved, this indeed shows that the council concludes its work not out of exhaustion, but rather with the vitality which has inspired all the meetings and which will, with God's help, lead it to resolving these questions after the council is dismissed.

Our council will hand down to posterity an image of the Church: this hall filled with holy pastors who profess the same faith and breathe out the same love; who are joined together in a society of prayer, discipline, and an eager devotion to the task; and who all — what is truly remarkable — have a single wish, namely to offer themselves like Christ, their teacher and Lord, for the life of the Church and the salvation of the world.

But our council hands down to posterity not only an image of the Church, but also the patrimony of her doctrine and precepts, the deposit entrusted to her by Christ himself. Her people have constantly reflected on this deposit through the centuries and have turned it into their own flesh and blood, as it were, by giving it expression in their way of life. This deposit of faith is now illuminated in so many of its parts and has come to be established and arranged in its fullness and integrity. This living deposit of faith constituted by the divine power of truth and grace is capable of giving life to everyone who receives it devoutly and by it nourishes his own life.

What this council was in reality, or what it accomplished, might have been the subject of our final mediation. But this would require too much time and attention; nor, at this last and solemn hour, would we venture to comprehend in a few words a matter of such importance. We desire rather to devote these weighty moments of time to a thought that both humbles our souls and lifts them to our highest aspirations. We desire, that is, to ask ourselves: What is the religious importance of our council? By the term "religious" we mean to signify our relationship to God, which is, after all, why the Church exists, what she believes, what she hopes for, what she loves; this personal relationship to God defines what she is and what she does. In this light then we must ask what we have done here: have we brought praise to God; have we sought knowledge and love of Him; have we advanced in our efforts to contemplate Him; have we increased our desire for His glory; have we developed our abilities to proclaim Him to men who look to us as pastors and teachers of the ways of God?

---

[1] December 7, 1965. *Acta Apostolicae Sedis* 58 (1966), pp. 51-59, trans. Michael Woodward and John P. Hittinger.

We sincerely believe the answer is yes. From the very outset we followed the fundamental intention according to which the whole reason for the council was established. Our predecessor of happy memory, John XXIII, rightly considered the author of this ecumenical council, gave the opening speech and his words still resound in this Basilica of St. Peter. At that time the pope said:

> The greatest concern of an ecumenical council is that the sacred deposit of Christian doctrine be guarded and taught with a more powerful and persuasive account.... Christ the Lord truly proclaimed this message: "Seek first the kingdom of God and his righteousness." The word "first" means that this is especially where our energies and thoughts should be directed.

And the result in fact corresponded to his intention. That we might appreciate the result in its reality we should recall the age in which the council took place: it is an age when, as all agree, men are more concerned with seeking mastery of this world than they are in seeking the kingdom of God; it is an age when forgetfulness of God has become a common habit of mind, as though the progress of the sciences warranted it; it is an age when the principle impulse of the human person, who had attained a clearer consciousness of himself and his freedom, claims an unabridged freedom not subject to any law beyond the order of natural things; it is an age when the ideology of "secularism," pushing ahead by privilege of today's advances in learning, is held as the wisest norm by which society should be governed; it is an age, moreover, when human reason has fallen so far as to embrace the "absurd" and complete despair; it is an age, finally, when the greatest religions of the world were subject to disturbances and changes never experienced before. It was in this age, then, that our council was celebrated to the praise of God, in the name of Christ, by the breath of the Holy Spirit "who searches all things" and even now animates the Church from within "so that we may know what God has given us" (1Cor 2:10-12). In other words, the Spirit brings the Church to a deep and comprehensive understanding of human life and the world.

With the help of this council, by a doctrine of human nature and the world which is theological and theocentric, as they say, the Church has turned the minds of men to herself, as it were provoking those who consider her alien and outside of the viewpoint of our time. She embraces what the world at first considers absurd – the claim that God exists. But we are strongly confident that the age will later of its own accord acknowledge this belief as humane, wise and beneficial. For God is; He actually exists; He lives; He is a person; He is providential, endowed with infinite goodness, and He is not only good in himself, but especially good in regards to us; He is our creator, our truth, our happiness; so much so that when a man tries to fix his mind and heart on God through contemplation he elicits an act of his own spirit which is the most fine and perfect of all; thus even in the modern world, in all fields of human endeavor, we can and should aspire to this contemplative act so that all human activity is raised and perfected in its own order from within.

Someone might say that the council focused less on the elaboration of divine truths than on its principal theme – the consideration of the Church, her nature, her composition, her ecumenical task, and her apostolic and missionary work. This ancient religious society, which is the Church, was eager to meditate on herself in order to know herself better, to define herself better, and from this, to present her mind and teachings. This is all true; but this awareness of herself was not the sole end she proposed to herself, nor was it simply to display her talents for earthly culture. Calling herself back to herself, the Church has penetrated the hidden recesses of her own being, not in order to please herself with scholarly investigations that delve into religious psychology or the history of her own past, not in order to describe her laws or regain, by dedicated effort, her own rights. But she does so in order that, alive in herself, and through the Holy Spirit, she might better understand the efficacious word of Christ, might search more deeply the mystery, which is the wisdom and presence of God around her and within her, and might nourish more and more in herself the flame of faith, that hidden power on which her strength and wisdom depend. This is the flame of love by which she is compelled to sing praises of God without end, since, as St. Augustine says, "it is the nature of the lover to sing." Yes, this particular religious purpose is clearly evident from the council's documents, especially those which discuss divine revelation, the liturgy, the Church, priests, religious, and the laity. From these it is shown how clear, fresh, and rich is that spiritual stream which, flowing out of a vital contact with the living God, breaks forth from the heart of the Church and is poured through her onto the parched and arid ground of our world today.

As we trace, however, the religious power of this council, we must not overlook a certain purpose that is of utmost importance, for it was very prominent in it: to examine the modern world. Never, perhaps, before the time of this synod, has the Church felt herself brought to such a necessity: that she had to understand and, as it were, draw near to the society of men around her, to know it and consider it rightly and bring herself into it, to serve it and deliver to it the message of the Gospel, even to seek it out, somehow pursuing a society that changes so quickly and continually. This disposition arose from the fact that the Church, in an earlier age and especially in this past century, remained apart and separated from secular culture. This disposition to understand and draw near to the society of men is always entailed by the Church's primary duty, the salvation of men; at no time has it not been so. It has prevailed constantly and successfully at this council. On account of this, a suspicion arose in some people who believed that a philosophy, found in the outside world from the teaching of "relativism," predominated in the men and acts of the synod, which paid too much attention to transitory matters, to new currents that thrive in human culture, to perceived needs of others that arise; all this to the detriment of a fidelity owed by the majority to accepted doctrine, and with the loss of a religious perspective and purpose, which should be the proper concern of the council. We, of course, do not think that such ruinous designs should be attributed to it, if its true and authentic resolutions and genuine acts are considered.

We prefer to notice that our council's spirituality was chiefly one of love, on account of which express purpose no one will be able to treat the council as though it were irreligious or deviating from the holy Gospel, when we remember how Christ himself taught us that "in this all may know we are his disciples, if we love one another." (*Jn* 13:35) We may also allow the words of the apostles to resonate within our hearts: "This is pure and unstained religion before our God and Father: to visit orphans and widows in their tribulation, and to keep oneself undefiled by the world." (*Jas* 1:27); and again: "Whoever...does not love his brother whom he sees, how can he love God whom he does not see?" (*1Jn* 4:20).

Indeed the Church, gathered together in the council, has devoted herself to reflect – not only on herself and the relationship by which she is joined to God – but also on man, and on man as he really shows himself at this time: man, we say, who lives; man who is devoted to promoting himself alone; man, who not only considers himself worthy to be the one that unites, as in a center, every study, but who is also not afraid to affirm that he is the center of everything, even a law unto himself. The whole man as a phenomenon – using an expression of the current age – clothed and appearing in countless roles, has set himself before the council fathers, who are themselves men, yet all pastors and brothers, endowed with an intense concern and love: man, who complains bitterly about his lamentable lot; man, who in the past and in our own time judges others as below himself, and is therefore always wavering and insincere, covetous and proud; man, who is dissatisfied with himself, who bursts into laughter and tears; man, who can adapt to everything and play any role; man, who is narrowly focused on the investigation of science; man as such, who thinks, loves, and strains in effort, ever turned to some desire, like that "growing son" (*Gn* 49:22); man, who must be considered to have a certain sacredness on account of the innocence of his childhood, the secret of his poverty, and the devotion that his griefs produce; man, on the one hand caring only for himself, on the other fostering society; man at once "praising the past" and awaiting the future, while happily dreaming of the past; man, on the one hand guilty of crimes, on the other hand adorned with the sanctity of morality; and so on.

Let us say that the fiercely ambitious ideology of secular humanism has now finally come forth to provoke the council to a fight. We stand confronting each other: the religion which is the worship of God who wished to become man, and the religion (for it should be considered such) which is the worship of man who wishes to become God. Yet what happened? A fight? A war? An anathema? This rightly could have been expected, but it clearly did not happen. That parable of the good Samaritan was the example and norm that directed the spirituality of our council. Indeed an immense love toward men completely pervaded the council. The needs and interests of men, observed and then examined more closely, which become ever more burdensome the more the son of this world grows, held the entire focus of this synod's study. At least ascribe this praise to the council, you of this age who are single-mindedly devoted to humanity, who deny any truths that transcend nature; acknowledge our new assiduity for humanity. For we too, or rather we above all others, are devoted to humanity.

What has this fullest gathering observed in human nature? Or, having gained light from God, what did it endeavor to know? It desired to look fully upon man's countenance, which always displays two appearances, the the grandeur and misery of man; both its greatest evil, in which it undoubtedly struggles as if with an incurable sickness, and its goodness that remains, marked by hidden beauty and extraordinary courage. The truth must be confessed openly, that our council, when it made its own judgment on man, turned more to regard his fair side rather than his harsh side, and with full awareness interpreted everything in its best aspect. The council brought much affection and admiration to the men of our age. Their errors were certainly rejected, just as love as well as truth demanded; but men were only admonished concerning their error, always under the sound precept of respect and love. And thus it happened that, instead of a study of the ills which destroy souls, saving remedies full of comfort were brought into their midst, in order that the council might speak to men of this time, not in dire prophecies, but in tidings of hope and words of assurance. The things in them that are good it treated with due respect, and even great honor, and it confirmed all its undertakings and studies, seeking to heal and raise these things from within to their full integrity. We shall mention but a few more prominent examples. The countless languages scattered about and being used today have been brought into the sacred order of rites, so that human words might be addressed to God and in turn divine words to men. Also of great import is that natural, deep-rooted inclination to affirm the full rights that are to be enjoyed by man insofar as he is man; this inclination of itself is a harbinger of a destiny that surpasses nature. Thus, we desire, with highest hopes, that this inclination may prosper and that man may enjoy his own dignity, genuine freedom, abundance of learning, improved social conditions, justice and peace; that all of these, we say, may be enhanced and encouraged to a richer perfection. Ultimately we must speak as pastors devoted to the sacred task of bringing the light of the Gospel to all men. At present, we can speak only too briefly of those many deep questions that touch the true flourishing of man, which the council discussed; nor was it the council's purpose to resolve all the more urgent questions of daily life. Some of these questions were set aside for more careful investigations, which the Church will establish later; many others were treated in a very brief and general way and, because of this, allow fuller explanations and various applications.

Now, however, it is good to notice that the Church, through her own magisterium, while she did not wish to define any point of doctrine with extraordinary dogmatic rulings, nonetheless articulated her own authoritative doctrine on many questions, to whose norms men are today bound to conform their conscience and reasons for action. Therefore the Church has entered into a dialogue, so to speak, with the men of our time, always retaining her authority and truth, and yet engaging in a willing and friendly conversation proper to pastoral love. She wants to be heard and understood by men. And thus she not only adapts her words to the understanding of men, but employs a way of speaking that is commonly used today in clear conversations. These words derive great power to attract and persuade from the experience of life on which they depend and from the decent sentiments of humanity by which they are affected. The Church spoke with the men of our age as they are.

There is another aspect of the council we think worthy of consideration: that it has examined the rich abundance of doctrine with a single purpose, to serve man in all matters connected with his life, in all his weakness and in all his need. The Church has, in a certain sense, professed herself the handmaid of the human race, and at a time when her magisterium and pastoral rule, because of the solemn celebrations of this ecumenical council, exhibited themselves in a brighter and more powerful way. Indeed the purpose of exercising her ministry occupied a central place.

In celebrating this council, has all we have said about it and all we could say further that pertains to its human importance, deflected the mind of the Church to a cultivation of today's perspective, which is focused entirely on man? It must be said that the Church has not departed from her straight road, but has directed it into that region. Those who correctly discern this particular focus, in which the council considered the temporal aspects of human good, must agree that such attention should have been paid to pastoral concerns, which the council wished to follow as the essential mark of its own efforts. And they should acknowledge that this same focus is never separated from the true core of religion, because of the love which moves it (for where there is love, there is God!), or because of the close bond, always confirmed and promoted by the council, which man's temporal good has with his spiritual, religious, and eternal good. The church turns herself toward man and the world, but at the same time she is lifted up toward God.

The men of our time, whose attitude forces them to judge the importance of things by their expediency, ought to recognize the gravity and significance of this ecumenical council because at least it addressed in a unique way its own usefulness toward men. No one, then, may claim that the Catholic religion is not useful. For when she particularly expresses the deliberate and efficacious nature of her own action, that is, when she celebrates this ecumenical council, she clearly declares that she exists for man's sake and promotes his flourishing. Since this is so, it must be admitted again that the Catholic religion and human life are joined to one another in a friendly agreement, and that both are striving together for one human good; in other words, that the Catholic religion exists for the human race and is, in a certain sense, the life of the human race. Indeed she should be called life because of her doctrine, which is excellent and perfect in every way, which she hands down to man (Is not man, left to himself, a mystery to himself?). And she rightly hands down this doctrine, because she derives it from the knowledge she has of God.

In order that we may fully know man, true man, integral man, it is necessary that we first know God himself. It will suffice at present to recall the burning words of St. Catherine of Siena: "In your nature, O eternal God, I know my own nature." Yes, the Catholic religion is life because it reveals man's nature and his final end, and gives his life a fuller meaning. It is life, finally, because it has the highest law of life and because it brings into man such hidden power of life that it actually makes him divine.

Venerable brothers and beloved sons, and all who are present here, if we remember that the face of Christ, the Son of Man, is to be seen in the face of every man, especially when it has become translucent with tears and sorrows. And if the face of our Heavenly Father is to be seen in the face of Christ, according to the verse: "He that sees me, sees also the Father," (*Jn* 14:9), then our way of judging human matters is transformed when it is brought into Christianity which is directed completely to God as its center. And so we may express the meaning in this way: that is necessary to see man in order to see God.

Is it not, then, the intention of this council, because it focused on man particularly and diligently, to propose to the world of our time a liberation and a consolation, to which it may ascend by steps? In the end, does not the council teach us by a simple, new, and solemn argument to love man in order that we may love God? To love man, we say, not as an instrument, but as a primary end so that we may attain our highest end that transcends human things. Thus is the entire council described and defined in terms of its religious meaning, since it is nothing else than a certain invitation, forceful and friendly, by which the human race is called to find, with the help of brotherly love, that God of whom Augustine says: "To turn away from him is to fall; to turn toward him is to revive; to remain in him is to be secure . . . to return to him is to be born again, to dwell in him is to live." (Augustine, *Sol.* I,3)

Certainly we are supported by this hope at the conclusion of this Second Vatican Ecumenical Council and at the beginning of the human and religious renewal that it has set for itself to reflect upon and promote. We have confidence, venerable brothers and council fathers, that this will come to pass for ourselves; and we hope the same will come to pass for the whole human race, which we have been taught to love more and to serve better.

Now, finally, that all these things may turn out well, we invoke again the prayers of St. John the Baptist and St. Joseph, patrons of the ecumenical synod, Saints Peter and Paul, the foundations and the protectors of Holy Church, together with St. Ambrose, the bishop whose feast we celebrate today, uniting in him, as it were, the eastern and western Church. At the same time we fervently implore the assistance of the Blessed Virgin Mary, Mother of Christ, whom we also call the Mother of the Church. And with a single voice and spirit we give thanks to God and proclaim his glory, who is the living and true God, the one and supreme God, Father, Son, and Holy Spirit. Amen.

# CONTRIBUTORS

J. Budziszewski (Ph.D. Yale University, 1981) is a member of the Departments of Government and Philosophy at the University of Texas, and studies the natural law and self-deception. His most recent books are *The Revenge Of Conscience: Politics And The Fall Of Man* (1999) and *Written On The Heart: The Case For Natural Law* (1997)

The Rev. Joseph M. de Torre is University Professor Emeritus of Social and Political Philosophy at the University of Asia and the Pacific in Manila, Philippines. He has published more than twenty books and numerous articles. His latest book is entitled *Contemporary Philosophical Issues in Historical Perspective*.

Gregory Doolan is on the faculty of the Catholic University of America. He has recently published an article in *The Thomist* 63 (1999) entitled "The Relation of Culture and Ignorance to Culpability in Thomas Aquinas".

Desmond FitzGerald is Professor Emeritus at the University of San Francisco. He attended the lectures of Maritain and Gilson at St Michael's, University of Toronto, as an undergraduate in 1940s. He holds a B.A. and an M.A. from Toronto and an M.A. in political science and a Ph.D. in philosophy from the University of California at Berkeley. He taught at the University of San Francisco from 1948 to 1998.

Timothy Fuller, professor of political science and acting president of Colorado College, is the editor of *Leading and Leadership* and *The Voice of Liberal Learning: Michael Oakeshott on Education*.

John R. Goodreau received his Ph.D. from the Catholic University of America.

Catherine Green is an Assistant Professor of Philosophy at Rockhurst University in Kansas City where she teaches general philosophy and ethics. She has an MS in Nursing from the University of San Diego, as well as an MA and Ph.D. in Philosophy from The Catholic University of America. She has published articles and reviews on Yves R. Simon's theories of freedom and practical knowledge as well as on ethical issues in nursing and the health sciences.

## Contributors

William Haggerty is the chair of the Philosophy Department at Gannon University. He has published articles and reviews in *Augustinian Studies*, *Laval Theologique et Philosophique*, and *The Catholic Social Science Review*.

James G. Hanink is a Professor of Philosophy at Loyola Marymount University, Los Angeles, and Associate Editor for the *New Oxford Review*. He is working on a study of the personalist movement, with a special focus on its implications for political transformation. With his wife, Elizabeth, he is active in a pro-life ministry in Los Angeles.

Jeanne M. Heffernan is Assistant Professor of Political Science at Pepperdine University. A political theorist with a strong interest in the Catholic natural law tradition, she has reviewed books on Jacques Maritain and Yves R. Simon for *The Review of Politics* and has recently published an essay on the Thomistic grounds for public support of the arts in *Beauty, Art, and the Polis*, published by the American Maritain Association (2000).

John P. Hittinger is professor of philosophy at the United States Air Force Academy and coeditor of *Liberalism at the Crossroads: An Introduction to Contemporary Liberal Theory and its Critics*, and author of articles on Jacques Maritain, Yves R. Simon, and John Locke

Russell Hittinger is Warren Professor of Catholic Studies and Research Professor of Law at the University of Tulsa.

Richard Lemp is Professor of English at the Air Force Academy. His most recent work includes co-editing *Genesis of Flight: the Aeronautical History Collection of Colonel Richard Gimbel* (University of Washington Press) and translating Brig. Gen. Lucien Robineau's "French Military Aeronautics Before and During the Great War" in *Airpower: Promise and Reality*, edited by Mark K. Wells (Imprint Press).

V. Bradley Lewis is assistant professor in the School of Philosophy of the Catholic University of America. His research concerns the nature and influence of classical natural right in political philosophy and jurisprudence. He has contributed articles to *Polity*, *History of Political Thought*, *The Southern Journal of Philosophy*, and *Communio*.

Nicholas C. Lund-Molfese, M.A., J.D. is Director of the Integritas Institute of the John Paul II Newman Center at the University of Illinois at Chicago. In addition to developing and implementing programs in ethics within the various professional colleges of UIC, he is currently editing one book on suffering and another on Christian approaches to healthcare.

John G. Trapani, Jr. has published several essays on various aspects of Maritain thought, most particularly aesthetics and epistemology. A Professor of Philosophy at Walsh University in North Canton, Ohio, he is currently serving as the President of The American Maritain Association. In addition, he is active as a professional musician and bandleader.

Deborah Wallace Ruddy received her Ph.D. from Boston College; she is presently on the faculty of The University of St. Thomas, St. Paul Minnesota.

Henk E. S. Woldring is professor of political philosophy at the Free University in Amsterdam and a member of the First Chamber (Senate) of the parliament of the Netherlands for the Christian Democratic Party since 1999.

Michael Woodward is Professor of Church History and Reference Librarian, St. John Vianney Theological Seminary, Archdiocese of Denver. He received his Ph.D. in Medieval Studies from University of Notre Dame.

# Index

## A

Acton, John, Lord, 43
Adler, Mortimer J., 8, 66
   on ambiguity in moral and aesthetic judgment, 166, 168
Alexander IV (Pope), 15
Alleinveille, Julio, 202
Aquinas, Saint Thomas, 3, 40n, 47n, 97, 118, 120–121, 157n, 160, 201
   on the common good, 20n
   criticized by Reinhold Niebuhr for his political and natural law teachings, 90–94
   his natural law teaching as evaluative social science, 142–147
   on killing in self-defense, 237
   as Maritain's principal inspiration, 2
   as a progenitor of liberal democracy, 26
   on the rational foundation of the natural law, 131–139
   on the self-evident principles of natural law, 127–131
   on the socio-political value of free associations, 14–17
   teaches that natural law must be learned, 159
Arendt, Hannah, 220n
Aristotle, 5, 40n, 50, 83, 145, 145n, 158, 165
   contrasted to Descartes on speculative vs. practical philosophy, 53
   on the five intellectual virtues, 167
   as a progenitor of liberal democracy, 26
Augustine, Saint, 4, 16, 29, 40n, 67, 90, 120, 146n, 205
   his affinity to Michael Oakeshott, 25, 29
   his teaching on humility and Maritain's cultural project, 223–227
   on humility, 213–219
   on humility and society, 219–223
   as a progenitor of Reinhold Niebuhr's Christian realism, 88–89

## B

Bacon, Francis, 30
Bacon, Roger, 67
Bellarmine, Robert (Cardinal), 97
Bergson, Henri
   and Étienne Gilson, 63
   influences Maritain, 1, 6
Berlin, Isaiah, 19
Bidault, Georges, 63
Bird, Otto, 66
Black, Hugo (Justice), 141n
Bloy, Léon, 203
Boland, Francis (Rev.), 93
Bonaventure, Saint, 15
Bondi, Roberta, 211–212
Bork, Robert, 152
Borne, Étienne, 202
Burke, Edmund, 2

## C

Caesar, Julius, 160
Cajetan, Tommaso de Vio (Cardinal), 97
Calvin, John, 45
Chenu, M.D. (Rev.), 202
Chesterton, Gilbert Keith, 118
Cicero, Marcus Tullius, 225
Clark, William, 119n

Clarke, Desmond M., 152n
Clerissac, Humberto (Rev.), 203
Cocteau, Jean, 197
Copernicus, Nicolaus, 56
Cortés, Donoso, 47
Costello, Declan, 153n

## D

Dante Alighieri, 67
De Gasperi, Alcide, 202
De Gaulle, Charles, 63
De Maistre, Joseph, 47
Delury, George E., 162, 163
Derrida, Jacques, 3
Descartes, René, 30, 63
   on the activity of the modern scientist and "generous" person, 50, 52–60
   compared to Yves R. Simon on work and rest, 50, 59
   distinguished from Maritain on mastery of nature, 194
Desclausais, Joseph, 202
Dewey, John, 85–86
Douglas, Stephen, 117
Dworkin, Ronald, 114

## E

Ely, John Hart, 152

## F

Fabro, Cornelio, 202
Favre, Geneviève, 62
Favre, Jules, 62
Fecher, Charles A., 226
Finnis, John, 117–118, 158n
Flint, Larry, 166
Fortin, Ernest, 143n
Frederick the Great, 108
Frederick William II, 108
Freud, Sigmund, 161
Fukuyama, Francis, 77

## G

Gallia, Adriano, 202
Gandhi, Mohandas K., 121, 232
Garrigou-Lagrange, Réginald (Rev.), 3, 202
Garve, Christian, 103
Gellner, Ernest, 13, 18–19
Gilson, Étienne, 202
   compared to Maritain on political democracy, 61–69
   compared to Maritain on world government, 66–67
   and "*l'Affaire Gilson*", 67–69
Goldstein, Valerie Saiving, 211
Guehenno, Jean-Marie, 73, 85
Gurian, Waldemar, 69

## H

Hecker, Isaac (Rev.), 43
Hegel, Wilhelm Friedrich, 26, 28
Heidegger, Martin, 3
Hobbes, Thomas, 29, 142
   and Kant, 104n, 107–108
   teaches an "unchristian" anthropology, 44
Hogan, Gerard, 152
Hume, David, 142

Index 259

Humphreys, Richard, 153
Hutchins, Robert M., 8

## J

Jagerstatter, Franz, 123
John Paul II (Pope), 118, 122, 200
   articulates a virtue of "solidarity", 19–20, 21
   cements the meaning of Vatican II, 191–192
   contributes to modern Catholic social teaching, 203
   emphasizes the problem of culture, 206–208
   has successfully related the Catholic tradition to contemporary thought, 3
   influenced by Maritain, 203, 206–208
   lauds Maritain for uniting faith and reason, 180
   and Maritain's "instrumentalist" conception of the state, 13
   and Maritain's teaching on means, 236–237
   on the "subjectivity" of society, 22
   on the value of "intermediate communities", 18
John XXIII (Pope), 122, 149
   articulates a virtue of "solidarity", 20
   contributes to modern Catholic social teaching, 203
   influenced by Maritain, 203, 205–206, 208
   and Maritain's teaching on means, 234–235
Johnson, Samuel, 119
Journet, Charles (Cardinal), 200, 202, 205

## K

Kant, Immanuel, 26, 29
   advocates a liberal political constitution, 104–108
   on church and state, 108–111
   critcized by Maritain for arguing for the autonomy of the human person from nature, 99
   distinguishes juridical and ethical lawgiving, 100–104
   his affinity to Maritain, 24, 28
   his political philosophy compared to Maritain's, 99–112
Kelly, J.M., 152
Kerwin, Jerome, 97
Kierkegaard, Søren, 90
Kimball, Roger, 120, 121
Kohlberg, Lawrence, 3
Korsgaard, Christine M., 99n, 104n
Küng, Hans, 3

## L

Lacombe, Olivier, 202
Lefort, Claude, 73, 77, 79, 82
Lenin, Vladimir Ilyich, 77
Leo XIII (Pope), 11n, 183
   contributes to modern Catholic social teaching, 203
   favored religious establishment, 93
   as a progenitor of 20th-century Thomism, 3
   as a progenitor of a virtue of "solidarity", 19n
   on a right to free association, 18
   softens catholic opposition to liberalism, 147
Lincoln, Abraham, 73
Locke, John, 18
Lott, John, 14n
Lucretius, 199
Luther, Martin, 44–45

## M

Machiavelli, Niccolo, 26, 120, 142
   critiqued by Maritain, 6
MacIntyre, Alasdair, 144, 158n
Madison, James, 89
Mapplethorpe, Robert, 166
Maritain, Jacques, 106n, 111, 115, 120, 121, 122–123, 167
   on the acheivement of Vatican II, 192–194
   and Augustine's teaching on humility and society, 223–227
   on Christian renewal, 196–201
   on church and state, 1–8, 180–187, 209
   on a common "secular faith", 7, 74–75
   compared to Étienne Gilson on political democracy, 61–69
   compared to Étienne Gilson on world government, 66–67
   compared to Michael Oakeshott on the modern state, 24
   compared to Philip Selznick on democracy, 80–84
   and the concept of sovereignty, 25
   criticized by Reinhold Niebuhr for his anthropology, 92
   critiques "substantialist" politics in favor of "instrumentalist" politics, 11
   on democracy, 73–77
   on democracy and Christianity as mutually sustaining, 209
   departs from Thomas Aquinas's natural law epistemology, 127, 131–139
   distinguishes civil law and morality, 101
   his natural law teaching applied to pornography, 172–175
   his political philosophy compared to Kant's, 99–112
   on human nature and society, 170–171
   influenced by Leo XIII, 3
   influences popes, 179–180, 191, 202–208, 234–237
   influences Vatican II, 2, 7, 187, 191, 235
   as a "liberal" Catholic, 43
   on the natural law foundation for human rights, 6
   on a personalist criterion for political legitimacy, 113
   as a political pluralist, 100
   and the problem of means, 228–240
   on the "sacral" vs. the "lay" state, 184
   on the Soviet Union, 6
   teaches that natural law must be learned, 159–160
   too sanguine on the affinity between Thomism and liberal democracy, 140
   on the use of force, 232–234
   on world government, 8, 66, 67
Maritain, Paul, 62
Maritain, Raïssa, 62
Markus, Robert, 215
Massineo, A., 202
Matthewes, Charles, 222
Maurras, Charles, 227
McInerny, Ralph, 4
Mill, John Stuart, 142
   his affinity to Maritain, 24, 28
Montaigne, Michel de, 134
Montesquieu, Charles de Secondat, baron de, 13–14

Mounier, Emmanuel, 113, 116, 121
Mulholland, Leslie Arthur, 107n
Murray, John Courtney, 12

## N

Niebuhr, Reinhold
    as a Christian realist, 88–90
    criticizes political Thomism and natural law theory, 90–94
    his criticisms of Thomism met by Yves R. Simon, 94–98

## O

Oakeshott, Michael
    compared to Maritain on the modern state, 24–33
    opposes a "politics of skepticism" to the "politics of faith", 30
O'Hanlon, Roderick, 155
O'Reilly, Peter, 68

## P

Paul, Saint, 195
Paul VI (Pope), 180, 188n, 207
    on church and state, 189, 191
    contributes to modern Catholic social teaching, 203
    influenced by Maritain, 2, 7, 179, 203, 205–206, 208
    offers Maritain a cardinalate, 226
    as a progenitor of a virtue of "solidarity", 19n
Péguy, Charles, 203
Percy, Walker, 116
Phelan, Gerald B., 68
Pius IX (Pope), 13
    opposed liberalism, 147
Pius XI (Pope), 13, 227
    as a progenitor of a virtue of "solidarity", 19n
    softens Catholic opposition to liberalism, 147
Pius XII (Pope), 13
    and Maritain's "instrumentalist" conception of the state, 12
    praises Irish constitution for its foundation in natural law, 147
Plato, 106n

## Q

Quill, Timothy E., 163

## R

Rahner, Karl, 3
Rawls, John, 73, 78, 79, 140n
Robinson, Mary, 154
Rommen, Heinrich A.
    adumbrates the Catholic political tradition, 34–48
    compares the conservative and liberal mindsets within Catholicism, 41–43
    distinguishes linear and spheric thinking, 36–40
    his philosophical anthropology, 43–48
Rosenblum, Nancy, 14
Rousseau, Jean-Jacques, 73
    criticized by Maritain for arguing for the autonomy of the human person from nature, 99
    teaches an "un-Christian" anthropology, 44
Ryan, John A. (Rev.), 93

## S

Salkever, Stephen G., 145n
Salleron, Louis, 202
Scalia, Antonin (Justice), 141
Schall, James V., 99n, 117, 120, 121
Schumann, Maurice, 63
Second Vatican Council, 179, 183
    assessed by Maritain, 191–201
    on the Catholic Church in the modern world, 187–191
    influenced by Maritain, 207
    inspired by 20th century Thomism, 4
    on the intellectual life of the Catholic Church before, 3
    and later turmoil in the Catholic Church, 194–196
    and Maritain, 2, 7, 12, 180, 184, 191–201, 207, 235
    and Maritain's teaching on means, 235
Selznick, Philip, 73, 80–84
Serrano, Andres, 165, 166
Shook, Laurence K. (Rev.), 62, 66, 67
Simon, Yves R., 1
    compared to Descartes on work and rest, 50, 59
    compared to Reinhold Niebuhr on democracy, 87
    influenced by Leo XIII, 3
    on the problem of work and modern man, 49–53
    as a respondent to Reinhold Niebuhr's criticisms of Thomism, 94–98
Sinatra, Frank, 174
Solomon, Andrew, 163
Solzhenitsyn, Alexander, 200
Stith, Richard, 115
Strauss, Leo, 1, 143n, 144
Suarez, Francisco (Cardinal), 97

## T

Teilhard de Chardin, Pierre, 3, 198
Teresa, Mother, 119
Thomas, Clarence (Justice), 141
Tocqueville, Alexis de, 14
    on the paradoxical relation of religion to liberty, 187
    as a progenitor of the Catholic Church's embrace of religious liberty, 193, 201

## V

Valera, Eamon de, 147
Vatican II. *see* Second Vatican Council
Voegelin, Eric, 1, 30
Von Ketteler, Wilhelm Emmanuel (Bishop), 11n, 13

## W

Walsh, Brian (Justice), 149–151, 152, 153, 157
Walzer, Michael, 82
William of Saint-Amour, 15
Williams, Howard, 108n
Wilson, Edward O., 199
Wilson, Woodrow, 24, 28
Wittgenstein, Ludwig, 3
Wolf, Naomi, 161

## Z

Zahn, Gordon, 123